Corporate Governance and Globalization

NEW HORIZONS IN INTERNATIONAL BUSINESS

General Editor: Peter J. Buckley
Centre for International Business,
University of Leeds (CIBUL), UK

The New Horizons in International Business series has established itself as the world's leading forum for the presentation of new ideas in international business research. It offers pre-eminent contributions in the areas of multinational enterprise – including foreign direct investment, business strategy and corporate alliances, global competitive strategies, and entrepreneurship. In short, this series constitutes essential reading for academics, business strategists and policy makers alike.

Corporate Governance and Globalization

Long Range Planning Issues

Edited by

Stephen S. Cohen

Professor and Co-Director, Berkeley Round Table on the International Economy, University of California at Berkeley, USA

Gavin Boyd

Honorary Professor, Political Science Department, Rutgers University, Newark, USA and Adjunct Professor, Management Department, Saint Mary's University, Canada

NEW HORIZONS IN INTERNATIONAL BUSINESS

Edward Elgar
Cheltenham, UK ● Northampton, MA, USA

Published by
Edward Elgar Publishing Limited
Glensanda House
Montpellier Parade
Cheltenham
Glos GL50 1UA
UK

Edward Elgar Publishing, Inc.
136 West Street
Suite 202
Northampton
Massachusetts 01060
USA

A catalogue record for this book
is available from the British Library

Library of Congress Cataloguing in Publication Data

Corporate governance and globalization : long range planning issues / edited by Stephen S. Cohen, Gavin Boyd
   (New horizons in international business series)
   Includes index.
     1. Corporate governance. 2. International business enterprises – Management.
   3. International finance. 4. International trade. I. Cohen, Stephen S.
   II. Boyd, Gavin. III. New horizons in international business.
HD2741   C77492000
658'.049 – dc21

00-028844

ISBN 1 84064 179 7
Printed and bound in Great Britain by Bookcraft (Bath) Ltd.

Contents

Figures

Tables

Contributors

Erik Berglöf is a Professor at the Stockholm Intitute of Transition Economics and East European Economies, Stockholm School of Economics, Stockholm, Sweden

Gavin Boyd is an Honorary Professor in the Political Science Department, Rutgers University, Newark, New Jersey, USA, and an Adjunct Professor in Management at Saint Mary's University, Halifax, Canada

John W. Cioffi is a Research Associate at the Berkeley Roundtable on the International Economy, University of California, Berkeley, USA

Stephen S. Cohen is Professor and Co-Director, Berkeley Roundtable on the International Economy, University of California, Berkeley, USA

Joseph P. Daniels is a Professor of Economics at Marquette University, Milwaukee, Wisconsin, USA

John B. Davis is Dean of Commerce at Marquette University, Milwaukee, Wisconsin, USA

William R. Emmons is an Economist at the Federal Reserve Bank of St Louis, St Louis, Missouri, USA

Paul J.N. Halpern is Professor of Finance and Toronto Stock Exchange Chair in Capital Markets at the Rotman School of Management, University of Toronto, and Chair of the Advisory Board of the *Canadian Investment Review*

Robert E. Hoskisson has the Rath Chair in Strategic Management, Michael F. Price College of Business, University of Oklahoma, Norman, Oklahoma, USA

Hincheon Kim is a Professor in the College of Business and Economics, Hanyang University, Seoul, Korea

Terutomo Ozawa is Professor of Economics, Colorado State University, Fort Collins, Colorado, USA

Frank A. Schmid is an Economist at the Federal Reserve Bank of St Louis, St Louis, Missouri, USA

Ernst-Ludwig von Thadden is a Professor in the Department of Economics, University of Lausanne, Switzerland

Ingo Walter is Director of the Salomon Center in the Stern School at New York University, New York, USA

Daphne Yiu is a PhD Student in the Michael F. Price College of Business, University of Oklahoma, Norman, Oklahoma, USA

Foreword

Literature on corporate governance has developed mainly in the USA, within the past decade and a half, as a response to increasing shareholder activism, in which large institutional investors (for example CALPERS in the US) have been very prominent. The focus has been on agency problems – issues in relations between corporate managements and shareholders. These issues have had extensive ramifications, with consequences for both the efficiency of firms and for the overall efficiencies of economies. For policy communities dealing with trade, competition, cross-border capital flows (both FDI and portfolio) and international finance, the issues have become increasingly significant because of the ongoing processes of globalization. The influence of differing systems of corporate governance and concomitantly, differing financial architectures on the strategic orientations and operations of firms has assumed more and more cross-border dimensions.

While the literature on corporate governance has been expanding, another stream of policy relevant studies, also of recent origin, has focused on the costs and benefits of globalization. These studies have drawn attention to problems of structural adjustment in the course of deepening integration, and to the burdens assumed by governments endeavouring to shelter and compensate sectors affected by competing imports and the entries of foreign firms. New currents of political representation associated with the adjustment problems, meanwhile, have had policy level impacts, as was evident with the failure to develop the MAI and, more recently, after the disturbances at Seattle which disrupted the Ministerial Meeting of the World Trade Organization in late 1999.

Academic specializations have tended to keep the literature on corporate governance separate from the studies of globalization, but important linkages have been evident, especially because of acute problems in global financial markets, notably those resulting from the crises that disrupted East Asian economies in 1997/98. With the development of international financial markets, corporate managements have to be sensitive to the interests of foreign shareholders: home country investor bias, although strong, will gradually diminish. Issues of corporate governance can thus become less domestic.

The problems of adjustment to globalization meanwhile tend to be sources of new perspectives on corporate governance. Broader concepts of agency responsibilities can assume relevance, as adjustment tasks involve workers, suppliers and distributors as well as managements and shareholders. Questions of intercorporate cooperation moreover demand attention, because of the complex sectoral interdependencies that develop in an industrialized state.

For interaction between experts on comparative corporate governance and scholars studying globalization, the Frank H. Sobey Faculty of Commerce at Saint Mary's University Halifax sponsored a conference and symposium on Corporate Governance and Globalization in September 1999. Following a lead paper by Paul Halpern, Professor of Finance at the University of Toronto, in the presentations and discussions that followed, diverse analytical approaches occasioned very productive exchanges between the professionals represented in this volume. Additionally, I had the privilege of reading, for Erik Berglöf and Ernst-Ludwig von Thadden, their paper on the changing corporate governance paradigm.

I wish to express my gratitude to all the participants at this event, and my deep appreciation of the involvement of Stephen Cohen, Co-Director of the Berkeley Round Table on the International Economy, as editor of this conference volume with Gavin Boyd. It is hoped that this book will advance the debate on corporate governance among academics, corporate decision makers, consultants, experts in corporate law and finance and officials in financial institutions.

J. Colin Dodds
Academic Vice President
Saint Mary's University, Halifax

Preface

This volume explores the ways in which systems of corporate governance, especially in the major industrialized states, influence the globalization process. Deepening integration, which increases levels of policy, as well as structural interdependence, results from the transnational activities of mainly US, Japanese and European firms. These enterprises evolved within national political economies that have distinctive cultures, structures, laws and financial systems. The formative effects of these differing political economies tend to endure. But globalizing product markets, and especially financial markets, create pressures for convergence in corporate governance, organizational development and strategies. They push questions of corporate governance from the back pages of recondite journals onto the front pages of the business press and into central arenas of international economic policymaking.

Questions of corporate governance systems have become central concerns for policymakers trying to promote deeper international economic cooperation. Of these questions, the most prominent and the most urgent are driven by the operations of international financial markets, but they quickly extend into a broad range of public policies and national preferences in political–economic organization. The study of corporate governance thus tends to become interdisciplinary.

A conference for discussion of our chapters was hosted by the Commerce Faculty at Saint Mary's University, Halifax, 17 and 18 September 1999. We are very grateful to Dr J. Colin Dodds, Academic Vice-President at Saint Mary's, for arranging this event and for delivering, on their behalf, the paper by Erik Berglöf and Ernst-Ludwig von Thadden. Exchanges at the conference were very stimulating and were very helpful for preparations of the final versions of the chapters. An incisive summing-up by John Cioffi identified important theoretical linkages between themes which had been prominent in the discussions. Faculty and students from Saint Mary's and Dalhousie University, Halifax, participated in the conference, and we wish to express our thanks to all who helped to make it a sustained and productive dialogue.

Stephen S. Cohen
Gavin Boyd

1. Systemic perspectives on corporate governance systems

Paul J.N. Halpern

1. INTRODUCTION

An economy's corporate governance system has a significant impact on the profitability and growth of corporations, their access to capital and the cost of their capital. The governance system can influence the decisions undertaken by firms and ultimately has an impact on the wealth created in a country. If the governance system results in a focus on investments in low-risk, low-expected-return projects, or on investments that reduce risk for a subset of investors but at a substantial cost, the wealth of the economy will be reduced or will grow at a low rate. Further, investors' perceptions of the managerial decision-making process can influence their confidence in the corporation, the price at which capital is provided to the firm and, thereby, the cost of capital. A higher cost of capital will reduce economic growth. The focus of this chapter is on the publicly traded limited liability company: this structural form, while important in most developed and many developing economies, does not define the total business activity in a country. A number of privately owned limited and unlimited liability companies control a substantial amount of wealth. It is possible that some of the governance principles identified for publicly traded companies have strong currency for private corporations.

There is a wealth of written literature on comparative corporate governance systems with the bulk of it focusing on the major economies – Germany, Japan, the United Kingdom and the United States. However, governance issues are equally if not more important for developing and emerging economies. Developing economies have highly concentrated shareholdings, usually held by founders or family members, and capital markets that are neither deep nor efficient. The governance issues in these economies relate to the constraints imposed by governments on the evolution of markets and the role of competition in the product and capital markets.

Governance systems differ across countries. Monitoring of managers and the monitoring entities vary as a function of the ownership structure of the equity, the structure of corporations, the role of the banking system in the economy, business circumstances, the efficient functioning of capital markets and the level of product market and capital market competition, both domestic and international.

This chapter reviews the two major corporate governance systems – market-based and bank-based – within the context of the generic problems they face and the success of each governance system in solving these problems. The problems include the principal–agent issue found in widely held companies, primarily but not exclusively found in the market-based governance system, and entrenchment issues found in concentrated share ownership. For the former, the evidence suggests that the market-based systems are the most effective in monitoring and disciplining management. The market-based systems provide flexibility to companies to use new structures and financing forms and will encourage the growth of companies based on knowledge as opposed to hard assets. The bank-based systems do not appear to provide appropriate monitoring.

Concentrated shareholdings are analysed in two different contexts: where cash flow and voting rights are identical and where voting rights exceed cash flow rights. While both scenarios can lead to management entrenchment and associated problems, the latter scenario presents more serious problems and is more prevalent in developing and smaller developed economies. The problems associated with concentrated holdings are found in both governance systems although they are most severe in Germany. We note that problems are not just due to concentrated holdings but in many situations may be exacerbated by the identity of the controlling shareholder – the founder or founder's heirs. It appears that the latter generate more serious problems. Neither governance system appears to deal effectively with this problem. Markets and monitoring appear to be ineffective and solutions rely on corporate law, product markets both internationally and domestically, and improvements in international capital flows.

We also investigate the convergence of governance systems: if convergence means a movement by bank-based systems to the use of capital markets and a reduction in bank share ownership and monitoring, and by market-based systems to increase bank monitoring, then it is difficult to believe that convergence will occur. Although there are changes designed to improve capital markets in bank-based countries, other organizational structures and share ownership patterns will impede any significant convergence. However, there are strong forces at play in domestic bank-based economies and along with international pressures on decision making in these economies they are leading to a functional convergence where managerial decisions and changes in corporate organizational structures are being made with shareholder interests as the objective. Whether these changes are the result of international investors such as pension funds, relaxation of domestic controls, international restructuring through mergers and spin-offs, or the pressures to counter a recession, the functional convergence is a reality.

Finally, the lessons from the major governance systems are interesting but the most important issue is how can developing countries structure their governance systems to maximize their economic wealth. The market-based system with its reliance on widely held shares and deep, effective capital markets is not a viable alternative in the short or medium term. These countries are faced with concentrated holdings, and government decisions that improve capital markets and increase product market competition will be necessary to address the problems.

The chapter is organised as follows: in Section 2 there is a discussion of the major governance systems. Section 3 identifies the significant problems observed with non-concentrated equity holdings and considers their solutions consistent with the governance system in place. Section 4 considers the extent of concentrated holdings in economies, the forms of and the problems associated with this type of holding, and the possible solutions to these problems provided by the different governance systems. Concentrated holdings are pervasive and solutions to problems associated with it are crucial to the ultimate growth of smaller developed, developing and emerging economies. In Section 5 there is a discussion of the forces leading to the convergence of governance systems or, more correctly, the convergence in corporate organizational structure and decisions that emphasize shareholder wealth. Conclusions are presented in Section 6. Throughout the chapter, references to developing and developed countries other than Germany, Japan, the United Kingdom and the United States are made to highlight a broader set of corporate problems that need to be solved by many means including corporate governance.

2.   CORPORATE GOVERNANCE SYSTEMS

Governance is defined in many contexts. From a societal perspective, governance is the power, influence and relationship between governments and citizens used to implement social and economic programmes thereby generating sustainable economic progress. Here governance is observed in the exercise of power in the management of resources, and involves the nature and extent of authority and the control and incentives provided to utilize human and other resources for the wellbeing of the general public. The issue of governance in the public sector and the management of public sector companies becomes an interesting issue as countries privatize many of their state-owned enterprises and decide on the financing of these new entities and the governance structure that is appropriate. The latter issue reflects our concern, the governance system of publicly traded corporations.

From the corporate perspective, a governance system is a framework of laws, regulatory institutions and reporting requirements that conditions the way the corporate sector is managed. The corporate governance system also incorporates the financial system since the latter has a role to play in conditioning behaviour of the corporate sector. The financial system is the structure of financial contracts that governs the distribution of claims on all cash flows generated from productive assets in the economy.

While governance is a broad concept referring to a system's internal and external forces, governance must be related to a particular objective. One possible objective focuses on the ownership of the firm and how decisions by the firm affect the wealth of the firm's owners – the shareholders. The governance system defines the relationship of the owners to their firm and the mechanisms through which the owners affect the institution's behaviour (Roulier, 1997, p. 450). Thus the governance system is concerned with the creation of wealth through the maximization of economic efficiency of the firm, and with shareholders as the residual claimants they have the greatest incentive to create wealth. The governance issue, therefore, is to ensure that management's interests are aligned with those of the shareholders.

This focus on shareholder wealth is justified by recognizing that other suppliers of capital (both human and financial) have mechanisms through which they can protect their interests after having committed their capital. For example, long-term debt holders insert covenants into debt contracts to constrain certain management's decisions; short-term debt holders have strong monitoring and information provision requirements; and labour has unions and pre-specified payments for services along with the labour market. Shareholders are unique in that they provide large amounts of capital on terms that are vague and, hence, subject to potential abuses through opportunistic behaviour undertaken by managers.[1] Further, by having a wider class of affected and interested parties, it is difficult to measure success and assess the trade-offs between classes.

A wider view of corporate governance is proposed by Deakin and Hughes (1997, p. 2) who state that corporate governance is 'concerned with the relationship between internal governance mechanisms of corporations and society's conception of the scope of corporate accountability'. In certain countries, society's view of corporate accountability is wide. For example in French company law, a good company is seen in terms of a wider social interest and management must reconcile the interests of different corporate stakeholders of which only one is the shareholder class; the weight of shareholders in this reconciliation is not pre-specified. Similarly, in Germany, the mission of the public limited liability company must incorporate a set of complex corporate goals. Decision makers in the company are 'obliged to thoroughly discuss conflicts of stakeholder interests and decide on these issues cooperatively. Executives may be viewed as market oriented but socially responsible balancers of stakeholder interests' (Schmidt et al., 1997, p. 38).

In Table 1.1 the various elements in corporate governance systems and the motivation of each element in its governance function are identified. The emphasis and functioning of the governance elements distinguishes corporate governance systems.[2] Also, the governance system that is in place is the result of the interplay of various forces that relate to the governance elements and the motivation behind their exercise of influence. The motivation for the governance activity and the importance of the governance elements can differ among governance systems. For example, reliance on capital markets and the market for corporate control along with dispersed equity holdings and a focus on shareholders as the prime stakeholders distinguishes a market-based governance system[3] or outsider controlled system from a bank-based or insider controlled system.[4] An outsider control system is distinguished by a small number of controlling shareholders and little intercorporate equity holdings. The US and UK corporate governance systems are market-based or outsider controlled. In this system, third party and other stakeholders such as bond holders and employees have their interests protected through the firm's

Table 1.1   Elements of governance and motivations

Elements of governance	Primary motivation
Equity holders	Dividends and capital gains
Markets	
● Capital market	Competition for funds and monitoring
● Corporate control	Generate wealth through restructuring
● Product market	Competitive forces to discipline management
Debt providers	
● Public debt	Principal and interest
● Private debt	Principal and interest
Employees	Compensation and job security
Business practices/corporate culture	Standards of practice
Legal system	Set standards and provide sanctions for specific prohibited actions
Public opinion	Indicate the weight to stakeholder interest in firm decision making

goal of long-run profit maximization and the operation of bond markets and labour markets.[5]

Another distinguishing characteristic of this system is the presence of widely held companies and the relative minor role played by banks in the governance function. This does not imply that concentrated (controlling) positions in the equity of companies are not found in this system; as discussed in Section 4, concentrated holdings can and do lead to serious problems due to inadequate independent monitoring.

Alternatively, reliance on banking relationships, intercorporate holdings and concentrated holdings of equity is the basis of a bank-based corporate governance system or insider system of control.[6] In this system, non-controlling equity holders, even though they have a claim to cash flows in proportion to their equity holdings, are not able to exert much control. With concentrated holdings, the market for corporate control is not very strong and the capital market may not perform a monitoring function. Even within bank-based systems such as Japan, equity can be widely held. However, in Germany, widely held firms are the exception and concentrated ownership is more frequent.[7]

The examples noted above are the end points on a spectrum and intermediate positions are observed in countries. For example in Canada, an economy that shares a number of similarities to the United States in terms of legal and corporate structures and with an active capital market, there are very important differences in the actual governance systems. In Canada, the widely held company is the exception and not the rule;[8] the banks are large and actively involved in corporate lending and recently in underwriting and brokerage activities. Finally there are a large number of situations in which control rights and cash flow rights of the controlling shareholder – typically the founder or the founder's family – diverge dramatically.[9]

2.1 Characteristics of the Governance Systems

An important ingredient in all corporate governance systems is monitoring of managerial activity by various elements of the system. Monitoring can be undertaken by the board of directors, individual shareholders, concentrated holdings of shares such as mutual funds and pension funds, bondholders, banks or workers. Monitoring is facilitated by the presence of information on the firm and this can be generated pursuant to loan agreements or general shareholder information. Information acquisition is costly and for some of the monitoring groups, the benefits are not worth the costs. While there is a 'hands-on' monitoring function provided by the board of directors in some systems and banks, in other systems monitoring is reinforced at annual meetings through shareholder proposals and proxy voting.

Monitoring is assigned an important role in all governance systems but it is necessary to recognize its limitations in order to evaluate the effectiveness of different governance systems. The monitor represents its own interests with the objective of maximizing its own expected utility. This is straightforward when the monitor is an individual representing himself or herself as a capital provider. However, the individual could represent an institution and still make decisions that maximize the monitor's expected utility; by meeting the objectives of the institution the individual will obtain compensation from the institution for good performance. If the monitor and the institution it represents have aligned interests, then monitoring is in effect maximizing the wealth of the institution.[10] Consider two examples. Suppose employees were assigned a monitoring role over the managerial investment decisions. Their self-interest would emphasize managerial decisions that increased or maintained the labour intensiveness of the firm and were not very risky so as to reduce the probability of a bankruptcy that would throw workers out of their jobs. Their influence on managerial decisions would maximize the value of their claim but not necessarily those of other claimants such as equity holders. The second example is a member of the board of directors, which in US law has an important monitoring function. This individual must make decisions that are in the best interests of the corporation. However, this does not necessarily align the board member's interests with any particular stakeholder class or grouping of stakeholder classes. If the equity holder is the stakeholder class for whom the monitoring is being undertaken, an alignment of interests would require that the board member have an equity holding in the firm either as a precondition of becoming a board member or more likely as payment for services.

In Table 1.2 some of the characteristics of the governance systems are presented. The US structure is used as the example of the market-based system. Under a banking-based system, two sub-categories are considered. First is the German universal banking system and the second is the Japanese main bank system. As can be seen in the table, the market- and bank-based systems have very different elements. We will consider each governance system in turn.

2.1.1 Market-based (market-centred) systems

While relying on markets to provide the governance of corporations, market-centered systems also have other monitoring arrangements, incentives and disciplinary techniques designed to achieve strong managerial performance. The unique aspect of the equity market in the market-centered system is the widely held nature of securities and the lack of significant intercorporate, individual/family and bank holdings. Financial institutions, such as mutual and pension funds and insurance companies, while holding shares, do so for portfolio purposes.

Table 1.2 Governance systems

Element	Market-based United States	Bank-based	
		Universal banking (Germany)	Main bank (Japan)
Internal control/board of directors	Primarily outside members with strong CEO influence	Two-tier board: management and supervisory	Primarily insiders
Equity ownership	Widely held	Concentrated in family, corporate, bank. Separation of cash flow and control rights	More diffuse, intercorporate and bank ownership
Share voting	Some concentration through investment funds and strong proxy system	Banks vote as custodians as well as owners on their own	Voting by ownership of shares
Equity market	Liquid and efficient	Illiquid	Minor influence
Corporate control	Vigorous	Little activity	Little activity

On the incentive side, there is the presence of senior management compensation that is tied to variables designed to align the interests of management and shareholders. The principles on which management compensation is based are presented in the annual report along with the salaries, bonuses and contingent compensation of senior management. By using compensation tied to share price, for example, management is expected to make decisions that lead to higher share prices. Share price performance, sometimes adjusted for overall market movements, provides an indication of management success and can be used as the basis to fire management.

Essential to the control of corporations is the board of directors who are legally and practically charged with directing and managing the business of the corporation on behalf of the owners. Some aspects are delegated to management. In meeting its obligations, the board must be vigilant in overseeing management's actions with the ultimate goal of shareholder wealth maximization. Their general responsibilities, beyond management oversight, are to adopt a corporate strategy, appoint and monitor senior management, communicate with shareholders and other stakeholders, and ensure that internal control systems and management information systems are in place and function effectively. The access to up-to-date information is crucial for the board to do an effective job.

In addition, it is shareholders' responsibility to monitor management and the board of directors. Thus they vote for directors at the annual meeting, and based on the proxy process they can introduce shareholder proposals. While management maintains the power to include or exclude shareholder proposals, many proposals are voted on at the shareholder meeting. The proxy process has been made easier to use in the United States and ultimately more effective with rule changes. To the extent that institutional shareholders have substantial equity positions in securities, they also monitor firm management.

In addition to the monitoring activities of shareholders and boards of directors, markets provide a monitoring and, in some situations, a disciplinary function. The markets considered are the securities (capital) market, the market for corporate control, market for managers and the product market.

Transactions in equity claims issued by corporations are undertaken in the securities market. With deep and liquid markets, the share price at any point in time is an unbiased estimate of the value of the equity of the firm under incumbent management and the impact of any entrenchment devices the management has introduced. The capital market monitors the firm in the sense that the security price provides a signal of management's success. Also, when the company issues new securities, the share price will react to reflect the expectations of the impact of new capital on the firm's performance.

The market for corporate control is a very important means to solve the principal–agent problem. In the prototypical case, poor management performance in a widely held company leads to a low stock price. A potential acquirer believing that it can improve the performance of the firm either by removing management, altering operations or generating economies of scale will either make a friendly bid for the equity of the firm or, if incumbent management is not inclined to the transaction, make a hostile bid. Friendly bids are the most common transaction by far although the contentious bids receive the greatest media exposure. In some situations there is an auction in which there are a number of bidders; in some jurisdictions securities regulation is designed to facilitate an auction. Incumbent management can engage in a number of defensive tactics intended to slow down the process or stop it entirely. The bids are frequently facilitated by the existence of one or more institutional stockholders who tender their shares to the bid and make it successful.

The market for managers is effective if management, in order to maintain its marketability, operates the firm to achieve strong returns. A poorly performing manager will have difficulty finding a new job. This market is an informal one but can be very effective in monitoring and disciplining managers; it provides the incentive for the manager to operate in the interests of the firm.

The final market in play is the product market where a firm that operates poorly relative to its competitors ultimately will find itself in financial distress and in the extreme, bankrupt. This outcome will result in a restructuring of the firm's operations and asset holdings and in some cases the replacement of management. If a firm has a large amount of physical assets and faces imperfect competition, product market discipline will occur only with a long lag. Government policies concerning domestic and international competition in product markets will be very important in the effective functioning of the product market.

Underlying the discussion of the market-based governance system is the assumption that the companies have widely held equity. The conclusions have to be modified if there are concentrated holdings of equity. This possibility is considered in depth in a subsequent section.

2.1.2   German system

An important element in the German system is the two-tiered board system: the supervisory board and the management and executive committee. As a result of the Codetermination Act of 1976, public and private limited companies with greater than 2000 employees must have a supervisory board. The board has specific control duties and powers such as appointing, dismissing and monitoring the management board, which includes screening of investment plans and vetoing investments of which it does not approve, and reviewing certain information sent to shareholders. The supervisory board cannot be involved in management. On the supervisory board, one half of the seats are allocated to labour.[11] The non-labour members are elected by shareholders. However, with the voting power of the banks, in essence these members are elected by the banks, may in fact be representatives of the banks, and in their role on the board could take the interests of the bank over those of the shareholders. The chair of the board, who is usually from the management group, can cast two votes in order to break a tie.[12] The management board is responsible for the day-to-day operations of the company.

There is a significant concentration of equity ownership in the German system along with a separation of cash flow and voting rights. The ownership concentration arises through families that control a large number of companies, corporations that hold shares of other corporations as investments (cross-holdings) and banks that hold shares of companies for investment/ portfolio purposes. The extent of these bank holdings can be quite large. For example, Deutsche Bank owns 28.3 per cent of Daimler Benz, 12.5 per cent of Allianz and more than 25 per cent of Karstadt. Where families do not have controlling blocks, banks have a large presence. Very few large German companies do not have a large blockholder. For example, 85 per cent of 171 of the largest non-financial firms have a single shareholder with a block of in excess of 25 per cent of the voting shares. Banks hold a small percentage of these blocks. Given the large block holdings, it is necessary to form coalitions to generate control in widely held firms. Management can form a coalition with employees and in order to maintain shareholder control it is necessary for the institutions to form a coalition (Roe, 1994, p. 182). Banks' control is obtained through a confluence of circumstances. First, banks are the custodians of shares left with them by clients. With written authorization, they can vote these shares. Second, there can be a voting right limitation introduced by a special resolution of shareholders. The limitation is set at 5, 10 or 15 per cent of total votes by any one shareholder in spite of the actual shareholdings. Since this limitation does not apply to the banks, they have a strong influence on voting.[13] To highlight the importance of the banks' position in the governance system even when they do not have a large ownership position, the direct holdings and voting percentage for three banks in Daimler Benz is shown below:

Daimler Benz	Direct holdings (%)	Voting percentage
Deutsche Bank	28.3	41.8
Dresdener Bank	1.6	18.8
Commerz Bank	1.6	12.2

Source: Roe as cited in Macey and Miller (1997).

While the loan market is well developed, equity markets are not. This state of affairs is a result of bank intervention to reduce the growth of the equity market. There is a German equity market but the depth of the market and the extent of listed companies is not large. Also, a large number of companies have majority blocks.

For widely held firms in Germany, the takeover market is inactive. During the 1980s, the total number of mergers in Germany was about one-half of the number in the UK. Hostile takeovers are very rare; three have occurred since the Second World War and these have been of recent vintage (see Franks and Mayer, 1997, p. 41). This inactivity should be no surprise given the banks' voting control, the existence of voting restrictions and the difficulty of changing membership on the supervisory board given the worker representation and their predilection to vote with management and in effect ensure their jobs. Of course, the concentrated ownership of other firms precludes hostile takeovers. All of the above factors can lead to entrenched management.[14]

There are benefits of this universal banking system and even without strong capital and corporate control markets, German banks are supposed to ensure that management operates effectively. The first benefit arises from the economies of scale and scope generated by the bank's size and operations in the loan and underwriting markets. The economies of scope arise as information gathered at one level, say by the bank for credit purposes, can be used at another level, say underwriting activities for the same firm. The result is a reduction of transactions costs of information that can lead to better monitoring. The economies of scale arise from the capital-intensive data processing and back office functions. Second, the banks hold both debt and equity claims to the firm. By holding both claims, expected default costs can be reduced. In addition, the bank should be interested in the overall cash flow of the firm and not just the cash flow to either set of claims. Thus monitoring should be based on maximizing firm cash flow and hence maximizing the value of the overall firm. If managerial decisions are consistent with this goal, all financial claimants are better off. However, this argument is strictly applicable when the bank holds proportionate claims of all securities of the firm. In the German system, the equity stakes in a firm are not as large as their debt exposure. Third, with other corporations having equity holdings of a firm, their self-interest should result in the effective monitoring of firms. Thus even without the market for corporate control, the monitoring agents should be able to achieve a similar result and provide forces of corporate control and incentives for management decisions. Whether the monitoring that does occur by banks and other corporations under this system generates the suggested benefits will be considered in subsequent sections.

2.1.3   Japan

Publicly listed Japanese companies are of three types: independent firms, members of a '*keiretsu*' and companies that were at one time members of a '*zaibatsu*', a conglomerate structure that was dismantled subsequent to the Second World War but with resulting 'independent' firms maintaining intra-group links.[15] The structure that has received the most attention is the *keiretsu* in which there is a core company, either a parent or a main bank, and a set of companies associated with the core company; all of the companies hold cross-holdings in the equity of each other firm in the group. The core company paternalistically controls the other *keiretsu* members even though there is no controlling share interest, and intervenes in the management process. In return the *keiretsu* companies are assured of survival by the parent. For the financial institution, the benefit of membership and the required equity investment is potential reciprocal services; business ties are established and implicit long-term contracts are instituted. Almost all non-financial firms are associated with a main bank.[16] While each member's holding is small individually, a coalition of firms and financial institutions could obtain a controlling position. A bank is not permitted to own in excess of 5 per cent of the equity of any firm but given the size of the banks and the relatively smaller size of Japanese companies compared to US companies, a 5 per cent holding can be obtained without a substantial undiversified dollar investment. The result of the *keiretsu* structure is a concentration of ownership for all sizes of companies. Five banks and financial institutions own approximately 20 per cent of the shares in major companies (see Roe, 1994, p. 171). However, there is still a large number of small shareholders in Japanese companies.

In the Japanese system there is a board of directors that manages the company and supervises management. Further, it must approve of the acquisition or sale of substantial assets, large borrowings and dismissal of managers. It thus appears to have an internal monitoring function. The board is composed typically of insiders who, while formally elected by share-holders, are in effect appointed by the CEO who is president of the board. The boards are large, from 20 to 35 members, with senior managers being members of the board. Outside, but not independent, members of the board are found in some companies; they can be from other companies in the group or infrequently from the bank. The true power in the board is a small executive group of managers, including the president, who are representative directors having special rights to represent the company. They make the important decisions that are rubber-stamped by the board of directors at board meetings.[17] There is the equivalent of a second tier in the board structure called the President's Council. This group meets monthly and is composed of financial intermediaries and intercorporate owners. No votes are taken at the meeting but the president of the firm feels constrained by the consensus of this group. Based on their direct dealings with the company and their interactions through the President's Council, banks are able to obtain information, even confidential information, at a low cost. This access to information should lead to improved monitoring of managers. Also, the long-term relationships within the *keiretsu* result in member firms making profitable reputational investments in non-opportunistic behaviour. Given the *keiretsu* structure, the control of the board by the managers, and the difficulty in obtaining a controlling equity position, the market for corporate control is inactive and monitoring is by the banks and the other *keiretsu* members who take disciplinary action when necessary.

Since there is no market for managers, poorly performing managers are disciplined in indirect ways.[18] Members of the keiretsu can threaten to sell their positions in the firm and thereby make a hostile takeover feasible. However, to be effective, this threat would require the agreement of a significant number of corporate owners. However, removal of a firm from a *keiretsu* may be a signal of poor managerial performance. The most direct method of controlling management is through bank participation on the board in the event of crisis. With a cash flow and liquidity problem that impacts the firm's ability to repay principal and interest (and not necessarily a reduction in share price), banks will take control of the board and in some situations dismiss the CEO. In the event of extremely poor stock performance, management has been replaced.[19] After appointment of bank representatives to the board, liquidity and cash flows return quickly to industry norms whereas growth in assets and sales grow more slowly to industry norms.[20] Even though the markets for corporate control and for management do not function, the banks along with the other corporate shareholders can change management at a lower cost than a takeover. Thus the main bank/*keiretsu* system provides an effective monitoring of debtors, protects bank clients against business failure of firms, and monitors management performance allegedly for the benefit of shareholders.[21]

This alleged benefit does not come without potential costs. First, since there is one dominant bank (or coalition of banks), the members of the *keiretsu* may be subject to creditor opportunistic behaviour. This behaviour could be observed in concessions made by the company to prevent a holdup problem in needed financing or a veto of projects that are not viewed favourably by the banks. Without viable alternative financing through the capital markets, this risk is serious. Further, the main bank charges an interest rate to debtors in excess of the market rate. While this can be interpreted as an agency fee for the monitoring function, it is also consistent with a rent obtained for protecting incumbent management from hostile takeovers and to compensate for earning sub-optimal equity returns on the bank's equity investment in the company (see note 18).

Finally, there is one unique aspect of Japanese corporate governance: Japanese bureaucrats who, as stakeholders of the firm, influence managerial behaviour. This influence is observed when a bureaucrat leaves government service and enters private management. An 'old boy network' of founders, owners and former presidents or former bureaucrats will influence the president of the firm. These are 'old buddies' who know each other well and meet regularly within and across industries. This group can influence corporate behaviour, but it is not clear whether its objectives are consistent with shareholder interests, a broader social concern, or a narrow individual one.

3.　ISSUES ADDRESSED BY CORPORATE GOVERNANCE: WIDELY HELD EQUITY

In this section we consider problems in firms with widely held equity that the corporate governance system is intended to address. The problems are identified and empirical evidence on their existence and severity is presented. Solutions to the problems based on the governance system are described and their potential success in solving the problems is assessed.

3.1　The Principal-Agent Problem

The classic problem identified by Berle and Means (1933) and formally developed and extended by Jensen and Meckling (1976) concerns the effect of splintered ownership on managerial behaviour. In the Jensen and Meckling model, management has delegated powers from the principals of the firm – the shareholders. Owing to the cost of information acquisition and the difficulty of monitoring management behaviour to ensure it is consistent with shareholders' interests, rational managers can undertake behaviour that shifts wealth from shareholders to themselves. The loss in market value relative to its value if no agency issues existed is called the agency cost of equity. This agency cost is also referred to as moral hazard behaviour since management undertakes unexpected behaviour not in the best interests of the principals.

Agency cost is related to the degree of separation of ownership and control. In the situation where managers have small equity holdings, gains from diversionary activity and shirking exceed any loss in value through a reduction in the market value of the manager's equity holding in the firm. This problem reaches its most serious manifestation in the case of widely held shares with professional management. Where managers have little or no equity holding and with widely held shares, individual shareholders will refrain from making costly investments in monitoring activity and information gathering due to the free-rider problem. Monitoring activity is of benefit to all shareholders yet only the monitoring shareholder bears the costs. In the absence of coercion, the rational decision is to eschew monitoring leaving the managers free to undertake wealth-decreasing activities. The wealth-decreasing activities include shirking, accepting projects that decrease the wealth of shareholders and reduce the risk associated with managers' undiversified human capital investment in the firm, and diverting corporate assets or cash flow to managers at shareholders' expense.[22]

3.2 Solutions

3.2.1 Market-based system
The market-based corporate governance system solution to this problem employs the full arsenal of internal, external and market techniques. In general, the solution is to employ mechanisms that align the interests of managers and shareholders. If these mechanisms are unsuccessful, other techniques must be used. However, with the introduction of management entrenchment devices such as poison pills and altered board structures or increases in the debt component in capital structures that serve the same purpose, all solutions to the principal–agent problem are blunted.

On the internal side there are a number of ways to improve managerial behaviour. The first is the use of compensation contracts related to the performance of the company. These contracts include stock options or similar contracts that pay-off to managers when the firm's share price increases above some threshold value. These contracts are costly to shareholders but the expectation is that with an improved alignment of interests, the expected benefits exceed costs. Of course there are problems with the asymmetric pay-off associated with stock options – there is no cost for poor performance except in the extreme cases where management is fired; in addition there is the possibility of excessive risk-taking by management intended to increase the value of their stock options.[23] In the latter scenario, the incentive to take riskier projects is a counterweight to the tendency to take less risky projects due to their undiversified human capital. However, board oversight and internal controls are essential to control excesses in this direction. Bonus pool schemes have been introduced to penalize negative managerial performance.

The second technique is monitoring by the board of directors. Suggestions to ensure an effective board are designed to align the interests of directors and shareholders and include directors' legal liability, the use of truly independent directors – directors who have no relationship with the firm including financial, legal and accounting personnel – and equity ownership by board members. The board comes under scrutiny since management, even without significant shareholdings, can influence the board's conduct through its *de facto* control of the nomination and agenda setting process and board members serve at the pleasure of management. While these issues are serious, there is no doubt that boards will remove poorly performing management. The question is how long does the poor performance have to continue until the decision is made and what is the quantum of poor performance that results in board action?

The third method is monitoring by shareholders (or a coalition of shareholders) whose holdings are large enough to overcome the free-rider problem. These shareholder groups need to have sufficient votes to pose a credible threat to management or have sufficient influence and stature to lead other shareholders to question management's behaviour and agitate for change. The obvious example of this monitoring is found in the activist behaviour of pension and mutual funds.[24] There is a large literature on the impact of pension fund activism on the performance of targeted companies. Karpoff (1998) presents an excellent review of the empirical literature. Pension fund activism includes the introduction of a shareholder proposal(s) at an annual meeting, private negotiations with the board concerning changes in the company, or a combination of both approaches. The growth of activism is attributed to the increasing holdings of financial institutions, especially index funds, the potential significant cost of unwinding equity positions, and the adoption of firm and state anti-takeover provisions that lead to entrenched behaviour. Karpoff concludes that shareholder activism does not have an impact on share values and earnings but can prompt changes in the target firm's governance structure. Negotiations with the board of directors and private proposals at shareholder meetings have been successful in prompting organizational changes. These negotiations reflect true monitoring and oversight by the pension funds and substitute for aspects of the board of directors' oversight.[25]

An alternative to pension fund monitoring is the activist behaviour of specialized investment funds that take equity positions in firms they believe to be undervalued relative to their value under new management or under a new corporate structure. Wealthy individuals and financial institutions including pension funds finance these funds. The specialized fund forms a coalition with other aggrieved large shareholders in the target firm and then launches a proxy contest to take control of the board and introduce changes. In many instances these specialized funds have succeeded in changing firm operations or structures.[26]

Corporate managements are very distressed by activist shareholders; management believes that even well run companies with sound business strategies are subject to activist shareholders who, based on investor pressure for strong performance, agitate for change. They prefer more patient, 'long-run' investors. However when investing capital and looking for returns, while patience may be a virtue, being overly patient and indulging management's poor performance is a sin.

On the external side, solutions are observed in the labour market for managers and the market for corporate control. In the former, managers, unless entrenched and insulated from the possibility of losing their position, must be interested in their marketability, which is related to their managerial performance and reputation. In the US system, managers are generally professional and their reputations are crucial for future employment at other corporations. Managers can leave their firms for reasons unrelated to their specific capabilities and performance. For example, there can be a disagreement with the board about the future strategy of the company or the managers' pay package. Managers will maximize their chances of obtaining a new position by performing well. Poor performance can lead to a difficulty in getting a replacement job or being placed in a tightly monitored position.

The corporate control market is a very important element in the market-based system. The market for corporate control will only work in a widely held company or one in which share blocks are held by institutional investors who have no interest in supporting incumbent management unless they are providing competitive returns. Thus the market for corporate control operates as a disciplinary mechanism for poorly performing managers or as a monitoring mechanism, whose existence leads incumbent management to make decisions that maximize the wealth to current shareholders. In the latter case, it is the possibility of a hostile bid that disciplines management. This market can be impeded with the introduction of management entrenchment devices either by the firm or by governments. These devices tend to prolong the problems and ultimately the product market solution of financial distress or bankruptcy will be invoked.

The market-based system has its problems, and even though there are a number of elements available to solve the principal–agent problem, they may not work perfectly. However, this system does provide flexibility and a number of approaches to address the issue.

3.2.2 Bank-based systems

The principal–agent problem exists in bank-based systems since there are widely held companies and professional managers. However, the bank-based systems face the same potential shortcoming – the lack of external control mechanisms such as a well functioning capital market, market for corporate control and market for managers. Thus any solution to the principal–agent problem must rely on internal mechanisms. In this section we examine the effectiveness of internal solutions found in the German and Japanese governance systems.

Germany   In the German system, market-related solutions are not feasible. The equity market is not well developed and hence there is no monitoring function. With some concentrated holdings through intercorporate invest- ments or concentrated voting in the banks, the market for corporate control is not operational. Further, senior management compensation contracts based on share price performance are generally not observed. Management receiving a fixed salary has every incentive to take on low-risk projects and construct diversified corporate structures thereby reducing the risk of financial distress and loss of firm-specific human capital through termination of employment. Therefore any monitoring activity must come from the supervisory board, any intercorporate shareholders, or the banks. Institutional funds typically are passive and mutual funds, which are more concerned about company financial performance, are quantitatively small.

The supervisory board may not be structured to provide the necessary monitoring. The labour component of the board is interested in continuity of employment for employees and thus will prefer low-risk or risk-diversifying corporate activities. The non-worker group on the supervisory board was elected by shareholders and given that banks have the controlling vote, this group could represent the bank's interests rather than the dispersed non-bank, non-corporate shareholders. The bank's interests are very straightforward. They are interested in the level and variability of the cash flow available to pay principal and interest on the firm's debt. Firms' liquidity and stability of cash flows are very important to the banks. Even if the banks owned both debt and equity in equal proportions, which they do not, their financial interests would still necessitate a low risk of default in the corporations in which they are invested. The costs of default are not trivial and there are other pieces of the banks' operations that could be affected by a bankruptcy of a customer.

The final monitoring group is the intercorporate shareholders who look upon their investment as a way of ensuring business ties and not as an actively managed portfolio. The managers of these companies would not want to upset the status quo of benign neglect. Therefore, active monitoring is unlikely to arise from this source.

Japan   Shareholdings of Japanese companies are divided among financial institutions, which include banks, trust banks, life companies, and pension and mutual funds, intercorporate holdings and individual shareholdings. This last group has less than 35 per cent of the shares and they are widely held. Just as in the other governance systems, managerial interests need to be aligned with those of non-corporate, non-institutional shareholder interests. One method is through managerial compensation contracts based on share price performance. These contracts, until recently, are rare in Japan and are inconsistent with cultural norms in which team and not individual effort is valued. Another method of internal control of management is the board of directors. Although expected to have a monitoring role, the board is ineffective; the executive committee makes decisions and there is a lack of serious questioning of managerial decisions by the board.[27] Further, there is a lack of techniques to align board and shareholder interests. Groups of shareholders such as pension and mutual funds and life companies that could monitor have decided not to engage in this activity, agreeing to waive all or part of their rights as shareholders for the sake of stable shareholding agreements and mutual trust (Baum and Schaede, 1994, p. 610). Another potential monitoring group is the intercorporate shareholders. These cross-holdings are large in aggregate although any individual company does not hold a large undiversified portfolio investment in a single company in the group. Companies in the group hold these share positions to maintain reciprocal insurance in the event of financial problems and to generate business ties. Any attempt to monitor a manager and agitate for change or dismissal, except in the extreme situation of financial distress, would be seen as a violation of maintaining business ties. Every manager of a company in the group would not want to be placed in the position of being monitored and hence will not engage in this activity. This group's self-interest is inconsistent with a strong monitoring presence for the sake of the non-corporate, non-institutional shareholders. Even the group that has the largest influence on the day-to-day operations of the company, the 'old boy network', does not necessarily have non-corporate, non-institutional shareholders' interests in mind. Their concerns may be much wider including the impact of corporate decisions on stakeholders such as the workers or on the economy and not the non-corporate shareholders.

The final potential monitoring group is the main bank, which alone or as part of a banking syndicate has loans outstanding to the companies in the group and a small equity interest in the group's firms. However, are their interests as monitors aligned with the non-corporate shareholders? Clearly, banks are concerned with the financial distress/default outcome and are interested in ensuring this does not occur even if their intervention in this regard does not maximize share returns. Given their small equity stakes in the firm relative to their position as creditors, this emphasis is not surprising; it is consistent with the observations that bank intervention is based on liquidity problems, not share price reductions and cash flow problems, and increasing liquidity after bank intervention.

Finally, the last market to provide any discipline of managers is the product market through domestic and international competition. While this is a slow route, it can provide the discipline as long as it is able to function effectively. The issue in the Japanese system concerns the speed with which management is replaced in the event of poor performance. Also, is bank intervention an attempt to bail out existing management with management replacement as the last case scenario? If so, the disciplinary role of the product market through reorganization or bankruptcy of poorly performing firms will not be effective. Of course, a series of poor performances by a firm whether due to old or new management will ultimately lead to changes in the firm's operations.

In general, the principal–agent problem is not well addressed by the Japanese governance system. Market-related monitoring approaches are non-existent or blunted by internal mutual insurance by the corporate share-holders. The internal mechanisms such as the board of directors' and share-holders' meetings are ineffective and the corporate shareholders, respecting implicit non-intrusion clauses, do not monitor. Banks' self-interest does not provide the type of monitoring of management that leads to shareholder gains. Finally, the informal monitoring of the 'old boy network' is effective but its objective may be inconsistent with non-corporate shareholder wealth.

3.3   Free Cash Flow

Management of certain types of firms are faced with an interesting problem – what to do with the cash flow remaining after having accepted all good investment decisions. Free cash flow (FCF) is defined as the annual cash flow available after all good investment decisions and all non-discretionary expenditures of cash have been undertaken. The FCF can be returned to shareholders or invested in assets. In the latter case, the value of the equity will fall since the accepted projects are not wealth-enhancing; however, managers, owning a small proportion of the firm's equity, if any, will have their wealth unaffected. In fact, it can be increased if salaries are a function of assets or managers receive non-pecuniary benefits of managing a large entity. Not all firms face this potential problem; only those whose products or services have a stable demand, require little research and development expenditures, have large and stable cash flows and face little competition are potentially affected. This example of the principal–agent problem is identified separately not because it is the most important manifestation of the problem but first, because it demonstrates the market-based governance system's flexibility, and second, the solution to the problem has been compared to monitoring by financial institutions/lenders within a market-based governance system.

Investments made with free cash flow are not acceptable from a present value comparison of costs and benefits and are typically made in hard assets and in low-risk projects. In the bank-based systems, these types of investments would be acceptable to the bank monitors since the increased assets improve the collateral available to the bank in the event of financial distress and the lower risk projects reduce the probability of financial distress.

Management views these investments as reducing their risk of losing a job in the event of financial distress and in the German system, labour on the supervisory board would support the investments since they reduce the probability of a job loss. Thus, even though shareholders are worse off, there is no monitoring mechanism available in the bank-based systems to address the problems of wealth transfer from shareholders to other stakeholders and a reduction in the overall firm value.

The market-based system is slightly more effective through the operations of the market for corporate control where incumbent management can be removed and new operations and monitoring are introduced. However, in the US the standard mechanism to control this problem seemed not to work given the reported excesses of some firms. The solution that evolved in the market for corporate control was the leveraged buyout (LBO). The LBO is a bid, sometimes hostile, for the equity of the firm financed by equity and a substantial amount of debt. If successful, the resulting firm becomes a private entity with a large amount of debt and a management holding of a significant amount of equity – 10 to 20 per cent compared to their very low holdings prior to the transaction. The debt and equity claims are purchased by pension funds, insurance companies, high wealth individuals and the LBO partner who initiated the deal and negotiated the final debt and equity holdings. The financial institutions hold both debt and equity claims and thus have incentives to ensure the maximization of the overall firm value and reduce the cost of financial distress in the event of problems. Management's equity holding aligns its interests with the other monitoring shareholders. The LBO structure manages, in order to meet principal and interest payments on the large amount of debt outstanding, to reduce unnecessary investments and run the firm to maximize its cash flow and ultimately share price.

It has been suggested that the LBO is an example of bank monitoring found in the bank-based systems. However, this comparison is not correct. In the LBO, monitors have not only a debt position but also a large equity position. Even though the financial institutions have well-diversified debt and equity portfolios, they have an incentive to monitor in order to increase the equity value of their investment. The holding of securities by the financing parties with pay-offs contingent on the success of the firm and the return of the firm to the public markets through an initial public offering reinforce this monitoring incentive.

4.   CONCENTRATED OWNERSHIP

The focus of this section is on the effective monitoring of companies by firms, individuals and financial institutions in which the controlling shareholder is involved in management either directly or indirectly as the chair of the board of directors. Thus, financial institutions that hold blocks of shares for portfolio purposes such as pension funds, mutual funds and financial institutions and which may provide a monitoring but not operational role, are not considered controlling shareholders in this discussion. The forms of control are presented in Figure 1.1.

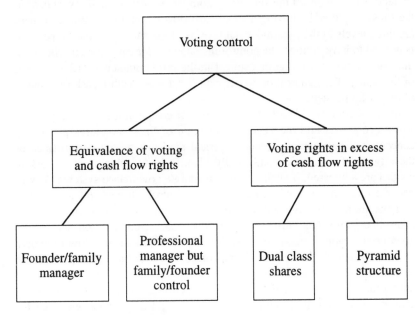

Figure 1.1   Control possibilities

Voting control is decomposed into two possible scenarios: the first occurs where the voting rights and cash flow rights of the controlling shareholder are identical. The controlling shareholder owns a proportion of the shares of the company and has votes and claims to cash flows from the company in the same proportion. The controlling shareholder can be either the founder of the company or the founder's family (heirs) where the controlling shareholder can act as manager or in the case of professional management, the controlling shareholder is active as chair of the board of directors. The second control scenario arises where voting rights exceed cash flow rights. The two examples presented are the dual class share structure and the pyramid company structure. In the former, the controlling shareholder owns enough shares to provide a large percentage of the votes. However, due to the existence of another class of equity securities with diminished or no voting rights, the controlling shareholder does not need to own an equal proportion of the overall assets of the company. Thus cash flow rights, which are based on the proportion of total shares held, are lower than the voting rights.[28] In the pyramid structure the parent or controlling company, which frequently is controlled by a founder or founder's heirs, has as its sole asset an equity holding in a subsidiary company. This company in turn can hold a controlling interest in another company and so on. In this way the original controlling shareholder can control the subsidiary companies with a small investment in the subsidiary thereby having a small cash flow claim. For example, if there are three levels in the pyramid, each level is of the same size and 50 per cent is needed to have control, the controlling shareholder can have control of the third tier company with an investment in the third company of 12.5 per cent of the equity. Thus control of 50 per cent is achieved with a cash flow claim of only 12.5 per cent.

In this section we identify the incidence of concentrated ownership in the world economies and the benefits and costs of these structures generating concentrated ownership; present empirical evidence on the performance of these types of companies; and finally identify how problems of ownership control are addressed, if at all, through corporate governance systems. As will become clear in the section, conventional controls through all governance systems are not effective and solutions to improve corporate performance of controlled companies must rely on product market competition and, where appropriate, capital market competition. These solutions are slow to evolve and are influenced by the legal framework of the countries. Here governance systems are less important and product and capital market competition lead to appropriate discipline. Insights from this section are relevant to developing economies as well as developed ones and should have some relevance for privatizing companies.

4.1 Importance and Incidence of Control Structures

La Porta et al. (1998) investigate the incidence of control structures by looking at the ultimate ownership of the 20 largest publicly traded firms in 27 of the (generally) richest countries that have significant stock markets. They conclude that the Berle and Means 'company' is not widespread, the separation of cash flows and voting rights is pervasive, occurring more frequently through a pyramid structure than dual class shares, and banks do not control many companies.

They also identify the ultimate ownership both of capital and voting rights.[29] Given that the data reflect the largest firms,[30] there should be a bias toward finding the Berle and Means corporation since the degree of ownership concentration of equity is inversely related to the size of the company – the larger the company the lower the ownership concentration. La

Porta et al. (1998) also segments the countries into two classifications related to the protection of minority rights.[31] The results for ultimate ownership are presented in Table 1.3. Defining control as a 20 per cent ownership stake, they observe for all countries that 36 per cent of the firms are widely held, 30 per cent are family controlled and 18 per cent are state controlled. The remaining firms are either controlled by a widely held corporation or financial institution or included in an 'other' category. Classifying the countries into above median (high) and below median (low) shareholders rights protection countries, they observe that 48 per cent of the firms are widely held in countries with strong shareholder protection whereas 27 per cent are widely held in 'low' protection countries. This difference is the only statistically significant one in all of the comparisons of 'high' and 'low' shareholder protection for all categories of company size and control definitions.

Family control is observed more frequently in the 'low' category for all control definitions and company size categories. When the control definition falls to 10 per cent, the incidence of widely held firms decreases and increases for family owned firms. Also, using the smaller company sample, the incidence of family control increases dramatically to 45 per cent for all firms, with 'low' protection countries having a higher percentage than 'high' protection countries. Within the shareholder protection categories, there is a large range of outcomes. For example, with the 20 per cent control definition and the large firm sample, Hong Kong has 70 per cent family ownership and 10 per cent widely held, the UK has 100 per cent widely held firms and the

Table 1.3   Incidence of ultimate control of corporations

	20% control definition			10% control definition		
	Widely held	Family owned	State	Widely held	Family owned	State
Large firms						
All	36	30	18	24	35	20
High	48	25	14	34	30	16
Low	27	34	22	16	38	24
Smaller firms						
All	24	45	15	11	53	16
High	38	39	9	17	51	10
Low	13	50	20	6	54	21

Source: La Porta et al. (1998, tables II and III).

US 80 per cent widely held and 20 per cent family controlled. In the 'low' category, France has 60 per cent widely held, 20 per cent family and 15 per cent state owned, Germany has 50 per cent widely held, 10 per cent family and 24 per cent state controlled, and Sweden has 25 per cent widely held, 45 per cent family controlled and 10 per cent state controlled.[32]

Based on this evidence, the Berle and Means company in which there is a separation of ownership and control is not the prevalent ownership structure. This conclusion is even more emphatic in the smaller company sample. While countries with a relatively strong incidence of widely held firms composes a substantial portion of the world market index, an understanding of governance structures, how they evolve and how they can be improved requires an understanding of the ownership structures of other countries.

La Porta et al. (1998) also investigate the incidence of dual class shares, pyramid structures and cross-shareholdings observing a significant difference in the 'high' and 'low' categories in the use of dual class shares. In the 'high' category, to control 20 per cent of the votes of a company, a holding of 19.7 per cent of the shares is necessary. The country in which dual class shares are most important is Norway in which 18 per cent of the shares are needed to control 20 per cent of the votes. In the 'low' category, 17.6 per cent of the shares is needed to control 20 per cent of the votes; in Sweden 12.6 per cent of the shares are needed to control 20 per cent of the votes. Thus the dual class structure does not appear very important overall although the differences between the 'high' and 'low' categories were statistically significant and there were individual countries where the dual class structures were important. These results are for the largest firms and the 20 per cent control value. Although not investigated, using the smaller firm sample should increase the importance of dual class shares.

Observing 18 per cent of the firms with a pyramid structure or a not widely held parent for the 'high' category and 31 per cent for the 'low' category, they conclude that the pyramid is a more effective method to separate control and cash flow rights. Cross-shareholdings were minor in all countries except Germany and Sweden.

Probably the most interesting results relate to family control in the large company sample.[33] They observe that in an average country the ultimate family owners control on average 25 per cent of the market value of the top 20 firms. In the 'high' category, the ownership is 20 per cent of the market value, whereas in the 'low' category it is 29 per cent. They also found that the ultimate family owner controls on average 1.3 of the largest firms in the country; in the 'high' shareholder protection category this value is 1.2, whereas for the 'low' category the value is 1.4. A high of 2 is found in Ireland, which is in the 'high' category; in the 'low' category Israel and Sweden have a value of 2.5. Although these firms are large in their domestic market and it is expected that professional rnanagement is more likely, it was found that on average about 69 per cent of families that control firms also participate in their management. This ranges from 75 per cent in the 'high' group to 64 per cent in the 'low' group.

Finally, the importance of banks/financial institutions holdings is investigated; the incidence of bank control is small, about 5 per cent on average for the large firm sample ranging from 2.5 per cent in the 'high' category to 7 per cent in the 'low' category. In the 'low' category, banks controlled 30 per cent of the firms in Belgium and 15 per cent in Germany.

Therefore, concentrated ownership is a pervasive phenomenon whose existence may generate serious problems for minority shareholders due to controlling shareholder activities that either shift wealth from the minority shareholder to the controlling shareholder or maximize the controlling shareholder's utility but not the wealth of all investors. Even more broadly, concentrated holdings can have a depressing effect on economic growth. Before considering governance system solutions to this problem, we investigate its impact.

4.2 Impact of Concentrated Holdings

4.2.1 Equivalence of cash flow and voting rights
In the principal–agent story, the misalignment of interests of managers and shareholders arises due to the small ownership of managers. As managerial ownership increases, managers bear more of the cost of non-wealth maximizing behaviour undertaken by them. If there is professional management, the controlling shareholder will monitor management carefully since there is no free-rider problem. With the increased holdings of equity the alignment of interests of managers and shareholders improves and minority shareholders should not be negatively impacted by management decisions.

However, there are potential costs to minority shareholders in firms in which there is a controlling shareholder. In general, the presence of a controlling position gives management an entrenched position. If decisions are made that do not benefit all shareholders and thus depress share price, the market for corporate control and the market for managers, if they exist, cannot operate to discipline poor managerial performance. While capital markets will produce a lower share price to reflect poor performance, the lower price is not a signal for a takeover but is just a cost to the controlling shareholder that is insufficient to offset any benefits that arise from a controlling position.

Benefits from a controlling position include managerial/controlling shareholder utility-maximizing decisions. These decisions include investments in pet projects and furthering political goals; engaging in costly investments intended to diversify the concentrated wealth of the controlling shareholder (see note 10); diversion of assets to companies owned by the controlling shareholder, and salary and bonus contracts unrelated to performance. Clearly the controlling shareholder values these benefits more than the costs associated with the reduced share price.

A large literature using US data addresses the performance of companies in which there are concentrated holdings where cash flow and voting rights are equivalent. Evidence shows that firm value, as proxied by a firm's q ratio,[34] increases in managerial equity at low levels of managerial equity and decreases in managerial equity at high levels of managerial equity (see Morck et al., 1988; McConnell and Servaes, 1990; and Anderson and Lee, 1997). There is also the same non-linear relationship between the q ratio and CEO ownership (Hermalin and Weisbach, 1991). While there is disagreement as to the level of ownership at which the relationship changes, there is no doubt that it exists. Problems of corporate performance and control are related to individual and not corporate ownership of a controlling position. Also the sale of a majority block had an impact on share price based on the identity of the seller and not the buyer. If the seller is an individual the share price increased by approximately 14 per cent, measured around the date of the announcement, while a corporate sale led to a 5 per cent increase. Thus the problems associated with entrenched behaviour are more acute when the blockholder is an individual rather than a corporation (Holderness and Sheehan, 1988).

The relationship of performance and managerial equity ownership is displayed in the form and mood of the acquisition of a company. Acquired firms whose prior managers had low equity stakes and engaged in non-value maximizing behaviour tend to be acquired in hostile takeovers whether by an investment group or by another operating company. Firms whose managers owned a large proportion of their firms' stock and engaged in non-value maximizing behaviour tended to be acquired by an investment group, typically organized by some of the managers, in friendly transactions such as LBOs. Finally, acquired firms whose prior management had a significant, but moderate, share of the firms' stock and did not engage in non-value maximizing behaviour tend to be acquired by another operating company in friendly transactions. For the first two classes of ownership, performance of the firms measured either by the q ratio or the stock price performance relative to a market index was inferior to that found for firms in the middle level of managerial ownership (see Halpern et al., 1999a, tables 5 and 6).

Another indication of the impact of entrenched management achieved through concentrated equity ownership is observed in the reaction by the board of directors to the poor performance of a founder controlled and managed company. Considering the replacement of founder CEOs for firms that performed poorly based on their two-year stock performance, a wealth gain to existing shareholders was achieved if the founder CEO was replaced as CEO and also removed from the board. Unless the latter occurred, improvement in performance was not observed. Thus, managerial entrenchment is a significant deterrent to improving the fortunes of poorly performing companies led by a founder CEO. Also founder-led firms were less likely than non-founder-led firms to replace the CEO due to poor performance, file for bankruptcy, engage in asset restructuring or be targeted for a takeover. This is consistent with the desire of founder firms to preserve capital and maintain control.[35]

Another way to look at the impact of large controlling positions is to investigate the impact on the share price of the unexpected death of founders who were also senior executives. Where the CEO was also the founder, the share price (adjusted for general market movements) increased approximately 3.5 per cent while for non-founder deaths, the share price changes were not statistically significant. This observation supports the conclusion that founders do not behave in a shareholder wealth-maximizing manner (Johnson et al., 1985). Also, the relationship of a change in share price to the size of the control position of CEOs and founders who died suddenly depends on the individual's ownership in the equity and not the employment status or whether or not the individual is a founder. Therefore, individuals with large ownership interests manage in ways consistent with entrenchment and an unexpected death leads to expectations of either a takeover or a change in internal control that will improve the firm's operating performance (Slovin and Sushka, 1993).

Given that there can be serious problems with concentrated holdings, can the governance system be expected to solve these problems and if not, what will? I consider the market-based governance system first and then the bank-based systems.

Under the market-based system, the usual market solutions are not feasible due to size of managerial equity holdings. The board of directors, while still concerned about shareholders, especially minority shareholders, cannot be expected to be effective. The directors recognize that the controlling share-holder has invested a substantial amount of wealth in the firm and it is unlikely that directors will disagree with the controlling shareholder's managerial decisions. However, a more diligent and less accommodating board would help to resolve this problem. Pension funds cannot mount a credible threat to force controlling shareholders to change their behaviour and thus are powerless. One potential solution is the equity market which, as a result of a lower share price for a poorly performing firm, will provide discipline if the company intends to issue equity. The only discipline remaining is the product market. With competition in the product market, non-value-maximizing decisions by controlling shareholders will ultimately lead to poor financial performance, financial distress and either bankruptcy, reorganization, or merger. This solution can take a long time but is assisted by pro-competitive policies within the economy including facilitating international competition in product and capital markets.[36] Where markets do not work, there is the substitution of corporate law. For example, in France there is a special responsibility given to controlling shareholders to reflect their influence in the decisions of the company. In Canada, an oppression remedy and a set of minority shareholder protections in provincial securities legislation protect minority shareholders. These protections include minority shareholder approval of certain transactions. In this instance, minority shareholder protection is found in required minority shareholder votes on certain issues. Even with this legislation there remains a question of its effectiveness.[37]

There is one solution that is effective but is a voluntary decision made by the controlling shareholder – the going private transaction through the LBO. In this transaction, the controlling shareholder joins with an LBO specialist and other financial backers to purchase the shares of the company through a combination of a large amount of debt and equity. The incumbent management typically ends up by having a larger proportion of equity in the new firm than in the pre-transaction firm but a smaller amount of personal wealth invested in the new firm. Thus the LBO permits the owners to diversify their wealth by taking some money out of the firm to invest in other financial assets. The incentive to engage in diversification activities through firm investment decisions is eliminated. The LBO partner has an equity interest in the firm so its monitoring function is consistent with the desires by management to increase shareholder wealth. For most of these transactions, the firm remains private since this is the optimal structure for the company (see Halpern et al., 1999b). However, this transaction occurs only for those controlling shareholders that want to diversify their personal wealth and are prepared to be monitored by an active investor. Further, the firm must have operating characteristics that permit the use of a substantial amount of debt in its capital structure.

In Germany the issue of family controlled firms is not very significant for the largest firms; they are either widely held or controlled by a widely held financial institution. The issue becomes relevant for smaller companies where family control is more important and widely held financial institution control is modest. In the German bank-based governance systems, the lack of market solutions does not functionally distinguish them from the market-based governance systems – market solutions do not work. In discussions on the widely held company and the bank-based governance system it was observed that there were ineffective boards and inadequate shareholder oversight. There is no reason to believe that board performance will improve in the situation of controlling shareholdings. The banks as monitors still have the same objective

– reduce the probability of default and maintain the value of their debt claims. If controlling shareholders wish to take advantage of their position, the banks will not be concerned as long as their claims are unaffected. The labour members of the supervisory board continue to have the same objective.

In Japan, family control and closely held companies are found within small firms. However, as noted previously, ultimate control is located in groups where no one member has control. Thus the governance issues of closely held companies are not as serious. The problem is one of entrenchment of the management where control is found in the group. However, for the situations in which it arises, the Japanese system performs no better than the German or the US systems in protecting minority shareholders from wealth loss.

In the bank-based systems, just as in the market-centred system, the solution is the product market and its impact on the efficient operations of the firms. Aided by pro-competitive behaviour by domestic governments in opening markets to internal and external competition, the product market can resolve many of the problems observed in closely held companies.

Although the discussion is couched in terms of bank- and market-based systems, the true distinction appears to be closely held and widely held companies with no controlling shareholder. This distinction is also relevant in emerging/developing economies. Even in countries with reasonably active capital markets, the potential problem of concentrated holdings is important. Finally, the issue has been framed as family concentration with companies run by founders or the founders' family. There is some empirical evidence that suggests the problems are more likely to arise in the latter situation (see Morck et al., 1998). We consider this issue in the section on pyramid structures.

4.2.2 Voting rights in excess of cash flow rights

When voting rights exceed cash flow rights and there is control through voting rights, there is a significant potential for non-controlling shareholder wealth to be diminished through actions of the controlling shareholders. The voting control prohibits a hostile takeover thus providing the controlling shareholder with an entrenched position through which wealth can be diverted; the wealth shifting techniques have been described in the previous section. However, there is the added factor that the controlling shareholder owns a small proportion of the total shares of the firm, that is, the cash flow rights are small. Thus the cost to the controlling shareholder of diversionary activity is small. This situation is identical to the principal–agent problem described by Berle and Means. The controlling shareholder has an entrenched position and since the cost of such activity to the controlling shareholder is less than under the situation of equality of cash flow and voting rights, there is a greater incentive to engage in wealth diversionary activities. While there are legitimate uses of corporate structures that separate cash flow and voting rights, the potential problems can be serious.

Dual class share structures   In a dual class share structure there are two classes of equity securities – superior and inferior voting shares. The number of votes per share for each class will differ; in some examples the inferior voting shares have no votes and the superior voting shares have one vote. The founder of the firm or the founder's family holds an interest in the superior voting shares and inferior voting shares so as to provide a controlling interest. The dual class share structure can be achieved in a number of ways, some of which are illegal in certain jurisdictions. In the situation where the two security classes are achieved by a stock split, existing shareholders have to agree to the recapitalization and if new inferior voting shares are issued, new shareholders will set a price that reflects potential diversionary activities. The fact that current shareholders must approve or that new shareholders must purchase the shares has led commentators to argue that whether or not dual class shares lead to problems, the shareholders have priced the securities for this contingency.[38] This incorporation of the contingency in the share price is certainly true in situations where there are alternatives to the securities being issued. However, in some countries controls on investments in foreign securities can reduce the size of the alternative investment set available for the increasing pools of funds that are being created in institutions through mutual and pension funds. In fact, in many countries with dual class share structures, the inferior voting shares are widely held by large financial institutions that can agitate for changes to address poor managerial performance within the firm but can only rely on the 'sunlight' principle to achieve any results.

There are generally two rationales for the dual class share structure. The first is to provide the firm with needed capital to grow while permitting the founder to maintain control. The founder is then free to undertake firm-specific investments that would have no value in the event of a takeover. The founder may have the technological and/or management expertise to help the firm grow, and the dual class structure protects the founder from takeover or other pressures to change the strategy of the firm. Without the dual class structure, a firm that has significant growth opportunities would have to issue voting equity with a result of a loss in control by the founder. The second reason relates to the desire by the founder or founder's family to reduce its investment in the firm and thereby diversify its personal portfolio or use the funds for personal reasons without losing control of the firm. For example in the stock split method, assuming that the founder has a controlling position, the founder will sell enough of the inferior voting shares so that control is maintained but the dollar investment in the firm is reduced. When the inferior voting share has no votes, the controlling shareholder can sell the entire inferior voting shares holding only the voting shares. With a diversified personal portfolio, the founder/family need not make investment decisions within the firm that reduce the risk of the company and the controlling shareholder's personal wealth.

One specific problem associated with dual class shares is the potential of the sale of the controlling interest without the sale of the entire company. Thus a takeover premium can be paid to the control block without an associated bid to the inferior voting shares. In this situation, there will be a difference in share prices to reflect this possibility.[39]

There have been a number of studies of dual class shares. Many investigated the differential in share prices between superior and inferior voting shares finding a large difference ranging up to a high of 82 per cent in Italy to 5 per cent in the US with a typical value of 10–20 per cent. Evidence on the impact of the dual class recapitalization on share prices is mixed. There are small statistically significant negative abnormal returns around the announcement of the dual class recapitalization with a much larger negative response while the controlling holder has large holdings ranging from 30 to 55 per cent (see Jarrell and Poulsen, 1988). In Canada the response of the share price to an announcement of a recapitalization while negative is not statistically significant (see Jog and Riding, 1986).

An interesting perspective on the impact of dual class share structures is achieved by looking at situations where dual class shares have been unified into a single class of voting shares. In Israel, following legislation that banned the use of inferior voting shares to raise new equity, all of the dual class share structures were unified. Prior to the legislation, 40 per cent of the companies on the exchange had dual class share structures. Also, one year prior to the unification, the price premium of superior over inferior voting shares was on average 54 per cent with a median of 21 per cent. This premium reflected the possibility of a takeover and the unequal premium that would be paid to controlling and non-controlling shareholders. In the unification there was in effect a payment to the controlling shareholder for the reduction in their control position. It was observed that the net of market share rates of return for the one year prior to the unifications were positive for both classes of shares but much greater for the inferior voting shares. Also the unification, while removing the separation of cash flow and control rights, kept the control group voting power approximately unchanged. Thus the observed increase in share value for both classes reflects the reduction of agency costs associated with separation of control and cash flow rights and not the higher probability of a takeover and equal sharing of any premium.[40]

Pyramid structures The pyramid structure relies on the control of companies lower down in the pyramid by those higher up, with the company at the top of pyramid usually controlled by a founder/family member.[41] The companies in the pyramid are operating companies and apart from the controlling position held by another company in the pyramid, the shares can be widely held; in economies where there are large pension funds, institutional investors have significant holdings. The companies in the pyramid have boards of directors, publicly traded shares and, in some cases, non-founder management.

There are a number of benefits accorded to the pyramid structure. First, as in the dual class share structure, the pyramid structure enables controlling shareholders to finance new growth without losing control. Second, the pyramid typically has holdings in more than one industry and thus provides a diversified portfolio to investors in the controlling company. To the extent that there are exchange controls that limit acquisition of foreign equities by individual shareholders but not by corporations, the pyramid can purchase foreign companies and provide foreign content to investors. Third, the pyramid structure provides an internal monitoring device and thus is an alternative to the discipline of the market. If subsidiary company management does not meet expectations, the poorly performing manager can be dismissed by the controlling family/founder quickly and without any external pressure or input. Of course, it is the controlling party's expectations of performance that are relevant and these expectations need not be the same as those of a non-controlling shareholder. Finally, if the economy has a lack of managerial expertise, the pyramid structure, through the controlling shareholder, provides this expertise and monitoring for other companies in the pyramid. However, if the other companies in the pyramid are in different industries it is hard to visualize any benefits from the controlling shareholder beyond general managerial assistance.

Pyramid structures can have serious shortcomings.[42] The general problem of control without significant investment in the company is the same as identified in the dual class share structure. However, in the pyramid structure there are some added concerns. With the ability of the controlling shareholder of a pyramid to control a substantial amount of the economic activity in a country, especially but not exclusively in developing economies, the controlling shareholder can have significant influence on the political system. This political access combined with lobbying activities can permit controlling shareholders to entrench their positions against foreign competition by raising barriers to capital mobility and international direct investment. The substantial wealth found in the pyramids can skew capital distribution and have a negative impact on the growth and functioning of domestic capital markets; all to the benefit of the existing set of controlling shareholders in the economy. In addition, there is preferential access to capital within the pyramid that provides an internal capital market permitting the controlling shareholder to bypass conventional capital markets and the associated monitoring function they provide. The internal capital market is based either on cash flows generated by operating companies in the structure passed through to the controlling shareholder for their investment purposes or through a subsidiary finance company. For example, in the Daewoo structure, there is Daewoo Securities Company that was used as a cash pipeline to support the automobile manufacturing business. The confusing corporate structures associated with a pyramid, often made more opaque by the existence of dual class shares, make it difficult for the capital market to value the overall operation. With small holdings in the subsidiary companies, an improvement in share price of individual companies in the pyramid will not be of benefit to the controlling shareholders.[43]

Just as in the dual class structure, shares of subsidiary companies have to be issued to finance growth, and investors price and purchase these shares, knowing full well the potential problems of the pyramid structure. In this sense the pyramid structure meets the market test. However, the caveats to this conclusion noted for the dual class structure apply here leaving the market test not very revealing.

Therefore, concentrated holdings, either directly or in situations where voting rights exceed cash flow rights, can have a negative impact on the firm and ultimately on the growth of an economy. Typically, the controlling shareholders are founders or families of founders. However, it is possible that we are too hard on the controlling shareholders; perhaps there is a difference in results depending on whether the concentrated holding reflects founder or heir control. By looking at economic growth within different economies and its relationship to founder versus heir control, a picture of the problems of control can be identified. Of course, due to the length of time over which development has occurred, developing countries have more entrepreneur/founder wealth whereas more developed countries have more heir wealth.

In economies where heir wealth is large relative to GDP, there is lower growth, more signs of rent-seeking and less spending on innovation compared to economies in which self-made/founder wealth is large relative to GDP. This does not suggest that the problems associated with concentrated wealth do not occur in the latter case, but with a lower frequency.[44] Further, heir controlled firms show lower financial performance, capital–labour ratios and R&D spending relative to control samples of the same size and age and it appears that concentrated inherited corporate control impedes growth. Morck et al. (1998) call this observation the 'Canadian Disease' based on empirical evidence on the Canadian market; further research on its applicability in other countries in which there are concentrated holdings may permit a more inclusive descriptor for the poor performance.

Solutions Whether companies are in market- or bank-based systems, solutions to problems of concentrated holdings with different cash flow and voting rights are not obvious. The same constraints on the operations of corporate governance systems identified in the discussion of concentrated holdings discussion are present here. Any technique that breaks down the pyramid and results in a number of independent companies with no controlling shareholders will improve capital markets and permit the domestic corporate governance system to operate. Once again we have to rely on the functioning of the product market to solve this problem. In one sense, the passage of time will transfer control from founder to heir and if the qualities that made the founder successful are not found in the heirs, the product market can be expected to have an influence. Even if family members decide to hire professional management, they have a difficult time stepping away from control. Moreover, there is some empirical evidence suggesting that heir controlled firms are not expected to perform as well under product market competition than founder controlled firms. Morck et al. (1998) observed stock price performance of heir and founder controlled firms upon the announcement that the Free Trade Agreement (FTA) between Canada and the United States would be signed. They observed that stock prices of heir controlled firms fell along with the price of widely held firms while firms controlled by business founders gained the most. The FTA would promote capital market openness and product market competition.

Germany is the only country of the four on which we have focused in which there is a pyramid problem. However, it is a major problem in the rest of the world. Movements to improve the economic framework in which companies operate and to reduce constraints on competition are ways to facilitate the end of the concentrated ownership with different voting and cash flow rights.

5. CONVERGENCE OF GOVERNANCE SYSTEMS

> The days of divergent governance systems presiding over convergent organizational forms, however, are likely to be numbered as seasoned international investors urge a common model. (Useem, 1998, p. 57)

There are many commentators that believe convergence in governance systems will occur in the major countries – Germany, Japan, the UK and the US as a result of a number of internal and external forces. However, looking at the major bank-based systems, there are many rigidities that inhibit significant changes in equity holdings of market participants and corporate organizational structure in a short period of time. Also the development and efficient operations of capital and takeover markets is a longer run phenomenon which will require significant changes in ownership structure. In the US, the Glass–Steagall Act prohibitions on universal banking may be loosened in the future but it is not clear that changes would result in structures that emulate existing bank-based systems. To do so, investments by banks in their clients' equity, in order to generate concentrated holdings and engage in monitoring, would have to generate an economic benefit or bank share prices would fall and market solutions to this inefficient behaviour would follow. In the UK there are no prohibitions against banks holding the equity of their clients yet it is not observed. While it is true that pressures for convergence exist at some level, and organizational changes are occurring where German or Japanese companies begin to organize themselves more like US companies, it is difficult to believe that full convergence will ever occur. Convergence would require changes in ownership structures, a relaxation of cultural constraints to certain types of behaviour and development of markets that require very basic changes in financial systems. What can be expected is a convergence in decisions intended to improve markets, to improve monitoring for the benefit of shareholders and directly to improve operations that will lead to better financial performance of relevance to shareholders. Therefore, we anticipate changes to occur in the companies in bank-based governance systems' countries leading to a convergence of corporate structure and managerial decisions and less so in governance systems.

Although the focus is on the major economies, a number of the changes identified as necessary to have convergence will be applicable to other countries and hybrid systems.[45] For the emerging and developing economies, infrastructure and in some situations legal systems are necessary.

To have governance system convergence in the Japanese and German governance contexts, it is necessary to increase the effectiveness of markets – capital and takeover markets; on the US side there would have to be a move toward more concentrated holdings to provide monitoring. In the former, the capital market would improve by increasing its liquidity with more listed companies and an increased volume of equity transactions. This improved equity market would provide monitoring as well as financing functions. Improvements in the market for corporate control require sufficient numbers of shares to be available so bids can be undertaken. In the German context there is the added problem of the voting control of banks far in excess of their equity holdings – this is the prototypical example of the Berle and Means separation of ownership and control.[46] A necessary condition for improvements in both of these markets is the reduction of concentrated holdings. This implies that banks and other corporations would need to reduce their investments in companies. Also the control of corporate funding by the banks would have to be reduced. On the US side, increasing concentrated holdings would arise through institutional holdings or specialized companies that make investments in order to monitor and where necessary engage in management for companies in which they invest.[47]

In both Germany and Japan, there is no evidence of decreasing bank equity holdings in the corporate sector. In Germany, bank ownership of large blocks of equity in firms is increasing whereas in Japan it has remained stable (Macey and Miller, 1997, n. 60). However, changes may be under way with the new capital adequacy requirements imposed by the Bank for International Settlements. The banks in both Germany and Japan may find it more productive to invest their funds in assets other than shares of corporations. In addition, the importance of German and Japanese banks in funding corporations is falling (Macey and Miller, 1997, n. 61). The banks had significant influence on funding when capital was hard to obtain. However, with alternatives more readily available as capital markets become freer, companies no longer need to rely on banks for funding.

In a functional sense, the US model has evolved to include the insider controlled system of large shareholder/financial investor monitoring. With the flexibility afforded by a capital market-based system, corporate structures have evolved that maximize the value of the firm and of shareholders in the firm. The LBO, whether friendly or hostile, permanent or transitory, has functionally replicated the monitoring services provided by financial institutions and large shareholders found in the banking-based system. For a subset of companies with specific characteristics, the LBO has introduced strong monitoring by a party with a financial interest in the equity of the firm and hence interests aligned with management. Further the financing of the firm is structured so as to minimize the cost of a change in control in the event of financial distress. The LBO, although not as frequently used as in the 1980s, has left an important legacy in the operations of firms, structures and ownership.[48]

Given the vested interests that have to be persuaded that a different system will provide greater wealth to them than the current system, the existing infrastructure, the existing structure of equity ownership (pyramid, dual class, bank-controlled and closely held) in insider systems that would have to be dismantled, and the lack of political will of governments to make some of these changes, it is unlikely that true convergence will ever occur.

In this section, the forces for change and actual changes in the companies in the bank-based countries are identified. We conclude that with these pressures on existing managers and governments, managerial behaviour will begin to converge and there will be movement in the bank-based systems toward shareholder wealth maximization.

5.1 Forces Consistent with Convergence of Systems (Managerial Behaviour)

5.1.1 Improvement of domestic equity markets

Institutional holdings   Bank-based systems need to improve their capital markets. Improvement can be achieved by increasing the size of the pool of funds available for investment in domestic equities and, given the size of the pool, the amount of capital that can be invested in domestic equities. Investments in equities can be undertaken on an individual basis where the investor purchases the securities directly or indirectly through institutional holdings. Individuals investing through institutions have generated very large capital pools. The institutions – whether mutual funds, corporate, individual or government pension funds, or other investment funds – have become large holders of companies' shares. For example, for the top 1000 firms in the US, institutions held approximately 43 per cent of the equity in 1985 whereas in 1997 the proportion was 60 per cent. Considering all equities, the proportion of institutional holding is less, but in 1994, for example, it was approximately 50 per cent. The institutional holdings in the UK are even greater than in the US. In 1994, institutions held approximately 80 per cent of the shares in the UK market. Non-individual holdings in Japan, France and Germany are also large, but these reflect bank and intercorporate holdings as well as institutional investments.

Pension plans, an important part of the institutional market and the owners of government bonds as well as corporate bonds and equities, are found in both the private and the public sectors. The pool of pension fund capital for the top eight pension asset countries as forecast for the year 2000 is presented in Table 1.4. As observed in the table, there is a large discrepancy among the countries not only in total pension assets but also in their per capita asset values. The variation reflects a number of factors including domestic country tax provisions facilitating private retirement planning and the use of pay-as-you-go versus funding of pension liabilities by governments as well as individual companies. For example, in Germany, which has surprisingly low values of pension fund assets in both absolute and standardized values, there is a history of pay-as-you-go pension financing and the social security system, just as in many other countries, invests in government bonds. In the private sector, some companies internally manage their pension funds; the company builds a reserve for pensions and invests it within the company. Companies engaged in this type of pension financing are required to engage in some form of insurance that guarantees the pension funds. Other firms invest pension pools through insurance companies; the insurance companies invest in bonds and equities consistent with life insurance investment regulations (Haupt, 1994, pp. 556–60).

Table 1.4   Pension fund capital around the world in 2000: top eight pension asset countries in $US billion

Country	Pension assets	Assets per capita	Largest public/industry fund (1996)	Largest corporate fund
United States	8 078	29 000	TIAA/CREF $185	General Motors $80
Japan	1 926	14 000	Local Government $82	Nippon Telephone $16
UK	1 261	21 000	Electricity Supply Group $25	British Telecom $34
Canada	607	20 000	Ontario Teachers $37	Canadian National $7
Switzerland	501	69 000	Canton of Zurich $10	CIBA–Geigy $8
Netherlands	440	27 000	ABP $143	Philips $16
Australia	242	13 000	NSW State $15	Telstra Super $4
Germany	199	2 000	N/A	Siemens $14

Source: Goldman and Sachs 1997, cited in Ambachtsheer and Ezra (1998).

Even though there is no necessity for the per capita pension assets across these countries to equalize over time, there is scope for growth for the countries with low per capita pension assets. The importance of pension funds as liquidity pools for the domestic capital markets in general and equity markets in particular will only increase in the future as individuals and governments face the need to finance the medical and physical requirements of an aging population. This will lead to pressures to reform private and government pension funding. In fact, some governments are reviewing their pay-as-you-go plans with a view to funding these plans thereby increasing the pool of funds available to invest in financial assets. In addition, standardization of investment rules and pension funding across European Union countries will have an impact on the size of the pool. All of these factors will assist in the improvement of capital markets.

Easing domestic investment restrictions   Many countries have investment restrictions on institutional pools of capital. These constraints, while in many cases nominally intended to reduce the risk of the investment portfolios, have serious consequences for the individuals who are the beneficiaries of the portfolios. In addition, the restrictions can impede the growth of the domestic equity market. In Table 1.5 a number of the investment restrictions on pension fund portfolios are presented for five countries as of 1995. The investment

Table 1.5 *Government-imposed investment restrictions on pension funds, 1995*

Country	International equities	Domestic equities	Property	Principal guaranteed	Foreign denominated
Canada	<20%	–	–	–	–
France	–	<65%	<10%	–	–
Germany	<5%	<30%	<25%	–	–
Japan	<30%	<30%	<20%	>50%	–
Switzerland	<25%	<50%	–	–	<30%

Source: Ambachtsheer and Ezra (1998, table 17.1) based on Goldman Sachs (1997) 'The Global Pension Time Bomb and its Capital Market Impact'.

restriction on domestic equities of 30 per cent in Germany and Japan limits the size of the equity market, negatively influences its efficiency and reduces the wealth of the beneficiaries of the pension plans since optimal portfolios cannot be constructed.

As an example of the problems associated with investment restrictions consider the restriction on investment in international equities. The purpose of the restriction is most likely an attempt by domestic governments, perhaps pushed by lobbying efforts of domestic companies, to build the domestic equity market. However, there are unintended negative consequences in two dimensions. First, domestic issuers can issue equities such as restricted voting shares or shares in operating companies in pyramid structures since there are no alternative investments in international markets available to domestic investors. Second, the investor does not obtain the benefits of international diversification and thus must accept a higher portfolio risk.

Increasingly, governments recognize investment restrictions can cause problems, although the movement to remove them is not rapid. In some government pension plans, funds were used to purchase government bonds and in some cases, a small amount of corporate bonds. With the need to generate higher returns and the recognition that equities outperform bonds over the horizons generally considered by pension plans, there is discussion of investing a significant proportion of the funds in equities. For example in 1995 the Dutch government introduced legislation to permit the Dutch civil service pension, ABP, to invest its pension assets without investment restrictions for the best interests of its stakeholders. This legislation ended ABP's previous investments in government bonds and residential mortgages. In the private sector Japan is undergoing significant changes in its regulations surrounding pension plans. The restrictions are being removed and foreign firms are now allowed to manage pension funds.[49]

In the private and public sectors, a relaxation of investment restrictions will ultimately increase the size of the pool of funds invested in domestic and international equities and ultimately will result in more effective capital markets.

Other changes in domestic markets   A number of changes in the domestic markets of countries with bank-based and even market-based systems are beginning to erase the differences in the structures. For example, in Japan, there was a revision to the criminal code to make it easier to sue companies. This change led to a number of shareholder suits such as a suit against Nomura securities for covering trading losses for preferred clients and Sumitomo for losses in corporate copper trading. With the ability to sue, shareholders become more involved and can address certain types of managerial behaviour. However, this technique is *ex post*; *ex ante* monitoring and control of behaviour requires more fundamental changes.

In both Germany and Japan, more use is being made of incentive-based compensation. In Japan there was concern that cultural norms would make individual incentive pay more difficult. While a consideration, a number of companies such as Toyota and Daiwa Securities have introduced incentive compensation. In Germany, Deutsche Telekom and Daimler Benz have introduced stock options for senior executives.

In terms of corporate structures, there have also been changes. Just recently Deutsche Bank has announced that it will transfer US$24 billion of its holdings of German companies into a new unit. The holdings in this unit could be sold to finance capital needs. Also, there has been a movement to eliminate complex shareholding structures in Canada, Switzerland and Scandinavia. Finally there have been examples of shareholder activism often precipitated by foreign investors. An example is the removal of the chair of Olivetti in Italy.

5.1.2   International influences

International investment in equities   The significant growth in cross-border financial transactions reflects the growing internationalization of markets and the relaxation of constraints on capital flows between countries. The information in Table 1.6 illustrates the growth in this area. Each of the countries experienced a large increase in cross-border transactions with the largest increase found in Italy and the smallest in Japan. Part of this increase in cross-border transactions is the purchase of foreign equities by domestic investors. Typically, this behaviour is found in pension funds that can reduce risk through international diversification. Also there are mutual funds that specialize in the construction of portfolios of securities of firms in a specific

Table 1.6   Cross-border transactions in bonds and equities (as a percentage of GDP)[1]

	1985	1990	1995	1996*
Canada	26.7	64.4	194.5	234.8
France	21.4	53.6	179.6	229.2
Germany	33.4	56.7	169.4	196.8
Italy	4.1	26.6	252.8	435.4
Japan	62.5	119.4	65.1	82.8
United States	35.1	89.0	135.3	151.5

Notes:
* 1996 data refer to January through September.
[1]Gross purchases and sales of securities between residents and nonresidents.

Source: Crockett (1997, table 1 p. 91).

foreign country. Investors can then purchase a combination of these mutual funds and generate their own diversification. Alternatively, an investor can purchase a mutual fund that already provides an internationally diversified portfolio. These investments are undertaken in foreign markets in which the institutional investor has little knowledge of the operations of the markets or good information on the company itself. This asymmetry of information tends to dampen investments in foreign countries and leads to a home bias in which investors prefer to invest in equities in their home country.

The initiation of cross-listing of equity securities has made the process of international investing much easier for the non-domestic investor. The growth in cross-listing has been significant. For example, in 1986 there were 266 cross-listed securities on NASDAQ and in 1996 there were 460. The New York Stock Exchange also has a large number of cross-listed securities with 365 cross-listed securities in 1996. The cross-listing can be accomplished either by listing the security directly on the market or indirectly through a 'depositary receipt' (DR). The latter is a derivative security issued by a financial institution in the country in which the DR trades and is based on an underlying foreign security that has been immobilized in a bank in the home market of the company listing the DR. The DRs trade on the non-domestic exchange and the basic security trades in its home country. Non-domestic holders of a DR can vote the shares. In Table 1.7 the number of foreign securities and DRs in the three US markets are presented for 1996.

By far the largest component of the foreign issues group is Canada with 162 issues on NASDAQ followed by Israel with 54. The largest number of countries

Table 1.7   Cross-listed securities, 1996

	Foreign issues	Depository receipts	Total
NASDAQ	318	142	460
NYSE	118	247	365
AMEX	58	7	65

Source: NASDAQ Fact Book, 1997.

use the DR approach with the UK having 40, Japan 16 and Australia 14 on NASDAQ. Germany does not make significant use of the cross-listed market.[50]

In a cross-listing, required information disclosure and the degree to which home country financial statements must be translated to US accounting standards depend upon whether the listing company intends to issue new equity or just trade existing shares, and if new shares are to be sold, to whom. For example if a private placement of new equity is being considered, the information disclosure is modest. However, if the company intends to issue new equity, conversion of domestic financial statements is required; this conversion can have embarrassing results. For example Daimler Benz, the first German company to cross-list on the NYSE, reconciled its statements to US accounting standards and due to the past treatment of hidden reserves, a profit of DM 615 billion was transformed to a loss of DM 1.6 billion. Daimler Benz did not intend to raise capital at the time of the listing and technically did not need to translate their home country financial statements to US standards.

There are a number of benefits to existing firms in cross-listing their securities; benefits which have been touted by the NYSE in its attempt to grow through the use of international listings. These include increases in share prices for first-time listing on US exchanges[51] and significant reduction in risk measures especially for companies that list in US markets for the first time. Both of these effects should result in a lower cost of capital to the firm.[52] It should also be recognized that it is the current, not new, shareholders that benefit from this reduction in the cost of capital. Whether the gain is sufficient to offset the benefits of control found in a number of the closely held foreign companies will determine whether foreign companies cross-list their securities. Other benefits include increasing liquidity effects,[53] the potential to expand its investor base, increased visibility of the company and its products,[54] and the possibility of using shares to finance future acquisitions. These benefits come at some cost. These costs include direct costs of converting financial statements and indirect costs of providing information to the market which until the time of listing had remained less visible, increasing the global risk exposure of the equity and possibly the acquisition of a large block of shares by a foreign entity. However, improved information availability for markets in which information was not readily available has resulted in an increase in price as investors removed the negative price impact associated with incomplete information.

In addition to existing firms, newly privatized companies have decided to cross-list their securities not only to expand the size of the capital pool in which the issue can be made but also to increase the visibility of the company and its products. Deutsche Telekom and Huaneng Power (a Chinese company) are examples of newly privatized companies that have cross-listed their securities. There is still scope for continued privatizations and thus cross-listings from this area along with additional equity issues from previously privatized companies will continue the trend to the purchase of equity by foreign investors.

Shareholder activism and the quest for performance Institutions have become increasingly active in corporate governance and corporate performance issues through the proxy process or through informal discussions with board members or management. Public sector pension funds are the most vocal in this respect. However, smaller investment portfolio companies have also been effective in instituting change by forming coalitions with institutional investors. Currently in North America there is a movement from defined benefit to defined contributions pension plans. In the former, the pension benefit is specified related to years of employment and average earnings with contributions by the company and the employee to fund the expected pension liabilities. With a pension payout independent of the performance of the plan, shareholders bear the risk of the pension plan and decisions about the pension plan are made through a pension committee recognizing the shareholder impact of its decisions. In a defined contribution plan, the individual employees along with the company fund a specified contribution that is then invested by the employee in one or more mutual funds. In this case, the employee bears the risk. In this scenario, the investor is more directly connected to the process, and with heightened interests will impose greater pressure on the fund to perform. This pressure can result in a more activist position being taken by the mutual funds.

With mutual and pension funds investing more in foreign equities either directly or through cross-listed securities, their equity holdings will place them in a good position to generate the same pressure on management and boards in international companies as is currently being done in some domestic markets. The results should be a greater pressure by management to make operational and real investment decisions that increase the value of the shareholders' wealth. However, there are caveats to this conclusion. Considering Germany, the companies most likely to have foreign institutional investors are widely held. Since the banks continue to have control far in excess of their equity ownership, the foreign investor may not have enough shares to have an impact either through the proxy process or even through moral suasion. In addition, the likelihood of forming coalitions with domestic financial institutions in Germany is low. In Japan, given the cross-shareholdings and the main bank system, there are few shareholders that trade securities. Pension funds invest through insurance companies who, along with trust companies, maintain their holdings, as do corporations who hold shares in the company. Only the mutual funds trade securities, but with their small size have no economic interest in monitoring companies.

Another influence on shareholder activism is the performance of the overall stock market. When the market was generating large returns, there was no reason for shareholder activism. However, with the long decline in the market, shareholders now need to find ways to increase the share price of their companies. Individual shareholders will agitate for changes to improve the performance of the equity of the firm. Similarly poor equity performance will shake the foundation for the cross-holdings of shares. Typically, corporations would accept a low rate of return on their portfolio investment as a cross-holding in exchange for long-term business returns. As long as the combined package was positive, the cross-holding made sense. However, if the package becomes negative, the incentive to maintain cross-holdings may be reduced leading to an increase in the shares available in the market and further reductions in share price.

With these changes, international institutional investors will be important, and at the margin for companies in which there can be a significant enough holding of equity or the possibility of building a coalition with domestic institutional holders, they can have significant impact on the company's operations and decision making. However, in much, if not most, of the world concentrated holdings are the rule, not the exception, and the influence of foreign institutional investors will not be large. Further, improved performance by companies that have responded to institutional pressure to improve shareholder wealth will be a good guide to other firms but will not be a leading force to generate change. Thus, conclusions that international institutional investors will urge a common governance mode cannot at present be justified. Any influence toward a common governance model will depend upon the influence of competition and the product market. Only with this pressure will ownership structure be forced to change if in fact it cannot compete with firms that have different structures.

5.2 Influence of Poor Economic Conditions

An important catalyst to change is the poor economic conditions in a number of countries. The recessionary economy of Japan and the currency crisis-induced recessions in a number of other countries have put pressure on governments to change regulations and on firms to alter their operations and structures. When the economy is booming, poor decisions can be buried under significant cash flows from corporate operations. However, with poor operations, inefficient decisions are brought into stark relief and change is necessary. In some situations change comes slowly since the infrastructure, regulations and years of corporate governance oversight and corporate operating decisions are hard to alter.

In Japan transactions have occurred to rationalize industries that are in financial stress. For example in the oil industry, Nippon Oil and Mitsubishi Oil Co Ltd combined to become Japan's largest oil company; in 1995 Mitsubishi Bank Ltd and Bank of Tokyo merged; just recently Dar-Ichi Kangyo Bank Ltd, Industrial Bank of Japan and Fuji Bank Ltd agreed to join and form a holding company that will have separate functional operating companies. The benefits from these mergers have to be found in reduced operating and administrative costs and generating economies of scale in all facets of the business including the introduction of costly technology. This strategy requires labour reductions, which historically have been difficult to implement. For example, the existence of government regulations make the use of temporary workers difficult and thus limit the ability of firms to convert semi-fixed costs to variable costs and hence reduce the business risk of corporations.[55]

While the above-noted transactions will result in more efficient organizations, the monitoring of managerial behaviour for the benefit of shareholders may not necessarily change. The impetus for the changes that occurred and the constraint on future wasteful managerial action is competition from international product markets. One transaction that could have a more focused impact on managerial behaviour and shareholder value is the investment by Renault in the equity of Nissan Motor Co Ltd making it the largest shareholder and an example of foreign non-portfolio investors entering Japan.

A similar change is occurring in South Korea where Daewoo, the country's second largest conglomerate firm (Chaebol) is in financial difficulty and its creditors are prepared to accept a restructuring plan. This plan requires Daewoo to sell or spin off about 40 subsidiaries, leaving it with six affiliated companies focused on automobile manufacturing. The government supports the restructuring with government regulators threatening to permit creditors to sell the assets if the restructuring plan is not implemented expeditiously. Kim Dae Jung, President of South Korea, stated that the 'concentration of economic power in the Chaebol is no longer accepted by the market. Individual firms must be able to compete on their own against the world's best rather than as part of a corporate grouping'.[56] With this restructuring, the capital market will have more securities to purchase, provided the companies are publicly traded, and the pressure of foreign competition will make these companies more efficient. Of course, the final outcome of this restructuring will depend upon the ultimate ownership structure of the newly created companies and the effectiveness of the corporate governance system in generating managerial decisions that make the firm's operations efficient and generate wealth for shareholders.

Other changes in the Japanese capital markets will improve their competition and ultimately the capital markets. For example, there is deregulation by the Japanese government to allow banks, brokers and insurers to enter each other's markets. Government-fixed trading commissions will end in the near future permitting competitive commission rates.

5.3   Convergence: The Ugly Side

In a perverse way, convergence of decision making has already arrived in the four countries under consideration. Regardless of the corporate governance system, there are companies, or more correctly individuals within companies, who engaged in behaviour that led to serious financial problems. Some of these were problems associated with the use of derivative securities[57] while others did not need esoteric securities to generate financial mayhem. Whether the company was Barings, Sumitomo, Daiwa Bank, Metalgesellschaft, the equity arbitrage group at the London office of Credit Suisse First Boston, Proctor and Gamble, Orange County or Long Term Capital Management, there were common elements: the use of compensation contracts that were structured to provide an incentive to take risk and managerial oversight of the decision maker that was inadequate at best and flawed at worst. In situations where there is potential for excessive risk taking, monitoring must be very thorough. Monitoring becomes even more important when the decisions concern strategies that can by their nature be very risky.[58]

Part of the problem was overall management's lack of knowledge of the derivative position that existed, of the decisions undertaken by individuals in this area and of the basic risk of derivatives. Monitoring systems were inadequate and individuals were able to make decisions without any controls. Even in governance systems where monitoring is supposed to be most rigorous, Japan and Germany, derivative problems arose.

Suggestions to ensure these problems do not arise again revolve around information, monitoring and written policies. It has been suggested that the board and senior management understand the nature of derivatives they are supposed to be controlling and that the organization of the company is conducive to managing risks. Further, the board should approve written policies that define the overall policy framework in which derivative activities should be conducted and the risks controlled. More effective policies and monitoring along with education of the financial instruments and their risks should control the problems. A focus on internal monitoring is crucial. Without it, regardless of the governance system, the product market will ultimately have to resolve the problem.

In conclusion, while there are two generic governance systems, bank-based (insider) systems and market-based (outsider) systems, variations in the two systems observed in many countries, both developing and developed, along with different equity ownership structures, render convergence of governance systems to one of the existing systems or a blending of the systems into a hybrid system difficult to visualize. Based on the observed pressures for change, there is a convergence in the large economies but it is on a functional not system basis. Changes in the bank-based systems are occurring and will continue to occur within corporate structures, organizations and managerial decision making, thereby providing a new focus on shareholder wealth creation and efficient operations of capital markets.

6. CONCLUSIONS

There is a large and extensive literature on corporate governance in general and on specific governance systems in particular. The literature describes the two major governance systems, their functioning and their different objectives. In the market-based system the objective is to maximize the wealth of shareholders whereas in the bank-based systems shareholders are but one of a number of stakeholders that has to be considered in managerial decisions. This latter perspective seems to be losing favour to the shareholder perspective as economies become less productive and governments are unable to cross-subsidize stakeholders through corporate actions.

Typically, the literature deals with the widely held companies and their monitoring in the market- and bank-based governance systems. In the former, monitoring is undertaken through markets and, to an increasing extent, large portfolio investors. In the bank-based systems monitoring is not through markets, since they are not well developed, but through large shareholdings by banks and intercorporate shareholders. The effectiveness of monitoring in the bank-based systems is questionable. Monitors typically are concerned with their self interest; in the case of intercorporate holdings this usually means maintaining good supplier/customer relations leading to a do nothing policy. For banks, monitoring is a way of ensuring that the firm is able to pay its principal and interest payments. Thus management and monitors' interests in maintaining a low-risk company reinforce each other. Further, in the German system, banks typically have substantial voting rights but less ownership of equity. The relevant question becomes who monitors the monitors who influence decision making through their voting power. The bank-based governance system could work in large, fixed asset-intensive businesses that do not have growth opportunities or do not face much product market competition. However, in knowledge-based firms with significant human capital, equity capital is needed and the use of bank lending is not relevant. Here a bank-based system would not work well.

However, applications of the widely held company perspective to other economies and of the pure market-based governance system beyond the US and UK is problematic. This conclusion does not mean that there are no effectively functioning capital markets in other economies, only that the prevalent ownership structure is concentrated shareholdings, not widely held companies. The concentration is either as holdings of equity such that voting and cash flow rights are identical, or situations such as dual class shares and pyramid structures in which the voting rights exceed the cash flow rights. In many countries the controlling shareholders are founders of the company or family members/heirs. Concentrated holdings such as dual class shares and controlling holdings with equal cash and voting rights are found in UK and US markets as well. Concentrated holdings can lead to serious problems of misalignment of interests of controlling and minority shareholders. These problems are exacerbated in economies in which concentrated holdings also lead to political pressures to forestall capital market and product market competition.

As demonstrated in this chapter, no governance system is well suited to solve the problems of concentrated holdings. Markets do not function well and monitoring by banks and intercorporate shareholders does not work. In both governance systems monitoring by boards of directors does not work. What is left to provide the appropriate constraint on non-wealth creating decisions is the product market. Promoting product market competition internationally will discipline poorly performing management although the time frame over which it happens can be lengthy. It was also noted that heir controlled firms appear to be less effectively managed than founder controlled firms. This observation also provides a long-run solution. Of course, government actions to improve competition will speed up the disciplinary impact. In addition, where markets do not work well, corporate law may be a substitute leading to a greater emphasis on minority shareholder protection.

Finally, the issue of convergence of governance systems is considered. In the market-centred systems convergence would require changes that permitted more bank/financial institution ownership and hence monitoring of companies. In fact, this has occurred through the levered buyout process, but the financial institution has a strong alignment of interests with the shareholders, something that is not found in the bank-based systems. For the bank-based systems, changes to induce convergence would require improvement in capital markets, reduction of control by banks, and monitoring for shareholder interests. These are fundamental changes and are unlikely to arise in the near term. However, there are pressures forcing a convergence in a functional not a corporate governance sense. The changes are observed in the restructuring of corporations in the bank-based systems and the emphasis on decisions that improve shareholder value. Pressures are found domestically and internationally and the resulting changes can make effective capital markets a reality.

While the emphasis on shareholder interests has arisen in the major economies, it is still primarily focused on the widely held companies. The unaddressed issues remain the monitoring of companies with concentrated equity and the effective governance of emerging and developing countries in which capital markets are not effective monitoring tools and concentrated holdings have significant influence on government policy.

NOTES

1. Scott (1998) describes the equity contract as the perfect example of an incomplete contract and describes the justification for having equity as the focus for the wealth-maximizing decisions.
2. The weights attached to each element are particularly important in the supervision of banks. There is a recognition that regulations of banks can be inflexible and can result in unintended consequences. Thus there is a greater emphasis being placed on the internal governance system to address the concerns.
3. This governance system is also referred to as a common law-based governance system. See Deakin and Hughes (1997) and La Porta et al. (1997).
4. Franks and Mayer (1997) make the distinction between insider systems and outsider systems.
5. Cornell and Shapiro (1987) argue that it is in the firm's long-run best interests to take into consideration the impact of its decisions on employees, bondholders and the environment. In the case of bondholders, evidence of unanticipated firm behaviour that attempts to shift wealth from bondholders to equity holders through financial or investment decisions will result in a loss of equity value as bondholders alter the cost of debt on future financing. Analogously, reneging by the corporation on promises to employees will result in a loss of wealth as the firm re-enters the labour market to obtain labour and has to make wage or other adjustments in the labour contract. They also argue that a firm with a number of divisions or businesses may not make decisions in one division that will hurt bondholders or employees of that division if the decision affects the stakeholders of other businesses or divisions. Thus there is an impact not only on the initial division but also on all the others. The basis of their argument is that shareholder value maximization will require the firm to consider the impact of its decisions on all of its operations. However, if the firm is not a 'repeat player' in these markets, an end game problem can arise and optimal decisions can result in wealth transfers to shareholders from stakeholders.
6. This is essentially the governance system in countries with a civil law background.
7. Roe (1994, 1997) addresses the genesis of the US system of companies with widely held equity, centralized management and a powerful CEO with a non-confrontational board of directors. Berle and Means (1933) explained the US structure by the need for capital to fund acquisition of new technology and to diversify personal holdings leading founders to sell

new shares and reduce their ownership position. Roe states that this explanation is not complete. His position is that populist sentiment in the United States against concentration of economic power and large financial institutions led to a constraint on the size and importance of banks and hence a bank-based system of governance could not exist. If left to their own devices, there would be some firms for which concentrated holdings and bank monitoring are preferable. Easterbrook (1997) and Carney (1997) take counter-positions. Easterbrook argues that the difference in governance structures is due to the efficient functioning of capital markets and not corporate law. The US and the UK have efficient capital markets and relatively few controls on cross-border capital flows. If these governance structures were not working, investors would find ways to improve governance through other means. In countries where capital markets are less extensive banks and/or restrictive corporate law act as substitutes. Carney takes a position similar to Easterbrook and argues that the current monitoring function of banks in the bank-based system of Germany can be explained partly by the banks blocking the development of capital markets and obtaining information advantages over other investors.

8.   In 1998 there were 28 widely held companies in the Toronto Stock Exchange (TSE) 100 and 63 in the TSE 300. This is a modest increase from the 1993 values of 23 and 46 firms respectively.

9.   Buckley (1997) argues that the Canadian banking and corporate structure are '*keiretsu*'-like, with the influence of Canadian banks being amplified by the Canadian bankruptcy code in which banks remain secured creditors and until recently only the largest companies could reorganize in the face of financial distress through a court process.

10. Generally, the utility function has as one argument the wealth of the monitor; however, it can include other arguments such as the utility to other stakeholders. While some governance systems stress interests beyond equity holders, it is very difficult to identify *ex ante* the true interest of monitors.

11. Forces in society and public policy wanted to use the public limited liability company for general welfare purposes; hence the influence of labour and the two-tier board system (Schmidt et al., 1997, p. 35 and citations). One rationale for the labour membership on the supervisory board is to prevent moral hazard problems associated with employees who make firm-specific investments. For a discussion on how these problems are addressed in a market-based system see Cornell and Shapiro (1987) and note 4 above.

12. Companies with fewer than 2000 employees and greater than 500 have a supervisory board with one-third of the members allocated to labour. The provisions of the Codetermination Act do not apply to firms with fewer than 500 employees.

13. Banks can block or impede resolutions to remove voting restrictions even if one shareholder has a greater than 50 per cent position in the equity. Also they have influence over the removal of members of the supervisory board which can be accomplished by a super-majority vote.

14. In May 1998, the law on control and transparency in business (KonTraG), the German Corporate Governance Reform was enacted. Siebert (1999) presents a summary of many of the changes in this legislation. Some of the changes are intended to address many of the shortcomings noted in the discussion. For example, existing multiple vote shares will be phased out over five years leaving a one share–one vote rule, the maximum voting right provision will be removed, and the responsibilities of the supervisory board and banks are identified. However, banks will continue to vote the shares held by them for custodial purposes.

15. Yamamoto (1997) describes these different structures and the related internal governance frameworks. He finds that these sets of companies have very different internal decision-making processes and monitoring and their strategic decision making is very different.

16. Banks act in a syndicate fashion when lending and one of the banks is designated the main bank. The main bank is in fact the marginal supplier of funds and the lender of last resort if the firm finds itself in financial trouble. The main bank is not the largest bank in the syndicate. These functions of the main bank are in contrast to the universal bank in Germany where financing of debt and equity is undertaken through the bank.

17. In some cases a 'paper' meeting is held where the board members sign minutes of a meeting

that was not actually held.

18. Consistent with general labour practices generally, poorly performing managers remain in-house but are placed on a side track. See Baum and Schaede (1994).

19. See Kaplan (1997a) who looks at management turnover after stock price and sales reductions of at least 50 per cent.

20. See reference to Morck and Nakamura in Macey and Miller (1997).

21. The bank picked by the Ministry of Finance in the event a bailout of a large company is deemed necessary is called the main bank. In this context the bank operates as a government agent.

22. Wealth diversionary activities include perquisite consumption, compensation contracts that bear no relationship to managerial performance, and unbargained for self-dealing transactions at non-market terms.

23. Tufano (1996) presents an example of this behaviour in the North American gold mining industry. He observes that management that has little equity but has stock options engages in less gold price risk reduction through the use of derivative securities than does management with significant equity holdings. In the former case, the unhedged gold position exposes the firm to commodity price risk and increases the value of the stock options held by management. In the latter, management engages in a costly transaction to protect its personal wealth.

24. The major activist financial institutions are the government or group pension plans. Corporate pension funds are not active in this area since the fund managers face a conflict of interest – do they vote against management initiatives in the stocks they own in the pension fund even if the initiatives reduce shareholder wealth, especially if the pension fund manager may want to manage the company's pension fund or does not want to infuriate management of companies for which it currently manages the pension fund. In some situations, the pension funds acquire anonymity by financing a third party to agitate for reform.

25. For a discussion of the results of the 1997 proxy season in the United States and the types of proposals accepted for inclusion by management, see Campbell et al. (1999).

26. A current example in Canada is Crescendo Partners LP which has requested a special shareholder meeting for Call-Net Enterprises Inc., a Canadian company in the long-distance and local services market. Call-Net introduced a poison pill prior to the Crescendo action but subsequently instructed its investment banker to look at strategic alternatives for the firm. Call-Net management owns about 1 per cent of the voting common and less than one half of one per cent of the non-voting shares. The company's share price has fallen about 70 per cent over a one-year period. Just before the meeting an agreement was achieved in which Crescendo-nominated directors would be appointed to Call-Net's board. Crescendo Partners has found a lucrative practice in Canada!

27. Baum and Schaede (1994) also report that shareholders do not have any control through the annual shareholders' meeting. The meetings are short and non-confrontational even though shareholders are supposed to review important matters such as mergers, changes in business charter as well as nomination of auditors and directors and approval of annual reports. Thus monitoring of management by shareholders at annual meetings is non-existent.

28. For example, if there are two classes of shares with one class having a single vote and the other no votes, and if there are an equal number of shares in each class, holding 50 per cent of the votes means that the controlling shareholder owns 25 per cent of the total shares of the company. The latter is the claim on cash flows. If there are twice as many non-voting as voting shares, a 50 per cent controlling interest can be obtained by a 16.7 per cent ownership of the total shares of the company.

29. To determine the ultimate ownership, the authors had to wade through a labyrinth of ownership structures.

30. In a second sample the companies were the ten smallest in the economy with market capitalization in excess of $500 000.

31. The classification is based on a number of provisions linked to proxy voting, minority shareholder legislation, and shareholder's preemptive rights. The classification with high minority shareholder protection is also related to the common law legal regime.

32. The incidence of family control is much greater when the smaller firms are considered. The percentages are 50 per cent, 40 per cent and 60 per cent for France, Germany and Sweden respectively, using the 20 per cent definition for control.

33. Some preliminary evidence by La Porta suggests that in about one-third of the family ownership sample founders controlled the firm while two-thirds of the firms were controlled by descendants of the founder or other family members.

34. The 'q' ratio attempts to measure the expected growth in the firm by looking at the market value of the firm divided by the replacement value of the firm's assets. If the ratio is greater than unity, the firm has profitable growth opportunities. The q ratio is measured in a number of different ways.

35. See McNabb and Martin (1998). They defined poor performance as two-year stock returns that placed companies in the bottom 5 per cent of all NYSE and AMEX firms.

36. In Canada, Eatons, a 130-year-old company in the department store business just recently filed for bankruptcy (August 1999). As a private company, it had financial problems and to reorganize its debt, it also had to raise equity by selling a 48 per cent interest in its equity in 1997. The shares issued at $15 per share are now worth pennies. The impetus for its demise was continuing poor management by the heirs of the founder in the face of strong competition.

37. See Daniels and Morck (1995, pp. 674-6) for a discussion of the effectiveness of minority shareholder protection. A comparison of minority shareholders rights in Canada and the US is presented in DeMott (1993).

38. There are two other reasons why minority shareholders may vote for the transaction even though it is expected to reduce their wealth. The first arises from the collective action problem where shareholders are rationally apathetic based on the costs of becoming informed. The second relates to strategic choices made by shareholders. For example, management can add to the dual class share transaction a sweetener that is of benefit to shareholders; an example is a dividend increase or an increase in share liquidity contingent on a successful transaction. If the shareholder believes the transaction will go through, it is in the shareholder's best interests to participate in the transaction and at least receive the dividend to partially offset the wealth transfer to controlling shareholders. If the shareholder believes the transaction will not go through she will vote for the transaction believing that her actions do not affect the outcome. Another strategic choice problem is found when the management states that unless the transaction is approved, profitable projects will not be undertaken since there will not be enough capital. While the wealth diversionary activities will occur with or without the transaction, the potential offset through good investment decisions will arise only if the transaction is consummated. Hence the shareholder will vote for the transaction to obtain the investments.

39. In Ontario, the Toronto Stock Exchange requires dual class shares to have 'coattail' provisions that are intended to ensure that in the event of a purchase of a control block, the inferior voting shares must also receive the identical offer. This provision affects shares after the date the provision was introduced and no 'grandparent' requirement was made. The prices of superior and inferior voting shares are approximately the same for firms affected by the coat-tail provision.

40. See Hauser and Lauterbach (1999). This change was debated in the Israeli parliament and was the subject of government reports. In October 1989, the Tel-Aviv Stock Exchange along with the Israeli Securities Authority banned new issues of inferior class shares. The new regulation came into effect in January 1990.

41. In South Africa there were two examples of companies at the apex of the pyramid being mutual life insurance companies. See Barr et al. (1995).

42. In the US the closest analogue to a pyramid structure is the closed end investment fund in which a fund acquires a portfolio of shares in other companies. The value of the closed end fund is almost always less than the sum of the market values of its holdings – selling at a discount to its asset value; the obvious question is why the fund is not opened up and its value increased. Barclay et al. (1993) concluded that there is a conflict in the closed end fund between large controlling shareholders and small shareholders. They observed a discount of 14.2 per cent for funds with blockholders and 4.1 per cent for those without.

With management affiliated blockholders there appeared to be private benefits in excess of the value that could be obtained if the fund were opened up. The private benefits to the blockholder in the closed end fund include the receipt of management fees, the payment for financial research, commissions for trading of securities, employment of relatives and friends, and purchase by the fund of IPOs underwritten by the blockholder company along with non-pecuniary returns such as having the fund named after the blockholder.

43. This situation is in contrast to that found in the pure conglomerate structure where the main company owns controlling interests in each of the subsidiary companies. Here the controlling shareholder is better off by cleaning up the structure since the benefits achieved are appropriate in part by the controlling shareholder.

44. See Morck et al. (1998). Their sample included 39 countries excluding the US and the UK whose ownership pattern is atypical. The authors collected data on billionaire wealth divided by GDP divided into the following categories: entrepreneur billionaire wealth, heir billionaire wealth, probable heir billionaire wealth, entrepreneur and heir control and political family billionaire wealth.

45. A major difference would be the existence of graft and corruption in some developing countries at levels that impact corporate decisions and the influence of various competitive based solutions to governance problems – for example, the role of the product market can be blunted by government intervention to support companies that provide significant cash flows to the government or individuals within the government.

46. The voting concentration also affects the proxy process. Köndgen (1994) argues that it may be better to have the banks having effective control over the proxy process than management, as in the US system. However, the bank voting concentration results in a difficulty in generating voting blocks of concerned shareholders to affect change in management. As will be discussed, this problem is exacerbated by the lack of large liquidity pools such as pension funds.

47. The most frequently noted example is Berkshire Hathaway but other investment banks have as mandates to invest in firms in which they can use their expertise to improve shareholder value. LBO firms such as KKR and Forstmann Little engage in monitoring and the provision of managerial expertise.

48. Kaplan (1997b) argues that the reduction in the number of hostile takeovers and LBOs at the beginning of the 1990s was due not to the excesses of those markets in the last half of the 1980s but to the integration of insights from the LBO market into corporate behaviour. He identifies three changes in corporate actions that are a result of the LBO era: impose a cost of capital on management so it does not behave as if capital is free; increase equity ownership of management and introduce performance based incentives for top management; introduce active monitoring of management by boards and shareholders. Note that these changes do not require the heavy reliance on debt typically found in the LBO and hence have currency for a wider class of firms than those with characteristics amenable to a LBO.

49. Fidelity manges $100 million of Honda's retirement fund.

50. As of 1 July 1999, Germany had 7 DRs and one non-DR listed on the NYSE. France had 15 DRs and Italy 12 DRs. For NASDAQ, France had 7 cross-listed firms, Italy 2 and Germany 1.

51. The increase in price is particularly strong for companies in which there are local controls on equity investments or capital controls. The DR provides a method of finessing these restrictions.

52. Karolyi (1996) observed large reductions in capital costs – 33 basis points for European firms and 207 basis points for Asian firms.

53. For a discussion of the factors that determine the trading of cross-listed securities either on the NYSE, London Stock Exchange or the home country see Pulatkonak and Sofianos (1999).

54. Baker et al. (1999) find that visibility as measured by security analysts' following, increases subsequent to the cross-listing. The increase is greater for firms that intend to issue equity.

55. In its continued emphasis on lifelong employment, the Japanese government pays subsidies to companies to hold onto their workers even when positions are no longer needed. Also,

temporary employment agencies are forbidden from securing work for anyone within one year of graduation even though only about one-third of Japanese college graduates were able to obtain full-time work. Mandatory fee schedules inhibit competition among agencies or a number of job categories are declared off-limits to temporary employment agencies.

56. M. Schuman in the *Wall Street Journal* as reported in the Globe and Mail, *Report on Business*, 14 August 1999.
57. It is well accepted that derivatives *per se* are not the culprit in the story since they are very effective tools in hedging risk and providing preferred risk profiles to investors and companies. However, to use them correctly requires sophisticated knowledge.
58. J. Dial, Commissioner of the Commodity Futures Trading Commission, stated 'Each of these financial debacles [Barings, Orange County, and Metallgesellschaft] has at least two things in common (1) a lack or break down of internal management controls; and (2) improper use of instruments that were characterized as derivatives' (1995, p. 5).

REFERENCES

Ambachtsheer, K. and D. Ezra (1998), *Pension Fund Excellence*, John Wiley & Sons.

Anderson, R. and S. Lee (1997), 'Ownership studies: the data source does matter', *Journal of Financial and Quantitative Analysis*, **32**, 311–29.

Baker, K., J. Nofsinger and D. Weaver (1999), 'International cross-listing and visibility', NYSE Working Paper 99–01.

Barclay, M.J., C. Holderness and J. Pontiff (1993), 'Private benefits from block ownership and discounts on closed-end funds', *Journal of Financial Economics*, **22**, 263–91.

Barr, G., J. Gerson and B. Kantor (1995), 'Shareholders as agents and principals: the case for South Africa's corporate governance system', *Journal of Applied Corporate Finance*, Spring, 18–31.

Baum, T. and U. Schaede (1994), 'Institutional investors and corporate governance in Japan', in T. Baum, R. Buxbaum and K. Hopt (eds), *Institutional Investors and Corporate Governance*, Berlin: Walter de Gruyter, chapter 22.

Berle, A. and G. Means (1993), *The Modern Corporation and Private Property*, New York: Macmillan.

Buckley, F.H. (1997), 'The Canadian keiretsu', *Bank of America Journal of Applied Corporate Finance*, **9**, 46–56

Campbell, C., S. Gillen and C. Niden (1999), 'Current perspectives on shareholder proposals: lessons from the 1997 proxy season', *Financial Management*, **28** (1), pp. 89–98.

Carney, W.J. (1997), 'Large bank stockholders in Germany: saviors or substitutes?', *Bank of America Journal of Applied Corporate Finance*, **9**, 74-81.

Cornell, B. and A.C. Shapiro (1987), 'Corporate stakeholders and corporate finance', *Financial Management*, **16** (1), 5–14.

Crockett, A. (1997), 'Global capital markets and the stability of banking and financial systems', in C. Enoch and J. Green (eds), *Banking Soundness and Monetary Policy*, IMF, pp. 89–105.

Daniels, R. and R. Morck (1995), 'Canadian corporate governance: policy options', in R. Daniels and R. Morck (eds), *Corporate Decision Making in Canada*, Calgary: University of Calgary Press.

Deakin, S. and A. Hughes (1997), 'Comparative corporate governance: an interdisciplinary agenda', *Journal of Law and Society*, **24**, 1-9.

DeMott, D. (1993), 'Oppressed but not betrayed: a comparative assessment of

Canadian remedies for minority shareholders and other corporate constituents', *Law and Contemporary Problems*, 181.

Dial, J. (1995), 'Status report on regulatory and self-regulatory responses to the Barings bankruptcy', Address to 18th Annual Commodities Law Institute and 4th Annual Financial Services Law Institute, Chicago (http://www.cftc.gov/opa/speeches/chic95s/html).

Easterbrook, F. (1997), 'International corporate differences: markets or law?', *Bank of America Journal of Applied Corporate Finance*, 23–9.

Franks, J. and C. Mayer (1997), 'Corporate ownership and control in the UK, Germany and France', *Journal of Corporate Finance*, **9**, 30–45.

Halpern, P., W. Rotenberg and R. Kieschnick (1999a), 'The influence of target managerial shareholdings on acquisitions of corporations', working paper, University of Toronto.

Halpern, P., W. Rotenberg and R. Kieschnick (1999b), 'On the heterogeneity of levered going private transactions', *Review of Financial Studies*, **12**.

Haupt, M. (1994), 'The equity market in Germany', in T. Baums, R. Buxbaum and K. Hopt (eds), *Institutional Investors and Corporate Governance*, Berlin: Walter de Gruyter, chapter 19.

Hauser, S. and B. Lauterbach (1999), 'The value of voting rights: evidence from dual class stock unifications', working paper.

Hermalin, B. and M. Weisbach (1991), 'The effects of board composition and direct incentives on firm performance', *Financial Management*, **20** (4), Winter.

Holderness, C. and D. Sheehan (1988), 'The role of majority shareholders in publicly held corporations: an exploratory analysis', *Journal of Financial Economics*, **20** (1/2).

Jarrell, G. and A. Poulsen (1988), 'Dual class recapitalizations as antitakeover mechanisms: the recent evidence', *Journal of Financial Economics*, **20** (1/2), 129–52.

Jensen, M. and W. Meckling (1976), 'Managerial behavior, agency costs and ownership', *Journal of Financial Economics*.

Jog, V. and A. Riding (1986), 'Price effects of dual class shares', *Financial Analysts Journal*, **42**, 58–67.

Johnson, B., R. Magee, N. Nagarjan and H. Newman (1985), 'An analysis of the stock price reaction to sudden executive deaths', *Journal of Accounting and Economics*, **7**, 151–74.

Kaplan, S. (1997a), 'Corporate governance and corporate performance: a comparison of Germany, Japan and the US', *Bank of America Journal of Applied Corporate Finance*, **9**, 86–93.

Kaplan, S. (1997b), 'The evolution of US corporate governance: we are all Henry Kravis now', Conference on The Power and Influence of Pension and Mutual Funds, New York University Salomon Center Stern School of Business.

Karolyj, A. (1996), 'What happens to stocks that list shares abroad?', *New York Stock Exchange Paper*, New York.

Karpoff, J. (1998), 'The impact of shareholder activism on target companies: a survey of empirical findings', working paper, University of Washington.

Köndgen Johannes (1994), 'Duties of banks in voting their clients' stock', in T. Baums, R. Buxbaum and K. Hopt (eds), *Institutional Investors and Corporate Governance*, Berlin: Walter de Gruyter, chapter 18.

La Porta, R., F. Lopez-de-Silanes, A. Shleifer and R. Vishny (1997), 'Legal determinants of external finance', *Journal of Finance*, **52**, 1131–50.

La Porta, R., F. Lopez-de-Silanes and A. Shleifer (1998), 'Corporate ownership around the world', mimeo, Harvard University.

Macey, J. and G. Miller (1997), 'Universal banks are not the answer to America's corporate governance "Problem": a look at Germany, Japan and the US', *Bank of America Journal of Applied Corporate Finance*, 57–73.

McConnell, J. and H. Servaes (1990), 'Additional evidence on equity ownership and corporate value', *Journal of Financial Economics*, **27**, 595–612.

McNabb, M. and J. Martin (1998), 'Managerial entrenchment and the effectiveness of internal governance mechanisms', working paper, Baylor University.

Morck, R., A. Shleifer and R. Vishny (1988), 'Management ownership and market valuation: an empirical analysis', *Journal of Financial Economics*, **20**, 293–316.

Morck, R., D. Strangeland and B. Yeung (1998), 'Inherited wealth, corporate control and economic growth: the Canadian disease', NBER Working Paper 6814.

Pulatkonak, M. and G. Sofianos (1999), 'The distribution of global trading in NYSE-listed non-US stocks', NYSE Working Paper 99–03.

Roe, M. (1994), *Strong Managers, Weak Owners: The Political Roots of American Corporate Finance*, Princeton, NJ: Princeton University Press,

Roe, M. (1997), 'The political roots of American corporate finance', *Bank of America Journal of Applied Corporate Finance*, **7**, 23–9.

Roulier, R. (1997), 'Governance issues and banking system soundness', in C. Enoch and J. Green (eds), *Banking Soundness and Monetary Policy*, International Monetary Fund, pp. 450–63.

Schmidt, H., J. Drukarczyk, D. Honold, S. Prigge, A. Schuler and G. Tetens (1997), *Corporate Governance in Germany*, Baden-Baden: Nomos Verlagsgesellschaft.

Scott, K. (1998), 'The role of corporate governance in South Korean economic reform', *Bank of America Journal of Applied Corporate Finance*, Winter, 8–15.

Siebert, U. (1999), 'Control and transparency in business (KonTraG): corporate governance reform in Germany', *European Business Law Review*, 70–75.

Slovin, M. and M. Sushka (1993), 'Ownership concentration, corporate control activity and firm value: evidence for the death of inside blockholders', *Journal of Finance*, **48**, 1293–321.

Toronto Stock Exchange, 'Transaction costs in Canadian and US equity markets: a study of institutional trading in cross-listed stocks'.

Tufano, P. (1996), 'Who manages risk? An empirical examination of risk management practices in the gold mining industry', *Journal of Finance*, September, 1097–137.

Useem, M. (1998), 'Corporate leadership in a globalizing equity market', *Academy of Management Executive*, 43–59.

Yamamoto, M. (1997), 'Strategic decisions and corporate governance in Japan', in V. Papadakis and P. Baruise (eds), *Strategic Decisions*, Kluwer Academic Publishers, chapter 10.

2. Corporate governance and corporate performance

William R. Emmons* and Frank A. Schmid*

Corporate governance mechanisms assure investors in corporations that they will receive adequate returns on their investments (Shleifer and Vishny, 1997). If these mechanisms did not exist or did not function properly, outside investors would not lend to firms or buy their equity securities. Businesses would be forced to rely entirely on their own internally generated cash flows and accumulated financial resources to finance ongoing operations as well as profitable investment opportunities. Overall economic performance would be likely to suffer because many good business opportunities would be missed and temporary financial problems at individual firms would spread quickly to other firms, employees and consumers.

This chapter investigates the links between distinctive national systems of corporate governance and the performance of firms and economies that employ them. We first review the recently released *OECD Principles of Corporate Governance*, an initiative designed to increase awareness of governance issues and to disseminate information on best practices. Then we describe the world's predominant corporate governance traditions and discuss the historical and legal roots of these traditions. We then trace the effects of different corporate governance traditions on the development of financial systems broadly defined, including such things as the amount of external financing that firms typically do and in what form they obtain funds from investors (for example, debt or equity, bank debt or bond market debt). Finally, we provide evidence on the effectiveness of each of the major systems of corporate governance in producing favourable economic outcomes both at the firm level and for national economies as a whole. We also consider reasons why traditional profit-based or economic growth-based indicators of performance may be inadequate for analysing the complexities surrounding a country's corporate governance environment. Our analysis is most relevant for developed countries; for a related discussion of transition and developing economies, see Chapter 9 by Berglöf and von Thadden in this volume.

To preview our conclusions briefly, we find that corporate governance traditions are distinctive, deeply rooted and difficult to change. Some sets of corporate governance institutions appear to encourage or support broad financial system development more than others, which in turn may have consequences for the types of firms that can access public capital markets. Financial system development may also have implications for long-term economic growth, although this link remains controversial. At the same time, corporate governance systems in some countries may excel in respects other than fostering capital markets, such as providing long-term financial stability and opportunities for intertemporal risk-sharing. In sum, there appears to be no 'perfect' system, so we view continued diversity among corporate governance systems as unsurprising. Nevertheless, there is limited evidence of convergence among corporate governance systems around the world.

THE CAMPAIGN FOR BETTER CORPORATE GOVERNANCE PRACTICES

We begin with a case study that documents persistent cross-country differences in the profitability of large internationally active commercial banks. This simple example is designed to motivate our search for the causes of underlying differences in corporate governance environments around the world. Then we discuss a newly released set of corporate governance principles. The Organisation for Economic Co-operation and Development (OECD), a grouping of 29 industrialized and newly industrializing countries, recently published a set of corporate governance standards and guidelines covering five major areas. The OECD document highlights the increased profile that governance issues have attained around the world. In part, the renewed focus on governance can be traced to the immediate challenges facing policymakers and business leaders in emerging markets and transition economies. It is also the case, however, that the globalization of financial markets more generally has brought into sharp relief the sometimes significant differences that exist among advanced market economies with respect to shareholder rights, creditor rights and the legal enforcement environment.

Why Corporate Governance Practices Matter: The Case of Bank Profitability

Comprehensive cross-country and cross-industry comparisons of corporate performance are extremely difficult to carry out and to interpret. We focus instead in this case study on the core profitability of one part of a single sector, namely, large internationally active commercial banks. Although regulatory regimes and local competitive conditions differ across countries, our narrow

Table 2.1   Profitability of large banks

Panel A. Average pre-tax return on assets (ROA), 1986–88

Group average	0.89%		0.54%		0.70%		0.76%	
Individual countries	United States	0.70%	Sweden	0.77%	Germany	0.83%	France	0.32%
	UK	0.97%	Denmark	0.31%	Japan	0.60%	Italy	0.72%
	Canada	1.02%			Switzerland	0.68%	Netherlands	0.71%
							Spain	1.29%

Panel B. Average pre-tax return on assets (ROA), 1996–98

Group average	1.32%		0.98%		0.05%		0.59%	
Individual countries	United States	1.67%	Sweden	1.02%	Germany	0.48%	France	0.32%
	UK	1.13%	Denmark	0.94%	Japan	−0.43%	Italy	0.34%
	Canada	1.15%			Switzerland	0.10%	Netherlands	0.74%
							Spain	0.97%

Panel C. Average pre-tax return on assets (ROA), 1996–98

Group average	1.11%		0.76%		0.38%		0.68%	
Individual countries	United States	1.19%	Sweden	0.90%	Germany	0.65%	France	0.32%
	UK	1.05%	Denmark	0.63%	Japan	0.09%	Italy	0.53%
	Canada	1.08%			Switzerland	0.39%	Netherlands	0.72%
							Spain	1.13%

Sources: Panel A, OECD (1992); panel B, OECD (1999b); panel C, authors' calculations.

focus on an internationally comparable performance ratio – pre-tax return on assets, or ROA – allows us to explore the hypothesis that persistent cross-country differences might be attributable to differences in the incentives and controls facing managers. Given that investors in all countries prefer the highest return possible, persistently inefficient use of corporate assets (from the standpoint of equity holders) is an indication that the prevailing corporate governance system has not aligned the interests of managers and owners adequately.

Table 2.1 provides snapshots of the core profitability of large inter-nationally active commercial banks from 12 countries for two three-year periods. The first row of panel A shows the average pre-tax return on assets of the largest banks in each group of countries sampled over 1986–88, while the second row gives the individual country detail (the reason for grouping countries in this way will become evident below). Pre-tax ROAs vary a lot across countries, particularly in view of the tiny margins facing large banks. Panel B of Table 2.1 provides the same information viewed exactly ten years later. Panel C shows the averages over the two three-year periods taken together.

The most striking pattern in the table is that pre-tax ROAs in the first column (including the United States, the United Kingdom and Canada) tend to be higher than those in other columns. It is less obvious what differences, if any, exist among the countries or country groups in columns two, three and four. Likewise, it is difficult to make any comparative statement about the relative profitability of large banks in the US, the UK and Canada. One question we confront immediately is therefore, what is different about the English-speaking countries *vis-à-vis* the other countries? It could be the case that corporate profitability is higher in these countries due to factors unrelated to corporate governance, such as access to a large (English-speaking) market or favourable tax laws. This possibility merely raises another question, namely, what is similar among the English-speaking countries?

Before investigating these questions, we introduce the core standards and guidelines recommended recently by the OECD to promote harmonization in and improvement of corporate governance systems around the world.

The OECD Principles of Corporate Governance

The OECD's recommended principles of corporate governance are listed in Table 2.2 along with a brief commentary highlighting what we think are some of their most noteworthy elements. Five areas of concern are covered: (1) the rights of shareholders, (2) the equitable treatment of shareholders, (3) the role of stakeholders in corporate governance, (4) disclosure and transparency, and (5) the responsibilities of the board.

The major thrusts of the OECD principles are for better disclosure of important information to shareholders and vigorous protection of shareholder interests, especially the interests of investors who hold a minority interest or are located abroad. The report stops short of advocating far-reaching reforms of existing systems of corporate governance or legal systems even though it recognizes significant shortcomings in some countries. These shortcomings are arguably entrenched in the governance environment in some countries, however, so it is not clear how effective a set of voluntary guidelines such as these might be. Examples of serious impediments to greater compliance with the OECD guidelines include deviations from one share–one vote corporate charters and a board that is effectively dominated by the firm's managers or a minority shareholder.

The OECD principles represent a compromise in a number of dimensions. There is a clear advocacy of greater shareholder rights, but the stakeholder view of corporate governance is also acknowledged (if not endorsed). Yet, is not conflict inevitable between these two perspectives in practice? How is a country or an individual firm to sort out the competing priorities of shareholder- and stakeholder-based systems of governance? The OECD document suggests that shareholders may benefit in the long run from a concern with stakeholder interests, but this provides little guidance in the short term in the real world of corporate decision making.

In another instance of ambiguity, minority and foreign shareholders are held up for special mention as deserving better treatment than they sometimes receive. However, the OECD calls merely for disclosing, rather than eliminating, the corporate governance practices that put these shareholders at a disadvantage. These practices include unequally weighted voting classes and other capital structures (for example, pyramids composed of multiple holding companies each with a controlling interest but less than full ownership in the company at the level below it) that give certain shareholders control rights that are disproportionate to their share of contributed capital. Foreign and minority shareholders have little reason to expect that the mere publication of the *OECD Principles of Corporate Governance* will greatly enhance their property rights. Fundamental reforms must be enacted in individual countries in the face of what is likely to be strong resistance by parties well served by the current system.

Finally, creditors are obliquely mentioned in the principles in the context of non-shareholder stakeholders in the firm, but no specific recommendations are made to enhance creditor rights in countries where these are neglected (we provide evidence of this below). We will give special emphasis below to the importance of creditor rights in an overall framework of adequate corporate governance practices and institutions. It is to the fundamentals that underlie the visible framework of corporate governance that we now turn.

Table 2.2 OECD principles of corporate governance

	Topic	Principle	Comments
I.	The rights of shareholders	The corporate governance framework should protect shareholders' rights.	General conceptual framework for establishing shareholders' property rights. Recognizes the inevitable separation of ownership and control in widely held firms but does not propose specific approaches to solving the agency problem. Does not argue for one share–one vote rules but advocates transparent takeover markets.
II.	The equitable treatment of shareholders	The corporate governance framework should ensure the equitable treatment of all shareholders, including minority and foreign shareholders. All shareholders should have the opportunity to obtain effective redress for violation of their rights.	Stresses the importance of protecting the rights of minority and foreign shareholders. Does not take a position on the desirability of one share–one vote rules. Major thrust is on better disclosure and information flows to shareholders.
III.	The role of stakeholders in corporate governance	The corporate governance framework should recognize the rights of stakeholders as established by law and encourage active cooperation between corporations and stakeholders in creating wealth, jobs, and the sustainability of financially sound enterprises.	Covers employees, suppliers, creditors and all other non-shareholder individuals and groups with an interest in some aspect of the performance of a corporation's obligations. No inevitable conflict is recognized between shareholders and other stakeholders.

IV. Disclosure and transparency	The corporate governance framework should ensure that timely and accurate disclosure is made on all material matters regarding the corporation, including the financial situation, performance, ownership and governance of the company.	Endorses the maximum practicable flow of information to shareholders. Implies that shareholders' property rights (ought to) extend to insiders' material information about the firm.
V. The responsibilities of the board	The corporate governance framework should ensure the strategic guidance of the company, the effective monitoring of management by the board, and the board's accountability to the company and the shareholders.	Argues that independence from management is necessary for a board to carry out its responsibilities effectively. In addition to serving as shareholders' representatives, the board's responsibilities include relations with stakeholders and the public at large.

LEGAL TRADITIONS AND THE RULE OF LAW

Despite their universal importance and a considerable international exchange of ideas and institutions, corporate governance systems differ, even among advanced market economies. Perhaps the most important cause of international diversity among corporate governance systems is the existence of several distinctive legal traditions across countries (La Porta, Lopez-de-Silanes, Shleifer and Vishny (henceforth LLSV) 1998). These traditions shape the specific rights and protections investors enjoy in their interactions with firms. In addition, the extent to which contracts are legally enforced – what we will call the rule of law – also influences how effective corporate governance is in a particular country.

This section describes the major legal traditions in existence today and sketches their impact on creditor and shareholder rights. We also discuss cross-country measures of the enforcement of the rule of law as it applies to investors. We summarize the adequacy of creditor rights, shareholder rights and the enforcement climate in each of the major country groupings proposed by LLSV (1998) to come up with an overall ranking of the corporate governance environments in which firms operate around the world. Finally, following LLSV (1997a, 1998), La Porta, Lopez-de-Silanes and Shleifer (henceforth LLS) (1999), Shleifer and Vishny (1997) and Levine (1998, 1999), we argue that the legal and political environments are critical influences on the nature of coporate governance and thereby on corporate performance in every country.

Legal Traditions

What are the key features of a legal tradition that define and differentiate it from other traditions? LLSV (1998) cite comparative legal scholars who have identified six criteria:

> Among the criteria often used for this purpose are the following: (1) historical background and development of the legal system, (2) theories and hierarchies of sources of law, (3) the working methodology of jurists within the legal systems, (4) the characteristics of legal concepts employed by the system, (5) the legal institutions of the system, and (6) the divisions of law employed within a system. (Glendon et al., 1994, pp. 4–5)

Following this approach, legal scholars have concluded that the two most important broad legal traditions are civil law and common law. Other traditions exist that have the character of rule-based systems of law – such as Jewish law, Canon law, Hindu law and Muslim law – but LLSV (1998) argue that religious and other quasi-legal traditions are not relevant for a cross-country study of investor protection and corporate governance.[1]

The common-law tradition is found in the United States, Canada, the United Kingdom, other English-speaking countries and countries whose modern development was heavily influenced by the English-speaking world. The civil-law tradition (or 'Romano–Germanic' tradition) is found in continental Europe and other countries that were heavily influenced by continental Europeans. LLSV (1998) further subdivide the civil-law tradition into three main branches: (2a) the Scandinavian civil-law tradition, (2b) the German civil-law tradition, and (2c) the French civil-law tradition.

Table 2.3 displays the LLSV (1998) classification scheme for the legal systems of 49 countries. Countries from all continents are included in the sample although great swathes of Asia, Africa and eastern Europe are absent. Data limitations prevented LLSV from including the more than 100 other countries that are in databases such as the Penn World Table, Mark 5 (Summers and Heston, 1991). Fortunately, the LLSV (1998) sample includes countries representing all the major legal familes. The sample countries also produce the vast majority of world economic output. China and Russia are the two largest and perhaps most important countries missing from the sample.

The four legal families are indicated along the horizontal dimension of the table and a rough proxy for each country's stage of economic development is used to allocate countries vertically. The two largest legal groupings are those with corporate governance traditions originating in England and France. The common-law grouping includes all the English-speaking members of the OECD as well as former British colonies and protectorates plus Thailand. The countries with French legal traditions include several long-standing European OECD members, recent members Mexico and Turkey, plus former French, Spanish and Portuguese colonies in South America, Asia and the Middle East. The Scandinavian and German legal traditions were not spread as widely around the world due to the relatively small colonial empires these countries amassed. It is interesting to note that China, Russia and most of eastern Europe are developing legal and financial systems most heavily influenced by the German legal tradition.

Table 2.3 allows a first crude attempt to identify patterns among corporate governance systems. First notice that the OECD and G7 countries are fairly evenly spread across three of the four legal traditions identified by LLSV (1998). Thus, there is no monopoly by a single legal tradition among rich countries today. The distribution of countries not in the OECD (mostly former colonies of European powers) is less uniform but is not dominated by any single legal tradition, either. In sum, it is not obvious how legal origins and broad economic performance are related. We must examine each of these traditions more closely and ascertain what corporate governance practices and financial system features are associated with them before we can draw any

Table 2.3 *LLSV (1998) country classification scheme: legal traditions and economic development*

	Common-law tradition	Civil-law tradition		
	English origin	Scandinavian origin	German origin	French origin
OECD member countries (G7 members in bold)	Australia **Canada** Ireland New Zealand **United Kingdom** **United States**	Denmark Finland Norway Sweden	Austria **Germany** **Japan** South Korea Switzerland Netherlands	Belgium **France** Greece **Italy** Mexico Portugal Spain Turkey
Other	Hong Kong India Israel Kenya Malaysia Nigeria Pakistan Singapore South Africa Sri Lanka Thailand Zimbabwe		Taiwan	Argentina Brazil Chile Colombia Ecuador Egypt Indonesia Jordan Peru Philippines Uruguay Venezuela

Sources: LLSV (1998, table 2).

conclusions about whether and how corporate governance and corporate performance are related.

The common-law tradition

The English common-law legal tradition is characterized by judges trying to resolve particular cases. That is, precedents from judicial decisions, rather than contributions of legal scholars, shape common law. While most of the common-law countries share a common historical root in the English system and continue to apply a similar procedural approach to the evolution of their respective bodies of law, subsequent independent development means that the various national systems resemble each other less closely as time goes on. Nevertheless, comparative legal scholars generally agree that members of the common-law tradition share more critical features with each other than with members of other legal families (LLSV, 1998).

The civil-law tradition

The civil, or 'Romano–Germanic', legal tradition originates in Roman law and thus is much older than the common-law tradition. Civil law uses statutes and comprehensive codes as the primary means of organizing its legal principles. It relies on legal scholars to interpret the code and draft new interpretations and rules rather than building on judicial precedents alone (LLSV, 1998). Having developed to some extent independently over many centuries, countries within the broad civil-law tradition in some cases have diverged from each other more than have countries within the common-law family. Therefore, LLSV (1998) argue that the tripartite scheme of subdividing civil-law countries mentioned above is appropriate.

The Scandinavian family of legal traditions has its roots in Roman law but in modern times (since the eighteenth century) the civil codes have not been used (LLSV, 1998). In this respect, Scandinavian law has converged some way toward common law. Nevertheless, the origins of the Scandinavian legal system are in the civil-law tradition and quantitative measures of its protection of investors are most similar to those of the German tradition.[2]

The German Commercial Code was written in 1897. It influenced the legal development of Austria, Switzerland, Japan, Greece and Italy, although LLSV (1998) assign the latter two countries to the French group because they give priority to the origin of a country's legal tradition. Legal developments in South Korea and Taiwan were heavily influenced by Japan and China, respectively, both of which in turn borrowed from the German legal system. Other countries that show strong influence from the German legal tradition include the former Czechoslovakia, Hungary and the former Yugoslavia, although none of these countries are included in the LLSV sample due to their underdeveloped private sectors.

The French Commercial Code was written under Napoleon in 1807 and was spread initially in the wake of his conquests. Later, French colonizers imposed French legal systems that still survive in the Near East, Africa, southeast Asia, Oceania and the French Caribbean islands. The Spanish and Portuguese empires in Latin America predated Napoleon, but their disintegration paved the way for the introduction of modern French legal systems (LLSV, 1998).

Creditor Rights and Shareholder Rights

Legal traditions matter for corporate governance and corporate performance because they are systematically related to patterns in the types of legal rights and protections provided to investors. These rights and protections, in turn, affect the types of financing available to firms and may encourage the participation of some groups of investors more than others (such as banks, non-financial corporations, or individuals). It is to these specific rights and protections – and their distribution across countries – that we now turn.

Creditor rights

LLSV (1998) point out that creditor rights are actually more complex than shareholder rights in at least two respects. First, there are typically multiple classes of creditors of large firms, including secured and unsecured lenders, as well as senior and junior positions within a security class. Disagreements among creditors can literally tear apart a firm as secured and senior creditors pursue their collateral while unsecured and junior creditors are much more likely to wish the firm to continue as a going concern. Related to this conflict is the second aspect of the complexity pointed out by LLSV (1998). In case of financial distress, creditors must somehow choose between two quite distinct – and risky – strategies. They can liquidate the firm, perhaps locking in losses that are especially large for junior creditors. Alternatively, they can attempt to reorganize and resuscitate the firm, albeit risking total loss in the future. Reorganization may be very difficult and contentious, especially if incumbent management retains control rights while the reorganization proceeds. In contrast, shareholders almost always prefer to continue operating the firm because their upside potential is unlimited while their downside losses are bounded by virtue of limited liability.

To simplify the analysis of creditor rights, LLSV (1998) adopt the perspective of a senior secured lender. They use four binary variables to proxy for creditor rights, including the following (assigning a value of one if the answer is 'yes' and zero if 'no'):[3]

● Is there an automatic stay on assets?

- Are secured creditors paid first?
- Are there restrictions for going into reorganization?
- Is management prevented from retaining operating control during reorganization?

LLSV (1998) sum these four binary indicators to form a broad index of creditor rights. They also check for the existence of a 'remedial' mechanism that may compensate to some extent for the weak protection of creditors:

- Is a legal reserve required, expressed as some percentage of capital?

A legal reserve requirement protects unsecured creditors, in particular, who might otherwise receive nothing in a liquidation.

Creditor rights vary considerably across countries. France is a prime example of a country with very little legal protection of creditors, scoring zero on the LLSV broad index of creditor rights. Perhaps unsurprisingly, French law imposes a legal reserve requirement (of 10 per cent of capital) as partial redress of the poor protection of creditors' rights otherwise. At the other extreme, several countries, including the United Kingdom, obtain a perfect score on the broad index of creditor rights. There is no legal reserve requirement in the UK, presumably because creditors are well protected in any case.

The first row of Table 2.4 provides a crude summary ranking of the four country groups according to their legal protection of creditor rights. The average score of the English-origin group on creditor rights dominates those of each of the other three groups in head-to-head comparisons (see LLSV, 1998, table 4, panel B, for an explanation of the head-to-head comparisons). The German-origin group on average offers stronger protections to creditors than either the Scandinavian or French groups, so we assign two stars to the German group. The Scandinavian group may be slightly more protective of creditor rights than the French group, but this is not entirely clear so we conservatively assign one star to each of these groups. Following LLSV (1998), our conclusion is that common-law countries provide the best legal protection of creditor rights. It remains to be seen how well shareholders are legally protected in each country group and, even more importantly, how consistently contracts and investor rights are actually upheld. Without a climate in which the rule of law prevails, investor rights are meaningless.

Shareholder rights
Company laws in force in a country largely determine the nature of shareholders' voting rights, the ultimate source of value in corporate equity shares (Hart, 1995). LLSV (1998) identify six different types of shareholder rights that may or may not be present in any country. In addition, they create indexes

Table 2.4 Between-group comparisons of shareholder rights, creditor rights and the rule of law

| | Common-law tradition | Civil-law tradition | | |
	English origin	Scandinavian origin	German origin	French origin
Creditor rights	***	*	**	*
Shareholder rights	***	*		**
Rule of law	*	***	**	
Total	7	5	4	3

Source: LLSV (1998, tables 2, 4 and 5). One asterisk is assigned to a country group for each other country group that has inferior scores in a head-to-head comparison on this dimension.

for three other measures of shareholder rights that affect dividend payouts and the conduct of annual meetings. If present, each of the following six shareholder rights provides an important investor guarantee:[4]

● one share–one vote;
● proxy voting by mail;
● shares are not blocked before a general meeting;
● cumulative voting or proportional representation (to allow minority interests to gain representation on the board);
● an oppressed minority mechanism (allowing either judicial redress or a mandatory buyout of shareholders who are opposed to fundamental changes in company bylaws, such as voting rules);
● pre-emptive rights to purchase new equity issues.

Each of these variables is coded zero if the right does not exist or one if it does exist for each country in the sample.

In addition to these binary indicators, LLSV (1998) construct three other measures of shareholder rights:

● percentage of share capital needed to call an extraordinary shareholder meeting, where a lower number signifies better shareholder rights;
● an index running from zero to six of 'antidirector rights', consisting of the sum of scores on all of the previous indicators except one share–one vote, and where a value of one is assigned when any percentage of share capital less than 10 percent is needed to call an extraordinary shareholder meeting;
● the percentage of net income that by law must be paid out as a dividend, if any.

As in the case of creditor rights, these indicators of shareholder rights reveal a vast diversity among countries. Among the rich countries, for example, Belgium (part of the French-origin group) scores zero on every single indicator where this is possible except for the relatively high (and unfavourable to minority shareholders) 20 per cent of shares needed to call an extraordinary shareholders' meeting. At the other extreme, Canada (assigned to the English-origin group by virtue of Ontario's dominant role in the financial system) achieves a perfect score on six of eight measures of shareholder rights and a near-perfect score on the ninth (only 5 per cent of shares needed to call an extraordinary shareholders' meeting).

The second row of Table 2.4 provides a summary ranking of the four country groups according to their legal protection of shareholder rights. The average scores of the English-origin group again dominate those of each of the other three groups in head-to-head comparisons (see LLSV, 1998, table 2, panel B); hence, we assign the English-origin group of countries three stars. Despite the example of Belgium noted above, the French-origin group on average offers stronger protections to shareholders than either the Scandinavian or German groups, so we assign two stars to the French group. The Scandinavian group appears in head-to-head comparisons to be somewhat more protective of shareholder rights than the German group, so we assign one star to the former and none to the latter.

Thus, the common-law countries appear to provide the strongest legal protection of both creditor and shareholder rights. If these were the only relevant dimensions of corporate governance, we could stop at this point and recommend that all countries not in the English-origin group of countries should simply copy one of its representatives. LLSV (1998) argue that this would be a mistake, however. Effective corporate governance requires not just a strong legal framework of investor protections, but also a strong culture of rule of law. It is to this vital consideration that we now turn.

The Rule of Law

Legal rights of shareholders and creditors to receive certain cash flows and to participate in various corporate decision-making activities are necessary but not sufficient conditions for effective corporate governance. A climate of respect for the rule of law is also needed. Conversely, the greatest respect for and enforcement of the law are of no use to investors if they have few or inadequate legal rights to enforce. Thus, a core set of shareholder and creditor rights and an established tradition of legal enforcement of these rights appear to be complementary features of an effective system of corporate governance.

LLSV (1998) identify five 'enforcement' variables that may proxy for the intangible degree of the rule of law in a country. In addition, they examine the quality of accounting standards in each country. The enforcement variables they investigate are the following:[5]

- the efficiency of the judicial system, as ranked by Business International Corp.;
- an assessment of the law and order tradition, provided by International Country Risk, a credit-rating agency;
- an index of government corruption, also from International Country Risk;
- the risk of expropriation, also from International Country Risk;
- the risk of repudiation of a contract by the government, also from International Country Risk.

Each of these ratings is rescaled to lie between one and ten. The authors also generated ratings of accounting standards in each country by checking for the inclusion of 90 items in the 1990 annual reports of at least three companies in each country.

In contrast to the previously discussed cases of shareholder and creditor rights, the rule of law appears to be consistently strong among the rich countries and somewhat weaker among poorer countries. As LLSV (1998) note, rule-of-law indicators may be strongly correlated with per capita GDP for more fundamental reasons than differing legal origins. The rule of law may be both a cause and an effect of a well-functioning economy and society. Nevertheless, there are significant differences between groups of countries sorted according to their respective legal origins.

The third row of Table 2.4 provides a summary ranking of the four country groups according to their observance of the rule of law. The average scores of the Scandinavian-origin group are highest on these criteria, but it must be kept in mind that there are no poor countries in this group. The German-origin group on average obtains higher scores on the rule of law than either the English or French groups, but this also may be related to the relative scarcity of low-income countries in the German group. Meanwhile, the English-origin countries score higher than the French-origin countries with respect to law and order, and this result does not appear to be distorted by the mix of different income levels among countries.

Legal Traditions and the Rule of Law as Corporate Governance Indicators

What can we conclude about the importance of legal traditions and the rule of law in evaluating corporate governance in major countries around the world? The pioneering work of LLSV (1998) documents a link between a country's legal tradition and its relative ranking in terms of providing rights to shareholders and creditors and in fostering the rule of law (with the caveat that the latter also is related strongly to the country's level of economic development). Table 2.4 provides our interpretation of LLSV's (1998) results in summary fashion. We find that, on average, according to a simple measure that assigns equal importance to creditor rights, shareholder rights and the rule of law, countries in the common-law tradition appear to provide a better corporate governance environment than countries that have civil-law traditions. Differences among the civil-law country groups do not appear as significant, particularly given the large number of low- and middle-income countries in the French-origin group that may depress this group's scores for reasons unrelated to corporate governance *per se*.

The connections identified by LLSV (1998) between legal traditions and corporate governance indicators fall short of a full explanation of corporate governance and its ramifications, however. We need to understand how the corporate governance environment discussed above translates into specific modes of financing and ownership. Furthermore, we must seek to establish a link between these objective measures of financial structure of firms and measures of ultimate performance, such as profitability or growth. Consequently, the next section explores the evidence regarding possible links between a country's corporate governance environment and the financial structure of its firms. In particular, we focus on the typical capital structures employed by firms and on the structure of corporate ownership.

CAPITAL STRUCTURE AND CORPORATE OWNERSHIP

For present purposes, differences in legal traditions and the rule of law are important only if they actually matter for corporate governance. More specifically, differences in corporate governance institutions are of interest only if they translate into differences in objective measures of firm behaviour. In this section, we focus on the impact of the previously discussed corporate governance environment on the sources of external finance used by firms in different countries and on the patterns of corporate ownership.

The Corporate Governance Environment and Firms' Capital Structures

We first examine two aspects of the financing of large firms across countries: (1) their typical capital structure, that is, broad patterns on the liability side of firms' balance sheets, and (2) the relative importance of external financing, that is, funds provided by parties who are not firm insiders.

Capital structure

We provide two views of capital structure that correspond to a 'macro' view and a 'micro' view of firms' balance sheets. The advantages of the macro view from national statistics are that we capture all firms in the economy and we can observe a large number of countries. The advantage of the micro view from firms' financial statements is that it provides a more detailed look at balance-sheet items for a few important countries.

Table 2.5 provides the macro view of capital structures in a large sample of countries. Panel A of Table 2.5, drawn from LLSV (1997a), shows the ratio of the debt of all firms to GDP in 1994 averaged over all countries within each of the four legal traditions discussed above. The numerator of this ratio is the sum of bank debt of the private sector and outstanding non-financial sector bonds. There is essentially no difference between the common-law countries

Table 2.5 Importance of debt and equity markets

	Common-law tradition English origin	Scandinavian origin	Civil-law tradition German origin	French origin
Panel A. Ratio of debt owed by the business sector to GDP (1994)				
Group average	68%	57%	97%	45%
Examples	United States 81% Canada 72% Singapore 60%	Sweden 55% Denmark 34%	Germany 112% Japan 122% South Korea 74%	France 96% Italy 55% Mexico 47%
Panel B. Fraction of the business sector's debt owed to banks (1986)				
Examples	United States 75% Canada 86% UK 96%		Germany 99.8% Japan 96%	France 93% Italy 98%
Panel C. Ratio of the market value of outside equity capital to GDP (1994)				
Group average	60%	30%	46%	21%
Examples	United States 58% Canada 72% Singapore 118%	Sweden 51% Denmark 21%	Germany 13% Japan 62% South Korea 44%	France 23% Italy 8% Mexico 22%

Sources: Panels A and C, LLSV (1997a, table 2); panel B, Rajan and Zingales (1995, table 8).

77

and the civil-law countries on this dimension, a surprising finding given the much stronger protection of creditors in the English-origin countries (recall the second row of Table 2.4). Individual country detail (in the second row of panel A) reveals that high-income countries tend to have larger debt-to-GDP ratios than low-income countries sharing the same legal tradition, a point to which we will return later. Another explanation for why common-law countries do not have much larger debt-to-GDP ratios than civil-law countries is that other sources of financing may be available more readily – for example, equity.

Panel B of Table 2.5 breaks down the debt owed by the business sector into bank debt and bond market debt for each of the G7 countries (Rajan and Zingales, 1995). Although these data are from the mid-1980s and bond markets have grown in virtually all major economies in the meantime, it is unlikely that the relative importance of bank debt has changed very much. Simply put, firms in the United States and Canada issue significant amounts of bonds but nowhere else in the G7 countries is this true. The fact that British firms turn to banks for the vast majority of their debt financing indicates that legal traditions are *not* primarily responsible for the unimportance of corporate bond markets around the world.

Panel C of Table 2.5 shows the relative importance of equity markets around the world. The figures shown are estimates made by LLSV (1997a) of the ratio of the market value of outside equity – defined as the total market value of equity of the top ten firms in each country less the amount controlled by the three largest shareholders in each – to GDP. In contrast to the measures of debt shown in panels A and B, the relative importance of equity markets is indeed strongly related to legal traditions. Common-law countries have nearly twice the market capitalization of civil-law countries except in the German-origin group, where the inclusion of East Asia is pivotal. The surprisingly high score of the German-origin group (46 per cent of GDP) is due to Japan, South Korea and Taiwan, whose average equity-to-GDP ratio of 66 per cent is more than double the three European members' average of 27 per cent.

The overall picture we obtain from Table 2.5 is that common-law countries have much larger markets for outside equity and, in some countries, also for corporate bonds. Most external financing done by firms in civil-law countries is in the form of bank loans, although banks are quite important in common-law countries, too.

Financing by corporate insiders and outsiders
The results in Table 2.5 provided some indication of the unimportance of public equity and bond markets for most firms in civil-law countries. The unavoidable implication of having 'underdeveloped' equity and bond markets is that most firms in most countries are dependent on three sources of insider or near-insider financing:

- owner-contributed funds;
- retained earnings;
- bank debt.

Narrow capital markets in turn mean that fewer new firms are likely to emerge; existing firms may be smaller or more financially fragile than would otherwise be the case; internal financing is likely to be predominant and closely linked to the business cycle; inefficient forms of retained earnings may emerge; banks may obtain unwelcome power over firms; and owners may remain relatively undiversified. We discuss the first five of these issues briefly here before turning to the structure of corporate ownership in the next subsection.

Table 2.6 presents indicators of how narrow capital markets may constrain the financial behaviour of firms. Panel A contains two indicators of the ease with which firms may obtain external equity financing. The number of initial public offerings indicates the flow of new firms coming to the equity market, while the number of domestic listed firms gives some idea of how broad the equity market has become. This reflects both the inflow of new firms as well as the outflow of existing firms that can no longer operate profitably. These two measures are very similar in pointing to a clear distinction between the common-law and civil-law countries with respect to effective access to public equity markets, although Scandinavian-origin countries resemble the common-law countries in this respect.

Panel B of Table 2.6 provides details on the mix of internal and external financing by non-financial firms in the G7 countries. Firms in the civil-law countries generally must rely more on internal sources of funds than their common-law counterparts, as indicated by slightly higher percentages of total financing due to cash flows from operations in some cases.

Two special cases should be noted. The United States presents an exception to our generalization during the period Rajan and Zingales (1995) studied because a sizable portion of cash flows at US firms were dedicated to repurchasing their own equity (the same phenomenon occurred in the 1990s). The consequence is that, rather than constituting a source of funds, net equity financing was a use of funds. In fact, reliance on external debt by US firms was not out of line with their English-origin counterparts relative to overall cash flows, while the contribution of equity financing was equivalent to nearly negative 8 per cent of total financing in the US versus positive 12–14 per cent for the UK and Canada (Rajan and Zingales, 1995, table 4). This results in a relatively high reported percentage of total financing by US firms from internal cash flows. Subtracting 20 percentage points from the US figure – 8 percentage points of negative equity financing plus the 'normal' English-origin rate of net equity financing of 12 percentage points – gives a

Table 2.6 Consequences of narrow capital markets

	Common-law tradition		Civil-law tradition	
	English origin	Scandinavian origin	German origin	French origin
Panel A. Number of new and existing firms (1994–96)				
Initial public offerings per 1 000 000 people	2.23	2.14	0.12	0.19
Domestic listed firms per 1000 people	35.45	27.26	16.79	10.00
Panel B. Reliance on internal financing (1984–91)				
Percentage of total financing due to cash flows from operations	United States 77% Canada 58% UK 51%		Germany 67% Japan 44%	France 65% Italy 67%
Percentage of total assets financed by untaxed reserves or 'other' liabilities	United States 5.8% Canada 2.6% UK 3.4%		Germany 30.4% Japan 4.8%	France 6.3% Italy 7.8%

Sources: Panel A, LLSV (1997a, table 2); panel B, Rajan and Zingales (1995, tables 4, 2).

figure of 57 per cent, perfectly consistent with the numbers shown for Canada and the United Kingdom.

The second special case is Japan, which experienced an asset-price bubble during the late 1980s. All kinds of financing were considered cheap by firms during this period so they may have borrowed more and issued more equity than is normal. Hence, because of the market boom, Japan's figure of 44 per cent may be abnormally low and should not be used as *prima facie* evidence of low reliance on internal sources of funds by firms in civil-law countries in general.

Firms in Germany, France and Italy, meanwhile, obtained approximately 10 percentage points less of their total financing from external sources than did firms in the UK and Canada. This constitutes more evidence that relatively narrow capital markets in the civil-law countries may have constrained firms' financial behaviour.

The second row of panel B shows the percentage of total assets financed by untaxed reserves or 'other' liabilities, which together may represent relatively inefficient sources of financing in the sense that they are not priced by the market and are likely to be inflexible. A massive 30.4 per cent of German firms' assets are financed by these special categories; the lion's share of these liabilities are pension reserves (Rajan and Zingales, 1995). In contrast to the common-law country 'prudent-man' rules dictating minimum off-balance sheet funding requirements for employee pension liabilities, German firms are allowed to fund their future pension obligations as well as financing their current operations – with on-balance sheet reserves.

The last consequence of narrow capital markets we discuss in this section is the power banks may obtain over borrowing firms by virtue of their dominant role in external financing. Table 2.5 showed that firms in civil-law countries rely to a great extent on banks for external finance. It is commonly asserted that banks in these countries wield a great deal of influence through a myriad of financial activities that are grounded in a lending relationship (Rajan, 1992; Emmons and Schmid, 1998). It is possible that the relatively large amount of internal financing done by firms in civil-law countries reflects their attempts to minimize their dependence on banks.

We have shown in this section that the amount of debt financing by firms is similar among all high-income countries. A well-developed rule of law that may be a feature of high-income countries probably contributes to this widely shared feature of corporate capital structure. This regularity obscures differences in details, however. First, a few English-speaking countries have flourishing bond markets, providing an alternative to banks for debt financing. The strong protections of creditors' interests found in the common-law countries may be an important factor contributing to the vitality of public debt markets. The continuing dependence of British firms on banks points out the fact that creditor protections are necessary but not sufficient for bond markets to develop, however. If creditor protections are in fact important, however, then future bond market development may be more likely in German-origin countries than in other countries with civil-law traditions.

Second, many of the common-law countries have large equity markets in which outside investors hold substantial stakes in firms. These countries provide greater opportunities for firms to obtain outside equity and stock market listings and greater opportunities for investors to share economy-wide risks. With the exception of the East Asian countries, few civil-law countries have large and liquid equity markets. Shareholder rights appear to be stronger in French-origin countries than in the other civil-law countries, so equity markets may develop faster in the former group.

Third, civil-law countries finance a substantially larger part of their total operating requirements with internal cash flows. This could be due to weaker investor protections and the consequent underdevelopment of external capital markets relative to common-law countries. It could also reflect firms' attempts to minimize the extent to which they rely on banks in order to maintain their own bargaining power.

Together, these pieces of evidence on firms' capital structures suggest that bank domination of external financing in civil-law countries may reduce firms' flexibility in some respects. This aspect of relatively underdeveloped capital markets must be kept in mind when evaluating some of the potential benefits of bank-centred financial systems. It may also be related to the existence of insider-oriented governance structures and relatively concentrated equity ownership structures in many civil-law countries, as the next subsection discusses.

The Corporate Governance Environment and Ownership Structure

The number and nature of investors in a corporation and the relative sizes of their stakes are important features of the ownership structure of corporations. We now turn to evidence on differences across countries and legal traditions in terms of: (1) the locus of effective control by shareholders, (2) concentration of equity ownership, and (3) the identity of controlling shareholders.

Control of large public firms
A common assumption among economists and management scholars is that large firms are widely held, that is, the shares are dispersed among many investors, each with an insignificant fraction of the total and no way of exerting control over the management. This has led to large theoretical and empirical literatures dealing with managerial agency problems and the inefficiencies these create.

Panel A of Table 2.7 shows that dispersed ownership is a good approximation of reality in only some countries. Using a definition of effective control of 20 per cent ownership or more by a single entity at the end of 1995, LLS (1999) found that only 36 per cent of a sample of large firms drawn from 27 countries had no effective owner, that is, were widely held. If a cut-off level of stakes amounting to l0 per cent oŗ more is applied, only 24 per cent of firms in the sample were widely held. Large firms in the United States, the United Kingdom and Japan are almost all widely held, but other high-income countries are just about as likely to be controlled by one shareholder as to be without a dominant owner. Widely held firms are virtually unknown in some middle-income countries such as Mexico and Argentina, while in 17 of the 27 sample countries, a majority of large firms were controlled by a single owner (LLS, 1999, table 2). Thus, we have some evidence that ownership is concentrated in many large firms, especially outside the English-speaking world. This feature of equity ownership structure may be a response to the lack of investor protections in many civil-law countries noted above (LLSV, 1998).

Concentration of ownership
We can also examine the ownership concentration of a small number of large owners to seek more evidence on concentrated ownership. After all, effective control could be exerted by a small group of shareholders rather than by a single owner. Panel B of Table 2.7 provides evidence of a high degree of concentration of ownership among the three largest shareholders in large firms in many countries (LLSV, 1998, table 7). Consistent with the results shown in panel A of Table 2.7, the least-concentrated ownership structures appear to be those in the English-speaking world and Japan.

Within the English-origin group of countries, there is a very strong negative correlation between an individual country's per capita income level and the degree to which ownership is concentrated in its large firms. That is, richer countries have more widely held firms. A similar, but weaker, pattern appears among the French-origin countries. Thus, if concentrated ownership is a response to weak investor protections, then our earlier conclusion that common-law countries have stronger investor protections than civil-law countries is consistent with the ownership patterns we observe among the rich countries. A second, income-related, effect appears to be operating, as well. Within any country group, richer countries have more widely held firms than other countries (see panel A of Table 2.7). This may reflect our conclusion that the rule of law, an important complement of explicit legal investor protections, is stronger in richer countries of all legal traditions.

Identity of owners
Given a high degree of concentrated equity ownership in many countries, we

Table 2.7 Equity ownership structure

	Common-law tradition	Civil-law tradition		
	English origin	Scandinavian origin	German origin	French origin

Panel A. Control: fraction of ten largest non-financial domestic firms that are widely held (20% definition of control)

Examples								
United States	80%	Sweden	25%	Germany	50%	France	60%
UK	100%	Denmark	40%	Switzerland	60%	Italy	20%
Canada	60%	Norway	25%	Japan	90%	Mexico	0%
Singapore	15%	Finland	35%	South Korea	55%	Argentina	0%

Panel B. Concentration: median ownership of ten largest non-financial domestic firms by three largest shareholders

Group average	42%		33%		33%		55%	
Examples								
United States	12%	Sweden	28%	Germany	50%	France	24%
UK	15%	Denmark	40%	Switzerland	48%	Italy	60%
Canada	24%	Norway	31%	Japan	13%	Mexico	67%
Singapore	53%	Finland	34%	South Korea	20%	Argentina	55%

Panel C. Control: fraction of ten largest non-financial domestic firms controlled by a family, the state or a widely held non-financial firm (20% definition of control)

Examples							
United States	20%	Sweden	55%	Germany	35%	France	35%
UK	0%	Denmark	50%	Switzerland	30%	Italy	65%
Canada	40%	Norway	60%	Japan	10%	Mexico	100%
Singapore	80%	Finland	50%	South Korea	40%	Argentina	95%

Panel D. Control: fraction of ten largest non-financial domestic firms controlled by a widely held financial firm or 'miscellaneous' (20% definition of control)

Examples							
United States	0%	Sweden	20%	Germany	15%	France	5%
UK	0%	Denmark	10%	Switzerland	10%	Italy	15%
Canada	0%	Norway	15%	Japan	0%	Mexico	0%
Singapore	5%	Finland	15%	South Korea	5%	Argentina	5%

Sources: Panels A, C and D, LLS (1999, table 2); panel B, LLSV (1998, table 7).

can ask who these owners are. Panels C and D of Table 2.7 provide details on the types of major shareholders observed in large firms in several countries at the end of 1995. The fraction of large firms controlled by a family, the state, or a widely held non-financial firm is typically around one-half or more in all but the high-income English-speaking countries and Japan (panel C). For example, one of the ten largest non-financial firms in Germany was controlled by a family and three others were controlled by the state (in one of which control was shared with a widely held financial firm). In South Korea, two of the ten largest firms were controlled by families and two others by the state. In Mexico, all ten of the largest firms were family-controlled. At the other extreme, all ten of the UK's largest firms were widely held when a 20 per cent definition of control is used and nine of ten still qualify when a 10 per cent cut-off is applied (LLS, 1999, Table 2).

Panel D of Table 2.7 focuses on control of large non-financial firms by widely held financial firms – that is, banks, insurance companies, or other financial institutions that are not closely held or controlled by other entities. This definition includes many of the German, Dutch and Swiss universal banks, and the Japanese city banks, for example, although it does not cover the French or Italian banks in which the State maintains a large equity position.

Do large banks exert a great deal of control over large non-financial firms in some countries? The evidence from LLS (1999) is that bank control is the exception rather than the rule even in Europe, the home of universal banking. Private German, Swiss, Scandinavian, Italian and French financial institutions control only one or two of the ten largest domestic non-financial firms in each country. As expected, this form of control is non-existent in the high-income English-speaking world. Perhaps surprisingly to some, Japanese financial institutions are also absent from the list of effective owners of large non-financial firms.

Our discussion of equity ownership structure across countries provided some evidence consistent with the idea that concentrated ownership may be a response to weak investor protections (in the rich civil-law countries) and/or to a weak climate for the rule of law (in low-income countries of all legal traditions). We saw that it is families, the state, and other non-financial firms, rather than banks or other financial institutions, that provide the bulk of concentrated equity investment in the largest firms.

DOES CORPORATE GOVERNANCE AFFECT CORPORATE PERFORMANCE?

Our argument to this point has been built up in two stages. First, we argued that different legal traditions contribute to notable differences in the degree of investor protection written into the commercial codes of various countries. At the same time, higher levels of economic development correlate with a better climate for the rule of law. The second stage in our argument was that these two dimensions of a country's historical, legal and political legacy are critical determinants of the actual financial structures used by firms. In particular, we found that non-financial firms in common-law countries generally used more external finance than their counterparts in civil-law countries. Both outside equity (that is, contributed by non-controlling shareholders) and bond market debt were more plentiful in English-origin countries, on average. Consistent with these findings, we found that firms were more likely to have controlling shareholders and that ownership structures were more concentrated outside the English-speaking world and Japan. Although banks are dominant providers of debt finance in most countries, they act as controlling share-holders in only a few of the largest non-financial firms in the civil-law countries.

We now turn to the third and final stage in our argument. In this section we ask, do the legal traditions and patterns of corporate governance sketched so far have any significance for corporate performance? Furthermore, do these firm-level differences in performance, if any, translate into differences in the performance of national economies?

It is worth noting that we have already presented one suggestive piece of evidence that bears on these questions. Table 2.1 reported differences in the pre-tax ROAs of large internationally active banks from 12 countries. The tentative conclusion from our earlier discussion was that banks from English-speaking countries appeared to enjoy consistently higher levels of core profitability than did other banks. In light of our subsequent discussion, it is plausible to assert that differing corporate governance practices may be in part responsible. We now turn to more comprehensive sources of empirical evidence that might confirm this conjecture.

Evidence on the Links between Corporate Governance, Corporate Finance and Corporate Performance

We will review briefly evidence from industry-level data as well as from national accounts. An empirical investigation at industry level allows a finer partitioning of the data and a larger sample size, important considerations when testing theories that may be difficult to distinguish. This is certainly the case here, since corporate governance explanations of corporate or national economic performance may not be obviously more convincing than a reverse causation explanation, according to which good performance leads to more external finance, for example. The national accounts data are important because they are capable, in principle, of picking up all of the indirect and possibly intangible ways in which corporate governance systems may matter for overall economic performance.

An industry-level view of corporate governance and corporate performance

Rajan and Zingales (1998) begin with a simple maintained hypothesis: firms in industries that require relatively large amounts of external finance to succeed will perform relatively better in countries where financial markets are better developed. First, they estimate the amount of external financing as a fraction of capital expenditures actually used by all the manufacturing firms in the Compustat universe for the United States. They find that drugs and pharmaceuticals firms use the most external finance, followed by plastics and computing. The sectors with the least need for external finance – in fact, these sectors have a negative need, or excess cash flow – are leather, pottery and tobacco.

Armed with estimates from US firms of external financing needs by industrial sector, Rajan and Zingales (1998) then apply these financial dependence measures to 36 industries drawn from 41 countries. They use several proxies for the level of a country's financial development, including accounting standards (their preferred measure), the ratio of total stock market capitalization to GDP, the ratio of domestic credit to the private sector to GDP, per capita income and the LLSV (1998) country groupings. Their empirical tests consist of regressions of the growth of real value added by industries in each country on measures of financial development by country.

Consistent with the hypothesis that corporate governance as we have articulated it matters for corporate performance, Rajan and Zingales (1998) find that firms in industries that require large amounts of external financing grow faster in countries with high scores on their measures of financial development (their tables 4 and 5). The results are almost identical when they use the LLSV (1998) country classification scheme instead of their own financial development measures to gauge how easily firms can access sources of external finance. Thus, corporate governance appears to matter for corporate performance in the way one would expect. Better accounting standards, larger capital markets, stronger legal protections of investors and a stronger rule of law are all good predictors of growth by firms that need external finance.

National economic performance and corporate governance

Another strategy for detecting possible effects of corporate governance on corporate performance is to compare measures of national economic performance while controlling for governance proxies. In a series of papers,

Ross Levine (1998, 1999; Levine and Zervos, 1998) has shown that numerous indicators of financial development – including the LLSV (1998) country groupings discussed above – are strong predictors of several measures of aggregate economic outperformance. This is also consistent with the hypothesis that corporate governance practices are important inputs into corporate performance which, in turn, is related to national performance.

Levine and Zervos (1998, table 3) find that GDP growth, growth of the capital stock and productivity growth are all strongly associated with several measures of financial development over the period 1976–93 in a sample of 47 countries. These include the ratio of bank credit extended to the private sector to GDP and the ratio of stock market turnover to market capitalization, proxies for the ease of access to debt and equity markets, respectively. These results are robust to the inclusion of various controls for the level of economic development of each country.

Levine (1998) repeats the analysis done in Levine and Zervos (1998) but uses the LLSV (1998) country classification scheme to motivate his search for specific measures of financial market development. In particular, Levine (1998) uses the LLSV (1998) measures to extract the component of bank credit to the private sector that is due to (that is, correlated with) these corporate governance features alone. Levine (1999) uses a similar methodology with several broader measures of financial development. In both cases, the results are strongly supportive of the hypothesis that the elements of corporate governance identified by LLSV (1998) are in fact important determinants of aggregate economic performance over long time periods. In other words, the corporate governance environment can make a measurable difference not only to individual corporate performance, but also to national economic performance.

A Broader Perspective on Corporate Performance

Despite strong support for the common-law framework of corporate governance that emerges from the performance studies just described, there may be reasons why there appears to be no international rush to jetison existing frameworks where they differ from the English-origin model. Is this due merely to national chauvinism or the inability to recognize a superior model? Or are the issues surrounding corporate governance more complex than might have been inferred from our previous discussions?

The persistence of distinctive systems of corporate governance could be due to the existence of other important aspects of corporate governance and corporate performance that are not reflected adequately in the profitability and growth regressions reported by Rajan and Zingales (1998), Levine and Zervos (1998) and Levine (1998, 1999). For example, common-law countries' financial systems may be proficient in fostering 'creative destruction', but some countries may choose a milder – if also less profitable – form of capitalism. Some countries may enjoy comparative advantages in industries that do not require large amounts of external finance, reducing the attraction of large and liquid capital markets. Active capital markets may interfere with various kinds of financial intermediary-based long-term relationships that provide efficient monitoring of non-financial firms (Hellwig, 1991) or allocative efficiency (Allen and Gale, 1999). Capital markets that provide 'transactional finance' may undermine financial intermediaries' ability to provide socially beneficial intertemporal smoothing of risk (Allen and Gale, 1997) or to resist credit cycles that result in macroeconomic stability (Kiyotaki and Moore, 1997). Transition or developing economies may not possess the economic and institutional underpinnings that would be necessary to support a market-based financial system (Berglöf and von Thadden, Chapter 9, this volume). We turn briefly to some of these qualifications to our previous conclusion that common-law-based corporate governance systems appear to produce superior performance.

The role of financial intermediaries in monitoring non-financial firms

We alluded earlier to the role of financial firms such as banks and insurance companies in exerting control and monitoring the behaviour of non-financial firms. Clearly, ownership of a controlling equity stake is not the only, or perhaps even the best, way for a financial institution to provide incentives for managers to act in the interests of investors in the firm. A lending relationship is also a potential source of discipline (Diamond, 1984). As we noted, bank lending is the primary source of debt financing in virtually all countries, but it is relatively less important in a few of the English-speaking countries. It is precisely in these countries where bond and outside equity markets are most active. Based on a comparison of the United States and Germany, Hellwig (1991) argues that active capital markets 'serve investors who want to reshuffle their portfolios', but do not provide a substitute for the disciplining role of banks that closely monitor their borrowers. Jensen (1993) concurs by observing that the profusion of hostile takeover activity in the United States may be a sign that, in the absense of strong lenders, external capital markets and internal control mechanisms often have failed to serve investors well.

The role of financial intermediaries in producing allocative efficiency

Innovation often involves creativity, entrepreneurial drive and long-sighted financing. Financial intermediaries such as banks and venture capital firms appear to be indispensable in providing opportunities for profitable innovation and efficient allocation of society's resources (Allen and Gale,

1999). Active capital markets may indeed play an important role at a later stage in a new firm's life cycle, but financial intermediaries are more important in early stages. Analogously, intermediaries that monitor firms closely are better able to initiate restructurings or liquidation when this is called for. To the extent that capital markets are able to 'skim the cream' of profitable investment projects and firms, financial intermediaries may be weakened and their role in producing allocative efficiency undermined.

The role of financial intermediaries in providing intertemporal smoothing of income

From the standpoint of an economy as a whole, market-dominated financial systems may be efficient in a cross-sectional sense (that is, funds are auctioned to the highest-value bidder) even when they are not efficient in an intertemporal sense (that is, buffering shocks to households' incomes, Allen and Gale, 1997). The source of this apparent paradox is that the liquidity created by financial markets is a public good, leading to overconsumption of the good. That is, every participant faces the incentive to economize on holding 'safe assets' when financial markets appear able to provide liquidity on demand. However, large shocks to asset values or confidence may induce an abnormally large number of investors to seek to convert risky into safe assets at one time. This flight to safety reveals the ephemeral nature of the liquidity provided by markets. Financial systems that reserve a large (and profitable) role for financial intermediaries, on the other hand, provide incentives for these intermediaries to invest in safe assets so as to provide a genuine store of liquidity. Thus, economies that allow capital markets to reduce the profitability of financial intermediaries too much may run a greater risk of acute liquidity crises.

A related idea is that lending based solely on collateral – as opposed to relationship lending – can lead to destructive credit cycles in an economy (Kiyotaki and Moore, 1997). When assets serve both as means of production and loan collateral, shocks to the value of the assets has two effects. First, by definition the shock reduces the productivity of the assets and hence the incomes of borrowers. The second, and potentially more damaging, effect is that loan collateral values shrink. Lending that is based solely on these collateral values, rather than stable long-term relationships, then declines. This also reduces income, reinforcing the first effect. Clearly, the Kiyotaki and Moore (1997) account is related to the Allen and Gale (1997) scenario in the sense that there is a public goods problem. In both cases, the existence of financial intermediaries with some degree of market power allows them to internalize and hence to eliminate this source of fragility in a market economy.

CONCLUSIONS

We have argued that distinctive legal traditions, based on common law and civil law, respectively, gave rise to distinctive sets of legal protections of investors. The common-law tradition generally provides stronger protections for both debt and equity investors than do any of the legal families derived from the civil-law tradition. A second important dimension of investor protection relates to the overall climate and tradition of contract enforcement and the rule of law. High standards of investor protection appear to be correlated positively with countries' levels of economic development, regardless of their specific legal tradition. Clearly, strong legal protections of investors and a consistent pattern of upholding the rule of law are complementary aspects of a strong corporate governance system.

Taken together, the degree of investor protection and the strength of the rule of law appear to explain some of the differences in the capital structures of firms and ownership patterns across countries. Strong systems of corporate governance are associated with larger amounts of external finance, specifically, minority holdings of equity and corporate bonds. We also reviewed evidence consistent with the hypothesis that better investor protection and a stronger rule of law are related ultimately to both better corporate performance of firms that require external finance and to any of several measures of aggregate economic performance. Thus, differences in corporate governance systems seem to be connected to differences in performance at firm and national levels.

These conclusions should not be taken to imply that there is a single, universally accepted model of superior corporate governance. Transition and developing countries face constraints that may preclude the adoption of an idealized market-based, common-law-type financial system. At the same time, financial systems in developed countries continue to differ significantly. Because legal, political, social and financial systems are, in reality, extremely complex and interconnected, changes dictated by corporate governance concerns alone are likely to be very difficult to implement.

There are legitimate objections to a financial system dominated by capital markets as in the English-speaking world. Financial intermediaries carry out many roles that may not be duplicated, or performed well, by financial markets alone. In the end, we can say only that corporate governance systems are deeply entrenched and corporate performance is too multifaceted to allow unambiguous recommendations for future change and reforms. Nevertheless, stronger legal protections of creditors and shareholders and a strong commitment to the rule of law appear to be no-lose propositions that every country can and should embrace for the purpose of enhancing corporate governance as well as the overall functioning of the economy.

NOTES

* The views in this chapter are those of the authors and not necessarily those of the Federal Reserve Bank of St Louis or of the Federal Reserve System. We thank Gavin Boyd and participants at the September 1999 Halifax symposium for helpful comments.
1. Interestingly, LLSV (1997b) suggest in a different paper that religious traditions may be important, after all. They find a strong positive link between 'trust' by individuals of other people and organizations in society and measures of government efficiency, participation in civic organizations, social efficiency and the size of business firms. They argue that trust, in turn, is lower in countries where the dominant religion is 'hierarchical', including the Roman Catholic, Eastern Orthodox and Muslim religions. Thus, differing religious traditions may be important in any search for ultimate determinants of social systems and behaviours.
2. LLSV (1998, tables 2 and 4) compute indexes of shareholder rights and creditor rights for each country in their sample. Tests of differences of means for various aspects of investor protections between the four legal traditions indicate that the Scandinavian and German legal traditions are the most similar among all pairs.
3. See table 1 of LLSV (1998) for a complete description of the underlying data series.
4. See table 1 of LLSV (1998) for a complete description of the underlying data series.
5. See table 1 of LLSV (1998) for a complete description of the underlying data series.

REFERENCES

Allen, Franklin and Douglas Gale (1997), 'Financial markets, intermediaries and intertemporal smoothing', *Journal of Political Economy*, **105** (3) (June), 523–46.

Allen, Franklin and Douglas Gale (1999), 'Diversity of opinion and financing of new technologies', *Journal of Financial Intermediation*, **8** (1–2) (Jan.–April), 68–89.

Diamond, Douglas G. (1984), 'Financial intermediation and delegated monitoring', *Review of Economic Studies*, **51** (3) (July), 393–414.

Emmons, William R. and Frank A. Schmid (1998), 'Universal banking, control rights and corporate finance in Germany', *Federal Reserve Bank of St. Louis Review*, **80** (July/August), 19–42.

Glendon, Mary Ann, Michael W. Gordon and Christopher Osakwe (1994), *Comparative Legal Traditions: Text, Materials and Cases on the Civil and Common Law Traditions, with Special References to French, German and English*, St Paul, Minn.: West Publishing.

Hart, Oliver (1995), *Firms, Contracts, and Financial Structure*, London: Oxford University Press.

Hellwig, Martin (1991), 'Banking, financial intermediation and corporate finance', in Albert Giovannini and Colin Mayer (eds), *European Financial Integration*, Cambridge: Cambridge University Press, pp. 35–63.

Jensen, Michael C. (1993), 'The modern industrial revolution, exit and the failure of internal control systems', *Journal of Finance* (July), 831–80.

Kiyotaki, Nobuhiro and John Moore (1997), 'Credit cycles', *Journal of Political Economy*, **105** (2), April, 211–48.

La Porta, Rafael, Florencio Lopez-de-Silanes, Andrei Shleifer and Robert Vishny (1997a), 'Legal determinants of external finance', *Journal of Finance*, **52**, 1131–50.

La Porta, Rafael, Florencio Lopez-de-Silanes, Andrei Shleifer and Robert Vishny (1997b), 'Trust in large organizations', *American Economic Review*, **87** (2) (May), 333–8.

La Porta, Rafael, Florencio Lopez-de-Silanes, Andrei Shleifer and Robert Vishny

(1998), 'Law and finance', *Journal of Political Economy*, **106**, 1113–55.

La Porta, Rafael, Florencio Lopez-de-Silanes and Andrei Shleifer (1999), 'Corporate ownership around the world', *Journal of Finance*, **54**, 471–517.

Levine, Ross (1998), 'The legal environment, banks and long-run economic growth', *Journal of Money, Credit and Banking*, **30** (3), Part 2 (August), 596–613.

Levine, Ross (1999), 'Law, finance and economic growth', *Journal of Financial Intermediation*, (1–2) (January–April), 8–35.

Levine, Ross and Sara Zervos (1998), 'Stock markets, banks and economic growth', *American Economic Review*, **88** (3) (June), 537–58.

OECD (Organisation for Economic Co-operation and Development) (1992), *Bank Profitability*, Paris: OECD.

OECD (1999a), *OECD Principles of Corporate Governance*, Paris: OECD.

OECD (1999b), *International Banking and Financial Market Development*, Paris: OECD.

Rajan, Raghuram G. (1992), 'Insiders and outsiders: the choice between informed and arm's-length debt', *Journal of Finance*, **47** (4) (September), 1367–400.

Rajan, Raghuram G. and Luigi Zingales (1995), 'What do we know about capital structure? Some evidence from international data', *Journal of Finance*, **50** (5) (December), 1421–60.

Rajan, Raghuram G. and Luigi Zingales (1998), 'Financial dependence and growth', *American Economic Review*, **88** (3) (June), 559–86.

Shleifer, Andrei and Robert W. Vishny (1997), 'A survey of corporate governance', *Journal of Finance* (June), 737–83.

Summers, Robert and Alan Heston (1991), 'The Penn World Table (Mark 5): an expanded set of international comparisons, 1950–1988', *Quarterly Journal of Economics*, **106** (2) (May), 327–68.

3. Capital markets and control of enterprises in the global economy

Ingo Walter

1. INTRODUCTION

With the organization of economies by means of central planning and command structures now totally discredited – and assessments of its cumulative damage surpassing even the expectations of the most vociferous critics – one long-standing model of economic organization no longer beckons. Countries that followed it (voluntarily or not) have by now adopted alternatives, sometimes under conditions of crisis and chaos rarely imposed on the general public. 'Market orientation' has been the key, but itself encompasses a broad array of more or less subtle historical and contemporary gradations.

It is arguable that the role the market played in such economic renaissance 'success stories' as West Germany or Japan in the 1950s, South Korea or Singapore in the 1960s and 1970s, Hong Kong or Chile in the 1980s and Mexico or China in the 1990s is more distinguished by differences than similarities. Certainly economically devastated countries followed a broad array of routes to recovery (Smith and Walter, 1992). And people in advanced market economies dissatisfied with their own economic performance have sometimes found much to admire in the variants tried in other, ostensibly more 'successful' nations. In both East and West, critical comparisons among different ways of harnessing the market to optimize social welfare continue, carrying with them prospects for change in the way economies are organized in the years ahead.

With the policy reorientations, however, questions about the performance of markets, especially financial markets, have demanded much attention. The internationalization of product markets, following reductions of trade and investment barriers, has caused issues of competition policy and anti-dumping policy to assume larger dimensions. Meanwhile, the more extensive linking of financial markets has proceeded rather apart from, but with potentially destabilizing consequencs for, the real economies which are being linked in rising structural interdependencies.

This chapter focuses on a single aspect of this issue: how does the organization and regulation of the financial system, notably the role of banks, influence critical dimensions of domestic and international economic performance through the processs of corporate control? That is, how does the institutional design of the financial system influence the character of the capital allocation process and national economic performance?

Following a discussion in Section 2 of alternative financial–industrial control structures, four quite different systems are compared in Section 3 – the Japanese, German, French and Anglo-American (Walter, 1993). Each is then evaluated in Section 4 in terms of how it appears to stand up against a set of performance benchmarks, with the role of financial institutions as the centrepiece of the discussion. In Section 5, the potential for the convergence of financial system architectures is discussed in the context of the evolving and changing national financial and corporate governance structures, particularly in Europe and the USA.

2. BANKS AS A CENTRAL ELEMENT IN CORPORATE CONTROL SYSTEMS

Corporate control has to do with the management of enterprises. A classic assumption underlying market capitalism is that management acts consistently in the best interests of shareholders, maximizing their long-term wealth as measured by the stock price. *Agency problems* – defined in terms of potential divergence between the interests of owners and managers – do not arise. Managers consistently meet their fiduciary responsibilities to owners in a firm's purchasing and marketing decisions, in investment projects and financing decisions, in the use of human resources and in maximizing available economies of scale and scope.

In the real world, agency problems do arise, and present one of the most difficult problems in market economics. How these problems are resolved, therefore, is of great importance. Four stylized approaches[1] to handling them can be described as in Figure 3.1. All assign central but quite distinct roles to financial institutions.

- • *The equity market system.* Shares of corporations are held by the public, directly or through institutional investors – mutual funds and pension funds – and are actively traded. Corporate restructuring is triggered by exploitation of a *control premium* between the existing market capitalization of a firm and that which an unaffiliated acquirer (whether an industrial company or an active financial investor) perceives and acts upon by initiating a takeover effort to unlock shareholder value

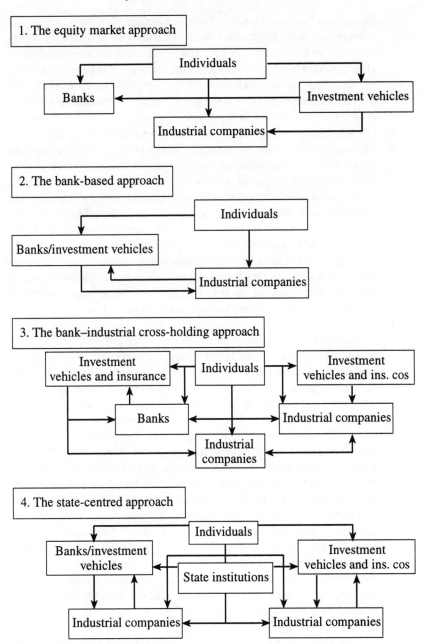

Figure 3.1   Alternative corporate control structures

through management changes. There is a high level of transparency and reliance on public information, with systematic surveillance by equity investors and research analysts. Concerns about unwanted takeover efforts prompt management to act in the interests of shareholders, many of whom tend to view their shares as put options – options to sell. The role of credit institutions in the control structure of this *outsider* system is mainly confined to arm's-length financing, including financing, advising and investing in takeovers and corporate restructurings.

- *The bank-based system.* Major equity stakes in corporations are held by banks, who act as commercial and investment bankers to their clients. With substantial equity as well as debt exposures, banks monitor the management of corporations, with active boardroom participation and guidance with the benefit of non-public (*inside*) information. The public holds shares in both banks and corporations. Markets for corporate equity and debt tend to be poorly developed, with relatively large investor holdings of public sector bonds as opposed to corporate bonds or stocks. Financial transparency tends to be relatively low, as does the free float of shares. External efforts to gain control of corporations against the wishes of management are rare.

- *Bank-industrial cross-holdings.* In this system, non-financial corporations hold significant stakes in each other and reciprocal seats on boards of directors. Both linkages may complement close supplier–customer relationships, with dependability and cooperation often dominating price as transactions criteria. Banks hold shares in industrial companies and play a significant role at the board level, and at the centre of equity cross-holding. The public holds shares in both industrial companies and banks. There is significant free float of shares and relatively well-developed corporate equity and debt markets. Managements of companies connected through cross-holding structures are generally felt to be acting in the interests of public shareholders, and the structures themselves may be viewed in the market as redefinitions of the boundaries of a 'firm' based on inside information, both among clustered industrial firms and between firms and banks. Unwanted corporate control change by active investors in this system is virtually unknown.

- The role of the state in the corporate control process can range across the three systems from *laissez-faire* to centrally directed. At one extreme, government may set macro policy, competition policy and international trade policy, and essentially all industrial outcomes are left to market forces. Alternatively, government involvement may include partial or full ownership of corporations, of banks with strong influence on investment and/or lending decisions, influence on credit allocation through the bank regulation and supervision process, or some

Type A: Full integration

Universal bank

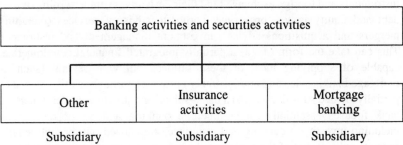

Type B: Partial integration

Universal bank

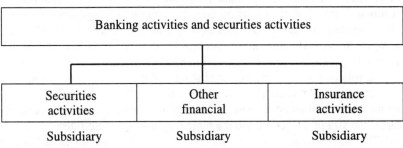

Type C: Bank parent structure

Universal bank

Type D: Holding company structure

Holding company

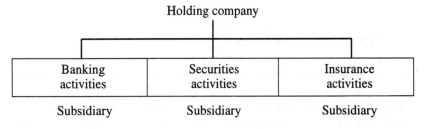

Figure 3.2   Stylized banking organization structures

combination of these conduits. The nature of the corporate control structure and bank–industry linkages may have a significant bearing on the ability of government to affect industrial outcomes.

The role of financial institutions depends importantly on how the banking system is structured, in particular the range of financial activities it incorporates (see Figure 3.2). Universal banking can be defined as the conduct of an array of financial services comprising credit, trading of financial instruments and foreign exchange (and their derivatives), underwriting of new debt and equity issues, brokerage, corporate advisory services (including mergers and acquisitions advice), investment management and insurance.[2] This can take the form of: (a) a partially-integrated financial conglomerate, capable of supplying most of these services but with several (such as mortgage banking, leasing and insurance) provided through wholly-owned or partially-owned subsidiaries; (b) a bank–subsidiary structure, under which the bank focuses essentially on commercial banking and all of the others, including investment banking and insurance, are carried out through legally separate subsidiaries of the bank; or (c) a holding company structure, where a holding company owns both banking and non-banking subsidiaries that are legally separate and individually capitalized, insofar as financial activities other than 'banking' are permitted by law. These may be separated by 'Chinese walls' and 'firewalls' if there are internal or regulatory concerns about institutional safety and soundness or conflicts of interest. The holding company may also be allowed to own significant shares in industrial firms. Or the holding company may itself be an industrial company.

The role of government and the structure of the financial system may be connected. An interventionist role of the state may be facilitated or hindered by the banking structure. The more universal the national banking system, the larger the size of the banks, and the more they are considered 'too big to fail' (TBTF), and the closer are bank–industry control linkages, the more likely it is that the state will seek to intervene in microeconomic and especially industrial restructuring outcomes.

3. FOUR SYSTEM PROFILES

In examining the role of the financial system in the process of corporate control, and its relationship to industrial restructuring, I shall begin by comparing four very different bank–industry–government control structures: Japan, Germany, France the United Kingdom and the United States – the latter examined jointly as the Anglo–American approach.[3] In each case, I first assess the structure of the bank credit relationship and the dependence of industrial firms on banks, which in turn is related to the comparative importance of earnings retention (self-financing) and disintermediation via capital markets as alternative sources of finance. Second, bank–industry linkages are examined at the level of equity shareholdings between banks and industrial firms, particularly the holding of stakes in industrial companies by banks. Third, the linkages are examined at the level of corporate surveillance and control, drawing distinctions between *outsider* systems – in which control runs directly from shareholders to companies – and *insider* systems, in which industrial companies and banks have interlocking control structures. Finally, each system profile addresses some of the informal structures, which in some countries play as important a role in binding industry and finance together as do the various formal institutional and legal linkages.

3.1 Japan

Japan's industrial and financial communities have historically been inter-linked more closely than in any other advanced economy. The state has exerted a powerful and multi-level influence on the financial and real sectors, using the financial sector – through the Ministry of Finance (MOF) – to influence the real sector in the implementation of a centrally guided industrial policy. The effectiveness of this guidance has been amplified by an institutional structure in which banks are normally part of interlinked groups of companies (*keiretsu*) tied together by long-standing supplier relationships, with banks often acting as the leading force in the groups. Leaders in finance, industry and government are closely bound together by very strong informal networks. While change has occurred over the years, especially with the reduced dependence of industrial companies on bank financing and the development of Japanese capital markets second only to those of the United States in size and depth, the Japanese approach to corporate control retains a number of unique features.

Japan has rebuilt its economic and financial systems twice since the Meiji Restoration of 1868. Both efforts were extremely successful – first, in converting a primitive, feudal economic system into one capable of competing with advanced industrial countries within a generation or two, and second, after the devastation of World War II. In the first restructuring, Japan looked mainly to Europe where large, family-dominated industrial groups with very close banking ties were common. The Japanese *zaibatsu* were not dissimilar to their European models – especially prior to the takeover by the militarists in the early 1930s. The rapid recovery after World War II benefited from a society of skilled and educated survivors whose motivation was enormous. The requisite human capital and technologies were largely in place not long after the war. The missing ingredient was physical capital. This was mainly provided by the resurrection and modification of Japan's prewar financial system – one that was accustomed to, and depended upon, the utilization of the maximum leverage available for the pursuit of growth.

In the Meiji tradition, financial leverage was as simple in concept as it is difficult to visualize in execution. All uses of credit were subject to the meticulous control of the Ministry of Finance. Bank loans were allocated preferentially to carefully researched industrial sectors based on government perceptions of long-term international comparative advantage (industrial targeting). From the outset, banks represented the dominant vehicle for capital allocation. To do this job efficiently, they were encouraged to maximize their loan-to-deposit ratios.

While systematically high bank leverage (gearing) was considered extremely risky in the United States or Europe, Japanese banks – although nominally owned by the private sector – for all practical purposes were controlled affiliates of the Bank of Japan and the MOF. To guard against 'errors' in credit allocation and financial 'accidents', banks were subjected to careful and tight regulation, constant supervision and strict limitations on the scope of their activities. The regulators could, in principle, have access to the details of every loan to every client, as well as the daily cash flows and, of course, the problem credits of all the banks.

A strong, centralized banking and credit system was thus used for postwar recovery. The encouragement of household savings (from a very low base), the marshalling of funds for economic expansion, the arrangement of foreign credits and the ruthless allocation of capital to targeted sectors of industry had already been among the vital attributes of the Meiji era financial system. The approach, dating back to the National Banking Law of 1882, was of epochal importance not only in the redevelopment of the currency and credit system after the war, but also in 'laying the foundation for the modernization of the Japanese economy and the growth of modern industries'.

It was fed by extraordinary levels of debt exposure – in stark contrast to so many other countries during the same period – because of the credibility of the intricate, finely-meshed web of mutually supporting mechanisms in the highly organized, centrally controlled Japanese system. Companies were encouraged to rely upon their linkages to banks, suppliers, agents and customers to maximize their borrowings, which in the end had to be for the 'right' purposes as defined by the Ministries of International Trade and Industry (MITI) and the MOF. In turn, the Japanese banks were so tightly regulated that companies could only finance new facilities and inventories. No credit was made available for unauthorized investments or for 'speculation'. The safety net erected by the regulators protected and nourished the prospects of its most promising industrial enterprises. In time, the system attracted both capital and talent from all types of domestic and foreign sources.

Several different kinds of banks and bank-like institutions were established in Japan, each confined to a prescribed function within the system. These included Japan's very large postal saving system, government owned development and reconstruction banks (specializing in private sector infrastructure projects), an export credit bank, agricultural cooperative banks, credit cooperative banks, trust banks (for managing institutional savings and pension funds), long-term credit banks to finance capital equipment for industry, large urban commercial banks and small (mainly rural) commercial banks.

The Ministry of Finance also regulated the non-banking financial sector, including the insurance and securities industries. Prior to World War II, Japan had no substantive separation between banking and securities activities. Banks monopolized the underwriting of government bonds and corporate securities under a cartel arrangement initially established in 1911. Securities distribution, brokerage and related functions were carried out by independent securities firms, as were equity underwriting and bond trading, mainly because banks were wary of the risks involved. Acceptance of proposals insisted upon by the US General Headquarters of the Occupation to introduce Article 65 of the Securities and Exchange Law of 1947, which separated the banking and securities industries, was based on the view that underwriting (even of bonds) was excessively risky for banks. However, Article 65 did not place limits on bank holdings of either debt or equity securities for investment purposes, which turned out to be an important source of competitive strength of Japanese banks in the 1980s – and a weakness in the 1990s during the dramatic and prolonged decline in the Japanese stock market. Another apparent purpose of Article 65 was to prevent bank monopolization of the securities industry. This was later reinforced by 'administrative guidance' from the MOF to prevent banks from underwriting local and government-guaranteed bonds, evidently in order to provide the securities firms with a monopoly that would help assure their competitive survival.

Japanese banks were allowed to own shares in their clients, who also owned shares in their main banks. Although the nominal value of these cross-holdings was small at the beginning, their practical impact on Japan's corporate control structure was critical. Cross-shareholding (*mochiai*) groups formed the basis for today's *keiretsu*, which in the early postwar years constituted an effective grouping together of dissimilar companies for mutual support and protection. Banks in Japan could hold up to 5 per cent of their assets (10 per cent prior to 1987) in the form of equity shares in industrial companies – about equal to the 4.9 per cent limitation for US bank holding companies – plus additional equity holdings in affiliated insurance companies. About 30 per cent of the equity of Japanese industrial companies has been held by banks in this manner within the cross-holding structures

(Pozdena, 1989). The banks act as treasurers to their particular *keiretsu* industrial groupings, and often represent the leading force within them. As much as 60 per cent of Japanese shares in the early 1990s were held in cross-holdings, up from about 50 per cent in 1980 (Mattione, 1992).

Beginning in the late 1970s, Japan has experienced substantial liberalization in its highly regulated financial system, although this process has been very gradual despite foreign pressure for improved access to Japan's financial markets. It is anchored in a number of deregulatory measures, such as greater flexibility in bank certificates of deposit, the introduction of money market certificates and the relaxation of interest rate controls. Japan's bond markets grew rapidly as well – spurred on by government issuance of large volumes of 10-year debt securities after the 1973 oil crisis – as did the country's equity markets. In the early 1970s, only about 10 per cent of Japanese external corporate funds came from the equity markets and 80 per cent from bank lending. By 1985, equity accounted for some 45 per cent of funds raised by industrial companies (with convertible bonds adding another 20 per cent), and the share of bank loans had fallen to only 20 per cent. By 1990, bank debt among the major Japanese companies was minimal, with reliance for external financing about equally split between bond and stock issues.

Gradual change also brought down the walls between the various types of financial institutions. In late 1992 the orderly phasing-out of Article 65 restrictions was implemented by the MOF. Beginning in 1993, separately capitalized subsidiaries of the ten Japanese trust banks were allowed to underwrite and deal in government and corporate bonds, underwrite (but not distribute) equity-linked securities and manage investment trusts such as mutual funds. The same limited privileges were extended to Japan's commercial banks in 1994. At the same time, securities firms were allowed to set up trust-banking subsidiaries to deal in investment trusts and currency instruments. Deregulation accelerated thereafter under Japan's 'Big Bang'. Foreign exchange deregulation, liberalization of asset management, a 50 per cent cut in the securities transaction tax, partial deregulation of commission rates and the introduction of financial holding companies occurred in 1998, while the transaction tax was abolished and fully negotiable commission rates were introduced in 1999.

A unique form of corporate control has been integral to the Japanese model of industrial development within the *keiretsu* system. Given the approach to financing enterprises and equity cross-holdings, the focus was on continuous surveillance and monitoring of management performance by the managements of affiliated firms and banks as well as, through them, the Ministry of Finance. Non-affiliated corporate equity holders were (and continue to be) largely passive investors except in cases of corporate emergencies, where the public shareholder was expected to go along with the policies of the group.

Efforts to exert control through unwanted shareholder actions have been minimal in *keiretsu* companies. The consequence was a system remarkable for its stability, continuity and (for the most part) single-minded pursuit of industrial objectives arrived at by management–bank–government consensus, one closely aligned to the national culture and the unique position of Japan in the international economy.

As a consequence, equity markets have not played a large role in corporate monitoring and control, initially because of their small size and later because the tightly-held nature of many listed companies resulted in very few shares available for purchase in the market. There was little or no opportunity for acquiring influential stakes. Takeovers most frequently take the form of 'rescues' organized by the government. Given the small free float, stock prices did not necessarily convey accurate information about the value of companies, and the potential for market-rigging was great – a fact that was evidenced on numerous occasions in the Tokyo market.

Informal connections play a very important role linking the banks to industry. The graduates of a few prestigious universities (notably *Todai*, the University of Tokyo) have been highly sought after by the civil service, the top banks and the major industrial groupings, and friendships formed at Todai tied individuals together from these groups throughout their careers. These links were reinforced by the fact that civil servants close to the top of their profession have often moved to industry, banking or politics. This 'descent from heaven' was not simply personal choice, but was embedded in the system itself, so that there has been a steady movement of senior civil servants into the private sector, ensuring the tightest of informal networks between government, industry and banking. All of these traditional structures came under substantial stress during the ten years of economic stagnation that began in 1990, which brought to the surface fundamental weaknesses and encouraged a search for alternatives and institutional reforms, however hesitant. The Asian financial crisis beginning in 1997 triggered similar rethinking in countries like Korea, which had their own versions of the Japanese approach – usually with strong links to founding families.

3.2 Germany

The interests of German finance, industry and government have traditionally been perceived to be largely coincident. The need to separate capital markets from credit markets was not perceived as a prerequisite to the maintenance of financial stability. The links between industry and finance were among the strongest in the world, and were exemplified by the traditional *Hausbank* relationship, in which many firms dealt principally with only one universal bank. The firm was bonded to its bank by the lending relationship, access to the securities market, bank holding of share stakes, bank voting of custodial shares and, often, supervisory board representation. The cumulative effect of these five aspects was an extraordinary potential for corporate control and monitoring.

German *Grossbanken* – Deutsche Bank, Dresdner Bank and Commerzbank – took shape in the early 1800s, during the country's initial period of industrialization. They remained a dominant force for almost two centuries, despite efforts by the Allies in the immediate postwar period to break them up as part of a policy to reduce the power of German industry and its principal banking sector 'tools'.

The German federal government does not have much *direct* influence on corporations or on the banks. Although public sector ownership of banks is relatively high (covering about half of all financial institutions and 36 per cent of total assets in the banking system), the majority are owned either by state (*Länder*) governments or by regional savings bank associations, so that local government can and does exert some influence on financial institutions. German public sector banks generally operate as commercial banks free from government intervention – except for occasional and controversial capital infusions and the presence of state guarantees. The three large German banks have a market share of only about 20 per cent of assets and 9 per cent of financial transactions.

Nor has the influence of the state been particularly strongly felt through the formal channels of bank regulation, which have traditionally been focused on self-regulation. After World War II, regulation was carried out at the state level, and it was not until 1961 that a uniform regulatory framework was established in Germany. Stricter rules were only introduced after the Herstatt Bank collapse in 1974, with bank regulation and supervision the joint responsibility of the Bundesbank in Frankfurt and the Bundesaufsichtsamt für das gesamte Kreditwesen in Berlin. Under German banking statutes, all financial activities can be carried out within the structure of the parent bank except for insurance, mortgage banking, building savings (*Bauspar*) activities and mutual funds, which require legally separate subsidiaries. Non-financial firms, especially insurance companies such as Allianz Versicherungs AG, also hold (sometimes substantial) stakes in universal banks as well as industrial companies.

There is a long-standing alliance between the large universal banks and large German industrial corporations – see Figure 3.3. A corporation can access both capital market services (stock and bond new issues, mergers and acquisitions transactions) and bank credit facilities from the same institution. This so-called *Hausbank* relationship has had, as its basis, a business firm's reliance on only one principal bank as its primary supplier of all forms of financing. The *Hausbank*, in turn, is deeply involved in its corporate clients' business affairs and, in times of adversity, might remain more committed to

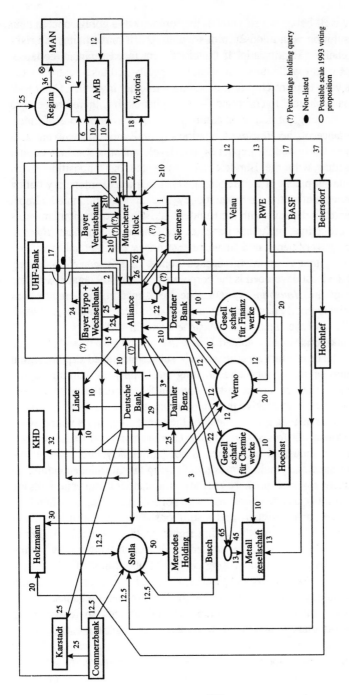

Source: Professor E. Wenger, University of Wurzburg, reproduced in M. Adams, *Anborung/Macht von Banken und Versicherungen-Wettbewerb im Finanzdienstleinstungssektor*, 8.12.1993, *Deuscher Bundestag*, Ausschuss fur Wirtschaft.

Figure 3.3   The traditional German shareholding structure

the continued well-being and survival of the company as a going concern than would an institution with a looser, arm's-length, profit-maximizing and risk-minimizing banking relationship. If the client firm faced financial collapse, the *Hausbank* might well convert its debt into equity and take control of the client, with a view to restructuring it or selling it to other investors. One result of the 'German solution' to corporate financial distress has therefore been to increase bank holdings of non-bank equity shares over long periods of time.

The importance of the *Hausbank* relationship and universal banking as a structure have clearly had an impact on the development of German capital markets, together with the Bundesbank's long-standing opposition (until 1990) to the development of a commercial paper market, for monetary policy reasons. Consequently, the German money market long remained almost entirely a market in deposits with the Bundesbank. The German bond markets have been more active, including issues of the federal government (*Bunds*), state and local governments, non-financial enterprises, commercial banks and savings banks – that is, mortgage-backed bonds, or *Pfandbriefe* – among which by far the least developed is the corporate bond market, again partly the consequence of the *Hausbank* system. The stock market in Germany was likewise relatively poorly developed by industrial country standards, although it grew rapidly after the creation of *Deutsche Börse* in 1992.

German banks traditionally gained *Hausbank* standing by providing all of the financing needs to start-up companies – subscribing seed capital, initial public offerings of stock, bond underwriting and supplying working capital (with a rolling line of credit often constituting essentially permanent financing). In return, they receive the long-term loyalty of the client company. They could also own a significant block of the client company's voting stock in their investment portfolios. Overall, the German universal banks' ownership of equity in industrial companies is not particularly large, due to the importance of the closely-held *Mittelstand* firms in the German economy.[4] In addition to share ownership, share custody is a standard universal banking function in Germany, as elsewhere, and large portfolios of stock are often held by banks in trust for individuals and institutions. While the ultimate share-holders theoretically exercise the voting rights, in fact the voting rights of depository shares are typically exercised by banks through proxy voting (*Depotstimmrecht*), giving them voting control of about half of all German listed shares in 1991 (Edwards and Fischer, 1992) – it is estimated that about 5 per cent of the equity of the top 100 companies is owned by banks.

The *Hausbank* relationship in sourcing financial services, share ownership and voting of fiduciary shares has been cemented by bank representation on supervisory boards of industrial companies (*Aufsichtsratsmandate*). Under German company law, supervisory board members are required to act in the interest of the firm and its shareholders, and bank representatives on client company boards are frequently called upon to provide advice on questions of financial management and capital structure. Bank supervisory board memberships appear to be concentrated among the largest German firms – the bank's representative is often the chairman of the industrial company's supervisory board – although they are also prevalent in companies below the German top 100. Bank members of supervisory boards have been said to be generally better informed and more actively engaged than traditional non-executive directors in the US or the UK system, although there is substantial disagreement on this point (Edwards and Fischer, 1992).

German banks have traditionally justified their share ownership, share voting and supervisory board roles by representing that:

- It permits orderly restructuring of enterprises and saves jobs, with firms that get into trouble taken over by banks, restructured, and then resold to new shareholders.
- It supports poorly capitalized *Mittelstand* firms directly though bank shareholdings and lending that would not otherwise be bankable.
- It can efficiently prepare government-owned enterprises for privatization.
- It provides an efficient vehicle for the sale of privately-held companies to the public, with shares taken over by the bank and subsequently sold in a public offering.

The first two points relate to the insider information issue as it bears on reducing asymmetry-of-information problems between banks and private shareholders.

Economic restructuring in Germany has always reflected heavily bank-oriented corporate finance, which provided the universal banks with both non-public information and (indirectly as well as through their non-executive board memberships) potential influence over management decisions involving corporate restructuring activities. Firms that did not meet bank performance expectations found themselves under pressure to restructure – restructuring that was often initiated, orchestrated and implemented by the banks (Rybczynski, 1989). Indeed, the German universal banks were repeatedly relied upon to carry out industrial restructurings in the absence of well-functioning capital markets in the past, following periods of war or economic collapse, and so were accustomed to this role.[5]

Things changed in the 1990s under pressure from institutional investors, including sharpening the rules to govern takeover activity (including extending share purchase offers to all shareholders), promotion of greater disclosure and transparency in takeovers, and elimination of voting restrictions and unequal treatment of shareholders. These clearly undermined the 'insider' character of the German system in the 1990s. Together with the beginnings of hostile bids in Germany – such as Krupp-Thyssen and Pirelli-Continental – this has led to significant corporate restructuring and greater attention to shareholder value.

Informal links between industry and finance in Germany have not traditionally been based on old boy networks stemming from educational or social backgrounds, but rather have been formed much later in business careers as part of the process of corporate supervisory board assignments and professional and industry associations. At the highest levels, the interlinking cross-representation on supervisory boards means the same people meet each other regularly.

3.3 France

The French financial and industrial systems have traditionally been dominated by the strong influence of central government. For more than 30 years following the end of World War II, the French system was highly *dirigiste*, controlling financial institutions and markets to ensure that capital was directed to those investments given priorities in 'indicative planning'. This domination eroded significantly in the 1980s and 1990s, however, with a shift in corporate funding away from intermediated (bank-dominated) finance toward open money and capital markets. Nevertheless, the power of the government remained much greater than in either the German or Anglo-American models, formally through regulation and state ownership and informally through the network of *grandes écoles* alumni.

In 1945, the government nationalized the four largest commercial banks. The principal French *Banques de Depôts* – Credit Lyonnais, Société Generale and Banque Nationale de Paris (BNP) – together with the co-operative bank, Crédit Agricole (until the 1980s the largest bank in the world) – dominated the French banking sector.

Until 1985, the French government effectively controlled lending to industry through the so-called *barème* system, whereby the state-owned banks shared out corporate business according to fixed percentages. Financial allocation by means of tight credit ceilings was combined with the refinancing of selected eligible credits with state-controlled bodies – such as real estate loans with Crédit Foncier or certain industrial loans with Crédit National. Moreover, the widespread use of subsidized loans – such as Crédit Agricole's agricultural *prêts bonifiés* – allowed the government to direct investment to those industries it wished to encourage. The commercial banking system was viewed more as an instrument of industrial policy than as an independent sector assigned the task of efficient capital allocation according to the dictates of the market.

There have been a number of governmental or quasi-governmental financial institutions which lie between the depositors and the borrowers in the French system – notably the Caisse des Depôts et Consignations (CDC). The CDC receives funds deposited with the savings banks (*Caisses d'Epargne*) and employs them in housing finance, in local authority finance and in the purchase of bonds and equities. Because of the dominance of the *Caisses d'Epargne* in the retail deposit market, the CDC commands vast resources. In 1988, over 17 per cent of total lending in France was through the CDC and *Caisses d'Epargne* (Kaufman, 1992). There are also various specialized financial institutions entrusted by the state with a permanent public interest financing task, such as real estate finance, capital goods finance or international trade and investment finance. For example, Crédit Foncier raises funds from other financial institutions as well as equity through the Paris Bourse for use in subsidized house purchase and house construction loans. Crédit National raises funds in the bond markets and makes medium and long-term loans for industrial investment, particularly in line with economic and social development plans at the regional level. While these institutions are not all government entities, they are in effect controlled by the state. An illustration of the power of the state in the French financial system is that an estimated 80 per cent of all medium- and long-term finance at some stage passed through government hands from the early 1970s until the mid-1990s.

The French system has also been characterized as compartmentalized and specialized, with different types of institutions targeting different financial activities. The *Caisses d'Epargne* have dominated the liquid savings market. The cooperative banks, especially Crédit Agricole, have dominated the agricultural sector. The *Banques de Depôts* (such as BNP or Société Generale) have been most active in short-term industrial finance, Crédit National in longer-term loans and Crédit Foncier in mortgage credit.

There are also the French *Banques d'Affaires*, which trace their origin back to the 1870s, when they were established for the purpose of investing in industry. By the end of the nineteenth century, they were not only making business loans, but also buying securities of companies in sectors such as electricity, iron and steel, transportation and gas. By 1967, when the regulatory wall between the *Banques d'Affaires* and the *Banques de Depôts* came down, two of these banks had established themselves as pre-eminent, Groupe Financière de Paribas and the Groupe Suez, along with a smaller firm, Lazard Frères & Cie. The first two of these institutions had more in common with large financial conglomerates than the traditional British merchant banks or US investment banks with which they are normally compared, tending to accumulate shareholdings much more readily than disposing of them and playing an active role in management.

At the beginning of the 1980s the French financial system was government-dominated, highly concentrated and compartmentalized. The Paris Bourse was very small, and offered no real alternative source of finance to industry. During the 1980s the system underwent a transformation, partly as a result of government efforts to promote Paris as a viable competitor to London and partly as a result of changing political fashion, with (limited) privatization replacing nationalization. The so-called Delors Law of 1983 was directed specifically at increasing the business use of the capital markets, providing a framework for the introduction of new financing techniques to French industry, and expanding tax incentives for individual shareholders. In 1985 the *barème* system was abandoned, encouraging competition among banks. Credit ceilings, which some commentators blamed for low investment levels in France, were abandoned. In 1986–87 Prime Minister Jacques Chirac undertook the privatization of the Groupe Financière de Paribas and the Société Generale, thereby reducing (albeit modestly) government ownership in the banking sector. The government's stated aim was to promote a capital freer market with less government control and direction.

France has traditionally had the highest level of corporate shareholding by banks in Europe. Wilth such a large share of the banking industry state-owned, these shareholdings could be viewed as indirect state ownership. Indeed, it has been suggested that some of the bank shareholdings were simply a device to feed public subsidies to nationalized industries, where direct subsidies would be banned by the EU on competition grounds.

Government influence apart, there was a long tradition in France of banks holding industrial shares, initially undertaken by the *Banques d'Affaires* but later followed by the main commercial banks – see Figure 3.4. The logic behind these equity stakes was threefold: (1) to generate capital gains through increases in the value of their shareholdings; (2) to capture the basic banking business of their non-bank affiliated companies; and (3) to win fee-based business such as mergers and acquisitions mandates for the group. In the traditional French model, industrial surveillance and control was through an 'insider' system although their role has fallen much more upon the state than on banks. The influence of the government was such that it was sometimes difficult to draw distinct lines between government and industry or between government and the banks. Indeed, the influence of the state was so pervasive in the private sector that managers in many corporations noticed little difference in the operations of banks when they were formally nationalized by the Mitterand administration after 1981 or when some of them were re-privatized under Prime Minister Jacques Chirac a few years later.

Even where formal ownership and regulatory control have been de-linked from the state, the government, the banks and major industrial enterprises

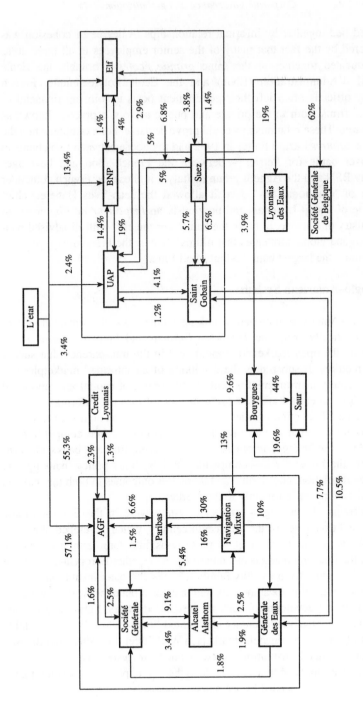

Source: François Morin, University of Toulouse.

Figure 3.4 Selected French cross-holdings

remained tied together by informal relationships. A degree of cohesion was engendered by the fact that many of the senior employees in all three areas were educated together at the same *grande écoles* - notably the Ecole National d'Administration (ENA) and the Ecole Polytechnique. French Treasury officials often left their government posts to join top financial or industrial firms, both in the private and public sectors, a practice known as *pantouflage*. These relationships could prove decisive. For example, when the *banque d'affaires* Lazard Frères in 1992 had to choose between two clients in a takeover battle for Perrier - between the French food and beverages company BSN and the Agnelli group of Italy - it chose the French contender because of 'emotional ties'. And it allowed the Jean-Yves Haberer, chief executive of Crédit Lyonnais and previously an *Inspecteur de Finance* with the Ministry of Finance, to drive the bank over the cliff with ill-advised pan-European and global strategies that ultimately cost the French taxpayer over $19 billion - the largest bank bailout of all time.

The Anglo-American System

The Anglo-American approach to linking industry and the financial system differs drastically from the Japanese, German and French systems in its reliance on the open market for capital, and in the transparency that such a system requires. It substitutes the discipline of an informed marketplace in debt and equity instruments for centralized control of capital allocation and pricing. It requires full and fair disclosure of all material information about the financial affairs of companies to work effectively, and an impartial system of corporate governance that favours the discipline of free competition, as opposed to close linkages among firms and between firms and banks. Government sets the broad rules - competition policy, trade policy, banking and securities regulation, and so on - and thereafter outcomes in both the real and financial sectors are left mainly to the markets.

The origins of the Anglo-American system were in the English capital markets and exchanges of the nineteenth century, which developed alongside the banking system to channel surplus funds into long-term investments. Initially, the financial markets of London and some other European cities were supplied by capital from wealthy families, banks and other institutions, which in turn was invested in local industry and in areas around the world engaged in capital-intensive development such as the United States, Latin America and Australia. In the twentieth century, the United States in turn became a global provider of capital, the financial markets in Wall Street flourished, and British-American financial institutions grew with their respective economies - expanding the supply of funds available to the marketplace and developing the skills and efficiency needed by the markets themselves.

The role of American bankers in the affairs of their clients was especially important in the latter part of the nineteenth century and in the early twentieth century. This was not because the banks owned significant stakes in corporations as in Germany, or because of *keiretsu*-like ties in Japan, but because the bankers had the capacity to place securities with their wealthy clients. These clients in turn wanted someone to look after their investments and to arrange for restructuring and reallocation of assets when those investments got into trouble. After about 70 years of increasing financial activity beginning during the Civil War, the US capital markets collapsed in 1929 following a decade of feverish financial innovation, rising prices and speculation. The markets were reconstituted in the 1930s under severe regulatory constraints, which separated the banking and securities businesses (as in the later case of Japan's Article 65), provided for government-backed deposit insurance and strict control of banking operations, and initiated top-to-bottom regulatory reform of the securities market. Another 60 years passed before regulators could be induced to loosen the system in order to allow US banks to adapt themselves to intensely competitive global banking conditions as they exist today.

It is useful to recall that American commercial banks provided investment banking services directly from 1812 to nearly the turn of the century, and thereafter through securities affiliates until 1933. The passage of the Glass–Steagall provisions of the Banking Act of 1933 (and later the 1956 Bank Holding Company Act) separated 'banking' – defined as taking deposits and making commercial loans – from everything else, defined as 'commerce'. Over the years, the dynamics of the financial intermediation process juxtaposed against a static regulatory framework left the commercial banks with a vastly diminished share of US national financial flows, a share which they only began to regain with regulatory liberalization in the 1990s. Relaxation of barriers in the US permitting banks to engage in underwriting and trading corporate securities through separately capitalized subsidiaries of one-bank holding companies have permitted them to enter the investment banking business in a meaningful way.

British financial markets, subject to international capital controls from World War I until 1979, grew in a considerably less ebullient way than did the American markets. On the other hand, the development of the Eurodollar and the Eurobond markets in the 1960s and 1970s enhanced the importance of the British financial houses and the role of London as a financial centre. In 1986, government authorities oversaw the complete reorganization and reform of the British financial marketplace which – together with enabling Parliamentary legislation – produced the most modern and efficient capital market in Europe. Banks in the United Kingdom are, in theory at least, universal – allowed since 1986 to own securities firms. In practice, they have found it difficult to operate successfully in the securities and investment banking markets and most have withdrawn from investment banking.

In the Anglo–American model there is no tradition of banks holding large shares in industrial concerns. The holding of shares in industrial companies is limited to 4.9 per cent of a bank's total assets in the United States, and while the same restrictions do not apply in Britain, it is the pension funds and the insurance companies (institutional investors) that dominate holdings in industrial companies, not the banks.

In the United States as well as the United Kingdom, the distribution of shares in public companies is sufficiently widespread that, in general, no single financial institution controls any particular industrial company. Large shareholdings by industrial firms in each other are also rare in the Anglo-American model, and where they exist they tend to be 'financial' investments rather than Japanese-style reinforcement of links with suppliers and customers. They may also represent early stake-building as a prelude to a takeover attempt. Long-term minority shareholdings among industrial companies have never been widespread in either the United Kingdom or the United States.

In both countries the pre-eminent role of capital markets has dominated industrial development for well over a century. Corporate financing has relied heavily on fairly regulated, freely traded securities markets – with debt holders exerting limited influence on managerial decisions under ordinary circumstances, and public equity holders exposed to the agency costs associated with management pursuing interests other than those which would maximize the value of their shareholdings. Even the large institutions present in the United Kingdom and the United States (mainly pension funds and insurance companies) have traditionally been passive investors, with significant shareholdings but with little or no influence in the boardroom. This 'outsider' system has produced, on average, the world's lowest cost and most ample supply of capital to industry for several decades.

Changes in corporate control in both the United Kingdom and the United States have been exerted by the capital market, often through hostile takeover attempts by outside parties that lead to major changes in corporate ownership and direction. Even if unsuccessful, existing management may engage in corporate restructuring activity not dissimilar to what an unaffiliated acquirer would do.

The Anglo–American system trades some aspects of safety and soundness for greater financial flexibility, innovation and adaptability. In order to foster the most efficient continuous redeployment of capital, the various elements of the system – disclosure and enforcement, competition, innovation, institutionalization of financial transactions and protection of depositors and investors – must be finely balanced. This balance can only be struck in an institutional arrangement dominated by mature and sophisticated participants in which the credibility and integrity of the market itself is high.

Finally, it should be noted that the Anglo–American system (like Germany) is also characterized by substantially less important government–bank–industry links in comparison to the French and Japanese models. The transparency inherent in the market-driven approach probably reduces the scope for effectiveness of such links in any case, even if they existed.

Although significant 'old boy networks' exist in the United Kingdom these tend not to be very strong in linking finance to industry. Indeed, in some ways the strength of this informal network serves to deepen the divide between finance and industry, on the one hand, and between government and industry, on the other. In the United States, with its more egalitarian, meritocratic and multicultural history, informal links are even less well established, and their influence is much less acceptable in the American social context than it is in more hierarchical cultures such as Japan and France.

4. COMPARATIVE ECONOMIC PERFORMANCE

Given the dramatically different characteristics of the Japanese, German, French and Anglo–American approaches to government–bank–industry linkages, it is not at all surprising that there has been continuing debate about the degree to which these differences have been responsible for the 'economic performance' of the respective national economies (Dodds, 1994 and Prowse, 1995). The arguments have been part of the economic policy scene for many years. Not least important is whether the structure of government-bank-industry links has anything to do with the flows of international trade and investment (both FDI and portfolio).

In the 1980s there was a vague popular feeling that control systems perceived (rightly or wrongly) to be significantly more interventionist outperformed those of the United States and the United Kingdom, while the reverse was popularly thought to be true in the 1990s. In order to judge the validity of such comparisons, one would have to define carefully the term 'economic performance' as some multidimensional, weighted composite of real economic growth – as determined mainly by the quantitative and qualitative development of the labour force, physical capital formation and technological change – as well as long-term unemployment, shifts in the terms of international trade and other familiar measures. Even if one could agree empirically that one approach has been demonstrably 'superior' to another, one would still have to graft that approach onto the economy in question and determine how things *might have gone* if the approach had been different.

In both the United States and the United Kingdom, admiration of the German and Japanese economies often centred on the differences in corporate governance. This usually involved heated discussions of the contribution of (or damage caused by) corporate takeovers, the proper role of pension funds and other institutional investors, management and/or employee holdings of equity stakes in their own firms, the nature of executive compensation schemes, inter-company equity linkages and strategic alliances, and the appropriate control function of banks and other financial institutions. The continuing debates on the 'optimum' system of enterprise governance, together with pressure for change in virtually all industrial countries, suggests that we are far from a resolution of these matters.

The notion that the German-style *Hausbank* shareholding and proxy voting systems and Japanese-style *keiretsu* linkages impart pre-emptive adjustment and stability to industrial firms is based on the idea that markets are short-sighted (that is, dynamically inefficient) and that placing a significant degree of corporate governance in the hands of bankers will achieve greater social welfare over the long term. This view was supported to some degree by financial theoreticians, who argued that a strong benefit may arise in resolving information asymmetries when the bank is both an equity insider and a creditor.

Some observers, such as Cable (1985), Sheard (1989), Prowse (1990) and Kim (1990), have argued that the success of the German as well as Japanese economies was partly attributable to the direct equity links and 'main bank' relationships. While lending makes a bank a privileged insider to the firm, the control of ownership stakes makes the bank even more of an insider to the operations of the firm than if it remained just a privileged creditor. As a result, a bank can exercise greater control over the riskiness of projects chosen by the firm. Full insider status internalizes and perfects information flows from the firm to the bank, allowing the bank to make more efficient and timely financing decisions. That is, German or Japanese-style organizational structures in which banks hold both debt and equity stakes in client firms could be seen as creating an internal (but informal) capital market between bank and firm.

In empirical work, Steinherr and Huveneers (1992) were unable to reject the hypothesis that universal banks better support the long-term financial strategies of non-financial companies than do financial systems based on capital markets. Research on the Japanese version of close-knit bank–industry linkages suggested that firms with a main bank relationship are less likely to be liquidity-constrained (Hoshi et al., 1991a) and more likely to be able to survive periods of financial distress by continuing their investment programmes (Hoshi et al., 1991b) – although errors may be made if short-term financial distress is in fact a signal of long-term inefficiency of the firm.

On the negative side is the problem of endemic conflicts of interest due to the breadth of the banks' involvement and weaknesses in internal controls. Especially in the German model, conflicts between the fiduciary responsibilities of a bank and its role as an investment banker, between its interest in completing an M&A transaction and its obligation to a target company that is (or has been) a client, between the profitabilty of stuffing or churning investment portfolios and its responsibilities to the asset holders, and between its interests as an investor and as a lender to the same firm, are some of the conflict issues extensively explored in the literature (Walter, 1985; Gnehm and Thalmann, 1989). Indeed, it may be that conflicts of interest which arise in serving various clients increases with the *breadth* of activities of a financial services firm. Economists generally rely on adverse reputation effects and on legal sanctions to check the incentives to exploit such conflicts (Krümmel, 1980), and some observers have pointed out that larger customers will in any case turn away progressively from closely-related banks if they are not as competitive as non-affiliated banks.

There is also the argument that large universal banks inevitably will not be permitted to fail due to the social costs of such failure and that they therefore have an artificial TBTF advantage in competing with institutions that have no such access to implied state support. Even in cases of failure of separately incorporated non-bank affiliates of TBTF banks (possibly including industrial companies), it may be necessary to bring the safety net into play, leading to unfair advantages in funding costs and the possibility of public bailouts of industrial companies. If the market perceives this to be the case, the safety net effectively stretches under such affiliates as well. Counter-arguments focus on the view that a broader range of activities increases the inherent diversification and stability of the financial institution, and therefore *decreases* the likelihood that the safety net will come into play.

Beyond corporate control issues, Japanese *keiretsu*-type and German *Hausbank*-type linkages, and to a lesser extent the French *dirigiste* approach, may have had an adverse bearing on the development of each country's financial markets as against the Anglo–American system, with possibly significant opportunity costs due to inefficiencies in financial intermediation. The interests of institutions with strong links to their clients rarely create fertile ground for innovations that compete with financial services already being offered, and possibly contribute to an erosion of the bank–client relationship itself. In view of this, market-oriented financial systems have often been credited with greater efficiency, greater innovation and dynamism, superior resistance to inherent conflicts of interests among the various stakeholders involved, and (through better transparency) less susceptibility to major uncorrected industrial blunders – as well as politically 'excessive' concentration of economic influence. Examples often cited include the role in

US economic history of universal banking houses such as J.P. Morgan during the 1920s and the contemporary role of the German *Grossbanken* (Smith and Sylla, 1992). Counter-arguments generally refer to the vigour and sophistication of current antitrust enforcement in many countries and at the level of the EU.

There is also the argument that universal banks, through their dominance of client relationships and presumed degree of economic influence, have the ability to suborn the political process and ram through political action that shifts the balance of risks and returns in their favour. This may include favourable tax legislation, access to government guarantees and bailouts, antitrust exemptions, and the like. Counter-arguments focus on the fact that special interest pressures from other types of financial institutions (for example, the savings and loan associations in the United States) or sectors of the real economy (for example, farmers in France) are no less capable of co-opting the political process, and that the root of any such problem may therefore lie in the political process itself.

If the market for corporate control is to be an integral part of an efficient capital allocation process, then 'control premiums' – the difference between what shares in a company are worth in the market and what they *could be worth* under optimum capital allocation circumstances should be at a minimum. That is, management is under pressure to consistently act in the best interests of its shareholders, so that other parties are unlikely to be able to achieve significant additional value should they be able to take over the company. One indicator of control premiums and their development over time is the difference between the price paid for a company's shares in a merger or acquisition and the market price five business days after the initial offer for the shares is made. Figure 3.5 shows that this premium has in fact declined in the United States over the years – that is, the US market for corporate control has indeed become more efficient (Estrich, 1999). The European bid premium has been somewhat higher that in the United States in recent years (35 per cent vs. 30 per cent in 1998), and has perhaps been somewhat less subject to erosion in recent years. As expected, bid premiums on hostile transactions in the United States during the period 1988–98 have been significantly higher than agreed transactions (60 per cent vs. 31.6 per cent) and for Europe during 1998 this was true as well (51 per cent vs. 30 per cent).

5. PROSPECTS

The global economy today consists of several competing systems of corporate governance. As noted in Table 3.1, they differ in several important and interrelated ways: (1) the sourcing of debt and equity financing for

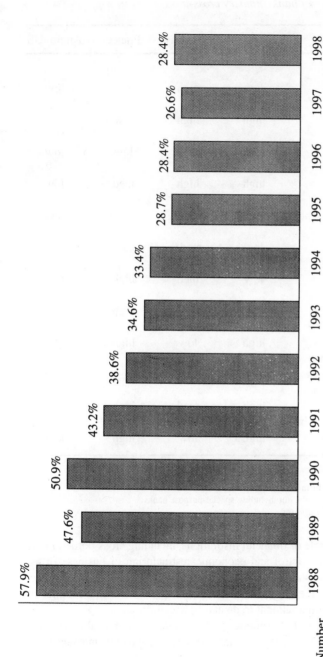

	1988	1989	1990	1991	1992	1993	1994	1995	1996	1997	1998
	57.9%	47.6%	50.9%	43.2%	38.6%	34.6%	33.4%	28.7%	28.4%	26.6%	28.4%
Number in sample	185	136	61	66	74	111	174	228	282	414	436

Notes: Includes acquisitions of US public companies where majority control is purchased. Only transactions over $50 million. Premiums calculated based on final offer vs. price five business days prior to initial offer.

Source: Securities Data Company.

Figure 3.5   Median control premiums paid for US corporations, 1988–98

Table 3.1   Summary of bank-industry cross-links

Issue	Japan	Germany	France	Anglo–US
Large-firm reliance on bank credit	low	high	med	low
Bank monitoring role	high	high	low	low
Industry–industry cross-holdings	high	med	low	low
Bank–industry shareholdings	high	high	med	low
Bank–industry monitoring and influence	high	high	med***	low
Industry–bank shareholdings	low	med*	low	low
Government–industry shareholdings**	low	med	high	low
Government–bank shareholdings**	low	low	high	low
Government influence on bank lending	high	low	high	low
Government influence on bank shareholdings	high	low	high	low
Informal bank–industry cross-links	high	med	high	low
Informal government–bank–industry cross-links	high	low	high	low

Notes:
*   Mainly on the part of insurance companies.
**   Central government only, not including special-purpose banks.
***   Primarily *banques d'affaires*.

enterprises; (2) the role of financial institutions, including cross-border, in the process of corporate control and economic restructuring of business firms; and (3) the role of the state as a source of capital and in corporate governance. They also differ in their implications for the formulation and conduct of policies bearing on international trade and financial flows.

The 'outsider-oriented' corporate control systems, in the absence of a government role in the process, favour the development and maintenance of a liberal international economic order.

Empirical assessment of the performance of different industry–bank–government models is basically impossible, due both to the complexity and essentially *political* definition of the dependent variable as well as tracking measurable performance attributes under different model assumptions, either longitudinally for a single country or cross-sectionally across countries. Nevertheless, the thought that the operation of free markets can be improved upon – even after broad interventions by the state to handle externalities and questions of fairness – is probably part of human nature.

In the end, there is today little question that the 'battle of the systems' will be won by Anglo–American corporate governance, perhaps modified by an as yet to be defined role by institutional investors acting as fiduciaries driven by portfolio performance in a highly competitive environment. The reasons have to do with: (1) increasingly competitive, liquid and transparent equity markets covered by the euro; (2) growing cross-border investments seeking higher returns and improved portfolio allocation which have little patience for corporate underperformance; (3) banks and insurance companies increasingly under pressure to perform, where long-term holdings in non-financial companies may not be a good way to compete with more performance-driven rivals; (4) the growing role of US and UK institutional investors in European capital markets – notably the single currency market of the euro zone – seeking superior returns that may come with economic restructuring in the region; and (5) the increasing acceptability of market-driven, potentially unwanted corporate actions to force changes in strategy, disposition of peripheral operations, declaration of special dividends and share repurchases, improvements in operating efficiency and other actions to enhance shareholder value. In all of these areas the euro is sure to serve as a catalyst in accelerating and amplifying developments that the globalization of markets has already set in train.

There is in any case likely to be some degree of convergence among the competing systems, as well as among the banking structures themselves. This is not inconsistent with financial liberalization and the wider use of securities markets by continental European corporations in the euro zone or with increasingly performance-oriented portfolio management by mutual funds, insurance companies and other institutional investors.[6] Both trends appear to be leading to a gradual shift away from bank finance, and a weakening of tight industry–bank relationships. Easing of bank activity limits in the United Kingdom and the United States is allowing them to play a larger role in industrial restructuring transactions, and to exploit some of the information and relationship advantages they have as lenders. Gradual convergence of Anglo–American style capital market orientation and Euro–Japanese style bank–firm linkages will test the relative merits of outsider and insider systems – that is, the importance of information asymmetries against the free market's capability of allocating and pricing capital within and across national frontiers.

In Europe there are strong pressures for change. Financial markets are being linked increasingly, institutional investors are expanding their operations and individual shareholders are becoming more active. Following the earlier approach of the UK, recent privatizations and sales of state assets are adding to the scope for investor holdings. Particularly in France, Germany, Italy, Belgium, the Netherlands and Spain (Lanoo, 1999) monetary union and liberalizing measures introduced in recent years by the European Union have given impetus to the integration of European capital markets. Institutional investors have been most active in this process, and are likely to become more involved in financing retirement and health care. Shareholder activism is growing within the EU, but not to the same extent as the US.

Capital market integration in Europe has not gone far because of home country bias in equity markets, and major contrasts in national regulatory environments (de Menil, 1999). In the complex trends that are evolving, a commonly recognized issue is a trade-off between liquidity and control. A degree of ownership dispersion is necessary for stock market liquidity, but entails monitoring and control problems which can be overcome by ownership concentrations, at the costs of reduced liquidity (Becht, 1999). At the Union level, there are major decisional problems that affect possibilities for enhancing economic growth through regulatory and deregulatory changes that can enhance competition. Regulatory systems in Europe are excessively restrictive, and the need for greater market dynamism is evident (Koedijk and Kremers, 1996). The reconciliation of national and sectoral preferences for Union policymaking is diffilcult (Kirman and Widgren, 1995). National administrative traditions and the influence of major interest groups have strong influence on the policies of EU member governments (Knill, 1998) and the overall effects in 'Union' decision making are potent, despite the lobbying of large firms, which appears on balance to favour greater regional market integration (Coen, 1998).

In the US, the development of highly liquid capital markets has been accompanied by strong upward pressures, causing asset appreciation at levels which have posed problems for monetary policy, which has been weakened by the strong growth of a securities industry. The Federal Reserve's responsibility for price stability has been challenged by the inflationary implications and potentially destabilizing dangers of stock appreciations and by the changing roles of US banks, as well as by the losses of monetary sovereignty associated with the internationalization of financial markets (Lamfalussy, 1994). The dangers of a sharp stock market reversal have been noted in IMF reviews (IMF, 1999).

The Federal Reserve's role in the maintenance of financial stability in the USA, dramatized by the orchestrated rescue of Long Term Capital Management, a highly leveraged New York firm operating outside regulatory surveillance (Edwards, 1999), could assume large dimensions if there is a sharp correction in US stock markets. Meanwhile, the continued linking of these markets with those in Europe is making it more and more probable that much Atlantic cooperation will be necessary if the US markets are destabilized. The linking results from high volume portfolio flows, and these, in addition to foreign direct investment, are having greater structural significance in Europe than in the US; in Europe the latter are contributing to agglomeration trends, and thus, indirectly, to change in the structural significance of corporate governance systems (Barrell and Pain, 1999).

Linkages between areas of economic policy have been tightened in different ways by the competitive effects of globalization in Europe and the US. In Europe the funding of industry has become a more urgent requirement because of the long-standing problem of lagging international competitiveness and the rising costs of welfare, as well as the still considerable degrees of segmentation in the single market. With the formation of the EMU the structural significance of fiscal policy choices has increased, and for structural policies the relative efficiencies of the various systems of corporate governance in member countries have become more important, but in contexts distinguished by different patterns of corporate interest representation. Monetary policy in the EU, however, operates more effectively through the banking system than in the US, as the monetary policy transmission mechanism has been less weakened by the growth of the securities sector. This will change over time.

Competitive pressures in the world economy, causing changes in corporate strategies, also cause adaptations in corporate governance systems, through policy shifts as well as through managerial adjustments. The funding of industry on an international basis, as stock markets become more globalized, does pose issues for national administrations concerned with the effects of world commerce on growth and employment. More fundamental problems, moreover, are presented by the speculative operations of institutional investors, using financial instruments which tend to move outside areas of regulatory supervision and which make financial markets more opaque (Lamfalussy, 1994).

Issues regarding the entitlements of investors, which have been given much attention in the literature on corporate governance, have assumed new dimensions with the vast growth of international securities markets. Questions about managerial responsibilities to investors have become complicated by the multiplication of sophisticated financial instruments in securities trading which has seen a *decline* in the demand for traditional supervisory functions, and the persistence of weak multilateral cooperation on the regulation of securities markets (Blommestein and Biltoft, 1995). At the same time, the broader interests of investors in the economic stability on which firms depend have become linked more closely with the endeavours of central banks, especially the Federal Reserve, to maintain that stability despite diminishing monetary sovereignty. With these changes, the basic interests of individual investors can be seen to diverge from those of institutional investors exploiting volatility on a large scale, with high risks. The competitive pressures in the real economy which tend to force adaptations in corporate operations, and thus gradually in systems of corporate governance, are active in the context of systemic changes in world financial markets. These raise questions of governance on a larger scale, and the exceptional prominence of the US securities industry in those markets has great significance for the development of a new international financial architecture (Gadziala, 1995; Eichengreen, 1999).

NOTES

1. Adapted from Mayer (1992) and Walter (1993) to include the possibility of industrial cross-holding systems, such as exist in Japan, and the role of insurance companies as holders of long-term equity positions.
2. For greater detail, see Saunders and Walter (1993).
3. The discussion presented here of the Anglo–American, German and Japanese approaches is elaborated upon in Story and Walter (1997). See also Dodds (1997).
4. The archetype of the German *Hausbank* arrangement is perhaps Deutsche Bank's relationship with Daimler-Benz AG, in which Deutsche held a 28 per cent equity stake prior to its merger into DaimlerChrysler, in which the bank initially was the largest shareholder, with a 19 per cent stake.
5. The case of Daimler-Benz, Germany's largest industrial company, has become a classic example of restructuring under the influence of universal banks in the 1980s. Evidently the early retirement in 1987 of the chief executive, Werner Breitschwerdt, and his replacement by Edzard Reuter was prompted by Deutsche Bank, whose position was that the company should adopt a strategy of rapid diversification and penetration of high-technology businesses, especially aerospace. This turned out to be disastrous, eventually triggering Reuter's ouster and further restructuring and merger with the Chrysler Corporation in 1998 under Jürgen Schrempp.
6. For a discussion, see Smith and Walter (2000).

REFERENCES

Barrell, R. and N. Pain (1999), 'Domestic institutions, agglomerations and foreign direct investment in Europe', *European Economic Review*, **43** (4–6) (April), 925–34.

Becht, M. (1999), 'European corporate governance: trading off liquidity against control', *European Economic Review*, **43** (4–6) (April), 1071–83.

Begg, D. and R. Portes (1992), 'Enterprise debt and economic transformation', Centre for Economic Policy Research, Discussion Paper No. 695, June.

Blommestein, H.J. and K. Biltoft (1995), 'Trends, structural changes and prospects in OECD capital markets', in *The New Financial Landscape*, Paris: OECD, chapter 9.

Cable, J. (1985), 'Capital market information and industrial performance: the role of West German banks', Economic Journal, xiv, 118–32.

Coen, D. (1998), 'The European business interest and the nation state: large firm lobbying in the European Union and member states', *Journal of Public Policy*, 18 (1) (January–April), 75–100.

de Menil, G. (1999), 'Real capital market integration in the EU: how far has it gone? What will the effect of the euro be?', *Economic Policy*, 28 (April), 167–89.

Dermine, J. (ed.) (1990), *European Banking After 1992*, Oxford: Basil Blackwell.

Dermine, J. and P. Hillion (eds) (1999), *Integration of European Capital Markets*, Oxford: Oxford University Press.

Dodds, J.C. (1994), 'The funding of Pacific industries', in G.K. Sletmo and G. Boyd (eds), *Industrial Policies in the Pacific*, Boulder, CO: Westview Press, chapter 3.

Dodds, J.C. (1997), 'Cross-border capital flows, corporate governance and developing financial systems in the Asia-Pacific Region', in G. Boyd and A.M. Rugman (eds), *Euro-Pacific Investment and Trade: Strategies and Structural Interdependencies*, Cheltenham, UK and Northampton, MA: Edward Elgar.

Edwards, F.R. (1999), 'Hedge funds and the collapse of long term capital management', *Journal of Economic Perspectives*, 13 (2) (Spring), 189–210.

Edwards, J. and K. Fischer (1992), 'An overview of the German financial system', Centre for Economic Policy Research Working Paper, November.

Eichengreen, B. (1999), *Toward a New International Financial Architecture*, Washington, DC: Institute for International Economics.

Estrich, R. (1999), *Mergers and Acquisitions Policy Group*, J.P. Morgan Securities Inc.

Gadziala, M.A. (1995), 'Structural changes in the North American capital markets', in *The New Financial Landscape*, Paris: OECD, chapter 10.

Gnehm, A. and C. Thalmann (1989), 'Conflicts of interest in financial operations: problems of regulation in the national and international context', paper prepared for the Swiss Bank Corporation, Basel.

Hoshi, T., A. Kayshap and D. Sharfstein (1991a), 'The role of banks in reducing the costs of financial distress in Japan', *Journal of Financial Economics*, xxii.

Hoshi, T., A. Kayshap and D. Sharfstein (1991b), 'Corporate structure, liquidity and investment, evidence from Japanese industrial groups', *Quarterly Journal of Economics*, xx, 33–60.

IMF Economic Reviews, May–August (1999), 2, *Consultation with United States*, 209–13.

Kaufman, G. (ed.) (1992), *Banking in Major Countries*, New York: Oxford University Press.

Kim, S.B. (1990), 'Modus operandi of lenders-cum-shareholder banks', Federal Reserve Bank of San Francisco, mimeo, September.

Kirman, A. and M. Widgren (1995), 'European economic decision-making policy: progress or paralysis?', *Economic Policy*, 21 (October), 421–60.

Knill, C. (1998), 'European policies: the impact of national traditions', *Journal of Public Policy*, 18 (1) (January–April), 1–28.

Koedijk, K. and J. Kremers (1996), 'Market opening, regulation and growth in Europe', *Economic Policy*, 23 (October), 443–68.

Krümmel, H.-J. (1980), 'German universal banking scrutinized', *Journal of Banking and Finance*, March, **v**, 121-7.

Lamfalussy, A. (1994), 'Central banking in transition', in Forrest Capie, Charles Goodhart, Stanley Fischer and Nortbert Schnadt (eds), *The Future of Central Banking*, Cambridge: Cambridge University Press, pp. 330-40.

Lanoo, K. (1999), 'A European perspective on corporate governance', *Journal of Common Market Studies*, **37** (2) (June), 269-94.

Mattione, R.P. (1992), 'A capital cost disadvantage for Japan?', *Journal of International Securities Markets*, September.

Mayer, C.P. (1992), 'Corporate control and transformation in Eastern Europe', paper presented at a SUERF conference on *The New Europe: Evolving Economic and Financial Systems in East and West*, Berlin, Germany, 8-10 October.

Pozdena, R.J. (1989), 'Do banks need securities powers?', *Federal Reserve Bank of San Francisco Weekly Letter*, 29 December.

Prowse, S.D. (1990), 'Institutional investment patterns and corporate financial behavior in the US and Japan', Board of Governors of the Federal Reserve System, Working Paper, January.

Prowse, S.D. (1995), 'Corporate govemance in an international perspective: a survey of corporate control mechanisms among large firms in the US, UK, Japan and Germany', *Financial Markets, Institutions and Instruments*, **4** (1), New York University, Salomon Center.

Rybczynski, T.N. (1989), 'Corporate restructuring', *National Westminster Bank Review*, August.

Saunders, A. and I. Walter (1993), *Universal Banking in the United States?*, New York: Oxford University Press.

Sheard, P. (1989), 'The main bank system and corporate monitoring and control in Japan', *Journal of Commercial Banking and Organization*, **vii**, 99-106.

Smith, G.D. and R. Sylla (1992), 'Wall Street and the capital markets in the twentieth century: an historical essay', New York University Salomon Center Working Paper, September.

Smith, R.C. and I. Walter (1992), 'Bank-industry linkages: models for Eastem European restructuring', paper presented at a SUERF conference on *The New Europe: Evolving Economic and Financial Systems in East and West*, Berlin, Germany, 8-10 October.

Smith, R.C. and I. Walter (2000), *Investment Banking in the Euro-Zone*, London: Financial Times - Prentice-Hall.

Steinherr, A. and C. Huveneers (1992), 'On the performance of differently regulated financial institutions: some empirical evidence', Universite Catholique de Louvain, working paper, February.

Story, J. and I. Walter (1997), *Political Economy of Financial Integration in Europe: The Battle of the Systems*, Manchester: Manchester University Press, and Cambridge, MA: MIT Press.

Walter, I. (1985), *Deregulating Wall Street*, New York: John Wiley & Sons.

Walter, I. (1993), *The Battle of the Systems: Control of Enterprises in the Global Economy*, Kiel: Institut für Weltwirtschaft.

4. Capital and labour market congruence and corporate governance: effects on corporate innovation and global competitiveness

Robert E. Hoskisson, Daphne Yiu and Hincheon Kim

Systems of governance in a national setting may provide a source of competitive advantage in the global arena (Kim and Hoskisson, 1997; Porter, 1992; Roe, 1994). The past decade has given rise to a debate over the relative efficiency and competitiveness of corporate governance systems in different countries. Not so long ago, it was fashionable to decry the short-sightedness of the Anglo-Saxon market-based governance system, and hear calls to incorporate features from the more relationship-based governance system which was credited with fuelling the miraculous growth of Japan in the 1980s (Porter, 1992). But today, with Japan's economy being in a depressed state, one hears more about the supremacy of the market-based Anglo-Saxon system. However, more work is needed to discern whether one system, market-based or relationship-based, is the better for competitiveness in all situations. If the market-based system is the superior one, does this mean that it will become the universal system and more relationship-based systems will disappear? Or as proposed by Porter (1997), should we blend the two systems together into one that combines the near-term efficiency of the US system with the greater willingness to invest in long-term capabilities that is said to distinguish the Japanese and German systems? These questions have a common assumption that there is no structural barrier for a national corporate governance system to be transferred across country boundaries.

In fact, one may argue that the structures of corporate governance are embedded in the idiosyncratic national institutions and ideologies of a country (Pauly and Reich, 1997). Using the concept of path dependence that views historical development as shaped by self-enforcing institutions (Arthur, 1988), institutional economists (for example, Knack and Keefer, 1997) propose that countries cannot easily improve their economic fortunes because they are often trapped in their own institutional matrix. Therefore, domestic institutional structures cannot easily be dismissed as a significant transfer barrier. Furthermore, from the view of complementary institutions (Milgrom and Roberts, 1995), one cannot analyse an economic institution apart from related societal and legal institutions. Complementary institutions function together and may work well only when all of them are in the same national economy. Milgrom and Roberts (1995) posited that the strength of institutions arises not just from their productivity, but also from making other institutions more productive. Complementary institutions will create a path dependency: institutions shape a development path by favouring new institutions that increase the pre-existing institutions' presence and outcomes. Hence, corporate governance systems may not be an isolated source of global competitiveness. Instead, they are shaped by and will shape corresponding institutions and, as such, it is the complementarity of related institutions that gives rise to governance efficiency and potential global competitiveness effects. We suggest that there may be no one best governance model. Accordingly, each governance system is likely to be efficient in its own configuration and it is not likely to be optimal to transfer one governance model to another country. This is no more evident than in the privatization experiment in Russia and other Eastern European countries. For example, through a voucher system in the former Soviet Union (Filatotchev et al., 1996), privatization of over 80 per cent of the formerly state-owned enterprises was accomplished in a very short period of time (1992–94). However, this implementation of radically different incentive and control mechanisms developed using a Western approach has not resulted in significant success.

In this chapter, we will specifically look into two institutional factors of a country, the capital market and the labour market. The reasons for choosing these two institutions are twofold. First, the functioning of both capital market and labour market is related to a country's ultimate competitiveness. Under 'investor capitalism' (Useem, 1992), the changing nature of competition and the increasing pressure of globalization make investment the most critical determinant of national competitive advantage (Porter, 1996). An effective governance system is one in which a country can achieve a more optimal allocation of capital which, together with the spillovers, creates benefits for the economy as a whole, apart from the private returns accruing to a firm's shareholders. Therefore, an examination of the relationship between capital market and corporate governance is critical to the global competitiveness of an economy.

Blair (1995) argued that the failure to represent the employees' interests in governance arrangements can lead to an underinvestment in job- and firm-specific skills. Under 'alliance capitalism" (Gerlach, 1992), co-specialized investment in inter-firm relations is essential to firm survival in the long run.

Investment in co-specialized assets involves the development of human capital through which cooperation is fostered. Boards of directors, even in the US market-based system, must not only look out for shareholders' interests, but also must hire executives from the labour market and establish a contract which facilitates the use of managerial decision making in an optimal way (Baysinger and Hoskisson, 1990). Therefore, the relationship between labour market and corporate governance is an important issue regarding firm competitiveness in the global context.

More importantly, the consideration of either capital market or labour market in isolation is not comprehensive enough to determine the global competitiveness of an economy because both institutions are complementary to each other. The second reason for choosing the capital market and labour market as the institutions of focus is that an effective governance system can bridge the two markets as implied above. Corporate governance can be thought of as a means used in firms to establish order between the firm's owners and its top-level managers whose interests may be in conflict. A primary objective of corporate governance is to ensure that shareholders' interests can be aligned with the interests of managers. More formally, from the agency perspective (Jensen and Meckling, 1976), corporate governance deals with the agency problem arising from the separation of ownership and control. The principal-agent view of corporate governance rests on the premise that the market for capital and the market for managerial labour provide the most effective restraints on managerial discretion, and that shareholders, as the residual claimants, should ultimately commit corporate resources to value-maximizing ends (Keasey et al., 1997). As such, a firm's existing governance system is an outcome of the negotiation process of owner-principals and manager-agents. More precisely, an effective governance system is one which can bridge the gap between the owner-principals who provide capital and the manager-agents who provide labour to a firm.

The purpose of this chapter is to present a contingency approach to examine how the congruency between the capital market and labour market of a country and the associate corporate governance system will affect corporate risk-taking behaviour and innovation activities, which in turn affects corporate performance and global competitiveness. To do this we first examine capital and labour market dimensions. Accordingly, in the next section, we define two main types of capital markets, contractual versus relational capital markets. The subsequent section will describe internal versus external labour markets. Following this, we will present a contingency framework, which predicts two optimal corporate governance systems based on the congruency between capital and labour markets. To illustrate the matches, we will look specifically at how the US and Japanese systems achieve separate but optimal efficiencies managerial systems. The effects of capital and labour markets on country innovation systems in terms of risk-taking propensities created for managers and entrepreneurs will be considered as well. In the final section, hybrid forms of corporate governance systems will be discussed. Finally, we conclude that there is no one best, universal corporate governance system. An efficient governance system requires complementarity among institutions in a society. The change of one component has to be accompanied by adjustments in a system of related components.

CAPITAL MARKET

Although each country has its unique capital market characteristics, at the risk of oversimplification we concentrate on two broad types of capital markets: one is more market-based which we call 'contractual capital market' and the other is more relationship-based which we call 'relational capital market'. The attributes of these capital markets, listed in Table 4.1, are described below.

Contractual Capital Market vs. Relational Capital Market

Contractual capital and relational capital markets are different in many aspects. According to Berglöf (1990), in general, there is a wide range of financial instruments in a contractual capital market. Households invest their savings into production. Banks primarily meet the short-term financing needs of the corporate sectors and are less important in the provision of long-term funds. They also receive a larger share of funds from sources other than households, primarily through borrowing in intermediate markets. The central bank is concerned primarily with the control of monetary aggregates, that is, money supply or interest rates. Government regulates the banking sector but normally refrains from active intervention.

On the other hand, relational capital markets are characterized by having less-developed financial markets, in particular for risky capital. The opportunities for investment portfolio diversification and hedging are more limited, when compared to contractual capital markets. Savings in the relational capital market are primarily transferred in the form of short-term and long-term credits through banks and other saving institutions. Government supports bank lending and actively intervenes to influence the costs of various forms of finance. In this section, we will summarize the major differences between the two capital markets through five dimensions of corporate governance.

Ownership structure
Contractual capital markets are characterized by diffused, non-corporate

Table 4.1 Attributes of contractual and relational capital markets

Governance characteristic	Contractual capital market	Relational capital market
Ownership	Low concentration	High concentration by families or financial institutions
Executive compensation	Managerial stock options	Seniority-based
Boards of directors	Outside directors dominate	Inside directors dominate
Market for corporate control	External groups pursue takeovers	Dominating shareholders and banks arrange
Role of financial institutions	Strong rules constrain financial institution involvement	Active participation by financial institutions
Debt vs. equity	High levels of equity	High levels of debt

shareholdings (Kaplan, 1997). More specifically, there is low concentration of ownership and insignificant commercial bank shareholdings. Interfirm shareholdings are less common and there is a relatively faster turnover of controlling blocs (Berglöf, 1990). On the other hand, relational capital markets are characterized by having more concentrated ownership by families, corporations or banks (Kaplan, 1997). Also, interfirm shareholdings are widespread and the turnover of controlling blocs is relatively slow (Berglöf, 1990). Investors in contractual and relational capital markets are also different in terms of their relative propensity for exit and voice behaviour (Hirschman, 1970). In contractual capital markets, the role of the individual shareholder voice is limited. The access to liquid stock markets gives the shareholder virtually unrestricted, low-cost exit opportunities. Therefore, given the high costs associated with collective action by shareholders who are small and dispersed, exit dominates voice in contractual capital markets (Keasey et al., 1997). Conversely, the less-developed markets for financial instruments in relational capital markets reduces incentives for investors to exit or leave established relationships. This 'lock-in' effect (Berglöf, 1990) induces voice behaviour by making exit very costly in the relational capital markets.

The ownership pattern may lead to other characteristics of a capital market. In a study of corporate ownership around the world, La Porta et al. (1999)

found that countries that restrict cross-ownership of shares (contractual capital market in this chapter) have more widely held average shareholdings in firms, as well as more liquid markets. Moreover, they found that greater ownership concentration in bank-oriented financial systems (referred to as relational capital markets in this chapter) with poor investor protection is reflected in such systems through greater reliance on debt rather than equity finance. This finding is consistent with that of Berglöf (1990): firms in bank-oriented financial systems typically have a capital structure characterized by low degrees of internal funding and high debt/equity ratios. The heavier reliance on debt in relational capital markets has made it possible for firms to grow without diffusing control to the same extent as in countries with contractual capital markets. The higher debt/equity ratios also imply that takeovers are not as common in countries with relational capital market systems as in countries with contractual capital market systems.

Executive compensation

The stock market economies in the contractual systems offer opportunity for providing high-powered incentives, for example, through managerial stock options. In contrast, close monitoring and well-functioning remuneration committees should promote stronger relations between executive compensation and firm performance in the relational systems. However, drawing implications from studies on the relationship between executive compensation and firm performance, Kaplan (1997) summarized that executive turnover increased significantly with poor stock performance and earnings losses in both contractual and relational capital markets. So, although executive compensation is relatively higher in contractual capital market, executive compensation as a managerial incentive mechanism appears to have similar effects in both contractual and relational capital markets.

Boards of directors

Contractual capital markets are often referred to as systems in which outside directors dominate the boards of directors, while in relational capital markets inside managers and employers are considered dominant, although other stakeholders often sit on boards. According to Mayer (1998), the main differences between outside- versus inside-dominated systems concern the formulation, implementation and adaptation of corporate strategy, rather than managerial incentives and disciplining, as well as finance and investment decisions. Outside-dominated systems are better at responding to change, whereas inside-dominated systems are superior at implementing policies which require the development of relations with other related stakeholders.

Board composition is also found to affect firm performance. From the perspective of agency theory, outside director prominence leads to superior firm performance as a result of their independence from firm management. This theoretical prediction on the positive relationship between outsider directors and firm performance through improved agency costs has empirical support (Baysinger and Butler, 1985; Ezzamel and Watson, 1993; Pearce and Zahra, 1992; Rosenstein and Wyatt, 1990; Schellenger et al., 1989). Quite opposite to agency theory, stewardship theory (Donaldson, 1990; Donaldson and Davis, 1991, 1994) suggests that more often than not insider managers are good firm stewards. Moreover, the superiority of the amount and quality of insider directors' information may lead to more effective evaluation of top managers and the strategies that they propose (Baysinger and Hoskisson, 1990). So, inside-dominated systems should lead to better firm performance based on improved strategic innovation (Kesner, 1987). Empirically, it is found that insider directors have positive effects on corporate R&D expenditure (Zahra 1996; Baysinger et al., 1991; Hill and Snell, 1988) and is related to the nature and extent of diversification (Hill and Snell, 1988).

Markets for corporate control
One of the major distinctions between contractual capital markets and relational capital markets is how the systems handle problems of financial distress (Zysman, 1983). In contractual capital markets, takeover by an external group of shareholders is the predominant mechanism in handling managerial failure; while creditor reorganization dominates in relational capital markets (Berglöf, 1990). Though markets for corporate control are regarded as an important discipline on the behaviour of firms in the contractual capital market, the process has high transaction costs due to the bidding process and regulatory requirements. In relational capital markets, markets for corporate control can be regarded as inactive or even non-existent because they are substituted by the close monitoring by the concentrated shareholders. In the case of financial distress, the dominating shareholders and banks normally assume control in such situations through their large share of claims (Kester, 1991).

The role of banks and other financial institutions
The differences between contractual and relational capital markets stand out clearly when the relative importance of various financial institutions is compared. In contractual capital markets, there are rules pertaining to commercial banks which limit the size of individual institutions, constrain their portfolio choices and prevent them from intervening when their client firms are in financial difficulties (Berglöf, 1990). However, relational capital markets are less regulated in all these respects. We find that banks hold a higher share of total domestic assets in the relational capital markets

(Goldsmith, 1985). Also, the lending activity of the banking sector is more directed to corporate financing. Furthermore, there is heavy concentration of share ownership held by banks and often substantial government ownership in relational capital markets.

Banks and other financial institutions are said to have significant monitoring and disciplining roles on firms' behaviour through their ownership of shares, appointment of bank directors and close intercorporate relationships (Kaplan, 1997). Therefore, agency costs are reduced. Moreover, as banks and other financial institutions have better information and more power to use that information, financing is readily available for value-increasing long-term projects. In addition, being the lender and a central risk-bearer, when a firm is in financial distress, banks and other financial institutions are willing to accept these higher debt levels since they can exercise control much more freely than their counterparts in the contractual capital markets (Sheard, 1994). Hence, the less restrictive regulations in relational capital markets reduce the costs of debt as an *ex-post* governance mechanism (Williamson, 1987). Finally, the domination of banks and financial institutions in relational capital markets is likely to hamper the development of markets for corporate control, thus saving the cost of expensive hostile takeovers found in contractual capital markets. Research has, indeed, found that banks have a significant role in reducing the costs of financial distress in relational capital markets (Hoshi et al., 1990).

LABOUR MARKETS

Labour markets can be classified into external labour markets and internal labour markets. We will compare the general characteristics of these two types of labour markets along three dimensions as discussed below and they are summarized in Table 4.2.

External Labour Markets vs. Internal Labour Markets

Mitigation of the adverse selection problem

In external labour markets, the manager finds workers in a well-organized labour market where each worker is priced according to the market assessment of his productivity. A well-functioning external labour market will reflect all the observable characteristics of the workers. Hence, market wages serve as good signals about workers' quality, thus mitigating the problem of adverse selection (Hoshi, 1998), which occurs when a potential employee misrepresents their skills and abilities. On the other hand, in internal labour markets, workers start at the lowest level of the firm hierarchy and get the

Table 4.2 Issues in external versus internal labour markets

Labour market issues	Externally-oriented market	Internally-oriented market
Adverse selection	Market wages serve as signal of quality	Management monitors worker performance
Monitoring	Reputations affects mobility	
Accumulation of skills and knowledge	General managerial skills	Firm-specific skills

same salaries. The managers monitor the workers' performance and promote them to the next rank if they meet a certain performance criteria. Over time, through the hierarchy (Aoki, 1988) managers observe workers' long-term performance. Thereby, managers obtain signals about workers' quality, which alleviates to a large extent the problem of adverse selection (Hoshi 1998).

Monitoring
In an effective external labour market, any misconduct by a manager to stakeholders may hurt the reputation of the manager in the labour market and adversely affect the probability of getting a lucrative management position in the future. This credible threat prevents managers from abusing their informational advantage against monitors and stakeholders. In this sense, a well-functioning external labour market for managers can be a substitute for internal corporate governance (Hoshi, 1998). However, external reputation is not a significant threat in an internal labour market because of the lack of exit, although internal reputation is crucial to promotion opportunities. Being unable to move to another firm, managers have to fully commit to existing firms and maintain a long-term relationship with stakeholders.

Accumulation of skills and knowledge
External labour markets tend to encourage the development of general managerial skills and knowledge. Since managers are mobile across firm boundaries, they will try to accumulate skills and knowledge that are applicable in a wide range of firms so as to increase their value in the labour market. Therefore, more general managerial skills are developed in external labour markets. Furthermore, in external labour markets, the uncertainty of the firm's employment may increase the employees' incentives to keep their industry-specific skills high (Gilson and Roe, 1998). Conversely, internal labour markets encourage accumulation of firm-specific human capital

(Hoshi, 1998). Internal labour markets require long-term employment relationships; hence, employees have incentives to invest in firm-specific skills and knowledge. Simultaneously, firms are willing to invest in firm-specific training programmes because they are not afraid employees will leave the firm once they are trained.

CAPITAL AND LABOUR MARKET CONGRUENCE

Based on the classifications of capital markets and labour markets described above, we propose four situations outlined in Figure 4.1. In our theoretical framework, we emphasize whether the capital market is congruent with the labour market in a national economy. We argue the importance of fit between the capital market and the labour market for two reasons. The first idea regarding fit concerns the issue of institutional complementarity. The strength of each institution arises not just from its own productivity, but also from its ability to make other institutions more productive. In other words, there should be a correspondence across the capital and labour markets so as to produce the most efficient corporate governance system. The second concern is path dependence. Complementary institutions will create path dependence which will shape new institutions that favour consequences of the pre-existing institutions. Hence, we propose that corporate governance systems are part of a set of institutions that create an opportunity for country global competitiveness. It is the complementarity and path dependency of these related institutions that gives rise to governance efficiency and the global competitiveness of a national economy. In our framework, we would argue that there are two cases in which the capital market is complementary with the labour market, thus giving rise to an effective corporate governance system. The first matched case is one which adopts a contractual capital market system and an external labour market. The second matched case is one in which relational capital and internal labour markets are the predominant modes in the economy. We will illustrate these two matched cases (see Figure 4.1) by looking specifically into the United States' corporate governance system (which corresponds to the first matched case) and the Japanese corporate governance system (which corresponds to the second matched scenario).

Match 1 – Contractual Capital Markets with External Labour Markets

The United States has a well-established contractual capital market in which the emphasis is on the specialization of management and the specialization risk-bearing by shareholders and creditors (Fama and Jensen, 1983). To deal

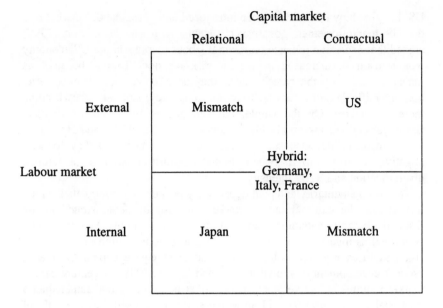

Figure 4.1 Corporate governance system congruence and mismatch

with the collective choice problems arising as a firm's stocks are widely held, control is delegated to management. However, it is this agency problem between shareholders and management which occupies the central position in the US corporate governance. To reduce the agency costs associated with the separation of ownership and control, external control mechanisms such as external managerial labour markets and markets for corporate control are necessary because they are complementary to the contractual governance system.

In the US contractual capital market system, corporate control is typically exercised through a change in the management by takeovers. Such a change is easier if firms do not have long-term relationships with other stakeholders. As such, the absence of a long-term relationship is conducive to arm's-length contractual capital markets in the US. Moreover, the lack of involvement of labour in the corporate governance process is favourable to the development of a contractual capital market because it will make takeovers smoother and reduce combination costs. Furthermore, to cope with frequent management changes under arm's-length financing, an external labour market which allows labour mobility and fixed market wages is necessary. The presence of strong creditor's rights and shareholder's rights are also contributory to an effective functioning of the capital markets in the US (Hoshi, 1998).

The external labour market also fits in the contractual capital market in the

US. Imagine how it would be if we introduced an internal labour market into the US market-oriented governance system. Kim and Hoskisson (1997) argued that excessive reliance on internal labour markets in the US economy would result in increased managerial risk-aversion. This is because, as managers move up the career ladder, they accumulate more firm-specific, non-diversifiable human assets. To minimize employment risks, they become more risk-averse. On the whole, innovation may be adversely affected. Baysinger and Hoskisson (1989), Hoskisson and Hitt (1988) and Hoskisson and Johnson (1992) also support this line of argument and they found a negative relationship between M-form (multidivisional) structures, diversification and R&D intensity.

The complementarity and path dependency between the contractual capital market and the external labour market can also be demonstrated in the distinctive venture capital market found in the US economy. Venture capital is defined as investment by specialized organizations in high-growth, high-risk and often high-technology firms that need equity capital to finance product development or growth (Black and Gilson, 1998). A venture capital market requires an active stock market (that is, a contractual rather than a relational capital market), and an active stock market requires a supply of entrepreneurs and deals, which in turn create the demand for a venture capital market. It is argued that a well-developed stock market that permits venture capitalists to exit through an IPO is critical to the existence of a vibrant venture capital market. The potential for exit through IPO allows the venture capital provider and the entrepreneur to enter into an implicit contract over future control of the company in a way that is not available in a relational capital market. This implicit contract over future control permitted by the availability of exit through an IPO helps to explain the greater success of venture capital in countries with contractual capital markets. Empirically, it is found that the US has a much more fully developed venture capital market than Germany and Japan (Black and Gilson, 1998).

Match 2: Relational Capital Market with Internal Labour Market

One cannot deny that the effectiveness of the Japanese corporate governance systems is derived from the complementarity between its bank-oriented relational system and the practice of lifetime employment. The Japanese governance system has been said to be one which maximize the interests of creditors and workers at the expense of the shareholders' interests. This may be due to two institutional mechanisms: a bank-oriented (relational) capital market and an internal labour market.

The Japanese capital market has historically relied on neither a source of external capital nor an external source of discipline on corporate management

(Gerlach, 1992). Market-based influence by independent and institutional investors is replaced by a closely connected community of mutually positioned, long-term trading partners. The forging of a stable relational governance system has gone hand-in-hand with the development of an internal labour market. Under lifetime employment, managers of large Japanese firms are sheltered by their affiliate firm shareholders from the pressure facing US managers for radical labour cost reductions when firm performance declines. Even when staff reductions are necessary, voluntary leaves and long-term phasing out of positions are preferred. Furthermore, alliance partners may offer a last-resort source of employment for group firms in financial distress. This has been called the 'Japanese-style layoff system', under which employees in firms in depressed industries are transferred to firms in growth industries (Gerlach, 1992). Furthermore, the lack of an external labour market motivates firms to invest in firm-specific and relationship-specific human capital (Gilson and Roe, 1998). At the same time, employees strengthen their commitment towards firms and trading partners because they lack external managerial opportunities. Hence, both the relational capital and internal labour markets reinforce each other, and produce a congruent system of monitoring and incentive for both owners and managers.

The development of institutions is non-recursive. The practice of lifetime employment will foster the closure of external labour markets. Similarly, the development of bank-oriented, relational capital market in the Japanese economy prevents the development of robust primary and secondary capital markets found in the contractual system. Macey and Miller (1995) have criticized the powerful banks in the Japanese corporate governance scheme by suggesting that the system prevents equity claimants from undertaking socially optimal risks, thereby hindering the development of robust capital markets. The relational system of corporate governance in Japan substitutes for the more market-oriented contractual system in the US. For instance, banks, affiliate firm shareholders and corporate group structures play a role that is similar to that of takeovers and proxy fights in the US (Kaplan and Minton, 1994; Kester, 1991). The pattern of cross-holdings among Japanese *keiretsu* firms is a deliberate anti-takeover defence system. It serves the same purpose as poison pills, greenmail and shark repellents do in US firms. Besides, the main bank system serves as a substitute for the market of corporate control (Aoki et al., 1994). In addition to being a substitute for a market-oriented governance system, the Japanese bank-oriented system is said to provide better monitoring and control of the moral hazard problem (see Macey and Miller, 1995 for details). The superiority of Japanese banks in controlling moral hazard reduces the banks' aggregate risk, which contributes to profitability. This superiority in controlling moral hazard suggests that

Japanese firrns would find bank financing more attractive than capital market financing. Although banks reduce the potential gain from investing in the stock market by limiting upside gains to residual claimants, concentrated ownership patterns reduce the need to pursue costly hostile takeovers and stock market illiquidity. This, together with the substitution for external monitoring mechanisms in contractual capital markets and the superiority of banks in handling moral hazard problems, contribute to why there is little need for a strong equity capital market in Japan.

Implications for Global Competitiveness

Porter (1997) posited that the nature of competition and the pressure from globalization have shifted in ways that make investment more critical to success in the global context. Corporate governance in both the external and internal capital markets is accordingly likely to play a major role because it forms a self-reinforcing national system for the allocation of investment capital (Porter, 1997). Besides the effect of governance systems on capital markets, systems of corporate governance are also important to labour markets because of the potential to add value through the human capital of a national economy (Prahalad, 1997). Capital and labour markets associated corporate governance systems also have effects on corporate innovation activities. As suggested by Franko (1989), research and development is the principal means of gaining market share in global competition. Hence, the relationship between corporate governance and corporate innovation activities may help us to predict national country competitiveness in the global context. The following considers the different effects of the two matches and associated systems of corporate governance on corporate propensities for innovation and risk-taking.

Contractual capital market, external labour markets and corporate innovations

Capital markets impose effects on corporate innovation activities in terms of their monitoring and risk-taking propensities. In regard to monitoring, contractual capital markets have been criticized as being inefficient in monitoring managers' opportunistic behaviour, thus giving rise to increased potential for agency problems. Holmstrom (1989) argued that the contracting costs associated with promoting inventive activity are especially high because of the five characteristics of innovation: the long-term, high-risk, unpredictable, labour-intensive and idiosyncratic nature of innovation. Furthermore, the prevalence of executive compensation contracts which rely on short-term bonus plans in diffusely held firms may discourage investments in innovation in favour of projects with more immediate and certain contributions to earnings (Froot et al., 1992; Holmstrom, 1989; Jacobs, 1991; Narayanan, 1985a, 1985b; Stein, 1988, 1989). This argument is empirically supported by Francis and Smith (1995). They found that diffusely held firms, which are the most common type of ownership in contractual capital markets, are less innovative along the dimensions of patent activity, growth by acquisition versus internal development and timing of long-term investment spending. On the other hand, a counter-argument is that in contractual capital markets managers have more managerial discretion and strategic autonomy to generate entrepreneurial rents.

As for the risk-taking propensity, in contractual markets, shareholders are more short-term oriented. This is because the pressures to perform and look good are very great in contractual capital markets in which past firm performance and reputation are important signals for the future potential of the firms and thus determines the availability of new capital. Therefore, there is a tendency for managers to act myopically by choosing short-term projects with faster paybacks (Holmstrom, 1989; Stein, 1987). Yet, managers still have the incentives to pursue innovation activities to minimize their employment risks and to get more external fund sources and potential investors.

In the context of the labour market, there are two dimensions which are related to firm innovation: risk-taking behaviour and learning and knowledge creation. As mentioned above, managers are not restricted by mobility barriers in external labour markets. Thus, they have only short-term commitment and high-powered market incentive to continually examine their employment options elsewhere (Williamson, 1985). As the labour market is open, there is high upside return and low downside risk when the existing organization fails because performance-based compensation schemes are usually applied in external labour markets. This provides incentives to pursue risky innovation projects. Conversely, the internal labour market is characterized by high long-term commitment and low labour mobility across firms. Organizations are taken as social institutions in which norms and role expectations are greatly emphasized (Zenger, 1992). Managers will then have low upside return but high downside risk because of the lack of mobility choice. Furthermore, due to long-term or even lifetime employment expectations, employees accumulate high firm-specific human capital, thereby increasing the costs of exit. So, managers in internal labour markets are more risk-averse in pursuing innovations.

In the context of learning and knowledge creation, external labour markets facilitate inter-firm mobility which acts as a mechanism of new resource combinations and knowledge creation. Macro-flexibility leads to good cross-boundary coordination; however, because of the lack of managerial commitment, within-boundary coordination and appropriability is poor. Owing to inter-firm mobility, innovation associated with external labour markets tends to revolutionalize industries (Utterback, 1994; Tushman and O'Reilly, 1996) and innovation can be made in the context of converging industry boundaries (Yoffie, 1996).

As a general prediction, in the quadrant of contractual capital markets and external labour markets (for example, the US), firms' opportunism in lowering wages or limiting promotion opportunities is mitigated by the existence of external labour markets. Because human capital is flexible in an external labour market, shareholders under 'investor capitalism' (Useem, 1992) will strive for short-term, high-risk innovations in order to maximize their returns. And the quickest way for short-term returns is having a broad market scope, suggesting more globalization. Hence, we predict that innovations in this quadrant tend to be exploratory (Levinthal and March, 1993; March, 1991), and revolutionary (Utterback, 1994; Tushman and O'Reilly, 1996). The strategic goal is to achieve dynamic efficiency which involves a continuous reconsideration of initial conditions (Ghemawat and Costa, 1993) where firms are in search of new break-through innovations. Moreover, firms are more likely to maximize shorter-term profits and the performance is relatively varied in the global competitiveness context, suggesting a stronger upside, but also a strong downside potential.

Relational capital market, internal labour market and corporate innovations

In contrast, the relational system can mitigate incentive, information and control problems (Williamson, 1985) through high ownership concentration, use of insider directors and the coalignment of interests between shareholders and managers in the form of compensation schemes. The effective monitoring system in the relational market results in a reduction of both agency costs and information costs. However, because of the close relationship and associated monitoring mechanisms in this market, there is limited managerial discretion and strategic autonomy. Managers, investing most of their non-diversifiable and non-tradable human capital in the firms, tend to avoid pursuing risky projects and strategic actions (Zajac and Westphal, 1994). Therefore, there is a significant probability of forgoing entrepreneurial rents.

Relational capital market is characterized by having long-term oriented shareholders, relatively fewer potential investors, and limited managerial discretion and strategic autonomy. This means that external factors such as environmental complexity, dynamism and unpredictability do matter. In this way, both shareholders and managers are more risk-averse. The unique role of banks and other financial institutions as both shareholders and debt holders in relational capital markets also means that they would not encourage the incumbent firms to pursue risky innovation projects. Next, we focus on labour markets in this quadrant.

The emphasis on internal labour markets have more 'micro' flexibility in that they can induce greater commitments to human capital, and employees can move and adapt well to modest technological changes (Gilson and Roe, 1998). Therefore, internal labour markets create more firm-specific knowledge, which is a source of competitive advantage. Yet, there is also an inward-looking myopia because of the general and firm-specific nature of the human capital in the internal labour market. Also, coordination is good within a firm but poor between firms (Kogut and Zander, 1992, 1996). Therefore, innovations in the internal labour markets tend to be more firm-specific. Cross-industries' innovations are relatively less, compared to situations where external labour markets are emphasized.

As mentioned above, the complementarity between the capital markets and the labour markets is essential in governing firms' behaviour. Countries with relational capital markets and weak external labour markets (for example, Japan) have firms which face less employee and competitor opportunism, because neither employees nor competitors can appropriate the returns on the firm's investment because the flow of human capital is curtailed. Although product market competition, for example, through systems of reverse engineering, may not be dampened, diffusion of innovation through the labour market is lessened with an emphasis on internal labour markets. As such, employee commitment is traded for flexibility and innovations tend to be in-house, less risky and with longer payback periods.

As a general prediction, firms in a national economy with a relational capital market and an internal labour market are more likely to pursue innovations that are exploitative (Levinthal and March, 1993; March, 1991), and evolutionary (Utterback, 1994; Tushman and O'Reilly, 1996). The goal is more towards static efficiency which involves continuous search for improvements within a fixed set of initial conditions (Ghemawat and Costa, 1993). Japanese firms, for instance, have focused on the adaptation and improvement of existing technology rather than the creation of new technology (Mansfield, 1988). Also, Japanese firms have focused on process R&D, which tends to be less risky than product R&D (Mansfield, 1988). Therefore, Japanese innovation-oriented projects may entail a much lower level of uncertainty than the US innovation-oriented projects. However, as Japanese firms more frequently engage in projects for the creation of new technology, the Japanese financial system may become a hindrance. Yet, risky innovations do exist in this quadrant. The special feature of alliance capitalism (Gerlach, 1992) in the relational system may help firms finance long-term, high-risk innovations in order to compete collectively in the global context. Thus, the potential problem may have been moderated by longer time horizons facilitated by the Japanese financial system. Furthermore, this may not have posed a serious problem until the last decade because the central issue regards the type of project that may receive funding in a more centralized system. Additionally, the success of the auto and consumer electronics industries in Japan fit well with their system governance. These are industries that require significant internal coordination challenges that fit with the internal capital market and have just been able to manage advancement through incremental innovations, which are often process-oriented.

A project is evaluated by a smaller number of sources of financial resources in the Japanese centralized financial systems than in decentralized financial systems. Accordingly, a project has a lower chance of getting funded in a centralized than a decentralized financial system because the project will be evaluated by more analysts in the decentralized system. In particular, an innovation-oriented project, which entails a high level of uncertainty by nature, would have a much lower chance of getting funded in centralized systems compared to decentralized financial systems (Sah, 1991). As we move more towards an information-oriented economy (Sampler, 1998), process innovation in manufacturing may not bring the returns that investment in information systems bring in a more 'virtual' economy.

Consequently, we can predict that firms in this quadrant will have longer-term profits and more stable performance in the global competitive context, but risks are evident as we move towards an economy that emphasizes more rapid innovation through investments in a more information-oriented context.

In conclusion, the match between the capital market and the labour market is critical in explaining corporate risk-taking and innovation behaviour as well as performance implications in the global context. The evidence of the success of evolutionary innovative Japanese manufacturing products (for example, auto and home electronics) and revolutionary innovative US high-technology products in the global market are examples of the match of these two institutional aspects.

The US approach to governance is said to have more 'macro'-flexibility (Gilson and Roe, 1998). The external capital market presses for change, and lacking large shareholdings that facilitate credible obligations to a firm's employees, the US has fewer commitments. Also, with a strong external labour market, workers pay for more of their general and industry-specific human capital. The Japanese and German systems, on the other hand, have 'micro'-flexibility (Gilson and Roe, 1998). The soft commitments slow down big, rapid adjustments. Yet, they can induce greater commitments to human capital, and employees can move and adapt well to modest technological change.

IMPLICATIONS AND DISCUSSION

In this chapter, we emphasize how the congruence between capital market and labour market influences corporate innovations and global competitiveness.

Although we have demonstrated how the US and Japanese corporate governance systems are built on separate congruences, each of these two systems is not without problems. While the level of bank control may be too high in Japan so that fixed claimants' interests are favoured relative to residual claimants, the level of financial institution control may be too low in the US because the ability to actively monitor and control on behalf of residual claimants may be impeded under the current system. Therefore, future studies can explore what is an optimal level of financial institutional control in each of the systems.

Another criticism is about short-termism versus long-termism. The US system is often criticized for its short-termism (Macey and Miller, 1995). However, the problem of short-termism is not just related to capital markets and opportunistic managerial mobility enabled by an external labour market, but intertemporal decisions are 'basic' in managerial work. Managers continually make decisions that maximize both long- and short-term valuations (Laverty, 1996). Moreover, firms that optimize intertemporal choices (the short-term and the long-term) maximize their stock price. According to efficient market theory, firms that optimize intertemporal choice create value and continue to survive (Laverty, 1996). Therefore, the pursuit of stock price maximization may not rule out the possibility of optimizing long-run value. In other words, even though US firms may have a system that emphasizes the short run, ultimate valuations also incorporate long-run considerations. Likewise, long-termism reinforced by the Japanese corporate governance system is criticized as detrimental to fast responses to market changes in industries such as software. Also, the focus on growth among Japanese firms instead of profitability may foster a focus on incremental innovation and in some instances a system focused on imitation only. This may impede its global competitiveness. Hence, the debate on short-termism vs. long-termism, and their relationship with global competitiveness, remains an important agenda item to be resolved. In fact, the 1998 Competitiveness Report lists Japan lower than other contractual market-oriented economies, but higher than the economies of France, Germany and Italy (Sachs, 1999).

In what follows, we discuss the hybrid forms of corporate governance systems in Germany, France and Italy. There is either a lack of a strong contractual capital market or external labour market, or they are undergoing changes in either the capital market or labour market. We examine how these hybrid systems supplement elements to enhance the effectiveness of their corporate governance systems. Corporate governance should be regarded as a system of complementary institutions. Given the existing institutions, one may improve the corporate governance systems by adding complementary elements.

The German corporate governance system is characterized traditionally by a relational capital market in which German banks play a major role. As commented by Gilson and Kraakman (1993), German banks have the position, information and power to effectively monitor the activity of management and, when necessary, to discipline management. To bridge the gap between capital and labour, a governance system labelled co-determination has been implemented. Co-determination refers to the creation of two boards of equal size representing capital and labour. Under this two-tier board structure, there is a management and executive committee (*vorstand*) and a supervisory board of directors (*Aufsichstrat*) which incorporates labour representation. The German governance system structure aims to achieve a balance between owner and employee participation, and a balance of control from both the residual claimants and fixed claimants.

Italy lacks both the continuous and textured monitoring by banks that characterizes the German system as well as the monitoring by outside equity investors that characterizes the US system (Macey, 1998). The lack of an effective governance infrastructure in the Italian economy discourages the development of capital markets and prevents large firms from realizing economies of scale and scope. A consequence resulting from these corporate governance problems is that small organizations dominate the Italian economy; 98 per cent of Italian firms have fewer than 20 employees (Macey, 1998). Most Italian firms rely on owner-operators to reduce agency costs. Due to a lack of legal protection for outside shareholders, a pyramidal ownership structure is often set up in which a single firm or entrepreneur controls multiple companies through mutual and overlapping investments. Under this arrangement, about 60 per cent of listed companies are part of corporate groups, and even relatively small companies tend to be part of such groups (OECD, 1995). The pyramidal ownership structure helps to prevent opportunistic behaviour of member firms and the complex shareholdings makes markets for corporate control impossible in Italy. In addition, the small size of Italian firms facilitates the development of firm-specific human capital and a stable workforce in the economy.

Traditionally, the French economy is characterized by family capitalism. About 32 per cent of the 200 largest French corporations are managed by their founders or the heirs of founders (Bauer and Bertin-Mourot, 1995). Nowadays, French family capitalism has not been transformed into managerial capitalism but rather has merged with modern forms of financial capitalism (Windolf, 1998). There are two main types of networks in the French economy. The first type is called a 'holding company network' (Windolf, 1998). In this network, entrepreneurs and family clans keep control over their patrimony which is threatened by economic concentration trends such as hostile takeovers. Most families construct complex networks which have a pyramidal structure. The parent firm holds shares of its subsidiaries which in turn dominate smaller firms on a lower level. These family networks consist of a cascade of intermediate holding companies in which the family is supported by an alliance with a financial institution (Windolf, 1998). The second type of network is called 'multitier control network' (Windolf, 1998). There are three levels of control within this type of network. At the lowest level, a parent company holds a relatively high proportion of the shares of its subsidiaries. At a second level, the different groups are linked to a financial network which is dominated by the large French financial corporations. At the highest level, the large financial institutions are linked to each other by capital networks and interlocking directorates. The high ownership concentration and large overlap of capital networks provide a link between ownership and control.

The hybrid forms of corporate governance systems imply that financial institutions, legal institutions and social institutions work hand-in-hand. The lack of effective development of one institution will be supplemented by other institutions. In regard to global competitiveness, the hybrid systems in Italy and France may help explain the relative success of the small- and medium-sized firms of these countries in the global arena. This may also be the reason why corporate governance is not a big issue in these small-firm dominated economies. Nonetheless, the globalization of capital markets may lead to changes in the local capital markets of these countries. As small firms have more access to global capital markets and as this induces these smaller firms to grow larger, corporate governance issues may become more prominent. Similarly, as the European Union fosters a united currency and its economic policy favours a strong market orientation, restructuring and rationalizing across European borders will also be likely to lead to larger firms and an associated focus on corporate governance issues. Accordingly, these hybrid governance systems will have to undergo further transformation. However, the direction of the transformation is uncertain.

CONCLUSION

The past decade has given rise to a debate over the relative efficiency and competitiveness of corporate governance systems in different countries. Building on the view of complementary institutions, we argue that complementary institutions create path dependency in corporate governance. Institutions shape a development path by favouring new institutions that are spawned by the pre-existing institutions. Our theoretical framework indicates that capital markets and labour markets will reinforce each other as an effective corporate governance system evolves. We also relate congruency among institutions and corporate governance systems to corporate innovation orientations and subsequently to global competitiveness.

With globalization, the barriers of resource mobility are removed. Firms can get financial resources in the global capital markets and human resources by implementing global human resource management practices. However, at a country level, firms are still constrained by the historical institutional positioning in a nation. We argue in this manuscript that such institutional path dependency creates a significant barrier to transferring national corporate governance systems across borders. The resulting national corporate governance system which emerges has a direct effect on firm investment. Since each country has its unique corporate governance system due to different inherent institutions, we predict a distinct pattern or cluster of investments and business activities in different countries in the future. For example, corporate venturing will be typically found in the US market capitalist system, industrial groups will be prevalent in the Japanese system and small to medium-sized businesses will dominate in southern European countries.

REFERENCES

Aoki, M. (1988), *Information, Incentives, and Bargaining in the Japanese Economy*, Cambridge: Cambridge University Press.

Aoki, M., H. Patrick and P. Sheard (1994), 'The Japanese main bank systems: an introductory overview', in M. Aoki and H. Patrick (eds), *The Japanese Main Bank System: Its Relevancy for Developing and Transforming Economies*, Oxford: Oxford University Press.

Arthur, W.B. (1988), 'Self-reinforcing mechanisms in economics theory', *Journal of Political Economy*, **58**, 211–21.

Bauer, M. and B. Bertin-Mourot (1995), *L'accès au sommet des grandes entreprises françaises 1985–1994*, Paris: CNRS/Boyden.

Baysinger, B. and H.N. Butler (1985), 'Corporate governance and the board of directors: performance effects of changes in board composition', *Journal of Law, Economics and Organization*, **1**, 101–24.

Baysinger, B.D. and R.E. Hoskisson (1989), 'Diversification strategy and R&D intensity in multiproduct firms', *Academy of Management Journal*, **32** (2), 310–22.

Baysinger, B.D. and R.E. Hoskisson (1990), 'The composition of boards of directors and strategic control', *Academy of Management Review*, **15**, 72–87.

Baysinger, B.D., R.D. Kosnik and T.A. Turk (1991), 'Effects of board and ownership structure on corporate R&D strategy', *Academy of Management Journal*, **34**, 205–14.

Berglöf, E. (1990), 'Capital structure as a mechanism of control: a comparison of financial systems', in M. Aoki, B. Gustafsson and O.E. Williamson (eds), *The Firm as a Nexus of Treaties*, Part IV, chapter 11, London: Sage Publications, pp. 237–62.

Black, B.S. and R.J. Gilson (1998), 'Venture capital and the structure of capital markets: banks versus stock markets', *Journal of Financial Economics*, **47**, 243–77.

Blair, M. (1995), *Ownership and Control: Rethinking Corporate Governance for the Twenty-first Century*, Washington, DC: The Brookings Institution.

Donaldson, L. (1990), 'The ethereal hand: organizational economics and management theory', *Academy of Management Review*, **15**, 369–81.

Donaldson, L. and J.H. Davis (1991), 'Stewardship theory or agency theory: CEO governance and shareholder returns', *Australian Journal of Management*, **16**, 49–64.

Donaldson, L. and J.H. Davis (1994), 'Boards and company performance: research challenges the conventional wisdom', *Corporate Governance: An International Review*, **2** (3), 151–60.

Ezzamel, M.A., and R. Watson (1993), 'Organizational form, ownership structure, and corporate performance: a contextual empirical analysis of UK companies', *British Journal of Management*, **4** (3), 161–76.

Fama, E. and M. Jensen (1983), 'Separation of ownership and control', *Journal of Law and Economics*, **26**, 301–25.

Filatotchev, I., R.E. Hoskisson, T. Buck and M. Wright (1996), 'Corporate restructuring in Russian privatizations: implications for US investors', *California Management Review*, **38** (2), 87–105.

Francis, J. and A. Smith (1995), 'Agency costs and innovation: some empirical evidence', *Journal of Accounting and Economics*, **19**, 383–409.

Franko, L.G. (1989), 'Global corporate competition: who's winning, who's losing, and the R&D factor as one reason why', *Strategic Management Journal*, **10**, 449–74.

Froot, K., A. Perold and J. Stein (1992), 'Shareholder trading practices and corporate investment horizons', *Journal of Applied Corporate Finance*, **2**, 42–58.

Gerlach, M.L. (1992), *Alliance Capitalism: The Social Organization of Japanese Business*, CA: University of California Press.

Ghemawat, P. and R.I.J. Costa (1993), 'The organizational tension between static and dynamic efficiency', *Strategic Management Journal*, **14** (special issue), 59–73.

Gilson, R.J. and M.J. Roe (1998), 'Lifetime employment: labor peace and the evolution of Japanese corporate governance', paper presented at the Sloan Project on Corporate Governance at Columbia Law School, May 1998.

Gilson R.T. and R. Kraakman (1993), 'Investment companies as guardian shareholders: the place of the MSIC in the corporate governance debate', *Stanford Law Review*, **45**, 985–9.

Goldsmith, R. (1985), *National Balance Sheets for 20 Countries, National Bureau of Economic Research*, New Haven: Yale University Press.

Hill, C.W.L. and S.A. Snell (1988), 'External control, corporate strategy, and firm performance in research intensive industries', *Strategic Management Journal*, **9** (6), 577–90.

Hirschman, A. (1970), *Exit, Voice, and Loyalty*, Cambridge, MA: Harvard University Press.

Holmstrom, B. (1989), 'Agency costs and innovation', *Journal of Economic Behavior and Organization*, **12**, 305–27.

Hoshi, T. (1998), 'Understanding Japanese corporate governance', paper presented at the Sloan Project on Corporate Governance at Columbia Law School, May 1998.

Hoshi, T., A. Kashyap and D. Scharfstein (1990), 'The role of banks in reducing the cost of financial distress in Japan', *Journal of Financial Economics*, **27**, 67–88.

Hoskisson, R.E and M.A. Hitt (1988), 'Strategic control systems and relative R&D investment in large multiproduct firms', *Strategic Management Journal*, **9**, 605–21.

Hoskisson, R.E. and R.A. Johnson (1992), 'Corporate restructuring and strategic change: the effect on diversification strategy and R&D intensity', *Academy of Management Journal*, **13**, 625–34.

Jacobs, M. (1991), *Short-term America: The Causes and Cures of our Business*

Myopia, Boston, MA: Harvard Business School Press.

Jensen, M.C. and W.H. Meckling (1976), 'Theory of the firm: managerial behavior, agency costs and ownership structure', *Journal of Financial Economics*, **11**, 5–50.

Kaplan, S.N. (1997), 'Corporate governance and corporate performance: a comparison of Germany, Japan, and the US', in D.H. Chew (ed.), *Studies in International Corporate Finance and Governance Systems*, New York: Oxford University Press, pp. 251–8.

Kaplan, S.N. and B. Minton (1994), 'Appointments of outsiders to Japanese boards: determinants and implications for managers', *Journal of Financial Economics*, **36**, 225–58.

Keasey, K., S. Thompson and M. Wright (1997), *Corporate Governance: Economic, Management, and Financial Issues*, New York: Oxford University Press.

Kesner, I.F. (1987), 'Directors' stock ownership and organizational performance: an investigation of Fortune 500 companies', *Journal of Management*, **13**, 499–508.

Kesner, I.F. (1988), 'Directors' characteristics and committee membership: an investigation of type, occupation, tenure, and gender', *Academy of Management Journal*, **31**, 66–84.

Kester, W.C. (1991), *Japanese Takeovers: The Global Contest for Corporate Control*, Boston, MA: Harvard Business School Press.

Kim, H. and R.E. Hoskisson (1997), 'Market (United States) versus managed (Japanese) governance', in K. Keasey, S. Thompson and M. Wright (eds), *Corporate Governance: Economic, Management, and Financial Issues*, New York: Oxford University Press.

Knack, S. and P. Keefer (1997), 'Does social capital have an economic payoff? A cross-country investigation', *Quarterly Journal of Economics*, 1251–88.

Kogut, B. and U. Zander (1992), 'Knowledge of the firm, combinative capabilities, and the replication of technology', *Organization Science*, **3**, 383–97.

Kogut, B. and U. Zander (1996), 'What firms do? Coordination, identity, and learning', *Organization Science*, **7** (5), 502–18.

La Porta, R., F. Lopez-de-Silanes and A. Shleifer (1999), 'Corporate ownership around the world', *Journal of Finance*, **54** (2), 471–517.

Laverty, K.J. (1996), 'Economic "short-termism": the debate, the unresolved issues, and the implications for management practice and research', *Academy of Management Review*, **21**, 825–60.

Levinthal, D.A. and J.G. March (1993), 'The myopia of learning', *Strategic Management Journal*, **14**, 95–112.

Macey, J.M. and G.P. Miller (1995), 'Corporate governance and commercial banking: a comparative examination of Germany, Japan, and the United States', *Stanford Law Review*, **48** (1), 73–112.

Macey, J.R. (1998), 'Italian corporate governance: one American's perspective', *Columbia Business Law Review*, **1**, 121–44.

Mansfield, E. (1988), 'Industrial R&D in Japan and the United States: a comparative study', *American Economic Review*, **78** (20), 223–28.

March, J.G. (1991), 'Exploration and exploitation in organizational learning', *Organization Science*, **2**, 71–87.

Mayer, C. (1998), 'Financial systems and corporate governance: a review of the internal evidence', *Journal of Institutional and Theoretical Economics*, **154**, 144–65.

Milgrom, P. and J. Roberts (1995), 'Complementarities and fit strategy, structure, and organizational change in manufacturing', *Journal of Accounting and Economics*,

19, 179–208.

Narayanan, M. (1985a), 'Managerial incentives for short term results', *Journal of Finance*, **5**, 1469–84.

Narayanan, M. (1985b), 'Observability and payback criterion', *Journal of Business*, **58**, 309–23.

OECD (1995), *OECD Economic Surveys: Italy*, Paris: OECD, 59–60.

Pauly, L.W. and S. Reich (1997), 'National structures and multinational corporate behavior: enduring differences in the age of globalization', *International Organization*, **51** (1), 1–30.

Pearce, J.A. and S.A. Zahra (1992), 'Board compensation from a strategic contingency perspective', *Journal of Management Studies*, **29**, 411–38.

Porter, M.E. (1992), 'Capital disadvantages: America's failing capital investment system', *Harvard Business Review*, **62** (3), 65–82.

Porter, M.E. (1996), 'Competitive advantage, agglomeration economies, and regional policy', *International Regional Science Review*, **19**, 85.

Porter, M.E. (1997), 'Capital choices: changing the way America invests in industry', in D.H. Chew (ed.), *Studies in International Corporate Finance and Governance Systems*, New York: Oxford University Press, pp. 5–17.

Prahalad, C.K. (1997), 'Corporate governance or corporate value added? Rethinking the primacy of shareholder value', in D.H. Chew (ed.), *Studies in International Corporate Finance and Governance Systems*, New York: Oxford University Press, pp. 46–56.

Roe, M. (1994), *Strong Managers Weak Owners: The Political Roots of American Corporate Finance*, Princeton, NJ: Princeton University Press.

Rosenstein, S. and J.G. Wyatt (1990), 'Outside directors, board independence, and shareholder wealth', *Journal of Financial Economics*, **26**, 175–91.

Sachs, J.D. (1999), 'The year in review', *The Global Competitiveness Report 1998*, Geneva: World Economic Forum.

Sah, RK. (1991), 'Fallibility in human organizations and political systems', *Journal of Economic Perspectives*, **5** (2), 67–88.

Sampler, J.L. (1998), 'Redefining industry structure for the information age', *Strategic Management Journal*, **19**, 343–61.

Schellenger, M.H., D. Wood and A. Tashakori (1989), 'Board of directors composition, shareholder wealth, and dividend policy', *Journal of Management*, **15**, 457–67.

Sheard, P. (1994), 'Interlocking shareholdings and corporate governance', in M. Aoki and R. Dore (eds), *The Japanese Firm: Sources of Competitive Strength*, New York: Oxford University Press, pp. 310–44.

Stein, J. (1988), 'Takeover threats and managerial myopia', *Journal of Political Economy*, **96**, 61–80.

Stein, J. (1989), 'Efficient capital market, inefficient firms: a model of myopic corporate behaviour', *Quarterly Journal of Economics* (Nov.), 655–99.

Tushman, M.L. and C.A. O'Reilly (1996), 'Ambidextrous organizations: managing evolutionary and revolutionary change', *California Management Review*, **38** (4) (Summer), 8–30.

Useem, M. (1992), *Investor Capitalism: How Money Managers Are Changing the Face of Corporate America*, New York: Basic Books.

Utterback, J.M. (1994), *Mastering the Dynamics of Innovation: How Companies Can Seize Opportunities in the Face of Technological Change*, Boston: Harvard Business School Press.

Williamson, O. (1985), *Economic Institutions of Capitalism*, New York: Free Press.

Williamson, O. (1987), 'Corporate finance and corporate governance, economic analysis and policy', Working Paper No. EAP-26, Berkeley, CA: University of California.

Windolf, P. (1998), 'The governance structure of large French corporations: a comparative perspective', paper presented at the Sloan Project on Corporate Governance at Columbia Law School, May 1998.

Yoffie, D.B. (1996), 'Competing in the age of digital convergence', *California Management Review*, **38** (4), 31–53.

Zahra, S.A. (1996), 'Governance, ownership, and corporate entrepreneurship: the moderating impact of industry technological opportunities', *Academy of Management Journal*, **39**, 1713–35.

Zajac, E.J. and J.D. Westphal (1994), 'The costs and benefits of managerial incentives and monitoring in large US corporations: when is more not better?', *Strategic Management Journal*, **15** (Winter Special Issue), 121–42.

Zenger, T.R (1992), 'Why do employers only reward extreme performance? Examining the relationships among performance, pay, and turnover', *Administrative Science Quarterly*, **37**, 198–219.

Zysman, J. (1983), *Governments, Market, and Growth: Financial Systems and the Politics of Industrial Change*, Ithaca, NY: Cornell University Press.

5. Macromanagement patterns and corporate governance

Gavin Boyd

Deepening integration in the global political economy is a vast process of largely ungoverned systems transformation and structural linking, through trade and transnational production and the internationalization of financial markets. Industrial capabilities are altered as more competitive firms gain cross-border market strengths, to the disadvantage of weaker enterprises. In this entrepreneurial activity the principal agents of change are large corporations that have emerged from systems of corporate governance in the major industrialized democracies. These corporations operate under the influence of policy level interactions between the US, the European Union and Japan. The interactions result as governments in this Triad pattern endeavour to increase the shares of their economies in the overall spread of gains from deepening integration through improvements in structural competitiveness and through bargaining over issues of market access.

Differing degrees of guidance and control over the evolution of structural interdependencies are possible for national administrations and corporate groups. The US, because of the size of its economy and its level of industrialization, has potent leverage to secure access to foreign markets, but has less policy level influence on the development of its nation's structural linkages than Japan, as international firms based in its economy operate very independently, and its political tradition obligates aloofness from industry and commerce.

The Japanese political economy is rather highly integrated, and thus has a superior capacity to enhance its structural competitiveness. Overall changes in the Triad pattern of structural linkages, however, tend to be advantageous for the US, as its firms, although relating distantly to its administration, are the largest and most numerous in the rivalry for world market shares. The Japanese political economy has been weakened by acute strains in its financial sector and in those of industrializing East Asian states which have drawn much of its direct investment. The European Union lags in structural competitiveness, and can exert pressures on issues of market openness only under constraints set by dependence on trade with and investment in the US.

There is a rough balance in cross-investment, on an historical cost basis, but the large US corporate presence in the Union is structurally much more significant than the European counterpart in the US.

A market-driven balance in the spread of gains from commerce in the Triad and in the global economy is not in prospect. Market forces become more active across borders, but firms with larger resources and higher levels of competitiveness gain international oligopoly power, and there are disparities in the spread of benefits from commerce because of contrasts in structural competitiveness and economic openness. The acquisition of international oligopoly power is not significantly hindered by collaborative competition policies, and the policy level interactions over issues of market openness, in which relative bargaining strengths have great importance, on balance work to the advantage of US firms, especially those operating in Europe.

Interdependencies between governments and firms become more significant, functionally and politically, in the Triad pattern, as rivalries in the uneven structural linking continue. Macromanagement achievements depend on the alignment of home country corporate strategies with structural policy objectives which have to be set in terms of the capabilities of national firms. These firms depend on the efforts of governments to build infrastructures, sponsor the development of social capital and provide efficient systems of contractual governance. The administrative–corporate interdependencies evolve more spontaneously and become more extensive in communitarian political economies, notably Japan and Germany, than in individualistic political economies, such as the US and Britain.

Corporate management of interdependencies with governments is influenced by systems of corporate governance, insofar as these shape intra-firm dynamics, intercorporate relations and managerial orientations towards ways of combining international expansion with the productive use of forms of policy level support. In communitarian political economies systems of corporate governance are based on concepts of social solidarity, focusing on interdependencies between management, workers, shareholders, suppliers, distributors, financing institutions and related firms. In individualistic political economies the systems of corporate governance identify management as the agent of shareholders, subject to discipline in markets for corporate control, and the interests of workers are virtually excluded from the agency responsibilities of management.

In the latter system of corporate governance the agency role of management relates exclusively to shareholder interests in maximum returns, over short terms. Macromanagement concerns regarding the overall development of the national economic structure tend to be excluded, and the policy level is dealt with distantly, while relations with other firms tend to be entirely competitive. Solidarity-based systems of corporate governance generate commitments to integrative intra-firm and intercorporate cooperation and to collaboration with structural policy endeavours. Deepening integration thus presents different challenges for policymakers in the two types of political economies with their contrasting systems of corporate governance.

ANALYTICAL PERSPECTIVES

Studies of macromanagement trends and issues in deepening integration have generally not been linked with research on the dynamics of systems of corporate governance. One reason for this has been a neglect of the significance of structural interdependencies in globalization, and of structural policies in the management of microeconomic policy interdependencies.[1] Macro- and microeconomic policies, however, have to respond to the opportunities and problems of deepening integration in ways that enlist corporate cooperation. At a fundamental input level globalization entails losses of government revenue as firms move production abroad, yet allocations to assist and shelter sectors disadvantaged by outward direct investment and by competing imports tend to increase.[2] The dynamics of interest representation in the policy process can therefore change. Outcomes in states with communitarian cultures may well be managed more effectively, through administrative–corporate cooperation, than in states with individualistic cultures.[3] This may be possible because of imperatives for technological collaboration which become stronger as advances in frontier research continue, and because imperatives to concert entrepreneurial endeavours also become stronger as industrialized economies become more complex, through the multiplication of specializations given impetus by technological advances.[4]

Research on corporate structures and functions in conditions of intensifying competition has included work on the efficiencies of coordinated intra-firm specializations made possible through the relational cooperation between management and workers in which tacit knowledge is developed and shared in very active communication flows based on organizational loyalties. This capabilities perspective, influenced by studies of Japanese firms, identifies functional logic associated with solidarity-based systems of corporate governance in which the stakeholders are workers as well as management and shareholders, and in which the interests of stakeholders are linked extensively in stable patterns of intercorporate relations.[5]

The corporate capabilities perspective has been developed with insights into innovation processes that have depended on accumulations of tacit knowledge, with synergies resulting from strong task orientations.[6] An alternative perspective, which has been more influential in Anglo–American studies of corporate governance systems, has focused on managements as agents of shareholders operating as opportunistic investors. Questions about managerial interests and efficiencies, and about the entitlements of investors, have been given much attention.[7] A stream of this literature has concentrated on problems of international competitiveness resulting from the emphasis on short-term profitability in US firms, under pressures from shareholders. The attention given to problems of competitiveness, meanwhile, has been related to research on policy level responses to the costs and benefits of globalization.[8]

Losses of economic sovereignty are associated with the losses of revenue experienced by governments as firms produce more abroad than at home for foreign markets and source more from abroad for their home markets. The transnational enterprises gain increasing scope for independent initiatives as they expand their international operations while exploiting alternative location advantages and the investment bidding of host governments.[9] Managements tend to lose home country attachments and loyalties and seek to reduce home country regulatory as well as tax exposure. The macro-management tasks of governments, however, have to cope with the costs of the outward movement of production processes and the restructuring of firms gaining international oligopoly power while driving weaker enterprises into declines.[10] The involvement of other governments in corporate rivalries which drive that global concentration trend also has to be reckoned with. Representations of interests by groups experiencing losses and insecurity in the course of globalization, meanwhile, obligate macromanagement endeavours to engage more actively with structural, trade, foreign direct investment and competition policy issues. Hence systems of corporate governance, because of their influence on the strategic orientations of firms, become more significant for the implementation of policy mixes.

General economic openness, facilitating further advances in globalization, does not promise harmonious interdependent development. Market failures as well as market efficiencies became internationalized. Governmental collaboration for constructive responses through structural, trade and other initiatives is not forthcoming, mainly because of competitive policy orientations.[11] Meanwhile independent corporate operations tend to contribute more actively to the internationalized market failures as well as efficiencies, notably by driving global concentration trends. This vast process gives rise to extremely complex asymmetric interdependencies, and these are all the more challenging for concerned policymakers because of the involvement of government failures as well as achievements. Prominent processes in the Triad pattern are the effects of prolonged heavy deficit spending and inadequately restrained speculation in the US, coupled with high-volume government debt. Assessments of the dynamics of globalization have to take into account the danger of losses of international investor confidence which could have severe effects through the Triad pattern.[12]

The significance of issues of advanced political development, in Europe and Japan as well as the US, becomes apparent when macromanagement deficiencies interact with problems of internationalized market failure. Imperatives for systemic adjustment and harmonious evolution become evident, and these have implications for systems of corporate governance as formative influences on the roles of firms in deepening integration.

GOVERNMENT AND CORPORATE INTERDEPENDENCIES

In deepening integration, because of the growth and employment effects of structural changes and of shifts in gains from global commerce, interactions between governments increase and become more complex. Efforts are made to change degrees of market access for the advantage of national firms, structural policy endeavours react to those of rival governments and each administration's macroeconomic policies have effects in conjunction with those of other administrations. Relative bargaining strengths alter, and for states disadvantaged in this respect imperatives to enhance structural competitiveness and to secure allies in the struggles for world markets become more compelling.

While there are rises in policy interdependencies there are also rises in interdependencies between governments and firms.[13] Enlisting corporate cooperation becomes more necessary for structural policies, especially to the extent that these are oriented toward forming balanced diversified patterns of sectoral linkages. Emphasis on providing market-friendly location advantages tends to be extended into offers of incentives to attract investment in production ventures, thus drawing enterprises into forms of dependence. Official support for the development of new technology, meanwhile, becomes an important means of encouraging firms to maintain operations in the home economy and of forming consultative links with them that can induce sensitivities to structural policy concerns.[14]

The pattern of policy interdependencies in the Triad is closely linked with the very extensive pattern of interdependencies between governments and firms. The market and structural effects are especially significant in relations between the US and Japan, as the Japanese administration's informal links with its economic associations and industry groups are essential for its efforts to maintain the structural competitiveness of its economy while interacting with the US government over issues of reciprocal market access.[15] For the US government its lack of close consultative ties with American firms is a disadvantage in the interactions with Japan. US policymakers have to cope with the same disadvantage in relations with the European Union, but the asymmetries are on balance favourable because firms in the major European states, although advantaged by collaborative links with their administrations, generally lack international competitiveness.[16]

Triad policy interdependencies are dominated by the US, because of its bargaining strengths, the persistence of national rivalries which hinder complete political and economic integration in the European Union, and the absence of substantial policy level and societal links between that Union and Japan. In this configuration the USA's policy mix, determined with little responsiveness to Europe or Japan, has the most extensive effects, through the strong import drawing effects of high internal demand, attributable mainly to prolonged fiscal stimulus and speculative asset appreciation.[17] The resulting balance of payments deficits motivate efforts to externalize the costs of adjustment by pressing for Japanese and European fiscal expansion. The European Monetary Union, as an institution obligating fiscal discipline, is a strong source of resistance to the pressure for expansionary policies, although these have considerable appeal to groups throughout the European Union that are concerned about its high rates of unemployment.[18]

The regulation of international financial markets has been an issue in Triad policy interdependencies, primarily because of the very active roles of US financial institutions in those markets. Taking advantage of low interest rates in Europe and Japan, these institutions have drawn investment into extensive foreign as well as domestic speculative operations. These have become more and more closely linked, with dangers of destabilization that have persisted mainly because of the reluctance of US financial interests and policymakers to support proposals for strong prudential regulation of the internationalized financial markets.[19] The dangers of destabilization have been very significant because of problems of informational market failure, which cause herd behaviour by the speculators and which result from the sheer volume of their operations. A critical factor in this context is the confidence of speculators in the US's overall investment position: this confidence can be affected by the US's high debt level, its large balance of payments deficits, and the uncertain sustainability of its levels of asset appreciation.[20]

European governments, especially the French administration, have sought international support for effective regulation of world financial markets, but political will for this has been lacking in the European Union, partly because of a lack of enthusiasm in the highly internationalized British financial community and its ties with that in the US.[21] Japanese financial interests and policymakers are not well placed to press for reform in international financial markets, because of the dependence of their manufacturing interests on exports to the USA, but in those markets they are advantaged by the solidarity of their intercorporate system and of their political economy as a system of alliance capitalism.[22]

Microeconomic policy interdependencies in the Triad form a very imbalanced pattern in which solidarity-based forms of protection in Japan and to a lesser extent in the European Union are countered by US trade policy activism, directed in part against European and Japanese structural policies. These structural policies, especially the latter, are facilitated at fundamental levels by national systems of corporate governance. These are the basic source of resistance to US pressures for reduced European and Japanese structural policy activism, but in Europe this opposition is fragmented and is to a degree countered by the European Commission's endeavours to enhance the region's structural competitiveness by promoting more active intrazonal corporate competition.[23]

Trade policy interdependencies, evolving to a considerable extent in separate interactions between the US and the European Union, and the US and Japan, evidence the effects of strong American bargaining strengths but also of constraints on the use of those strengths because of the great importance of the European market for US firms and the dependence of the US administration on the confidence of Japanese investors holding US government debt. American management of the Atlantic trade policy interdependencies seeks wider access to the European Union market, but the relationship tends to become more difficult as the Union adds new members and as its monetary union provides conditions for more comprehensive integration in its single market and for initiatives to enhance its structural competitiveness. Market opening leverage applied against Japan can be more potent, but Japanese investor confidence remains a critical factor while stock market speculation in the US approaches unsustainable levels and the overall US investment position becomes more negative.[24]

Competition policy interdependencies, notably relating to large-scale Atlantic mergers and acquisitions, are managed on an ad hoc basis between US anti-trust authorities and the European Commission, with sensitivities to the high levels of cross-investment that have been rising since the formation of the Union's single market.[25] European direct investment in the US has been responding to high production costs and government costs in the home economies, and to the US's higher growth rates, while US direct investment in the Union has been attracted by opportunities to consolidate the strong American corporate presence, which is still advantaged by the generally weaker resources of Union firms. European structural policy endeavours, which could be supported by increases in solidarity in response to Atlantic trade frictions, may well reduce competition policy cooperation between the US and the Union.

Competition policy issues between the US and Japan, resulting from American efforts to encourage Japanese implementation of measures that would reduce the pervasive relational cooperation in the national intercorporate system, have been intractable.[26] Reciprocity, sought because of the openness of the US system, has not been acceptable on the Japanese side because of the intensity of intercorporate solidarity. The cultural and moral basis for this is a source of efficiencies that can offset the strengths which US firms acquire through entrenched positions in their large home market.

In Atlantic relations the competition policy interdependencies are related to the interactive effects of US efforts to provide market-friendly environments for international firms and European endeavours to provide such environments with competing attractions, including diverse subsidies. On each side there are concerns to encourage national firms to maintain very substantial operations in the home economy, but the incentives motivating direct investment each way remain strong, in part because of very uncertain prospects for transregional trade liberalization.[27]

Interdependencies between firms, domestically and internationally, multiply in deepening integration: technological advances expand the scope for complementary specializations and wider information-sharing is necessary for the advantages of entrepreneurial cooperation. Management of the interdependencies can aggravate or overcome problems of market failure as these assume cross-border dimensions and may assist adjustment to problems of government failure.

The corporate interdependencies are especially evident in centres of agglomeration where there are dynamic clusters of innovative activities. Agglomerative logic is more advanced in the well-integrated US market than in the still somewhat fragmented European market, where industrial clusters are less developed but more numerous. In the US, close and intense interactions within the industrial clusters raise levels of trust and general awareness of potentials for entrepreneurial collaboration, thus contributing to interdependent growth that can meet shareholder expectations and provide greater stability in the pattern of intercorporate relations.[28] The European industrial clusters constitute more restricted applications of agglomeration logic, because of the influence of different systems of corporate governance and structural policies. The systems of corporate governance are gradually being interpenetrated with the evolution of cross-border subregional patterns of industrial activity, but it clearly will be difficult for the Union to develop a common system of corporate governance.[29] Cross-border European mergers and acquisitions have been increasing since the formation of the European Monetary Union but regional financial markets remain quite segmented.[30]

In Japan corporate interdependencies are at high levels because of strong solidarity in its integrated political economy, which has been continually reinforced by the collective efficiency effects of that solidarity – effects which thus sustain consensus in support of the system of corporate governance.[31] Agglomeration logic is operative because of severe spatial limitations, and the resultant levels of intercorporate cooperation tend to be extended into the formation of integrated systems of international production in areas receiving major flows of Japanese foreign direct investment.

Intercorporate interdependencies in the US outside its areas of industrial clustering receive limited recognition in entrepreneurial decision making because of informational problems, low levels of trust and intensely competitive relations between firms. The strongly individualistic culture which pervades the system of corporate governance tends to perpetuate the informational problems and the low levels of trust – that is in conjunction with the ways in which antitrust enforcement discourages cooperation between firms.[32] Incentives to form alliances based on emerging or planned complementarities influence managements, notably in high technology sectors, but opportunities to develop these in foreign operations appear to assume greater significance, because antitrust enforcement has a mainly domestic orientation.

MACROMANAGEMENT IN DEEPENING INTEGRATION

Because of the rises in corporate, corporate–government and inter-governmental interdependencies, deepening integration tightens functional and political linkages between macro- and microeconomic policies. This happens more coherently in communitarian political economies than in those with individualistic cultures, as these tend to be sources of problems of governance that become more serious because of the difficulties of managing the costs of globalization.

Government resources decline because of tax losses associated with outflows of investment into foreign operations. In varying degrees these may be balanced by inward direct investment, but this can involve limited tax exposure and both the inward and outward direct investment may involve increasing emphasis on production in low-cost locations. The costs of sheltering and compensating adversely affected sectors increase because of the structural and market changes resulting from competitive pressures in globalization. The attractions of lower–cost foreign locations thus increase for firms, and these attractions can be all the more significant if shifts in interest representation cause governments to adopt policies less favourable to corporate operations.[33]

Imperatives to enhance structural competitiveness are thus recognized in varying degrees as primary tasks of macromanagement, and tend to demand comprehensive engagement. A fundamental requirement is to increase the utility of the entire policy mix through securing extensive corporate cooperation – inducing national firms to plan and contract more with each other, and to locate substantial shares of their operations at home. The encouragement of intercorporate cooperation can increase managerial interest in maintaining and extending home country operations, but firms expanding their international activities have increasingly important incentives to exploit foreign location advantages in their quests for world market shares. These incentives tend to be more potent for firms based in individualistic political economies than for those operating out of communitarian states; in the latter stronger intercorporate bonds, higher levels of trust, and closer as well as more productive links between management and the policy level cause retention of home country ties. These ties are advantageous in the management of foreign operations and can balance tendencies to build industrial capacity at external locations, as has been evident in the strategies of German firms, which have emphasized serving external markets mainly through exports.[34]

In individualistic political economies liberal policy orientations, it must be stressed, cause reliance on the provision of market-friendly environments: these are intended to ensure the enhancement of structural competitiveness while balancing the attraction of foreign locations. Relatively weak home country ties, however, tend to be evident as firms devote more and more resources to high volume production abroad, exploiting foreign location advantages in generally independent quests for world market shares. Meanwhile national policy processes, more internally conflicted than in communitarian states, tend to result in less functional policy mixes, in effect diminishing the value of home country ties for firms seeking opportunities in global markets.

Systems of corporate governance in communitarian political economies function within patterns of internalization logic that constitute advanced forms of alliance capitalism. Firms, operating as relational rather than arm's-length expressions of internalization logic, are active in virtual applications of that logic at industry group levels, where corporate operations are coordinated through information flows and consultations, on the basis of shared concepts of interdependent specializations and reciprocal obligations. These patterns of network coordination, moreover, tend to evolve in alignment with structural policies, through mutually responsive interaction.[35]

Destabilization threatens, however, when international competitive pressures cause structural disruptions, prodution costs increase because of the demands of employees as stakeholders and government costs rise because of adjustment allocations. Such strains have been evident in Germany, causing its system of corporate governance to conform less to the stakeholder model in an integrated political economy.[36] A high degree of integration has to be maintained in a communitarian political economy in order to cope with competing imports, adapt structurally and avoid increases in government costs while becoming more deeply involved in the world economy. The linkages between macro- and microeconomic policies have to be managed very effectively and much effort has to be devoted to building solidarity, especially insofar as this can moderate and cope with intrusions into the economy through trade and foreign direct investment.

Germany's situation is exceptional, as the communitarian political economy has to function within an integrating regional political economy. The limited mobility of capital in the Union and the superior resources of German firms are advantages, but gradual penetration of the economy by other Union firms through exports and direct investment has to be accepted while German enterprises expand within the Union. Penetration by US corporations also has to be accepted while German exports to and direct investment in the US increase, partly in response to slack growth in the rest of the Union.[37]

Macromanagement in individualistic political economies, relying on market-friendly structural endeavours, depends very much on the dynamics of autonomous corporate evolution. A very demanding requirement is the implementation of highly functional macro- and microeconomic policies, without the alternating biases, disjointedness and experimentation that can be caused by strong pluralism in contexts of weak institutional development. Problems of macromanagement that increase the costs and uncertainties of operating in the home economy will increase corporate interest in foreign operations, and the capacities to engage in such operations are likely to be substantial if the home economy is large and major firms have been able to consolidate domestic market positions. In the US, the principal Triad political economy with an individualistic culture, firms that have gained strength by exploiting the opportunities of its large internal market have superior resources for the support of international operations. The degree of market friendliness at home, however, is affected by the costs of government and by the dangers of a financial crisis, in view of the overall debt level and the strong speculative thrust in asset appreciation.[38]

Triad macromanagement endeavours to enhance structural competitiveness, while concerned with balances between the development of industrial capacity at home and investment in foreign production, have to deal with issues in industrial funding. The dimensions of these issues are affected by systems of corporate governance and by the evolution of financial markets. With the internationalization of these markets, institutions compete to provide investors with opportunities to maximize short-term yields. Firms thus have to compete more and more on a global basis for funding by demonstrating potentials for high short-term returns, and this obligates much emphasis on financial management, generally with low spending on research and development and neglect of opportunities for long-term planning.[39] Managers have incentives to exploit funding opportunities in financial markets but also to limit dependence on such funding by using internal funds for expansion. Across the Triad reliance on internal financing is very high.[40] Contrasts in industrial funding between communitarian and individualistic political economies, however, are very significant.

Stable preferential 'insider' industrial financing on a relational basis accords with macromanagement objectives in a communitarian political economy. Drifts of investment into international financial markets would work against those objectives, and would tend to increase if opportunities were provided by regulatory changes and any weakening of systemic solidarity. In macromanagement perspectives giving prominence to that solidarity, moreover, vulnerabilities to the destabilizing potential of very high volume speculative flows in world financial markets have to be avoided.[41]

Macromanagement in an individualistic political economy has to reckon with the consequences of securities-based industrial financing. While this funding tends to obligate short-termism, investor pressures give managements significant incentives to expand production abroad, because of its higher profitability and its opportunities to reduce dependence on home country investors while securing funding from foreign investors remote from those in the domestic economy. Increased use of securities funding enables firms to extend foreign production while exploiting investment-bidding rivalries between home and host governments.[42] Motivations to take advantage of such rivalries can be strong because of weak solidarity in an individualistic political economy.

Throughout the Triad macromanagement endeavours depend, at fundamental levels, on forms of social capital. These become increasingly significant, in deepening integration, for efficiencies in intercorporate cooperation and for productive political cooperation. Both types of cooperation are necessary on a large scale for the development of a political economy as a system capable of managing complex structural interdependencies.[43] Solidarity-based corporate governance can make large contributions to the development of social capital. Changes in business practices that can help to introduce stakeholder concepts of corporate governance into individualistic political economies can assist governmental performance: with the promise of increasing X efficiencies there can also be prospects for more developed forms of alliance capitalism.[44]

CORPORATE GOVERNANCE IN DEEPENING INTEGRATION

As basic determinants of corporate cultures, structures and dynamics the Triad systems of corporate governance influence the evolution of American, European and Japanese structural interdependencies. Differing degrees of firm level efficiencies, industry group efficiencies and structural capacities in the leading industrialized states evidence the effects of functional contrasts between corporate governance patterns associated with competitive or cooperative managerial capitalism. Arm's-length low-trust contracting with a short-term financial focus, organized with strong top-down bureaucratic discipline, drives the first type of capitalism and has distinctive structural effects in deepening integration. Relational high-trust long-term contracting with stakeholder and community orientations, organized collegially, drives the second form of capitalism, with capacities for coordinated adjustment in the multiplication of structural interdependencies.[45]

The structural linking of highly industrialized states in deepening integration is a context in which interactions of competitive and cooperative corporate activity evidence the functional logic of coordinating specializations in forms of alliance capitalism. How such ventures evolve depend on basic orientations influenced by the differing systems of corporate governance. These systems are in turn influenced by forms of political change, with the multiplying interdependencies between firms and governments. Because of the increasing functional significance of coordination imperatives for management of those interdependencies the logic of alliance capitalism can be complemented by a logic of alliance politics. This develops spontaneously in communitarian political economies, in recognition of the efficiency and welfare effects of consensual rather than adversarial policymaking.[46]

Deepening integration tends to have divisive effects in highly industrialized states that lack capacities for coordinated adjustment to market and structural linking caused by the independent operations of numerous foreign and home country firms. Stakeholder corporate governance in a system of alliance capitalism and alliance politics tends to facilitate harmonious market and structural linking, although with dangers of opportunistic exploitation of established patterns of trust. Securities-based corporate governance in a system of competitive managerial capitalism and adversarial politics leaves the way open for disjointed market and structural linking, posing coordination problems which are difficult to resolve.

In securities-based corporate governance firms operate under pressures from managements motivated by high rewards who are responsive primarily to shareholder demands and to the dangers of an active market for corporate control. Radical innovations of potential significance for international competitiveness have been claimed to be possible because of the dynamism of managements and their scope for forceful direction of their staffs, but their concerns with short-term financial returns have been considered to be responsible for myopic attitudes to investment in new technology.[47] Contributions to the development of social capital have been generally considered to be negative, with effects in intercorporate relations that have hindered adjustment to the strains of deepening integration, while also making constructive policy level responses more difficult.

Solidarity-based systems of corporate governance are sources of more collaborative dynamism, with efficiencies resulting from more spontaneous concerting of task orientations. Managements are freer to concentrate on long-term strategies for technology development, product improvement, and diversification, with confidence in supportive financing and collaborative bonds with other firms.[48] The solidarity facilitates the development of foreign production with more intercorporate partnering that is normally possible for firms based in individualistic political economies and can promise more effective coordination of international operations with industry group and other partners in the home economy.

For all Triad international firms the benefits of operating in numerous host countries tend to be increasingly substantial, in terms of reduced home country tax and regulatory exposure, income-shifting, opportunities for foreign acquisitions and the exploitation of investment-bidding rivalries between governments, as well as the expanding scope for access to external financing. All these advantages are exploited on a larger scale by American enterprises than by their European and Japanese rivals, as the dimensions of US international corporate activities are much greater. The pattern of these activities, exhibiting a concentration on Europe that has tended to increase with the economic strains in East Asia, has indicated how home country shareholder pressures can be managed while foreign financing becomes more available and larger internal resources are acquired. Home country investors' expectations of high short-term returns can thus be met. As most research and development activity remains in the home country, however, the restrictive effects of emphasis on financial management on investment in new technology may remain significant.

The formative influence of national systems of corporate governance is more significant and more enduring in Europe, where firms have generally weaker resources for ventures in international production, and therefore less scope for foreign operations that can become increasingly independent.[49] The evolution of a common securities-based system of corporate governance for the European Union has been advocated for the financing and expansion of the region's firms. However, the structural policy concerns of member governments, which have been noted, and their sensitivities to the interests of their economic elites, which have been influenced by national systems of corporate law and corporate finance, make convergence toward a common system very unlikely.[50]

The US economy is the main external attraction for European foreign direct investment, but this constitutes a fragmented pattern in which Britain has the largest direct investment position in the US, on a historical cost basis, and Germany's position is small in relation to the size of its economy, but is more significant in mature and high-technology sectors. In this pattern German firms are advantaged by the solidarity of their home intercorporate system, which is all the more significant because of the size of the Germany economy and its central role as a base for expansion into the rest of the Union.[51]

The systemic significance of corporate governance in Japan is the principal contrast with the American system's influence on the incentives for its home country firms to expand internationally. Japanese managerial motivations draw on the strengths of intercorporate solidarity at home in the development of foreign operations, which thus assume integrated patterns and facilitate concerted management of the home country's structural interdependencies, with asymmetries that limit vulnerabilities to foreign penetration through trade and direct investment. The resources supporting this expansion of foreign production and trade are larger than those sustaining the extra European operations of German firms, and the Japanese corporate presence in the US is strategically much more significant than that of the Europeans and much less open to assimilation into the US system of corporate finance.[52] The Japanese involvement in the US, moreover, is more extensive than it is in Europe, where corporate and government resistance to its penetration has been substantial, especially in France and Italy. US firms experience less Japanese competition in Europe than they do in their home economy, and the representation of their interests in Brussels, which is on a large scale and highly operational, encounters no significant Japanese competition.[53]

In the Triad pattern the American system of corporate governance is exceptional because of the high volume of US foreign direct investment (stock and flow) and because, with related volumes of portfolio investment, it has great significance in international financial markets. The massive trading of securities in these markets has developed primarily because of the availability of forms of US corporate finance, in vast numbers, and because these have benefited from upward pressures associated with the general asset appreciation in US stock markets, and with the attraction of European and Japanese investment by large American financial institutions for speculative global operations.[54]

The internationalization of financial markets has led to increased efficiencies as investments have flowed to institutions offering higher returns, mainly with overall benefits for US firms, including those reducing dependence on home financing by extending their foreign operations. There are very serious risks of instability, however, because competitive pressures tend to motivate risky speculative manipulations, and failures of these can trigger herd behaviour. In this context the significance of corporate financing arrangements in the US has great importance, not only because they are major sources of the flows into world financial markets but also because destabilizing potentials in those markets, attributable in a large measure to the scale of operations by US financial institutions, have serious implications for the US. The risks for the US economy are greater than those for Europe because of the more limited involvement of Union firms in global finance, and because of the uncertainties confronting international investors, as noted, on account of the US's high debt levels, its large current account deficits and its degrees of speculative asset appreciation.[55]

MACROMANAGEMENT, CORPORATE GOVERNANCE AND STRUCTURAL CHANGE

Liberal macromanagement in the US facilitates and in effect gives impetus to the most substantial process of structural change in the Triad: the evolution of imbalanced Atlantic structural linkages. These are altering the settings in which US and European systems of corporate governance are changing. The large-scale structural linking is ungoverned, except to modest degrees on the European side; it represents the effects of market forces, with efficiencies and failures that are challenges for governments and firms. Imperatives for microeconomic policy cooperation are evident, with imperatives for spontaneous corporate endeavours to produce dynamic Atlantic structural harmony.

The most active market forces in the Atlantic pattern are the operations of US firms in Europe. Their sales in the Union are several times larger than Germany's exports to other Union members, and they are well placed to consolidate their positions because of the weaker roles of Union firms in the single market and in the rest of the world. Their expansion is aided by superior internal funding and their capacities to draw investment from European sources as well as from their home economy; they are also aided by investment bidding rivalries between member states in the Union, in which Britain is prominent because of the liberal environment provided for foreign firms. There are incentives to strengthen the involvement in Europe in advance of Union structural initiatives that might attempt to enhance the competitiveness of firms in member countries while introducing regulatory restraints on activities by outside enterprises.[56]

The American corporate presence in Europe is an influential force working for Atlantic trade and investment liberalization, in line with US foreign economic policy. Modest Union restraints on imports from the US, however, receive broad support in Europe because of the weaker competitiveness of Union firms, despite general awareness that US market penetration can stimulate increases in the efficiencies of European enterprises. Reactions to American market opening pressures contribute to the consensus on maintaining some degrees of protection for the single market: these pressures are directed mainly at the Union's agricultural protectionism, and arouse especially strong antipathies in France. Union attitudes are also influenced by US opposition to the large-scale subsidization of the Airbus consortium; for the industrialized members especially this large high-technology project has great cross-sectoral significance.[57] Further development of the project is a clear structural imperative, and its success thus far raises questions about the evolution of the automobile sector, which has wide-ranging implications for numerous Union industries. A relatively larger number of moderately-sized firms in the Union automobile industry have to contend with strong competition by American enterprises, advantaged by their strengths in their home market. The formation of a stronger European sector is hindered by the stuctural policy rivalries between the larger member states and, it must be stressed, the distinctly national characteristics of their systems of corporate finance and law.

The capacity of the American corporate presence to promote structural change is all the more significant because highly competitive financial services are components of that presence and are backed by large resources in the home economy. US financial institutions, basing their operations in Britain because of London's pre-eminence as an international financial centre, are extending their activities in continental cities with relatively small stock markets. These have been expanding because of the efforts of a growing number of German, French and other Union firms to secure financing for larger European operations. A lack of consensus between Union financial authorities hinders the development of a common policy which could establish an integrated European financial system for balanced interdependence with its American counterpart.[58] In the absence of consensus rivalries to attract international investors provide opportunities for US financial enterprises. Their services can be especially important for US manufacturing firms in the Union and for Union firms investing in the US.

The formation of a stronger US manufacturing, financial and trading presence in Europe is increasing the urgency of structural policy issues for member states as participants in a regional integration venture confronting asymmetries in its Atlantic interdependencies. The options of most significance for the Union are those posed for Germany as the largest, most industrialized and most integrated European political economy, with a system of corporate governance significantly resistant to penetration, and a basis for maintaining internalization logic above the corporate level. For a structural policy that will be sufficiently effective in the national and Union interest, however, comprehensive collaboration with France will be essential, and this will be difficult to develop because of the divisive forces in the less integrated French political economy.[59] Partnering with Britain would also be desirable, but British corporate interests, while fragmented, have a dominant financial orientation which reinforces cultural affinities with the US. The social democratic political philosophies of ruling political parties in France and Britain do not provide an adequate basis for rapport with that in Germany's more consensually-oriented political system.[60]

The establishment of European Monetary Union is obliging member governments to focus on issues of regional financial integration, especially for the regulation of securities trading. There is an unevenly shared continental consensus on the need to reduce very high-volume speculation in international financial markets and bring them into line with the needs of the real economy, while coping with the danger that European investment will be drawn increasingly into American corporate financing, because of its higher profitability.[61]

The importance of working toward more balanced Atlantic structural interdependence demands recognition in American policy communities. These, however, tend to be narrowly focused, under shifting pluralistic pressures, and are influenced by concepts of the efficiencies of free market forces, as well as by impressions that European interventionism tends to thwart those forces while giving Union firms unfair advantages in Atlantic commerce.[62] Strong leadership and intensive policy learning would be required to build commitment to a policy of promoting Atlantic structural complementarities based on understanding of Europe's need for autonomous development of its regional economy in a relationship that would move toward more equal partnering.

Outside the Atlantic relationship US firms contending for global market shares are advantaged by the scale of their operations and are in rivalry mainly with Japanese enterprises. There is a drain of Japanese investment to the US, as US financial institutions exploit the availability of funds at low interest rates in Japan and use these, with similar funds from Europe, for global placement at higher yields. Major Japanese manufacturing enterprises, however, have very large resources for internally financed expansion,which is given modest but secure support from home country banks.[63] Capacities to provide such support are becoming more significant as the financial sector recovers from losses in the late 1990s.

The Japanese system of corporate governance generates greater solidarity than that in Germany and this is expressed in more active alignment between corporate strategies and structural policy. Resistance to foreign penetration remains high, while involvement in the US economy through exports and direct investment constitutes a major process of external structural change. This has effects across a narrow range of sectors, principally automobiles and electronics and, on account of Japanese cost as well as quality competitiveness, has contributed to considerable movement of manufacturing activity by US firms to locations in industrializing East Asia. This direct investment has resulted from generally independent US corporate decisions and has been accompanied by extensive sourcing from East Asia by US importers. With the Japanese direct investment in the US, meanwhile, there has been related investment in manufacturing at sites in industrializing East Asia. Deindustrializing effects in Japan have been moderated by intercorporate cooperation which has retained much value-added activity in the home economy[64]. An integrated Japanese production system in North America is expanding while a related system in East Asia has begun to recover from financial crises in 1997–99.

Questions about Japanese corporate governance have been raised by risk-taking tendencies in the financial sector, the dangers of which were aggravated by the financial distresses in industrializing East Asia. The sector has become more stable, under apparently more effective supervision by the Finance Ministry; and its informal regulation of the securities industry, which on the whole remains strongly national, is in effect ensuring continuity in the system of corporate governance while large manufacturing and trading firms gradually increase financing their operations through securities and lower their dependence on banks.[65] The main external focus of these operations is the US market, and next in priority is industrializing East Asia, where the adjustment and development of production bases in South Korea, Taiwan, Malaysia, Thailand, Singapore and the Philippines has become vital for the assertion of a strong role in the global economy. A relative decline in the American corporate presence in industrializing East Asia was reversed after that area's financial crises.

Japanese firms in the US, retaining the solidarity of their home pattern of corporate governance, are not drawn into assimilation with the American system, but US firms in Japan are not able to operate effectively without adapting to the Japanese system, and this virtual requirement discourages US direct investment. The imbalanced bilateral pattern of market and structural linking is not changing, but more symmetry may evolve in the larger context of US–East Asian relations through increased US production in and trade with industrializing East Asian states. For their economic recoveries these states are drawing increased foreign direct investment, and they offer much scope for outside firms to operate without adaptation to the host country systems of corporate finance and law. The financial systems in this area are underdeveloped, and are under relatively weak regulation. Under pressure from the IMF, and thus indirectly but also directly from the US, South Korea and Thailand are increasing the openness of their financial systems, in line with established views of the American economic presence as an advantage in interacting with Japanese firms and their home administration.[66]

The market and structural linking between the US and East Asia is evolving quite apart from that in Atlantic relations. The contrasts regarding social distances, cultural affinities, communication flows, policy level exchanges, structural and policy interdependencies, and bargaining strengths indicate very different potentials for building trust, understanding and cooperation. Policy communities in the Atlantic context receive streams of economic advice to governments from North American and European social scientists in frequent communication with each other who to a considerable extent share understandings of the dynamics of their political economies. There is a potential to work toward convergence between European concepts of government–corporate cooperation and American economic liberalism: the cultural basis for dialogue is well established. In the Pacific setting, however, American and Japanese policy communities relate to each other across longer social distances and benefit from smaller cross-flows of economic advice. The contrasts in cultures, structures and dynamics are sharper, and strains in the relationship have lowered trust, understanding and goodwill.

POLICY LEVEL INTERACTIONS

Fundamentals in the Triad pattern of structural change are being shaped mainly by the operations of US firms deriving strategic orientations from their system of corporate governance: this gives strong thrust to their independent and self-reliant international expansion, while preserving an intensely competitive business culture that is distrustful of government. Very active quests for world market shares are aided by resources gained from established positions in the large internal market, and competitive strengths gained internationally are enhancing advantages in rivalries with European and Japanese firms. The former are endeavouring to function in a regional market that is still not fully integrated and that is not evolving a common system of corporate governance. The latter are recovering from severe strains in their home economy and in the integrated production system which they were building in industrializing East Asia.

In Triad policy level interactions the US has strong bargaining strength, subject to the constraints of vulnerabilities in interdependence, and this strength is exerted for the promotion of global trade and investment liberalization. This diplomacy is aligned with the interests of US firms seeking world market shares. US corporate strategies, however, it must be stressed, are directed more toward the service of external markets through international production rather than through exports, despite policy level concerns to encourage export expansion that could begin to bring the current account into balance. In the absence of a structural policy capability that could help to increase exports US foreign economic policy tends to concentrate on market opening leverage directed at major trading partners, but has to contend with strong European resistance and with the danger of provoking Japanese investors to reduce their holdings of US government debt.[67]

Shareholder pressures on the managements of US firms add to their incentives to expand international production, as it has higher profitability and increases potentials for internal financing of new ventures. The planning of these firms, moreover, has to reckon with the prospect of higher taxation at home, due to shifts in the pattern of interest representation occasioned by deindustrialization and the other costs of globalization. Stakeholder hopes for greater emphasis on outward-oriented production in the home economy are not encouraged by the priority given to shareholder interests in the business culture.

The European Union's maintenance of modest restraints on imports of manufactures, while intended to benefit efforts by its own firms to enhance their competitiveness, is a factor sustaining US corporate interest in production within the Union. Because of the Union's relatively high degree of openness to American direct investment, US policy level interest in discussions of further Atlantic investment liberalization is only moderately active, and appears to be tacitly limited because of the importance of increasing exports to Europe. On the Union side there is little interest in securing increases in the US's substantial openness to foreign direct investment, and as flows of such investment from Europe can reduce the funding of industry in the Union there are tacit interests in avoiding measures that would encourage it. Britain is the main source of the outflows, and on the continent they are limited by the influence of national attachments and loyalties associated with systems of corporate governance and with established patterns of state aid to industry.[68] The European Commission, although obligated to enforce general prohibitions of such aid, allows most forms of it to continue, in line with the clear preferences of most member governments. Yet for major continental European firms direct investment in the US tends to become increasingly attractive because of the size of its market and the persistence of slow growth and high government costs and production costs in the Union.

As the macroeconomic dimension of Atlantic relations has been altered by the formation of the European Monetary Union, the US is no longer able to press for fiscal expansion that would have import-drawing effects in Europe.[69] Hence market-opening leverage against the Union has become more important for improvement in the balance of payments. Yet only small results can be anticipated, because the Union's bargaining strength is substantial and, while these could not be expected to be significant in the balance between US exports to and production within the Union, the prospect of trade friction could well cause US corporate interest in production in the Union to increase more than would be expected from trends before any major resorts to leverage.

The evolution of Atlantic relations has vital significance for US endeavours to promote general trade liberalization through the World Trade Organization and to link with this an agreement for multilateral investment liberalization. The preferences of most Union member governments, however, are likely to shift toward increasing the single market's moderate import restraints, because of hopes of raising levels of domestically-based growth. For such hopes, within each member state, government–corporate links can be expected to become more important, and in this process the established systems of corporate governance will probably tend to be strengthened, through the influence of structural policy rivalries and increased use of state aids to industry.[70] Cross-investment between the member states may make the systems of corporate governance more open to each other, but this tendency is likely to be offset by the use of subsidies in structural policy rivalries, which can be expected to perpetuate the distinctly national processes of interest representation in most members, especially Germany, as the most integrated political economy of the region.

In relations with Japan its system of corporate governance has much greater structural significance than those in Europe, and is maintained with stronger economic nationalism, roused by strains over trade issues and the East Asian financial crises. The main imperatives in Japanese policy are to resume high outward-oriented growth, with increasing emphasis on rebuilding trade and investment links with industrializing East Asia, while retaining access to the US market, without yielding to pressures for the reduction of structural impediments to trade and investment. US policy continues to focus on those impediments, but remains sensitive to the importance of Japanese investor confidence for the management of government debt and the operation of US financial institutions taking advantage of low Japanese interest rates.

The scope for US corporate endeavours to alter the imbalanced structural interdependence with Japan, it must be stressed, is significant mainly in industrializing East Asia. Rivalry in that area is likely to become more difficult as its economic recoveries continue and as the collective advantages of Japanese firms, based on intercorporate solidarity, are increased by renewed growth in the home economy. Japan's management of the rivalry may well be aided by preferential Chinese treatment of its trade and investment interests, following adverse shifts in Chinese attitudes to the US during the war in Yugoslavia.

COLLECTIVE MANAGEMENT ISSUES

As the major structural and policy interdependencies of the Pacific are evolving quite separately from those in the Atlantic, more so than in the recent past because of the economic reverses in East Asia, issues of collective management have been receiving less attention in the Triad. The US policy style has tended to become more unilateral, because of executive responsiveness to domestic concerns with the costs of globalization, and because of the increased bargaining strength resulting from Japan's recession. European interest in commerce with East Asia has been discouraged and has to reckon with the prospect of stronger American corporate competition in that area, as well as a more active Japanese role. The focus of US policy communities on Europe has been tending to increase with the Union's enlargement, its endeavours to develop a unified foreign and defence policy and the establishment of its Monetary Union, which has signified a political will for further advances in economic integration. Decisional problems within the Union limit its scope for initiatives on questions of Atlantic or Triad economic cooperation, despite the great importance of these issues, and accordingly the US's options can have potent effects on the dynamics of the relationship.

The prospective benefits of the US's Atlantic policy choices are heavily predicated on its handling of difficult macromanagement problems – the high debt load, the balance of payments deficits and the doubtful sustainability of speculative asset appreciation which draws European and Japanese investment. The demands of these problems, in terms of policy learning and the development of a functional consensus that can overcome the negative effects of pluralism, are challenges to achieve progress in advanced political development. These could be aided by European as well as American efforts to sponsor intensive dialogues between Atlantic policy communities.

Vigorous engagement with the US's macroeconomic policy problems could encourage similar endeavours in Europe, to increase growth that has been lagging because of the decades of slow progress toward market integration and the high costs of maintaining welfare states. On each side there could be more awareness of fiscal, monetary and financial policy interdependencies. Meanwhile greater comprehension of microeconomic policy interdependencies could result. Requirements to introduce more balance into the structural basis for Atlantic commerce could thus become evident, but with understandings that structural policy initiatives would have to seek corporate cooperation through intensive consultations. The roles of governments could be identified in terms of facilitating services, assisting managements to explore potential complementarities between strategic planning alternatives, and to build trustful relationships in support of entrepreneurial partnering, with surveillance by US and European agencies. This approach to the management of microeconomic policy interdependencies would be preferable to managed trade, because of the efficiencies attainable through concerted entrepreneurship, and its promise of more substantial public goods.[71]

Systems of corporate governance would assume new significance in structural consultations sponsored for corporate cooperation. Stakeholder concepts would be broadened as managerial perspectives and motivations became attuned to the wider accountabilities and synergies of Atlantic intercorporate partnering, which would tend to become relational on a long-term basis. The logic of alliance capitalism in an emerging Atlantic social market economy could gain acceptance, with productive results that could contribute to the development of forms of alliance politics, supported by expanding forms of social capital.

An important strand of the logic of alliance capitalism is visible in the development of international production networks. In these the specialized capacities of numerous firms are organized by lead enterprises, with interdependencies that multiply as the specializations become more innovative, aided by the synergies of frequent interactions. For the evolution of these networks, on the basis of dense trustful accumulations of tacit knowledge, much organizational continuity is required in the interests of long-term planning.[72] Accordingly stable shareholding arrangements are desirable, so that managerial task orientations will not be affected by pressures for short-term profits: these task orientations will have to be focused increasingly on the development and application of new technology.

The development of international production networks has been a major Japanese achievement in East Asia, where it has demonstrated the efficiencies of the nation's industry groups (*keiretsu*). European, mainly German, firms have been setting up such networks in Eastern Europe, while moving operations out of their high-cost home bases.[73] In Atlantic structural consultations there could be many occasions for American and European corporate identification of opportunities for wider development of international production networks and for exploration of diverse other potentials for ventures in alliance capitalism.

In the US's relations with Japan the promotion of structural consultations would be more difficult than in the Atlantic context but could well have more dynamic consequences, especially because of the efficiencies of the Japanese system of alliance capitalism. A major source of strain in the recent history of the relationship, it must be reiterated, has been US pressure to overcome structural impediments to trade on the Japanese side: fundamental changes in the Japanese system of corporate governance have been demanded, especially to weaken the relational ties of the *keiretsu*. For the Japanese economic elite such demands have threatened the foundations of a superior system for the concerting of productive activities on a grand scale. The substitution of an entirely competitive form of capitalism has not seemed to be a rational choice in the public interest.[74] Implicit in the external pressure, moreover, has been US interest in forcing change in the Japanese system of alliance politics, so that more competitive political trading as a source of policy would ensure the development of competitive rather than cooperative capitalism.

Despite the frictions in the relationship there is a clear imperative to work cooperatively for change in the structural foundations for bilateral commerce, so that higher and more balanced growth will result. Collaborative ventures between Japanese and American international firms could be encouraged, through discussions of structural issues between Japanese and American corporate and government representatives. On the Japanese side there would be interest in the potential for stable long-term partnering, and for this US shifts toward stakeholder concepts of corporate governance would be desirable. These would be shifts in managerial, shareholder and worker attitudes that have been advocated for reform of the US system of corporate governance. The rationale for such shifts has been presented in terms of efficiency and equity considerations directly affecting the public interest,[75] but has very important implications regarding the evolution of the USA's structural interdependencies and of its domestic patterns of interest representation that are being influenced by reactions to the costs of globalization.

In the relationship with Japan, as in Atlantic relations, the US has superior scope for initiative, although disadvantaged by problems of governance caused by very strong pluralism which invites analysis in public choice perspectives. The scope for initiative has to be studied with a focus on structural trends and issues, and the knowledge-intensive policy learning that can be hoped for will have to recognize that corporate stability and capabilities for long-term planning will be essential for building the structural foundations for orderly and dynamic growth. Policy learning and managerial learning with this understanding that may develop in Atlantic consultations could assist and benefit from similar learning in US–Japan interactions.

In the larger context of policy issues and corporate planning issues evolving in globalization competition between governments to provide attractive business environments for their own and other firms may lead to neglect of public goods imperatives. This possibility has been recognized in abstract modelling and is evident in some of the empirical literature on globalization. Taxation and spending decisions can certainly express bias at the expense of the public interest, notably by shifting the costs of government through indirect taxes and thus burdening the immobile workers.[76] Representations by groups pressing for redistributive benefits can thus increase, but may have limited effects in high-level political bargaining.

A highly important public good which should be recognized after identifying the problem of destructive competition between governments relates to the imbalances and strains of largely ungoverned globalization. The international public good which has to be striven for is an orderly evolution of structural and policy interdependencies, in line with common interests in achieving balanced dynamic growth through extensive cooperation between firms and between firms and governments, as well as between governments. The influence of systems of corporate governance on the activities of firms will have to be aligned with imperatives for such extensive collaboration, that is for the development of advanced forms of alliance capitalism, and also of forms of alliance politics.

The US, because of its status as the largest and most highly industrialized state, and its scope for initiative in the international political economy, has a special responsibility to promote collective management of the structural interdependencies which are being shaped increasingly by the independent strategies of its firms. For this responsibility a primary task will be to set out a doctrine of consultative structural partnering, in terms of developmental imperatives in the international political economy, that will relate especially to corporate orientations and policy level orientations in Europe and Japan. Such a doctrine will have to be based on clear recognition of market and structural changes in the present evolution of globalization.

In the linking of markets through trade and transnational production, as contests for global market shares intensify, concentration trends increase:[77] the more competitive firms, deriving superior resources from worldwide operations, drive weaker enterprises into declines. This trend is facilitated by the absence of competition policy cooperation between governments, and by diverse forms of government assistance to home country and foreign firms.[78] Meanwhile externalities associated with the concentration trend and with often-related processes of restructuring have deindustrializing effects and contribute to shifts in the overall spread of gains from world commerce. Technology factors are increasingly important in the concentration trend and in the pattern of externalities, especially because the high and rising costs of advanced innovations can be met only by very large firms.

Recognition of the concentration trend and the externalities would have to be asserted with the understanding that these problems would remain serious even if all forms of state aid to industry and commerce were eliminated. An equilibrium in an integrating global market could not be anticipated while the strategic orientations of many if not most firms remained almost entirely competitive rather than cooperative, because of values imparted in systems of corporate governance and in national political economies. The rationale for consultative structural partnering could be affirmed with reference to corporate orientations at the basis of the concentration trend and the problem of externalities, as well as to the vital requirement for order and equity in the development of complementary forms of entrepreneurship. The basic principle to be asserted would be that policy level obligations to provide the international public benefit of harmonious deepening integration would have to be met through interactive learning in dialogue with corporate decision makers. This necessary affirmation could be made with explicit recognition of the logic of technocratic–corporate and intercorporate consultative learning in Japan.

A US endeavour to promote consultative structural partnering in relations with the European Union and Japan would be a highly significant advance from an enlightened shift in corporate and policy level attitudes toward interfirm cooperation which developed in the 1980s.[79] That shift was a response to perceptions that Japan's structural competitiveness was based on intercorporate collaboration and that the lack of such collaboration was disadvantageous for US firms. The manifest logic of cooperation that would avoid duplications of efforts and destructive competition was seen to promise enhanced efficiencies. The prospect of more balanced structural inter-dependencies was implicit in justifications for the emphasis on collaboration, but this was obscured because of the prominence of concerns about attaining greater competitiveness.

In US policy communities and business associations, understanding of the importance of intercorporate cooperation for structural competitiveness could lead to recognition of the efficiencies and equities of structuring firms on the basis of stakeholder concepts. The functional significance of these increases as technological advances continue because the development and accumula-tion of tacit knowledge by workers becomes more vital for productive achievements. Meanwhile managerial development of entrepreneurial expertise, linked with tacit working level knowledge, also becomes more necessary. Patterns of collaborative corporate dynamism thus have to evolve with much organizational stability as intrasectoral and sectoral inter-dependencies become more intricate and more extensive with technological progress and the multiplication of cross-border structural linkages. Corporate organizational evolution, in the comon interest, has to be consistent with the developmental logic that can be seen in the innovative potentials of tacit working level and managerial knowledge. That logic, moreover, has to be expressed in intercorporate relations, for the development of collegial rather than instrumental alliance capitalism.[80]

In further exploration of requirements for structural competitiveness and, more importantly, for cooperative management of structural inter-dependencies, imperatives can be seen for accumulations of *tacit technocratic knowledge*, for the management of consultative structural policies. This tacit technocratic knowledge would have to be acquired through interactive learning with corporate managements, absorbing and contributing to their tacit knowledge, while developing a capacity for structural forecasting and for the sponsorship of managerial explorations of potentials for concerted entrepreneurship.[81] This tacit technocratic knowledge would not be used as a basis for interventionist measures, but would contribute to the shaping of infrastructure policies, in consultation with corporate groups, especially to facilitate the development of dynamic industrial clusters.

In relations with the European Union and Japan a new US policy of structural partnering, supported by a shift toward stakeholder concepts of corporate governance, would seek to extend this partnering through processes of reciprocity in discussions of potentials for balanced, diversified and complementary specializations. The interactions would be influenced by traditions of close government–corporate relations in Europe and even more in Japan, and thus would confront issues posed by special interests active in those relations. Degrees of objectivity about the scope for promoting the development of broad complementarities could be quite limited. The quality of knowledge-intensive leadership in the common interest would therefore be of great importance in the official contributions to sponsorship of the structural dialogues, especially from the American side, because of the pivotal significance of the US role.

ECONOMIC ADVICE TO GOVERNMENTS

The thinking of policy communities and corporate associations about problems of collective management in deepening integration is influenced by immediate issues of stress, dislocation, imbalance and adjustment but also, at a general level, by policy literature about imperatives for broad collaboration to provide common benefits. Such benefits are lacking because of neglect and because of destructive competition between firms and between governments. Initiatives to provide the necessary benefits are discouraged by the pressures of disadvantaged and endangered groups demanding compensation or protection in coping with the costs of globalization.

The policy literature advocating collaboration to serve the international common good refers to environmental, health, trade and security problems, but generally neglects questions about structural policies, despite the increasing significance of market linkages resulting from direct investment and trade, and the asymmetries in gains from those linkages.[82] Important strands of the literature propose measures to fully liberalize foreign direct investment policies, but recognize numerous political factors which cause governments to maintain lists of sectoral exceptions in which domestic interests are to be protected.

A basic theme in much of the policy literature is that the economic policies of industrialized states have been guided by rationales stressing the efficiencies of free market forces. Policies allowing wide scope for corporate international operations have been identified as some of the factors accounting for neglect of the international common good, but perspectives influenced by the free market rationales have tended to preclude consideration of structural policy endeavours which could introduce more order and dynamism into the international economy. Understanding of the inter-dependencies between governments and firms has been evident only in some of the literature, and has not tended to broaden into reflections on questions of structural policy cooperation.[83]

Close study of the interdependencies between governments and firms can yield insights into processes of interdependent growth. For industrialized democracies linked increasingly in deepening integration, growth is increasingly knowledge-based: more and more advanced technology is made productive. This growth, however, occurs in contests for world market shares, in which stronger firms position themselves more effectively, with the advantages of being able to finance large investments in frontier innovations. Interdependent growth thus tends to become more oligopolistic as well as knowledge-based, and it must be stressed that the emergence of a common political will to cooperate in the management of competition policies tends to become less and less likely as policy level commitments are made to favoured national firms, despite formal endorsements of free market principles.

Studies of corporate behaviour, it must be stressed, have indicated that growth is knowledge-based because of adoptions of new technology but also because managerial perceptions of entrepreneurial opportunities, including opportunities for concerting strategic plans, are increasingly significant. A major consequence is that *interdependencies between firms* are more and more important factors in the interdependencies *between governments and firms*. All these interdependencies are knowledge-based, and offer more and more significant opportunities for generating new knowledge through interactive learning focused on potentials for concerting productive operations and developing complementary organizational capabilities.[84]

Concerting entrepreneurship through intercorporate learning with technocratic inputs can promise higher and more stable interdependent growth. This is a vital theme to be expressed in economic advice to policymakers in the US, as the basis for a creative structural policy to be implemented in collegial interactions with elites in Europe and Japan, in recognition of the potential for building systems of advanced alliance capitalism. The rationale for this innovative policy would have to be set out with the clear recognition of the importance of institutional development to ensure the accumulation of tacit technocratic knowledge, focused on the public interest. Imperatives for this institutional development would have to be affirmed with acknowledgement of the danger that special interests could seek to influence the technocratic sponsorship of consultations with firms.

The problem of international oligopoly power would also have to be confronted in the structural policy rationale. This power is commonly viewed as a challenge for competition policy regulators, but in view of the difficulties of international cooperation between such regulators it could be affirmed that the consultative activities sponsored under the new structural policy would entail broad surveillance of oligopolistic trends and issues. This could contribute to the work of competition policy regulators, but also to the development of informal restraints on oligopolistic behaviour, as the consultative activities would evolve with general acceptance of accountabilities for reciprocity, based on concepts of fairness and on understandings of obligations for building trust.

The structural policy rationale could be presented with a pragmatic emphasis on the intricate pattern of incentives that could be arranged in the public interest, to motivate cooperative responses from which all would benefit. This, however, would not be sufficient to inspire high-principled dedication for full development of the potential for consultative structural partnering. For this, the concept of solidarity can be invoked, with memories of the heroism which this inspired in Poland. This concept has special relevance for the change in thinking which Margaret Blair has called for in her plea for the introduction of stakeholder concepts of corporate governance in the USA.[85] A consultative structural partnering policy *could* be implemented without a general change to a stakeholder philosophy, but such a change would provide a very appropriate foundation for such a policy. Political entrepreneurship to introduce a policy of this kind, with broad corporate support, would be a highly constructive response to the macromanagement challenges in deepening integration.

The scope for promoting harmonious adjustment, more order, and higher and more balanced interdependent Triad growth through ambitious collegial structural partnering is very great. A policy and an intercorporate outlook focusing on this vast prospect could derive vital support from a reorientation of elite thinking toward stakeholder concepts of corporate governance. This, moreover, could help to rectify the US's own macromanagement problems, especially by increasing the service of foreign markets from production in the home economy while introducing more systemic developmental logic into the growth of the US's structural interdependencies through foreign direct investment.

Emphasis on the highly constructive potential of the US's role in the international political economy is appropriate, it must be stressed, because of the size of the American economy, the wide range of policy initiatives open to the US in the current pattern of Triad policy interactions, and the critical importance of basing American economic development on sound fundamentals, averting the dangers of debt-led growth and speculation-led growth. The developmental logic of collegial alliance capitalism and of collegial alliance politics can be manifested in this context. This can be done with due acknowledgement of the efficiencies and equities in Japanese alliance capitalism, with its emphasis on social solidarity. There can also be acknowledgement of the strains of humanistic thought and elements of social solidarity in Europe's political economies, with affirmations that its welfare state burdens have to be greatly reduced through the growth effects of structural partnering within those economies in the development of their regional economy, and in its external relations.

Advances in the development of Triad alliance capitalism could promise more order and higher growth, with greater equity, in North–South relations, to end the long record of trade discrimination that has hampered industrialization in developing countries. The evolution of systems of corporate governance in those countries, and in the Triad, could be aligned with imperatives for structural partnering on a large scale.

NOTES

1. Much of the literature has focused on issues of trade policy cooperation and macroeconomic policy collaboration. See, for example, John Llewellyn and Stephen J. Potter (eds) (1991), *Economic Policies for the 1990s*, Oxford: Blackwell.
2. See Dani Rodrik (1997), *Has Globalization gone too far?*, Washington, DC: Institute for International Economics.
3. On the dynamics of interest representation see Geoffrey Garrett (1998), *Partisan Politics in the Global Economy*, New York: Cambridge University Press.
4. On the increasing importance of inter-firm technological cooperation see Thomas M. Jorde and David J. Teece (1989), 'Competition and cooperation: striking the right balance', *California Management Review*, **31** (3), 25–37.
5. See Patrick Cohendet, Francis Kern, Babak Mehmanpazir and Francis Munier (1999), 'Knowledge coordination, competence creation and integrated networks in globalised firms', *Cambridge Journal of Economics*, **23** (2), March, 225–41; Richard N. Langois and Nickolai J. Foss (1999), 'Capabilities and governance: the rebirth of production in the theory of economic organization', *Kyklos*, **52** (2), 201–18; and Nickolai J. Foss and Brian J. Loasby (eds) (1998), *Economic Organization, Capabilities, and Coordination*, London: Routledge.
6. See references to tacit knowledge in Daniele Archibugi and Jonathan Michie (eds) (1997), *Trade, Growth, and Technical Change*, Cambridge: Cambridge University Press, and in Jonathan Michie and John Grieve Smith (eds) (1998), *Globalization, Growth, and*

Governance, Oxford: Oxford University Press.

7.   See Andrei Shleifer and Robert W. Vishney (1997), 'A survey of corporate governance', *The Journal of Finance*, **LII** (2) (June), 737–84.

8.   See Andrew P. Dickerson, Heather D .Gibson and Euclid Tsakalotos (1995), 'Short-termism and under-investment: the influence of financial systems', *Manchester School Papers*, **LXIII** (4) (December), 351–67.

9.   See observations on the weakening of structural policy instruments in *Globalization of Industry*, Paris: OECD, 1996, pp. 11, 12.

10. On problems of international competition policy cooperation see the symposium on competition policy, *The World Economy*, **21** (8) (November) 1998.

11. See comments on rivalries between governments in Raymond Vernon (1998), *In the Hurricane's Eye*, Cambridge, MA: Harvard University Press.

12. See Bank of International Settlements (1998), *68th Annual Report*, Part II.

13. See John Stopford and Susan Strange (1991), *Rival States, Rival Firms*, Cambridge: Cambridge University Press.

14. See Bruce L.R. Smith and Claude E. Barfield (eds) (1996), *Technology, R&D and the Economy*, Washington, DC: Brookings Institution and American Enterprise Institute.

15. An important consideration has been the development of dynamic balance between the home economy and external production systems. See Tamim Bayoumi and Gabrielle Lipworth (1998), 'Japanese foreign direct investment and regional trade', in Bijan B. Aghevli, Tamim Bayoumi and Guy Meredith (eds), *Structural Change in Japan*, Washington, DC: International Monetary Fund, ch. 6.

16. See Paolo Guerrieri and Carlo Milana (1997), 'High technology industries and international competition', in Daniele Archibugi and Jonathan Michie (eds), *Trade, Growth, and Technical Change*, Cambridge: Cambridge University Press, pp. 188–207.

17. On US fiscal deficits see Alan Auerbach (1998), *Quantifying the Current US Fiscal Imbalance*, Cambridge: National Bureau of Economic Research Working Paper 6119.

18. On fiscal discipline under EMU see Alessandro Sciamarelli (1998), 'Fiscal policy in the member states under EMU', *EIPASCOPE*, **3**, 32–7.

19. On the need for more effective regulation see Address by President of the Bank for International Settlements, 7 June 1999, at Annual General Meeting of the Bank – Press Release 25/1999E. See also Franklin R. Edwards (1999), 'Hedge funds and the collapse of long term capital management', *Journal of Economic Perspectives*, **13** (2) (Spring), 189–210.

20. See address by President of the Bank of International Settlements, cited in note 19.

21. See Brian Scott-Quinn (1994), *European Community Regulation of Securities Markets*, Discussion Papers in Accounting, Finance and Banking, Series D, Vol. v, No. 40, March, Department of Economics, University of Reading.

22. See Dennis J. Encarnation, *Rivals beyond Trade* (1992), Ithaca: Cornell University Press.

23. On EU corporate governance see Erik Berglof (1997), 'Reforming corporate governance: redirecting the European agenda', *Economic Policy*, **24** (April), 91–124. See also Kees Koedijk and Jeroen Kremers (1996), 'Market opening, regulation and growth in Europe', *Economic Policy*, **23** (October), 445–67.

24. On US government debt see Jill Ouseley (1997), 'United States: primary market auctions and government debt management', in V. Sundararajan, Peter Dattels and Hans J. Blommestein (eds), *Coordinating Public Debt and Monetary Management*, Washington, DC: International Monetary Fund, 1997, ch. 14. See also Russel B. Scholl (1998), 'The International investment position of the United States in 1997', *Survey of Current Business*, **78** (7) (July), 24–33.

25. On the cross-investment see Raymond J. Mataloni (1998), 'US multinational companies operation in 1996', *Survey of Current Business*, **78** (9) (September), 47–73 and Mahnaz Fahim-Nader (1999), 'Foreign direct investment in the United States', *Survey of Current Business*, **79** (6) (June), 16–23.

26. See references to solidarity in the Japanese intercorporate system in W. Carl Kester (1996), 'American and Japanese corporate governance: convergence to best practice?', in Suzanne Berger and Ronald Dore (eds), *National Diversity and Global Capitalism*, Ithaca: Cornell

University Press, ch. 4.

27. See David Soskice (1998), 'Openness and diversity in transatlantic economic relations', in Barry Eichengreen (ed.), *Transatlantic Economic Relations in the Post-Cold War Era*, New York, Council on Foreign Relations, ch 2.

28. On the efficiencies of industrial clustering see John H. Dunning (1998), 'Globalization, technological change and the spatial organization of economic activity', in Alfred D. Chandler Jr, Peter Hagstrom and Orjan Solvell (eds), *The Dynamic Firm*, Oxford: Oxford University Press, ch. 13.

29. See Berglöf, cited in note 23.

30. See Benn Steil et al. (1996), *The European Equity Markets*, London: Royal Institute of International Affairs.

31. See Shumpei Kumon and Henry Rosovsky (eds) (1992), *The Political Economy of Japan*, vol. 3, Stanford: Stanford University Press.

32. See Lawrence J. White (1993), 'Competition policy in the United States: an overview', *Oxford Review of Economic Policy*, 9 (2) (Summer), 133-51.

33. See Geoffrey Garrett (1998), *Partisan Politics in the Global Economy*, New York: Cambridge University Press.

34. The effects of this emphasis have been evident in balance of payments figures. See *OECD Economic Survey, Germany*, Paris: OECD, 1998.

35. These trends have been evident in Japan and Germany. See W. Carl Kester (1992), 'Industrial groups as systems of contractual governance', *Oxford Review of Economic Policy*, 8 (3) (Autumn), 24-44.

36. On the strengths of the German political economy, despite its strains, see Kirsten S. Wever and Christopher S. Allen (1993), 'The financial system and corporate governance in Germany: institutions and the diffusion of innovations', *Journal of Public Policy*, 13 (2) (April), 183-202.

37. The US direct investment position in Germany, although much smaller than that in Britain, is by comparison quite substantial in the manufacturing sectors and in transportation equipment is almost double that in the UK. See Russell B. Scholl, cited in note 24.

38. On the dangers of a financial crises see Victor Zarnowitz (1999), 'Theory and history behind business cycles: are the 1990s the onset of a Golden Age?', *Journal of Economic Perspectives*, 13 (2) (Spring), 69-90.

39. On the effects of this emphasis in the USA see William Lazonick (1998), 'Organizational learning and international competition', in Jonathan Michie and John Grieve Smith (eds), *Globalization, Growth, and Governance*, Oxford: Oxford University Press, ch. 11.

40. See Jenny Corbett and Tim Jenkinson (1966), 'The financing of industry, 1970-1989: an international comparison', *Journal of the Japanese and International Economies*, 10 (1) (March), 71-96.

41. On the benefits of 'insider' systems see Andrew P. Dickerson, Heather D. Gibson and Euclid Tsakalotos (1995), 'Short-termism and underinvestment: the influence of financial systems', *Manchester School Papers*, LXIII (4) (December), 351-67.

42. Increases in reliance on securities markets have accompanied the increases in US outward direct investment noted by Scholl, cited in note 24. The reliance on securities is examined in Marc R. Saidenberg and Philip E. Strahan (1999), 'Are banks still important for financing large businesses?', *Current Issues in Economics and Finance*, 5 (12), September, Federal Reserve Bank of New York.

43. See Carles Boix and Daniel N. Posner, 'Social capital: explaining its origins and effects on government performance', *British Journal of Political Science*, 28 (4) (October), 686-93.

44. See Rajneesh Narula and John H. Dunning (1999), 'Technocratic–corporate partnering: extending alliance capitalism', in Gavin Boyd and John H. Dunning (eds), *Structural Change and Cooperation in the Global Economy*, Cheltenham, UK and Northampton, MA: Edward Elgar, ch. 6.

45. See *The Political Economy of Japan*, cited in note 31.

46. See comments on Germany in Wever and Allen, cited in note 36, and comments on issues of monetary policy effectiveness in Iris Biefang-Frisancho Mariscal, Hans-Michael Trautwein, Peter Howells, Philip Arestis and Harald Hagemann (1995), 'Financial

innovation and the long-run demand for money in the United Kingdom and in West Germany', *Review of World Economics*, **131** (2), 302–25.

47. See Soskice, cited in 1998 , and Lazonick, cited in note 39.
48. See Kester, cited in note 35, and Giovanni Dosi, David J. Teece and Josef Chytry (eds) (1998), *Technology, Organization, and Competitiveness*, Oxford: Oxford University Press, Part B.
49. This theme runs through Berglöf, cited in note 23.
50. See references to structural policy rivalries between member states in Mitchell P. Smith (1996), 'Integration in small steps: the European Commission and member state aid to industry', *West European Politics*, **19** (3) (July), 563–82. See also Thomas Brewer and Stephen Young (1995), 'European Union policies and the problems of multinational enterprises', *Journal of World Trade*, **29** (1), 33–52.
51. See Scholl, cited in note 24, on German direct investment in the USA.
52. See details of Japanese direct investment in same.
53. See Maria Green Cowles (1997), 'Organizing industrial coalitions: a challenge for the future', in Helen Wallace and Alasdair R. Young (eds), *Participation and Policymaking in the European Union*, Oxford: Oxford University Press, ch. 6.
54. On the volume of trading in international financial markets see 69th Annual Report of the Bank of International Settlements, cited in note 12, Part VII.
55. Details of foreign holdings of US secrities are in Scholl, cited in note 24.
56. The European Commission has expanded its role mainly by extending its regulatory functions. On the technological lag, which could motivate regulatory measures against external firms, see Jonathan Eaton, Eva Gutierrez and Samuel Kortum (1998), 'European technology policy', *Economic Policy*, **27** (October), 405–38.
57. On the dynamics of aid to industry in the EU see Daniel Verdier (1995), 'The politics of public aid to private industry', *Comparative Political Studies*, **28** (1) (April), 3–42.
58. See Steil et al., cited in note 30.
59. See Vivien A. Schmidt (1996), 'The decline of traditional state dirigisme in France: the transformation of economic policies and policymaking processes', *Governance*, **9** (4) (October), 375–406.
60. The German party is more responsive to national corporate interests, which are organized more effectively than those in France and Britain. See references to Germany in Wallace and Young, cited in note 53.
61. On the internationalization of financial markets see H.J. Blommestein and K. Biltoft (1995), 'Trends, structural changes and prospects in OECD capital markets', in *The New Financial Landscape*, Paris: OECD, ch. 9.
62. For an influential expression of this view see Laura D'Andrea Tyson (1992), *Who's Bashing Whom?'*, Washington, DC: Institute for International Econonics.
63. See David E. Weinstein and Yishay Yafeh (1998), 'On the costs of a bank-centered financial system: evidence from the changing main bank relations in Japan', *Journal of Finance*, **LIII** (2) (April), 635–72.
64. See Bayoumi and Lipworth, cited in note 15.
65. See Hiroshi Nakaso (1999), 'Recent banking sector reforms in Japan', *Economic Policy Review*, Federal Reserve Bank of New York, **5** (2) (July), 1–8.
66. US investment in industrializing East Asia was lagging behind Japan's before the 1997/8 regional financial crises. The US direct investment position in 1997 is shown in Sylvia E. Bargas (1998), 'Direct investment positions for 1997', *Survey of Current Business*, **78** (7) (July), 35–45. See also Robert E. Lipsey, *The Location and Characteristics of US Affiliates in Asia*, Working Paper 6876, National Bureau of Economic Research, Cambridge, Mass.
67. Scholl, cited in note 24, indicates that as at the end of 1994 Japanese official and private investors held $bn38.8 in US Agency bonds and $bn127.7 in US Treasury Bonds.
68. See contrasts in British and other European direct investment in the US in Fahim-Nader, cited in note 25.
69. See C. Randall Henning (1998), 'Systemic conflict and regional monetary integration: the case of Europe', *International Organization*, **52** (3) (Summer).
70. Market integration accelerates the displacement of weaker enterprises by more competitive

ones. See John Cantwell (1987), 'The reorganization of European industries after integration: selected evidence on the role of multinational enterprise activities', *Journal of Common Market Studies*, **XXVI** (2) (December), 127-52.

71.   The logic of alliance capitalism has increasing international sgnificance as advances are made in widening areas of frontier technology; these enlarge the potential for productive cooperation between firms, and identification of those potentials can be aided by technocratic expertise. The international benefits that can be envisaged can be viewed in the context of the underproduction of public goods in the globalizing world economy - see Inge Kaul, Isabelle Grunberg and Marc A. Stern (eds) (1999), *Global Public Goods*, New York: Oxford University Press.

72.   See Michael Delapierre and Lynn Krieger Mytelka (1998), 'Blurring boundaries: new inter-firm relationships and the emergence of networked, knowledge-based oligopolies', in Massimo G. Colombo (ed.), *The Changing Boundaries of the Firm*, London: Routledge, pp. 73-94, and Patrick Cohender, Francis Kern, Babak Mehmanpazir and Francis Munier (1999), 'Knowledge co-ordination, competence creation and integrated networks in globalised firms', *Cambridge Journal of Economics*, **23** (2) (March), 225-42.

73.   See John Zysman and Andrew Schwartz (1998), 'Reunifying Europe in an emerging world economy: economic heterogeneity, new industrial options and political choices', *Journal of Common Market Studies*, **36** (3) (September), 405-30. See also Hans-Werner Sinn and Alfons J. Weichenrieder, 'Foreign direct investment, political resentment and the privatization process in Eastern Europe', *Economic Policy*, **24** (April), 177-210.

74.   See *The Political Economy of Japan*, cited in note 31.

75.   See Margaret M. Blair (1995), *Ownership and Control*, Washington, DC: Brookings Institution.

76.   On the costs of globalization for workers see Dani Rodrik, cited in note 2.

77.   See Cantwell, cited in note 70.

78.   See symposium on competition policy, cited in note 10.

79.   See Jorde and Teece, cited in note 4.

80.   This extends the themes in Cohendet et al., cited in note 5.

81.   A basic justification for more consultative policymaking can be seen in *Issues and Developments in Public Management*, Paris: OECD, 1997. See also Bart Nooteboom (1999), 'Innovation, learning, and Industrial organization', *Cambridge Journal of Economics*, **23** (2) (March), 127-50.

82.   See *Global Public Goods*, cited in note 71.

83.   See Dunning, cited in note 72.

84.   See observations on networking in Delapierre and Mytelka, cited in note 72.

85.   See Blair, cited in note 75.

6. US corporations in globalization

John B. Davis and Joseph P. Daniels

1. INTRODUCTION

The major force affecting corporations and economic institutions over the last two decads is globalization. A recent survey of the members of the American Economic Association, interpreted by Pryor (2000) reveals that economists see globalization as that factor (out of ten) most likely to have a major impact on the economic system or its important institutions. In contrast to past theories of trade, where firms could choose between exporting goods or exporting capital, that is, producing abroad, globalization has given rise to a 'disintegration of the production process in which manufacturing or service activities done abroad are combined with those performed at home' (Feenstra, 1998, p. 31). Hence, the old views of location of production activity are no longer appropriate and relationships between trade, investment and production activity are much more complex.

In the broadest sense, corporate governance consists of an interrelated set of mechanisms relating boards of directors, ownership structures, institutional and relational investors, and government and other stakeholder groups that influence firm-level decisions over resoure allocation aimed at maximizing shareholders' returns.[1] The purpose of this chapter is to understand these firm-level decisions in terms of the evolution and extent of globalization of US industries as revealed by trade, production and investment data, and relate these findings to theories regarding different systems of corporate governance. We offer a number of insights into how the distinctive characteristics of the US corporate governance system have helped US firms respond to opportunities presented by global integration through changes in trade, production and investment activities. We do not present original empirical work, but rather use the empirical findings of other studies to throw light on the US system. We also conclude that further research based on a similar attempt to link evidence and theories will require much more disaggregated data.

We begin our analysis in Section 2 by considering the duality of forces at work, the strategic pursuit of profits as influenced by the corporate governance system and the pressures and opportunities of increased globalization. Section 3 examines the extent of globalization of US industries, quantifying the trade and investment channels of the process, as well as the disintegration of the production process and increased global outsourcing. In Sections 4 and 5 we use the economic theory of corporate governance to explain how the US system of corporate governance influences how US firms are likely to approach global competition given the strengths and weaknesses of that system in promoting capital investment. Section 5 relates the theories of capital allocation to the quantitative data presented earlier. Section 6 offers general conclusions on the globalization of US corporations in relation to the US model of governance.

2.   GLOBALIZATION AND CORPORATE GOVERNANCE: DUALITY OF FORCES

As the economies of the world become increasingly integrated, the extent and effects of globalization have received greater and greater attention. The political economy literature has rightly tended to focus on the macroeconomic effects of globalization. Issues such as earnings inequality, employment security, tax base stability and the role of the welfare state challenge free trade positions grounded on the welfare gains from exchange (for example, Rodrik, 1997). Less research has been done on how corporate governance influences global trade and investment in light of the strengths and weaknesses of different types of governance structures in promoting capital investment.

As is well known, the forces of globalization and deeper integration are numerous and affect different industries and firms unevenly. The effects of globalization can be both direct and indirect, with contagion occurring far down the customer and supply chain. Few industries and firms, then, can escape the effects of globalization regardless of their choice to participate in, or avoid, the international arena. Hence, corporate governance necessarily occurs in a global environment. In addition, the globalization process and corporate governance structures each influence one another, and accordingly we must consider a duality of forces at work. The globalization process forces changes in corporate governance structures through direct and indirect channels, requiring that these structures adapt to the new opportunities available and the competition firms face, as determined by political and economic forces. At the same time, structures of different corporate governance systems influence firms' strategic approaches, and therefore the pace and pattern of globalization.

In the past, US firms exercised influence over the formation of trade policy and management decisions of suppliers and competitors by acquiring sizable market shares. More recently, however, soaring levels of US global equity holdings combined with the advantages of the US securities-based system of corporate governance have given US firms and institutions new channels of influence. Consider, for example, that the California Public Employees' Retirement System (known as Calpers) garnered support from an array of German pension funds, and forced changes in the two-tier shareholder structure of a large German utility. Steinmetz and Sesit (1999, p. 1) comment that the most significant effect of the surge in US global equity investment is that it 'forces European companies to change the way they do business and adopt American corporate values'.

Regarding corporate governance, we distinguish between management thinking on corporate governance, and appropriate an international political economy perspective and the economic analysis of corporate governance, based on the theory of efficient capital allocation. An economic analysis of corporate governance explains how principal–agent and insider–outsider relationships affect firms' investment plans and, therefore, location of production activity. Management thinking on corporate governance, built upon general systems theory, describes how firms may be constrained by possible conflicts with stakeholders, or groups affected by, and/or that can affect, a firm's decisions, policies and operations. Though we focus on the economic perspective, we contend that both perspectives are necessary, since one reflects how unhindered firms would choose to invest domestically and internationally, while the other reflects the political economic realities involved in globalization.

The US system of corporate governance is a securities-based system of corporate governance (sometimes called a neoclassical system of regulation) which favours competitive capital markets, discourages intercorporate cooperation, tips the balance of power between shareholders and corporate management in the direction of the former, and tends to be associated with a relatively unconcentrated corporate ownership structure, all reinforced by a competition policy based in antitrust law. We argue that the US system of corporate governance creates strong incentives for US firms involved in certain types of production to avoid regulatory exposure through foreign operations, while US firms involved in other types of production will have weak incentives to do so. These developments, it should be noted, need not be consistent with US macromanagement goals (cf. Daniels and Davis, 2000).

3. THE EXTENT OF US GLOBALIZATION: TRADE, PRODUCTION AND DIRECT INVESTMENT

Dunning (1993, p. 54) argues that the activities of multinational enterprises are motivated by stakeholder interest, where stakeholders include employees, management and shareholders. In contrast, neoclassical economic theory asserts that residual income accrues to a firm's shareholders in the form of profits paid as dividends, and that therefore profits motivate the actions of the firm (and its managers). In discussing the 'OECD Principles of Corporate Governance' Emmons and Schmid (Chapter 2, this volume) observe that both shareholder and stakeholder rights are acknowledged, but ask whether conflict between the two is not inevitable. Dunning also stresses that multinational activities may produce conflict between shareholders and stakeholders. Further, globalization strategies and the various exposures to risk globalization may generate considerable stress between these constituencies even when each includes profit maximization in their objective functions. Hence, globalizing firms may pursue a variety of different paths reflecting conflict over both objectives and strategies.

Trade economists have generally considered two routes of global expansion; globalizing through trade or globalizing through foreign direct investment (FDI). Traditionally these strategies were viewed as being separate or alternative means to globalization. That is, the exports of goods and capital substitute for each other. Recent theoretical (for example, Markusen and Venables, 1995) and empirical research (for example, Fontagné and Pajot, 1997) show that the relationship between trade and foreign direct investment is much more complex, and that trade and foreign direct investment may actually complement each other. That is, foreign direct investment may spur greater amounts of trade, and trade may spur greater amounts of foreign direct investment. Hence, the pursuit of profit maximization and the attempt to balance various stakeholder groups may well require a mixed approach to globalization. The approach in some industries may be increased trade channels, in others the acquisition of a controlling share in a foreign establishment, and yet others a mix of both.

There is a further reason that the relationship between trade and investment is complex. Global integration may be accompanied by a 'disintegration' of the production process (Feenstra, 1998, p. 31) whereby a formerly integrated domestic production activity becomes fragmented as portions of the production process are outsourced to foreign production. This outsourcing activity allows firms to concentrate on the highest value-added portions of the total production process, making many US firms only responsible for final stages of production. This complicates our standard model of comparative advantage which explains advantage in terms of *final* goods and services. In effect, a US manufacturing firm may find that it has a comparative advantage in high value-added stages such as design and marketing, but a comparative disadvantage in mass production. This may not be reflected in industry-level data, and thus makes clear-cut conclusions about trade, production and investment difficult, though not impossible.

3.1 Manufacturing

We begin our analysis of the evidence by considering global integration in the manufacturing sector. We are not concerned with defining globalization or integration *per se*. Neither do we classify industries as domestic or global (see, for example, Makhija and Williamson, 2000). Rather we consider industries along a continuum from relatively low to relatively high degrees of integration.

3.1.1 Integration of the manufacturing sector

Campa and Goldberg (1997) examine the external orientation of manufacturing in four different countries by considering the share of exports, imports and imported inputs for 20 categories of manufactures. The purpose of their study is to ascertain the exposure of these industries to international events such as changes in trade policies and exchange rates. Their results are particularly interesting in that they illustrate both direct and indirect exposures that may exist from globalization. Direct exposures refer to changes that affect the firm directly through effects on its price competitiveness or costs of inputs used in the production process. Indirect exposures refer to changes that affect the firm indirectly by impacting upon the firm's competition, suppliers and customers.

Campa and Goldberg capture direct exposure by measuring the extent to which an industry relies on exports and imported inputs. They capture part of a firm's indirect exposure through the degree of import competition. The levels of these shares are provided in Table 6.1 as are the changes in these shares over a 20-year period.

Campa and Goldberg calculate each industry's external orientation by netting the export and imported-input shares. The rationale for this measure is that it shows how export-oriented firms are at least partially insulated against exchange rate movements. For example, a firm facing appreciation of its currency and loss of export sales, benefits from the reduced domestic currency cost of imported inputs. Industries with the highest external orientation, such as instruments and related products (15 per cent), industrial machinery and equipment (14.8 per cent), electronic and other electrical equipment (12.6 per cent), and tobacco products (11.9 per cent), do not rely heavily on imported inputs, and therefore may be hurt by a domestic currency appreciation. Goldberg and Crockett (1998) claim that industries with more labour-intensive production processes are likely to have a lower imported-input share and, therefore, a higher external orientation. Comparing capital

Table 6.1 Export and import market shares for manufacturing, 1995

	Export share	Import share	Imported-input share	Change in export share*	Change in import share*	Change in input share*
Food and kindred products	5.9	4.2	4.2	2.6	0.5	1.4
Tobacco products	14.9	0.6	2.1	8.0	0.0	0.7
Textile mill products	7.6	9.1	7.3	2.5	4.8	4.3
Apparel and other textiles	7.4	31.4	3.2	5.4	22.9	1.9
Lumber and wood products	7.6	10.3	4.3	0.4	3.4	2.1
Furniture and fixtures	5.5	14.1	5.7	4.2	11.1	2.1
Paper and allied products	9.0	10.0	6.3	3.1	4.1	2.1
Printing and publishing	2.4	1.6	3.5	0.8	0.6	0.8
Chemicals and allied products	15.8	11.0	6.3	5.7	7.4	3.3
Petroleum and coal products	3.9	5.7	5.3	2.2	-4.0	-1.5
Rubber and miscellaneous products	9.2	12.8	5.3	4.4	7.9	2.6
Leather and leather products	14.4	59.5	20.5	10.5	41.8	14.9
Stone, clay and glass products	5.6	9.5	4.7	2.2	6.1	2.6
Primary metal products	11.2	17.4	10.6	6.1	7.6	5.6
Fabricated metal products	7.9	8.5	8.7	1.6	5.5	4.0
Industrial machinery and equipment	25.8	27.8	11.0	2.5	21.5	6.9
Electronic and other electric equipment	24.2	32.5	11.6	13.1	24.0	7.1
Transportation equipment	17.8	24.3	15.7	2.0	13.9	9.3
Instruments and related products	21.3	20.1	6.3	4.5	12.7	2.5
Other manufacturing	13.5	41.1	9.9	3.6	27.7	5.3
Total manufacturing	13.4	16.3	8.2	5.0	10.0	4.1

Note: * Change from 1975 level.
Source: Campa and Goldberg (1997, p. 57).

expenditure–labour unit ratios with the external orientation measure, as shown in Table 6.2, does not reveal such a pattem.[2] Goldberg and Crockett also argue that exchange rate changes disproportionately affect profitability and investment spending in industries with the highest external orientation.

Table 6.2   Capital expenditure to labour unit and external orientation

	Capital expenditures to labour	External orientation
Leather and leather products	1 386.8	−6.1
Petroleum and coal products	50 971.5	−1.4
Printing and publishing	4 293.8	−1 1
Fabricated metal products	5 407.6	−0.8
Furniture and fixtures	2 654.8	−0.2
Textile mill products	4 538.8	0.3
Primary metal industries	11 383.4	0.6
Stone, clay and glass products	9 114.9	0.9
Food and kindred products	8 058.2	1.7
Transportation equipment	8 916.3	2.1
Paper and allied products	15 355.6	2.7
Lumber and wood products	5 061.9	3.3
Misc. manufacturing industries	3 861.6	3.6
Rubber and misc. plastics products	7 670.5	3.9
Apparel and other textile products	1 192.7	4.2
Chemicals and allied products	24 927.2	9.5
Electronic and other electric equipment	15 081.0	12.6
Tobacco products	18 837.2	12.8
Industrial machinery and equipment	6 696.0	14.8
Instruments and related products	6 698.4	15.0

The data for all three measures shows that manufacturing has become much more integrated in the global economy over the 20-year period, as the share of exports increased an additional 5 per cent representing a 60 per cent gain overall. The share of imports increased an additional 10 per cent, a 159 per cent increase, while the share of imported inputs doubled to 8.2 per cent. Campa and Goldberg further compare the ranking of the twenty industries for the three share measures over the 20-year period. The industry rank correlations are positive and significant, indicating that the most export-oriented industries remained so over the entire period. Likewise, the most import-oriented remained so, though the increase in import shares differs significantly across industries. The authors find that the difference in the import shares widens considerably with import penetration increasing at a much faster rate in high import-share industries, such as leather and leather products, as compared to low import-share industries, such as tobacco and printing and publishing. Using Spearman rank correlations, we find that capital expenditures–labour unit ratios and *changes* in import shares are significant and negative indicating that the increasing spread in import penetration falls disproportionately on labour-intensive industries – industries in which the US is at a comparative disadvantage.

3.1.2 Disintegration of production in manufacturing

The industry import and export shares cited above do not reveal the extent of international trade in intermediate products. Advances in technology, particularly communications technology, coupled with reductions in transportation costs have allowed firms to outsource various stages of the production process, and focus on those segments of the value-added chain in which the firm has a comparative advantage. For firms in the US, this means increasingly that the manufacturing component of production is contracted out to foreign sources, allowing traditional manufacturing enterprises to concentrate on such high value-added activities as design and marketing. Firms such as Ford now see their future in design, branding, marketing and service operations, as opposed to automobile manufacture and traditional final assembly (Burt, 1999). Others, relying on new information technology combined with robotics and advanced production techniques, concentrate on 'mass customization' or customization of products on a large scale. Huffy, for example, recently announced that the last of its US bicycle plants would shut down, completing the firm's evolution into a 'multibrand design, marketing and distribution company' (Aeppel, 1999, p. A1).

Evidence that outsourcing has become more important for the United States is suggested by the rising ratio of US merchandise trade (the average of imports and exports) to merchandise value-added since the 1980s (Irwin, 1996). A higher ratio of merchandise trade to value-added indicates a greater share of imported inputs in final product value. Also, that advanced countries' final product value tends to be high relative to final product value in developing countries suggests that a higher share of imported inputs reflects inputs having a higher degree of processing. Further evidence that this higher share may reflect an increasing tendency on the part of advanced countries to outsource the low-wage stages of the production process associated with light assembly and manufacturing, while retaining domestically the high-wage portions of the production process associated with design and more complex, less standardized forms of manufacture, comes from changing shares of US exports and imports by end-use categories. To estimate the extent of outsourcing, Feenstra (1998), following Irwin (1996), calculates the share of exports and imports by end-use categories for the US. For the United States, as shown in Table 6.3, the first half of the century saw higher shares of raw materials and industrial supplies in exports and imports, while since the 1980s manufactured goods, including capital goods, at increasingly advanced stages of processing, have occupied a larger share of total end-use categories.

Thus the US appears to be importing products that are closer and closer to the final stage of production, allowing more and more of the earlier stages of the production process to occur in foreign countries. But industry-level trade data aggregates all stages of the production process and does not reveal the degree to which US firms concentrate on the high value-added stages of production, the stages of production in which they have a comparative advantage. A more thorough examination of this phenomenon would require us to consider firm-level data, which is generally unavailable.

3.1.3 Foreign direct investment shares in manufacturing

Expanded trade activity, whether vertical or horizontal, is but one path of globalization. Another is through foreign direct investment: investment in the form of capital, technology, management skills and so on, which is outside of the country but within the structure of the investing company (Dunning, 1993, p. 5). Table 6.4 provides the stock of FDI (historical basis) and share of outstanding stock for the 20 manufacturing industries considered in Table 6.1.

It is important to note that the measures in Table 6.1 are flow measures as they reflect the flow of goods and services over the course of a given period whereas the measures in Table 6.4 are stock measures, indicating the level of accumulated direct investment. Nonetheless, it is interesting to note that three of the five industries with the highest FDI shares (chemicals, industrial machinery and electronic equipment) are also in the top five for export shares, yet no relationship appears to exist at the bottom of the categories. In general, however, a positive ordinal relationship does appear to exist between FDI shares and export shares. No relationship is evident between FDI shares and import shares or imported input shares, or the changes in these shares. Spearman rank correlations lead us to the same conclusion.[3] We conclude, therefore, that the relationship between trade patterns and FDI stocks are complex and FDI is not a clear substitute for exports. This relationship is revisited later in the chapter.

3.2 Services

The service sector is extremely important to the US economy as most recent

Table 6.3 Shares of exports and imports by end-use categories

Category		1925	1950	1965	1980	1995
Foods, feeds and beverages	Imports	21.9	30.0	19.1	11.3	5.0
	Exports	18.7	15.5	19.2	16.9	9.2
Industrial supplies and materials	Imports	68.2	62.4	53.3	31.3	18.2
	Exports	59.8	45.5	34.8	32.2	25.6
Capital goods (except autos)	Imports	0.4	1.3	7.1	19.0	33.6
	Exports	8.7	22.4	31.4	35.0	42.4
Consumer goods (except autos)	Imports	9.4	6.1	16.0	21.5	24.3
	Exports	6.0	8.9	7.0	7.8	11.7
Automotive vehicles and parts	Imports	0.02	0.3	4.5	16.9	18.9
	Exports	6.8	7.8	7.5	8.1	11.2

Source: Feenstra (1998).

Table 6.4   Stock and shares of FDI for manufacturing, 1995

Industry classification	FDI stock*	FDI share
Food and kindred products	28 896	11.8
Tobacco products	3 962	1.6
Textile mill products	1 538	0.6
Apparel and other textiles	1 248	0.5
Lumber and wood products	1 861	0.8
Furniture and fixtures	805	0.3
Paper and allied products	11 748	4.8
Printing and publishing	2 344	1.0
Chemicals and allied products	61 374	25.2
Petroleum and coal products	19 597	8.0
Rubber and miscellaneous products	5 291	2.2
Leather and leather products	134	0.1
Stone, clay and glass products	2 786	1.1
Primary metal products	3 927	1.6
Fabricated metal products	7 628	3.1
Industrial machinery and equipment	29 626	12.1
Electronic and other electric equipment	27 514	11.3
Transportation equipment	34 076	14.0
Instruments and related products	11 676	4.8
Other manufacturing	7 520	3.1
Total manufacturing	243 954	100.0

Note: *Millions of US$. Historical cost basis.

Source: Bureau of Economic Analysis, *International Accounts Data*.

figures show (OECD, 1999a) that services contribute over 70 per cent of GDP whereas manufacturing contributes slightly more than 18 per cent. It is unfortunate, however, that private services transactions and US direct investment abroad are not classified the same and are not directly comparable.[4] Table 6.5 provides the export and import shares of total private services for the 11 broad categories used by the Bureau of Economic Analysis.

Table 6.6 provides the levels and shares of foreign direct investment for the major categories tracked by the Bureau of Economic Analysis.

Because the import and export shares and FDI shares are not directly comparable, there is little we can draw from their patterns. We note, however,

Table 6.5   Industry share of total private services exports and imports, 1995

Private services transactions	Share of total exports	Share of total imports
Travel	31.1	34.2
Passenger fares	9.4	10.7
Other transportation	13.4	21.0
Royalties and licence fees	13.4	4.8
Affiliated services	9.9	10.1
Education	3.7	0.7
Financial services	3.4	1.8
Insurance, net	0.7	4.0
Telecommunications	1.6	5.8
Business, professional and technical	8.7	3.5
Other	4.8	3.3

Source: Bureau of Economic Analysis, *Private Services Transactions by Type*.

the importance of exports to business services. We also note that the overall stock of FDI in finance and services is slightly higher than in manufacturing, though one would expect this to be a recent phenomenon. The relatively high FDI shares in finance, insurance and business are also apparent.

3.3 The Link Between FDI, Trade and Production Activity

The data presented thus far shows that there are complex relationships among trade, FDI and production activity. To add further support to this while trying to clear the picture as much as possible, we next present data on the geographical distribution of FDI and recent empirical evidence on the relationship between trade and FDI.

3.3.1 The geographical distribution of FDI
The geographical pattern of FDI is likely to vary across sectors as were export, import and FDI shares. Table 6.7 provides recent data on the geographical distribution of FDI stocks, delineating between the service sector and manufacturing sector.

The geographical pattern of FDI stocks reveals the concentration of investment in the United Kingdom and Canada. For manufacturing, these two countries account for 32 per cent of the share of FDI among the top 15 destinations. For the service sector FDI stocks are even more concentrated in

Table 6.6　Stock and shares of FDI for finance and services, 1995

Industry classification	FDI stock*	FDI share
Finance	68 135	27.5
Insurance	32 767	13.2
Real estate	1 194	0.5
Holding companies	11 6217	46.9
Services		
Hotels and lodging	2 044	0.8
Business services	15 043	6.1
Automotive rental and leasing	2 795	1.1
Motion pictures	1 682	0.7
Health services	267	0.1
Engineering	1 094	0.4
Management and public relations	2 354	0.9
Other		
Automotive parking and repair	68	0.0
Miscellaneous repair	235	0.1
Amusement and recreational	1 076	0.4
Legal services	145	0.1
Education	41	0.0
Accounting and auditing	225	0.1
Research and development	980	0.4
Other commercial services	1 670	0.7
Total finance and services	248 032	

Note: *Millions of US$. Historical cost basis.

Source: Bureau of Economic Analysis, *International Accounts Data*.

Canada and the United Kingdom as their combined share is in excess of 40 per cent. In addition, US FDI stocks are highly concentrated in the developed economies, particularly so in the service sector with 95 per cent of stocks located in Canada and the EU. Though the developed economies account for the majority of FDI stocks in both manufacturing and services, and though Canada and the United Kingdom are the top two nations in each sector, rank correlations show no significant relation among the pattern of nations across the two sectors. Hence, location strategies are likely to differ between the service and manufacturing sectors.

Table 6.7   Geographical distribution of FDI for manufacturing and services, levels and shares, 1995

Manufacturing	FDI* stock	FDI share	Services	FDI* stock	FDI share
Canada	41 248	19.0	United Kingdom	5 764	24.1
United Kingdom	27 865	12.9	Canada	4 014	16.8
Germany	23 671	10.9	Belgium	2 829	11.8
Brazil	17 651	8.1	France	2 324	9.7
Japan	16 664	7.7	Switzerland	1 440	6.0
France	16 555	7.6	Italy	1 257	5.2
Netherlands	10 451	4.8	Australia	1 055	4.4
Sweden	10 377	4.8	Netherlands	1 040	4.3
Italy	9 822	4.5	Germany	955	4.0
Mexico	8 856	4.1	Japan	686	2.9
Belgium	8 508	3.9	Denmark	651	2.7
Australia	8 466	3.9	Ireland	621	2.6
Ireland	6 894	3.2	Sweden	488	2.0
Spain	5 806	2.7	Spain	421	1.8
Switzerland	3 843	1.8	Mexico	412	1.7

Note: * Millions of US$. Historical cost basis.

Source: von der Ruhr (1999).

3.3.2 The impact of FDI on bilateral trade flows

Traditionally FDI and exports were viewed as being substitutes to each other. In other words, a firm could choose between exporting goods or capital. Recent theoretical and empirical research show that the relationship between trade and foreign direct investment is much more complex, with trade and foreign direct investment actually complementing each other.

Table 6.8 provides recent empirical evidence by Fontagne and Pajot (1998) on the impact of FDI *flows* on trade for the manufacturing sector. Because the authors consider FDI flows, the results below indicate the impact of *bilateral* FDI flows on *bilateral* trade. Countries in the columns are the exporting countries and countries in the rows are importing countries. The measures are generated from log-linear export equations that control for such things as market distance, income levels and market sizes, and reflect the change in trade flows resulting from the bilateral FDI flows.

As an example, the table indicates that Japan's exports to the United States

Table 6.8 *Trade creation resulting from bilateral FDI flows, 1994*

	US	Japan	Germany	UK	France	Italy	Netherlands	Denmark	Sweden	Switzerland	Spain	Canada	Australia
US	–	86	70	98	63	35	0	7	14	47	18	99	17
Japan	149	–	12	22	5	2	16	0	1	2	8	8	13
Germany	9	1	–	38	21	–7	20	2	–3	–1	8	0	0
UK	101	3	21	–	14	9	62	1	9	6	7	–3	33
France	42	2	19	35	–	14	15	1	–2	3	4	2	0
Italy	6	1	4	7	11	–	14	1	0	3	4	1	0
Netherlands	17	0	17	38	7	6	–	1	20	20		3	3
Denmark	11	0	3	13	2	0	5	–	9	2	10	1	0
Sweden	10	1	–4	6	–10	0	58	15	–	7		0	0
Switzerland	47	–2	16	23	11	1	11	1	8	–	–1	1	0
Spain	21	3	15	–1	14	9	12	0	0		–		
Canada	86	6		–14								–	2
Australia	20	2	0	29	3		3					2	–

Note: Expressed as a percentage, the additional trade created by bilateral FDI flows.

Source: Fontagné and Pajot (1998).

are 149 per cent higher than they would have been in lieu of bilateral FDI flows. In turn, US exports to Japan are 86 per cent higher than they would have been without the bilateral FDI flows. Hence, the US's FDI relationship with Japan results in a trade deficit as the FDI flows generate more exports to the US than imports to Japan. In contrast, the bilateral FDI flows between the United States and Canada and the United Kingdom, whose importance is demonstrated in the previous table, appear to be trade-balance neutral as they spur roughly equal amounts of imports and exports. What is evident in the table is that the bilateral FDI flows complement US imports *and exports* as opposed to substituting for them. The authors conclude that because exports increase, rather than being substituted for, US FDI results in greater US competitiveness in foreign markets boosting exports from home. Likewise the increase generated in imports reflects global relocations strategies with exports from foreign subsidiaries to home.

Fontagné and Pajot consider FDI stocks as well as FDI flows. The complementary relationships hold for stocks as well as each dollar of outward FDI stock results in 70 cents of new exports and $1.3 of imports. Hence, outward US FDI stocks are trade-deficit generating. Inward FDI stock, on the other hand, has a net substitution effect as each $1 of inward stock results in a 16 cent decline in imports and a 10 cent decline in exports. Fontagné and Pajot (1997) include FDI stock for services in these estimates and find that the negative trade effect of outward FDI and the positive effect of inward FDI disappear. The authors reason that FDI in services pertain to subsidiaries in wholesale trade which explains this outcome.

3.4 Conclusions

Our general conclusions in this section are summarized as follows:

- Manufacturing has become much more integrated in the global economy. Market shares of export, imports, and imported inputs have all increased significantly since 1975.
- The most export-oriented and the most import-oriented industries in 1975 remained so over the last 20 years.
- Import penetration increased at a much faster rate for high-import share industries than low-import share industries.

  (a) Changes in import shares are negatively related to the industry's capital–labour ratio. Hence, increasing rate of import penetration fall disproportionately on labour-intensive industries.

- The rising ratio of US merchandise trade to merchandise value-added indicates that outsourcing has become more important for the United States. Data on the share of exports and imports by end-use categories confirms this conclusion. Hence:

> (a) The US is importing products that are closer to the final stage of production and concentrating on the high value-added stages of production.
> (b) The phenomenon of outsourcing clouds the industry-level data as comparative advantage now takes place at a level of production rather than at the industry level. Firm-level data is required to conduct a more thorough examination.

- Manufacturing industries with the highest FDI shares (chemicals, industrial machinery, electronics) tend to have the highest export shares.

> (a) Overall, a positive ordinal relationship exists between FDI shares and export shares.
> (b) There is not an apparent relationship between FDI shares and import and imported-input shares.
> (c) Hence, the relationship between trade and FDI appears to be more complex than the traditional export substitution hypothesis.

- US manufacturing FDI shares are highly concentrated in the United Kingdom and Canada, and even more so in the service sector. Canada and Europe account for a high share of FDI stocks, particularly in services.

> (a) Though Canada and the United Kingdom are the top two locations of US FDI stocks, rank correlations between manufacturing and services do not verify an ordinal relationship among the pattern of nations.

- Bilateral FDI flows between the US and partner countries have differing effects on the US trade balance.
- Bilateral FDI flows are complements to both US imports and exports. Hence, FDI flows result in greater US competitiveness abroad in addition to global relocation strategies which result in exports from foreign subsidiaries.
- Outward US manufacturing FDI stocks complement US exports and imports whereas inward FDI stocks substitute for both imports and exports. Adding service stocks mitigates the trade deficit effects of outflows and positive trade effect of inflows.

In a more general sense, the evidence above shows that US corporations have effectively pursued globalization strategies over the last 30 years. In regard to production activity and FDI, outsourcing of low-value-added stages of production has become more important to US corporations while FDI continues to be directed to developed nations. In addition, FDI appears to complement trade as opposed to substituting for it. We conclude, therefore, that FDI strategies are primarily driven by ownership characteristics with acquired assets, whether tangible or intangible, complementing the corporation's existing comparative advantage.

4. CORPORATE GOVERNANCE AND CAPITAL ALLOCATION: ALTERNATIVE MODES[5]

The economic theory of corporate governance is rooted in theories of efficient allocation of capital. Efficient allocation of capital depends first upon investors having the knowledge needed to correctly estimate the expected return and risk of available investment portfolios. (1) *Misallocation costs* arise in the absence of such knowledge when scarce capital is not allocated to its highest yield use, and reflect costly efforts on the part of investors to acquire better knowledge regarding future states of the world and their probabilities. But capital markets also link investors who provide capital to firms which use it for investment purposes, so that the efficient allocation of capital also depends upon the relationship between investors and firms. (2) *Governance costs* are incurred when investors and corporate executives pursue conflicting goals, and adopt costly measures to achieve their respective goals. They include: (2a) agency costs (Jensen and Meckling, 1976; Spence, 1973; Stiglitz, 1975), including signalling costs on the part of firms seeking to demonstrate reliability and trustworthiness to investors and screening/ monitoring costs on the part of investors; and (2b) non-diversification costs incurred by investors who increase their degree of governance in order to lower screening and monitoring costs.[6]

Alternative modes of capital allocation and corporate governance may be distinguished according to the different regulatory regimes countries adopt to manage misallocation costs and governance costs. Dietl (1998, pp. 23ff) identifies two polar extremes in a wide spectrum of regulatory regimes, neoclassical and relational systems of regulation, and uses these polar extremes and a hybrid combination of the two to characterize the US, German and Japanese modes of capital allocation and corporate governance.

Neoclassical regulation, based on theoretical neoclassical economics, emphasizes allocative efficiency and competitive capital markets, and concentrates on removing capital market imperfections due to information asymmetries, manipulated markets and market power. Information asymmetries are addressed through accounting, disclosure and auditing rules, manipulated markets by prohibiting insider trading, and market power with anti-takeover laws and prohibition of universal banking (separation of commercial and investment banking). The latter combined with strict diversification requirements prevents financial intermediaries from acquiring control over non-financial institutions. Competitive capital markets are consequently associated with ownership fragmentation. One consequence of this is that investors do not commit themselves to long-term investment relations, since inability to earn governance rents means that investors discount future cash flows at high rates. Another consequence is that small corporations have good access to capital markets, since investors are protected by accounting, disclosure and auditing rules, insider restrictions, and so on.

Relational regulation, based on the property rights literature, focuses on governance efficiency and the economics of governance. Ownership concentration and market manipulation are not considered capital market imperfections, but rather as means of economizing on governance costs. Ownership fragmentation favoured in neoclassical regulation is seen as likely to attenuate property rights, and discourage efficient investments in governance and control. Concentrated ownership internalizes governance costs while it limits risk diversification. To compensate for undiversified investment portfolios, higher returns to investments in governance are needed. This implies weak accounting, disclosure and auditing rules, an absence of prohibitions against insider trading and market manipulation, and takeover-oriented regulations. Universal banking, the combination of commercial and investment banking, is also favoured in order to protect highly specific investments in corporate governance. Banks acquire greater ability to govern loans to non-banks, while the latter avoid credit rationing and undergo smoother restructuring when in financial distress. The resulting investment perspective is long term in contrast to neoclassical regulation.

Comparing actual national systems of regulation in terms of how well they address misallocation costs and governance costs requires that we consider the types of industrial production in which they specialize. Two characteristics of industrial development are central to this evaluation: industry maturity and investment plasticity. (1) *Industry maturity* occurs when market expansion is limited and typically occurs at the expense of competitors, product improvement is gradual and insiders have large amounts of knowledge for predicting the return and risk of new investments (for example, auto, steel). Immature industries have low entry barriers and high rates of innovation, while instability reduces the advantage of insider knowledge (for example, biotechnology, telecommunications, entertainment, financial services).

(2) *Investment plasticity* (Alchian and Woodward, 1987) concerns the relationship between the investor as principal and corporate executives as agents. High investment plasticity is associated with discretionary use of investment funds on the part of corporate executives, and occurs most commonly in industries especially reliant on human skills (for example, research laboratories, software, education). More technologically rigid industries (for example, mining, rail, power generation) have more implastic investments as investments are more clearly dedicated to identifiable purposes.

Here we focus on what these two industrial characteristics specifically imply about national systems of regulation that tend toward the neoclassical end of the spectrum, since this best describes the US case with which we are concerned.[7] Though US anti-trust law dates from the beginning of the century, much important legislation dates from the Depression of the 1930s. Key shareholder-oriented laws include: the 1933 Securities Act and the 1934 Securities Exchange Act which require registration and extensive disclosure concerning securities offerings, provide criminal penalties for false and misleading statements, and prohibit insider trading and market manipulation; the 1933 Glass–Steagall Act and subsequent laws that separate commercial and investment banking; and in the 1980s a variety of Supreme Court decisions allowing states to pass anti-takeover laws. In general, small investors in the US have many protections and corporate ownership is highly fragmented compared to Germany and Japan.

As a result of these laws and regulations, the US capital market is the largest in the world, yet US banks are not large relative to their German and Japanese counterparts. US holding companies are different from German joint stock companies and the Japanese equivalent (*kabushiki-kaisha*) in being subject to anti-trust regulation, so that intercorporate relationships are less common in the US. Finally, in recent years the power of corporate insiders has been increasingly curtailed through the greater presence of outside directors on corporate boards, a greater role for institutional and relational investors, shareholder resolutions, separation of CEO and board chair functions, and so on.

(1) *Mature vs. immature industries.* Neoclassical systems of regulation such as the US system are likely to have lower misallocation and governance costs in connection with immature rather than mature industries. In *immature industries* with considerable innovation and product development, the neoclassical system of regulation has low misallocation costs because competitive capital markets transmit knowledge on the part of outside investors, who have an informational advantage over insiders. Governance costs of the screening/monitoring variety are low, because accounting,

auditing and disclosure rules protect small investors and limit the control of executives. At the same time, accounting, auditing and disclosure rules also reduce signalling costs on the part of firms seeking investment funds. In contrast, since in *mature industries* insider knowledge is necessary and outside investors are at an informational disadvantage, a system that encourages their participation may actually impair allocative efficiency. In addition, screening/monitoring governance costs will be high for outside investors when insider knowledge does not transfer readily. These latter costs are likely to deter investment, and thus unintermediated capital markets tend to direct insufficient investment funds to firms.

One organizational response to this is the intermediation of capital markets. Intermediated capital markets in the form of investment banking allow outsiders to direct capital to mature industries, lowering both misallocation and screening/monitoring costs. But diversification requirements in neoclassical systems of regulation prevent banks from acquiring strong positions in non-bank firms, and thus capital markets are still likely to under-allocate financial resources to mature industries. Holding companies and multidivisional organizations[8] are a further organizational response to the presence of mature industries in neoclassical systems of regulation, because they channel investment funds to insiders while allowing them flexibility in their use. However, anti-trust law and enforcement in neoclassical systems of regulation also limits this organizational response.

(2) *Plastic vs. implastic investment.* Neoclassical systems of regulation such as the US system are also likely to have lower misallocation and governance costs in industries having implastic rather than plastic investments. Completely *implastic investments* create no governance problems, as screening/monitoring costs are minimized, and investors may be confident that executives will use investment funds as anticipated. At the same time, unintermediated capital markets are efficient as misallocation costs are minimal in the presence of accounting, auditing and disclosure rules. But with *plastic investments* firms exercise more discretion over use of investment funds and high screening/monitoring costs tend to deter investment, producing insufficient capital flows to firms. Additionally, should regulations favour outsiders at the expense of insiders, high misallocation costs are also likely since investors are unlikely to be in a position to recognize best investment fund uses.

Bank intermediation is an organizational response that may permit higher levels of investment in virtue of banks' specialization in screening and monitoring. However, diversification requirements still limit banks and other financial intermediaries from exercising control over non-bank firms. Holding companies and multidivisional organizations are also an efficient organizational response, since they may integrate firms engaging in highly plastic investment in larger organizations with stronger governance structures (especially where there are strong markets for corporate control). Again, antitrust law and its enforcement limit this organizational response.

5. IMPLICATIONS FOR US CORPORATION GLOBALIZATION

We turn to implications of this analysis for US firms in global competition. As a neoclassical system of regulation, we expect US firms that are successful in the global economy to more often be in immature industries and involved in implastic types of investment.

First contrast the case of mature industries. We distinguish among mature industries according to low or high capital expenditure–labor ratios. The US should have a sizable comparative disadvantage where this ratio is low, and we would accordingly expect the US to have low levels of FDI shares and high import shares in these industries. Corresponding to this, the six industries with the lowest FDI shares (leather and leather products, furniture and fixtures, apparel and other textiles, textile mill products, lumber and wood products, and paper and allied products) also have the lowest capital–labour ratios. (The category of other manufacturing is the exception.) These industries also have the lowest external orientation, ranging from a negative 6.1 per cent to just 4.2 per cent. Alternatively, in mature industries in which the capital expenditure–labour ratio is high (and where economies of scale can be achieved), US firms may overcome comparative disadvantage by locating outside the reach of US laws and regulations. While US firms are prevented from forming domestic intercorporate relationships by antitrust law, they may form joint ventures in foreign markets (recent examples include DaimlerChrysler, and Mattel-Bandai). This would imply high levels of foreign direct investment in such industries, and indeed we find that five of the six industries with the highest FDI shares (chemicals and allied products, petroleum and coal products, food and kindred products, electronic equipment and transportation equipment) have among the highest (top half) capital-labour ratios. (Industrial machinery is the exception.) Other than food and petroleum, these industries also have high export shares. However, their respective external orientation varies.

In the case of immature industries where US antitrust law is not at issue, we expect FDI to be low, both because there is no need to escape US laws and regulations, and because the domestic market is still being developed. We take engineering, management, legal, accounting and research and development services to be examples of immature industries, and find that their FDI shares are indeed low. We also expect the import share to be relatively low in immature industries, since US firms should be highly competitive in the domestic market. Examples here include business, professional and technical services where the export share is more than double the import share. But there is likely to be additional support for supposing that US firms have comparative advantage in immature industries when we emphasize the increasing importance in the global economy of the disintegration of production. Though there is not sufficient firm-level data on this development, the tendency of US firms to outsource low value-added stages of production and retain high value-added stages reinforces our conclusion that business, professional and technical services, such as design, branding, marketing and service operations, are areas of US comparative advantage.

It is more difficult to determine whether US firms are more successful in regard to relatively implastic as compared to more plastic investments, since an efficient organizational response of firms in neoclassical systems of regulation is the development of holding companies to carry out modest levels of plastic investment within comparatively large volumes of implastic investment. Thus firms in industries where plastic investments do occur, such as biotechnology giants with important laboratory divisions (for example, a Cargill or an Archer Daniels Midland), also engage in large amounts of relatively implastic investment. At the same time, the tendency of US firms to retain the high value-added portions of the production process may still provide some evidence of an emphasis on implastic forms of investment. When a firm such as Ford announces that it will reduce its involvement in manufacturing and assembly in order to concentrate on design, branding, marketing and service operations, it signals its intention to concentrate on implastic forms of investment, since these are relatively stable and transparent forms of business activity (though they are also relatively undeveloped and immature). Thus we take US firms' observable global activity in business and professional services as reflecting an increasing comparative advantage in immature industries and implastic forms of investment.

6.   CONCLUSION

The continuing global integration of markets presents US corporations with an interesting landscape of opportunities for expansion and profit realization. The corporation governance system, the set of relationships that yield a structure through which the corporations' objectives and means are determined and its progress in reaching those ends are monitored, influences management's approach to global market opportunities. The forces of global competition and the relational aspects of the governance system create a duality of forces that corporations encounter when expanding globally, and this duality is captured in the complex relationship that exists among trade and FDI strategies.

This chapter attempts to detail the alternative paths of globalization that US industries have followed, and relate this to views of corporate governance theories of capital allocation and market penetration. The economists' traditional view of comparative (dis)advantage at the industry level, at least in manufacturing, now only pertains to a few industries, primarily the most labour-intensive industries. Rather what exists today is a 'kaleidoscope comparative advantage' (Bhagwati and Dehejia, 1994) where US corporations outsource low-value-added levels of production and focus on high-value-added levels of production in which the US has a comparative advantage.

Furthermore, the traditional view that corporations may either export goods or export capital, which means that trade and investment are substitute strategies, has given way to a realization that the relationship between trade and FDI is quite complex with a complementary relationship existing, at least among the developed nations. The bulk of US FDI, as it is directed to other developed nations, is directed by ownership-specific characteristics that complement US corporations' comparative advantage in the high-innovation, high-value-added levels of production. Hence, the empirical evidence on the complex trade–investment relationship reflects a complicated pattern of US corporations in globalization.

Because we need to relate the data and theories at a much more disaggregated level, the clear predictions of the neoclassical economic model of corporate governance are somewhat blunted. Nonetheless, we do find evidence that US firms are successful in the global economy in immature industries and also mature industries which engage in high FDI and/or focus on high value-added stages of the production process. In addition, we find good reason to suppose that US firms are also successful in relatively implastic forms of investment, whether these types of investments are carried out in mature or immature industries. Further research into US firms' areas of comparative advantage in the world economy awaits better evidence and better understanding of the processes causing the disintegration of production while creating 'kaleidoscopic comparative advantage'.

NOTES

1. The OECD defines corporate governance as a set of relationships between a company's management, its board, its shareholders and other stakeholders, providing a structure through which the objectives of the company are set, the means of attaining those objectives are determined and performance is monitored (OECD, 1999b).
2. These ratios were calculated from the 1996 *Annual Survey of Manufactures*, Department of Commerce. Capital expenditures include new and used capital expenditures.
3. The Spearman Rank Correlation between the rank of FDI shares and export shares, 48 per

cent, is positive and significant at the 1 per cent level. The Spearman Rank Correlation between the rank of FDI shares and external orientation, import shares, imported-input shares are statistically insignificant.

4. See Quijano (1990) for information on the Bureau of Economic Analysis' statistics on foreign direct investment.
5. This section draws on Dietl (1998).
6. Misallocation costs may also take the form of non-diversification costs.
7. Dietl (1998) argues that Germany exhibits a relational system of regulation, and Japan exhibits a hybrid system of regulation with origins in the relational system.
8. Holding companies and multidivisional organizations own 100 per cent of their subsidiaries and are entitled to allocate 100 per cent of their subsidiaries' earnings. The legal structure of the former places more restrictions on doing so than that of the latter.

REFERENCES

Aeppel, T. (1999), 'Why making things is out of fashion', *Wall Street Journal*, p. Al, 8 November.

Alchian, A.A. and S. Woodward (1987), 'Reflections on the theory of the firm', *Journal of Institutional and Theoretical Economics*, **143** (1), 110–36.

Bhagwati, Jagdish and Vivek Dehejia (1994), 'Freer trade and wages of the unskilled – is Marx striking again?', in Bhagwati and Kosters (eds), *Trade and Wages: Leveling Wages Down?*, Washington, DC: The American Enterprise Institute, pp. 36–75.

Bureau of Economic Analysis, *International Accounts Data*, Various issues, http://ww.v.bea.doc.gov/bea/

Burt, Tim (1999), 'Ford to farm out key final assembly jobs to contractors', *Financial Times*, p. 1, 4 August.

Campa, José and Linda Goldberg (1997), 'The evolving external orientation of manufacturing: a profile of four countries', Federal Reserve Bank of New York, *Economic Policy Review*, July, pp. 53–81.

Daniels, Joseph and John Davis (2000), 'American macroeconomic issues and policy', in T. Brewer and G. Boyd (eds), *Globalizing America: The USA in World Integration*, Cheltenham, UK and Northampton, MA: Edward Elgar.

Department of Commerce (1996), *Annual Survey of Manufactures*, http://www.doc.gov

Dietl, Helmut M. (1998), *Capital Markets and Corporate Governance in Japan, Germany and the United States*, London: Routledge.

Dunning, John (1993), *Multinational Enterprises and the Global Economy*, Reading, MA: Addison-Wesley Publishing Company.

Feenstra, Ronald (1998), 'Integration of trade and disintegration of production in the global economy', *Journal of Economic Perspectives*, **12** (4), 31–50.

Fontagné, Lionel and Michaël Pajot (1997), 'How foreign direct investment affects international trade and competitiveness: an empirical assessment', CEPII Working Paper (November), No. 97-03.

Fontagné, Lionel and Michaël Pajot (1998), 'Is foreign direct investment a substitute for trade?', *The CEPII Newsletter*, 9 (Summer), Centre D'Études Prospectives et D'Informations Internationales, pp. 3–4.

Goldberg, Linda and Keith Crockett (1998), 'The dollar and US manufacturing', Federal Reserve Bank of New York, Current Issues in Economics and Finance, **4** (November).

Irwin, Douglas (1996), 'The United States in a new world economy? A century's perspective', *American Economic Review*, **86** (2), 41–51.

Jensen, M.C. and W.H. Meckling (1976), 'Theory of the firm: managerial behavior, agency costs and ownership structure', *Journal of Financial Economics*, **3** (1-4), 305–60.

Makhija, M. and S. Williamson (2000), 'The globalization of US industries', in T. Brewer and G. Boyd (eds), *Globalizing America: The USA in World Integration*, Cheltenham, UK and Northampton, MA: Edward Elgar.

Markusen, J. and A. Venables (1995), 'Multinational firms and the new trade theory', NBER Working Paper, No. 5036 (February).

Organization for Economic Cooperation and Development (1999a), *National Accounts: 1985-1997*, Paris: OECD, p. 22.

Organization for Economic Cooperation and Development (1999b), 'OECD Principles of Corporate Governance', www.oecd.org/daf/governance/principles.htm.

Pryor, Fredric (2000), 'The millennium survey: how economists view the US economy in the 21st century', *American Journal of Economics and Sociology*, **59** (1).

Quijano, Alicia (1990), 'A guide to BEA statistics on foreign direct investment in the United States', *Survey of Current Business*, Feburary, 29–37.

Rodrik, D. (1997), *Has Globalization Gone Too Far?*, Washington: Institute for International Economics.

Spence, M. (1973), 'Job market signaling', *Quarterly Journal of Economics*, **87** (3), 355–74.

Steinmetz, Greg and Michael Sesit (1999), 'Rising US investment in European equities galvanizes old world', *Wall Street Journal*, p. A1, 4 August.

Stiglitz, J.E. (1975), 'The theory of "screening", education and the distribution of wealth', *American Economic Review*, **65** (3), 283–300.

von der Ruhr, Marc (1999), 'Foreign direct investment in producer services', working paper, Indiana University, prepared for International Business and Economics Conference, St Norbert College.

7. Japanese firms in deepening integration: evolving corporate governance

Terutomo Ozawa

1. INTRODUCTION

In the pure neoclassical paradigm of capitalism, stockholders oversee and govern the management of business corporations by exercising their voting rights (collective power) in choosing, appointing and overseeing a team of business executives who can maximize profits and dividends in the stock-holders' interest. This model of 'shareholder capitalism', however, seems to have lost much of its conceptual relevancy even in the United States, the citadel of capitalism. This is because of the deepening chasm between the providers of capital and the users of capital – ever since the separation of ownership from management as celebrated by Berle and Means's seminal work, *The Modern Corporation and Private Property* (1932).

On this issue, Michael Jacobs, who headed a special office set up to study the competitiveness of American business during the Bush administration (1988–92), puts it:

> Lack of communication prevents investors from understanding management's long-term goals and objectives. Shareholders trade stocks *so often* and hold such *broadly diversified* portfolios that they cannot possibly keep up with the business activities of the companies they own. Because most U.S. investors are *detached* from the businesses they fund, they rely on outward manifestations of what is really going on within the company; namely, quarterly earnings and other accounting measures of performance ... When they are dissatisfied with corporate performance shareholders *sell stock rather than trying to discern the causes of poor performance and using their collective voice to communicate their concerns to management.*
>
> Companies exacerbate the problem by stacking their boards with directors handpicked by top management and *insulating themselves from the oversight traditionally provided by shareholders and lenders ...*
>
> This is in stark contrast to the practices followed in Japan and Germany where banks and shareholders are *long-term* investors. Capital providers become *intimately involved* with the companies in which they invest, either directly or

through agents, thereby establishing *a much greater degree of comfort and mutual trust*. (Jacobs, 1991, p. 10, italics added)

Americans were deeply concerned about their declining industrial competitiveness toward the end of the 1980s. It was in such a context that Jacobs made the above observation. Yet the onset of the bull market in the United States has reversed their whole perceptions. Now, America triumphs and considers its brand of capitalism the wellspring of superior corporate performance (hence governance). America's triumphalism is buttressed by the dramatic turn of fortunes in Japan and Germany, whose economies have slipped into lacklustre performance. Furthermore, Japanese banks are in a shambles with hundreds of billions of dollars in dud loans – and certainly appear in no position to claim their expertise for corporate oversight.

Why is it that the American system of corporate governance castigated as 'short-termism' (Jacobs, 1991) only several years ago has been capable of producing the longest period of economic prosperity in history – to the euphoric delight of stockholders? Is it a mere speculative 'bubble' which temporarily covers up some fundamental 'flaws' of American-style capitalism – just as Japan's 1986–90 bubble economy did to their underlying weaknesses? Or does this demonstrate that the American system of corporate governance is, after all, the best among the advanced countries? Conversely, why is it that the so-called 'main bank' system of corporate finance and governance in Japan, once touted as a more effective (more long-term-focused and competitiveness-inducing) alternative to its American counterpart (Aoki and Patrick, 1994), has crumbled, failing to monitor even its own reckless lending operations and causing 'the decade of lost growth' in Japan? Whatever happened to Japan's acclaimed main bank system? By citing Jacob's observation, I surely have opened a Pandora's box. My assigned task is, however, to explore only those questions related to Japan. But it should be kept in mind that Japan itself is now compelled to adopt some American practices under the forces of global financial capitalism.

The following themes will underlie this chapter:

(i)   Japan's main bank system was effective in capital allocation only during the early stages of Japan's postwar catch-up growth (at least until the early 1980s with 1975 as its watershed year) – but has been *over*-credited for corporate accountability (namely for successful performances of Japanese corporations, especially non-*keiretsu* affiliates);

(ii)   Japanese-style management has supplemented the main bank system as an instrument of self-governance. But it, too, has largely outlived its usefulness, now that the Japanese economy has entered an entirely different stage of growth that requires a new modality of corporate management; and,

(iii) being currently burdened by the overcapacity problem of corporate Japan (a legacy of *bank-loan capitalism*), its whole structure is in the throes of restructuring by adjusting to American-style *securities-market capitalism*, especially in connection with Japan's current Big Bang financial reforms.

In short, the leitmotif of this chapter is that Japan's system of corporate governance has gone through – and is now most dramatically going through – the *evolutionary* stages of adaptation along the path of its economic growth, from the initial catch-up industrialization to its emergence as the world's second largest economy – and presently in its struggle to dismantle the old (early postwar) institutional arrangements.

In what follows I will first briefly describe in what ways indirect finance was once used as a tool of corporate finance and governance under the main bank system of bank-loan capitalism, then explore how effectively Japanese corporations (*keiretsu-* and non-*keiretsu* firms alike) have been governed ever since they became practically 'independent' from banks in the mid-1970s, and finally look at how corporate Japan is groping for a new mode of corporate governance in the wake of financial liberalization and globalization, especially under Japan's Big Bang programme.

2.   BANK-LOAN CAPITALISM, JAPANESE-STYLE

In any economy banks serve as intermediaries in channelling savings into spending (investment and consumption). Indirect finance is ubiquitous across the world, although in the advanced capitalist countries such as the US, direct finance (stocks and bonds) plays a proportionately more important role in corporate finance. Hence indirect finance itself is nothing unique about Japan's heavy reliance on bank loans. What is distinctive about it is that indirect finance was once strategically controlled and micro-managed by the Japanese government (that is, by the Ministry of Finance which kept the Central Bank of Japan in its bailiwick) as an industrial policy tool to finance its catch-up growth by channelling funds into target industries, notably during its high-growth period.[1] Moreover, Japanese-style bank loan capitalism has only until recently been hugely biased against savers and in favour of borrowers and intermediaries such as banks and securities firms – all for the very purpose of keeping the cost of capital low for investment activities at home.

Under this policy, Japan's *keiretsu* banks became *conduits of capital investment* by their closely affiliated corporations in capital-intensive modern industries in the early postwar period. Furthermore, a key instrument of direct finance, stocks, actually came to be used as a *tool* of intricate organizational networking and relational coordination mostly within the *keiretsu* groups through cross-shareholdings – not so much as an object of investment to earn the market rates of return on capital (the normal use under capitalism). (In addition, stocks were frequently used as an instrument of unsavoury favours for organized crime, politics and big business, as revealed by the recently divulged scandals in post-bubble Japan.)

2.1. Central Bank-based Finance and the Main Bank System

Any fast-growing economy like postwar Japan requires increased finance. How to organize this is a critical issue in formulating a successful strategy for rapid industrialization.

In essence, two possible solutions exist. One is to borrow from overseas by running a current account (CA) deficit, that is, external borrowing. This, however, makes a debtor country vulnerable to the vagaries of foreign capital – and to a control of domestic productive facilities by foreign interests. The other is to create credit *internally* through a country's banking system with the help of its central bank. This second approach is self-reliant in development finance (though it risks inflation unless properly managed) and allows the country freedom from dependence on foreign capital. The first approach may be identified as 'CA deficit-based finance', and the second as 'central bank-based finance' (Ozawa, 1999a, 1999b).

In its early stages of postwar economic recovery and expansion (especially during the 1950s and 1960s), Japan relied more heavily on the second approach by minimizing borrowings from overseas. It also promoted domestic savings – indeed, very successfully – to raise funds internally. This self-reliant approach of financing economic development has been an ingrained policy ever since the start of Japan's modernization in the mid-nineteenth century. Japan's postwar financial industry came to be shielded from the global financial markets by way of regulations and protective measures. Foreign capital did not flow in freely, neither did domestic capital flow out freely.

In the early postwar period, the stock market initially did play a relatively important role as a source of funds for corporate investment, but it soon came to be overwhelmed by bank loans.[2] In order to control credit expansion, the government prohibited corporations from issuing bonds. A bond-issuing privilege was granted only to those institutions (mainly, three long-term credit banks and utilities) that the government specifically created to finance infrastructural facilities and services.[3]

Under central bank-based finance, the Bank of Japan pumped reserves into

Japan's major city banks, which in turn extended industrial loans to their own groups of closely affiliated corporations, the groups known as the bank-led *kinyu keiretsu* (financial conglomerates). There were six such major *kinyu keiretsu* that competed vigorously in arranging a core set of heavy and chemical industries (such as steel mills, petrochemical complexes, heavy machinery shops and shipyards) under the so-called 'one-set' principle. These *keiretsu* groups were led by their major banks (the Mitsui Bank, the Mitsubishi Bank, the Sumitomo Bank, the Fuji Bank, the Sanwa Bank and the Dai-Ichi Kangyo Bank), which supplied both short-term and long-term loans to, and exercised oversight on, their borrowers. All other Japanese corporations, large and small, tended to have similar banking arrangements in order to secure scarce funds in those days. Hence, this unique institutional set-up came to be known as the main bank system, a system of corporate finance and governance.

For example, this system is cogently described in Aoki (1988, pp. 148–9):

> Although the management of the [Japanese] firm may be *insulated from the discipline exercised through the stock market*, it is placed *under close monitoring by financial intermediaries*, particularly when it has to rely on borrowing from the bank for financing investment. The so called 'main bank' of a company, which is a major stockholder of the company and serves as an organizer of long-term loan consortiums to the company on a regular basis, plays an especially strategic role in monitoring. The main bank is in the position of being briefed about the company's general business and affairs in the capacity of a major stockholder and is able to scrutinize the company's strategic investment plan in the capacity of a major lender. It often sends its representative to the company's board of directors. Thus the main bank cum major stockholder has considerable ability to closely monitor its customer companies . . .
>
> . . . the individual stockholder is willing to delegate the monitoring function to the main bank cum major stockholder. The deviation from share price maximization by the company at the sacrifice of individual stockholders ... may in part be thought of as serving as the 'agency fee' paid by individual stockholders to the bank for that service.

In short, under this main bank system: (1) the banks were the major lenders of long-term and short-term capital and the major stockholders, (2) intercorporate stockholdings served to insulate the management of member companies from the threat of a takeover raid, (3) the main bank closely monitored management of the company to reduce bankruptcy risk, and (4) when a client company experienced a business difficulty, the main bank often took over management of the ailing company until the latter was restructured and revived.[4]

Setting aside the question of how the interest of savings-bent households was disregarded, proponents of this system conclude:

> The cross-country historical evidence, and the case of Japan, indicate that under

certain conditions banks are *better (or less expensive) able than* securities market institutions to evaluate the credit-worthiness of borrowers and the viability of new projects, to monitor the ongoing performance of firms, and to rescue or liquidate firms in distress. (Aoki and Patrick, 1994, pp. xxi–xxii, italics added)

Yet, the main banks are *only part of* a more intricate and multifarious macro-governance structure set up by the government to facilitate catch-up growth at the cost of household savers.

To begin with, Japan's postal savings programme played another key role in financial intermediation for policy purposes. During the high-growth period of heavy and chemical industrialization (1950–73), it captured nearly one-third of total private savings. Under interest rate controls the postal savings programme has been able to pay higher interest rates than city banks in attracting deposits from households. Its far-flung network of branch offices (33 000) throughout Japan, especially in rural regions, is a clear advantage.[5]

A huge amount of funds thus collected was channelled into the Trust Fund Bureau of the Ministry of Finance and distributed by its Investments and Loans Authority to various policy agencies such as (just to name a few) the Japan Development Bank, the Export–Import Bank of Japan and the Small Business Finance Corporation.[6] It was also from this source of funds that the government frequently *intervened* in the stock market for the purpose of 'stabilizing' (that is, manipulating) share prices.

In this sense, the stock market in Japan has frequently been 'tampered' with. Until the mid-1980s, for example, the share prices of major Japanese banks remained nearly constant for long periods of time, since regulators wanted 'to limit stock price fluctuations in an effort to influence the public's perception of risk at banks' (Genay, 1999, p. 2). Besides, until 1970 new stock had been usually issued at par (50 yen in most cases) rather than at market value and sold to existing shareholders on a pre-emptive right basis. This practice normally accounted for 80–99 per cent of new issues, for example, throughout the 1960s.[7] Hence, 'stock prices largely reflected the fixed cash dividend streams as though they were fixed income obligations infinite without maturity, combined with option values of the pre-emptive rights for new issues' (Ide, 1998, p. 82). But during the 1970s this peculiar arrangement began to be challenged, and altered, as new companies (mostly those that are not affiliated with the *keiretsu*) issued stocks at market prices.

In addition, dividends played a somewhat different role in Japan. They symbolized an assurance of the company's health to shareholders rather than a market rate of return on investment *per se*. Japanese companies used to pay a certain percentage (about 10 per cent) of the par value of the stock, even when they did not make any profit. 'Most Japanese companies try to pay this and will borrow or even sell assets to do so because missing this payment risks their ability to attract additional future funding from banks as well as from shareholders' (Abegglen and Stalk, 1985, p. 169).

Under heavy regulations and controls, furthermore, Japan's financial institutions were also compartmentalized into specialized activities and markets (for example, separation of the lending business from underwriting of, and trading in, securities and the trust business; separation of short- and long-term finance; separation of markets by size of customers via a two-tier banking system of city and local banks) – all for the purpose of channelling funds into specific areas. Three long-term credit banks were created for the specific purpose of promoting the development of capital-intensive heavy and chemical industries. Only these banks (along with public utilities) were authorized to issue debentures (bonds) to raise funds, but these debentures were not purchased by the public at large, but distributed solely to city banks through a complex 'subsidized monetization' scheme.[8]

Here it is thus important to keep in mind that this supposedly benign main bank system was merely one subset (though critical) of a much larger macro-organizational national scheme, *dirigiste* bank loan capitalism, that was specifically aimed at channelling scarce capital into Japan's big business sector under the direction of the Ministry of Finance, which in turn worked closely with the Ministry of International Trade and Industry, the major guardian of Japanese industry. The 'moral hazard' effect of government support was initially deliberately created and capitalized on for the purpose of inducing capital investment to build up heavy and chemical industries. But as will be detailed below, the moral hazard effect came home to roost to cause a bank loan supported bubble in the late 1980s.[9] *Therefore, the main bank system needs to be evaluated in terms of the whole dirigiste scheme of bank loan capitalism and not by just making a partial analysis of this intricate whole.*

In short, both saver–lenders (surplus units) and borrower–investors (deficit units) were completely snared in Japan's bureaucrat-run financial system and totally controlled for the national purpose of directing funds into strategic investment. The former, being prohibited to move money across borders, had to accept low interest rates at home, while the business sector was tied to the domestic banking industry as captive borrowers, since foreign borrowings were restricted in the early postwar period. Proponents have so far presented this government-controlled main bank system as an efficient ('better able than securities markets') set-up for corporate governance. But the system has eventually created troublesome problems as the Japanese economy became more capital-abundant and restrictions on overseas capital borrowing began to be gradually lifted. In other words, such a dirigiste system was certainly efficient as a mechanism of corporate finance when capital was scarce – but not so much as a system of corporate governance as might have been made out to be.

3. THE 'DEPARTURE FROM BANKS' PHENOMENON

In the final analysis, ironically, the main bank system has proved to be self-destructive; the more effective it was in facilitating Japan's catch-up indus-trialization in heavy and chemical industries (1950–74) by way of subsidized capital infusion, the faster its loss of effectiveness. And as will be made clear below, the process of globalization (that is, inevitable deregulations Japan had to implement in its financial sector) also has accelerated this paradoxical process.

Thanks to the relatively low-cost capital made available under Japan's bank loan capitalism, large-sized firms, especially those in the *keiretsu* groups, began to grow and accumulate internal reserves very rapidly.[10] Here, indeed, such a rapid expansion of internal reserves itself (i.e., a liberator of firms' dependence on banks) was made possible because the firms did not need to pay out much dividends (that is, after-tax payments) but made only interest payment (that is, pre-tax payments). In other words, the main bank system *itself* was responsible for promoting a quick accumulation of retained earnings and thereby making the banks' clients less dependent on loans – hence, less susceptible to monitoring and managerial interference. Further-more, in those days, Japanese firms paid dividends only as a certain percentage of the par value of shares. Hence, when they made a large profit, only a small fraction of it was paid out in dividends, leaving greater surpluses in retained earnings. In short, the rapid growth of individual firms' internal reserves inevitably reduced their reliance on bank credit and weakened banks' monitoring authority by the mid-1970s.[11]

In addition to rapidly accumulating internal funds, furthermore, new maverick companies began actively to issue new stocks at market prices, breaking the *keiretsu*-pleasing custom of issuing new equities at par value on a pre-emptive basis. Some successful Japanese corporations were also soon able to tap the international capital markets for their financing needs at lower costs as restrictions on borrowings from abroad were lifted with the amend-ment of the Foreign Exchange Control Law in 1980.[12]

As the result of ever-increasing internal funds and the opportunity to raise capital in the securities markets both at home and abroad, there was thus no reason for them to be subservient to their banks and dictated to about how to run their own businesses by bank officials. Besides, the main bank system might not have been as beneficial for the affiliated firms as described by its proponents, who emphasize the magic of the system in solving the problems of information asymmetry and transaction costs. One empirical study (Weinstein and Yafeh, 1998) reveals (i) that the cost of capital of Japan's bank-affiliated firms was higher than that of their peer (nonbank-affiliated ones) and (ii) that most of the benefits from relation banking were appropriated by the banks. No wonder, then, that the 'departure from banks' syndrome intensified.

Given these developments, a question naturally arises: if the main bank began to lose its monitoring capability – if not totally but substantially, how were its affiliated firms overseen and governed?

On this issue, Aoki (1988, p. 149) raises a question but leaves it unanswered:

> as the [Japanese] firm becomes less dependent on the bank in its corporate financing, the monitoring capability of the bank starts to weaken. Whether individual stockholders exercise their own monitoring through the corporate governance structure of the [Japanese] firm or the stock market, or whether management of the firm is comfortably left in a vacuum of effective monitoring *remains to be seen.* (Italics added)

4. HOW, THEN, WAS CORPORATE GOVERNANCE MAINTAINED IN JAPAN?

Although 'comfortably left in a vacuum of effective monitoring [from the banks]', Japanese corporations continued to be quite efficient and productive. In fact, many corporations emerged as world-class performers, especially after the Japanese economy moved into what may be called 'differentiated Smithian' industries which are assembly-driven, components-intensive and consumer-oriented (notably automobiles and electronics) in the late 1960s.[13] The question is, how have they been so effectively governed even after they escaped from intrusive (but supposedly effective) monitoring by their main banks – and especially more recently, after the banks themselves were bogged down in an unprecedentedly serious bad debt problem in the wake of the bubble burst and became preoccupied with their own oversight imbroglio?

Although it is not so widely known, many of Japan's best-performing corporations actually did *not* originate as *keiretsu* affiliates, ones which were supposedly best supervised by their main banks. These high performers started out as outsiders (non-*keiretsu* upstarts) and have largely remained as such ever since. A prime example is the Toyota Motor Corporation, the world's most efficient car maker, which has had no affiliation at all – either with any *zaibatsu* (in the prewar days since its birth in 1937) or any major *keiretsu* (in the postwar period). In fact, it has persistently avoided external debts.[14] Yet the company has been quite innovative and exemplary in management. Indeed, it is Toyota that innovated a world-renowned manufacturing technology, lean (or flexible) production (Ohno, 1978; Womack et al., 1990), and revolutionalized the automobile industry worldwide . The company also set up its own auto finance company out of its huge profits. Its internal reserves became enormous

– so much so that Toyota itself came to be known as the 'Toyota Bank'. In short, Toyota's growth and excellent performance practically had nothing to do with the main bank system.

Another example is Honda, which early on had a hard time securing bank loans because of its status as an independent entrepreneurial firm. (Only later on, the company came to be loosely 'affiliated' with the Mitsubishi Bank.) Similarly, Sony was once even slighted by Japan's industrial guardian, the Ministry of International Trade and Industry (MITI), when it sought permission to secure a Bell Laboratory's licence on the transistor, because of its unknown status (that is, non-affiliation with any *keiretsu*). (By comparison, for example, Mitsubishi Electric would not have such a problem dealing with MITI). Likewise, Matsushita Electric Industries quickly accumulated huge internal reserves and has ever since been practically free from external debt.[15] It is also often known as the 'Matsushita Bank'.

For all these cases (Toyota, Honda, Sony and Matsushita – just to cite a few), it is clear that we cannot give credit to the main bank system for their astonishing success in business performance. In fact, they were the very non-*keiretsu* upstarts which challenged the practice of stock issue at par by selling new shares at market prices in the 1970s and also took advantage of the overseas capital markets for their finances as capital liberalization occurred in the 1980s. They thus became independent from banks. But how did they manage to govern themselves so effectively and profitably?

In terms of American perspectives, an appropriate mechanism of corporate governance (an *independent* mechanism away from executives and the board of directors) is required, since corporate managers have a strong proclivity to maximize their own interests (executive compensation and 'perks') at the cost of stockholders. This is essentially served by the stock market. Stock prices are supposed to indicate approval or disapproval of corporate managers' performances. Hence, executives are highly sensitive to the stock prices, always worried about the bottom line. And threats of takeovers keep managers on their toes.

No doubt, there is a strong tendency for American managers to reward themselves 'excessively' in executive compensations and perks – excessively, particularly judged by the Japanese standards.[16] This is because managers' attitudes and behaviour critically affect the morale of employees and the *esprit de corps* (hence the productivity) of organization. Executives' salaries and perks should not be excessive lest they alienate and demoralize employees. Here, Japanese management usually stresses the 'we-are-all-in-the-same-boat' corporate ideology to secure maximum cooperation (hence maximum possible devotion) from workers.

In 1993, for example, Japanese executives earned, on average, less than 32 times the pay of the average factory worker (not including bonuses for workers that can boost their annual salaries by a third). This contrasts sharply with American executives who earned roughly 157 times average factory worker's pay.[17] More recently, this pay differential has surely increased, since American executives, especially CEOs, receive generous – often exorbitant – stock options. Nowadays, the average American CEO makes as much as *419 times* the wage of the average factory worker.[18] (Some Americans, such as the Fed's chairman, Alan Greenspan, are critical of this excessiveness in executive compensations.)

Why is it, then, that Japanese executives have been, on the whole, relatively better self-disciplined yet highly motivated to run businesses effectively – without much banks' and shareholders' oversight?

4.1 Self-governance

Japan is basically an egalitarian society, and Japanese businessmen have been traditionally beholden, with a strong sense of loyalty and obligation, to their own group and subordinates. Unlike American society which is strongly embedded in individualism, selfish and opportunistic behaviour is not looked upon favourably in Japan. Besides, against the backdrop of the adverse economic conditions in early postwar Japan, the Japanese company came to be organized and governed as a multi-stake *sharing unit*, representing the interests of its employees (in job security and income), its creditors (in loan obligations) and its suppliers (in steady and reliable orders for sub-assemblies, parts, components and accessories) – in addition to the stake of its stock holders (in long-term corporate growth). Collaboration and cooperation were a necessity for survival in the war-devastated Japanese economy.[19]

Thus, the self-discipline of managers, who are devoted to the welfare of their business organization rather than to their own pecuniary and material wealth, cannot be disregarded, since it does constitute an effective instrument of corporate governance. And self-discipline was all the more enhanced by the presence of fierce rivalries in Japan's domestic markets, a high level of share-grabbing competition which has often been described as '*kato kyoso* [excessive competition]'.[20] Vigorous competition makes Japanese companies – and their executives – frugal and conscious of cost reduction. When business slumps, executives are usually the first to cut their own salaries, and the rank-and-file follows suit. In a sharing unit everyone shares the burden of adjustment for survival.

In addition, the idea of a company as a sharing unit is closely related to the (now legendary) 'Japanese-style management' characterized by a combination of three distinctive features: (i) lifetime employment (career job); (ii) seniority-based (experience-gauged) promotion and compensation; and (iii) enterprise-based labour unions. These managerial practices were actually compatible with, and facilitated by, the high-growth environment Japan once enjoyed during the four decades of 1950–90.

Indeed, Japanese-style management worked very nicely in those high-growth days. As the firm grew, demand for workers expanded, and a guarantee for lifetime job security was offered without any difficulty. Expansion of the firm size in a pyramidal shape made it possible to create new managerial and supervisory positions quickly, accommodating the seniority-based procedures for promotion and remuneration. Enterprise-based unions, whose *raison d'être* and interests are identical with the fate of their specific firms, collaborated with management in the interest of corporate growth and profitability. Bi-annual bonuses (the amount of which was determined by corporate performance) came to be paid to workers. This system enabled companies to form human capital development among employees via job rotations for multi-skilling and to benefit from the knowledge and information possessed by employees through the suggestion system and quality circle (QC) activities. The net result was the strong competitiveness of Japanese corporations.

As emphasized before, Japanese-style management saw its best days during Japan's high-growth environment, which was made possible during its consecutive stages of 'heavy and chemical industrialization' (1955–74) and 'assembly-driven components-intensive, assembly-based growth' (notably 1970–90). And the availability of low-cost long-term funds (created by the policy of central-bank-based finance) facilitated firms' entries into the capital-intensive heavy and chemical industries in particular. Here, formation of the *keiretsu* groups was instrumental in avoiding 'coordination failure' (Aoki et al., 1997), thereby promoting their entries into otherwise highly risky, scale-driven industries. During the stage of 'assembly-driven, components-intensive industrialization' (notably automobiles and semi-conductors), non-financial corporations (manufacturers) became more or less independent because of accumulated internal reserves, equity issues and the opportunities (created through gradual deregulations) to tap the overseas capital markets. All these factors helped Japanese corporations grow in size, facilitating the practice of Japanese-style management – and corporate self-governance.

4.2   Interlocking Shareholdings for Mutual Monitoring

In addition to the self-governance mechanism, cross-shareholdings are supposed to serve as another means of monitoring. Especially in the case of the *keiretsu*, 10–25 per cent of each constituent firm's stock is held by other firms in the group. In addition, directorships are interlocked with each other in two-thirds of these firms; in other words, they have full-time executives dispatched from affiliated firms. 'With access to senior management and confidential data, these related company shareholders are better prepared to monitor and influence corporate decisions than a fragmented group of public stock owners' (Jacobs, 1991, p. 68).

Corporate Japan exhibits highly dense crisscross patterns of mutual stock ownership among related companies. The main bank owns shares of its affiliated corporations and other affiliated (usually smaller) banks (up to the legal limit of 5 per cent in each), and vice versa (no limit for non-financial firms, so long as they own other non-financial firms). In general, corporations own stocks in each other – mainly within their *keiretsu* group. The bank's holdings of stocks are said to serve as an important means of influencing the course of business in their client firms, while intercorporate stockholding in the non-banking sector is also a symbol of mutual trust (and hostage exchange) and long-term relations.[21] In fact, the interlocking of stock ownership and directorship is what characterizes the *keiretsu* system, both of the financial (*kinyu*) and industrial (*sangyo*) types. It is expected to serve as a mutual monitoring mechanism. Under this system, executives of related firms are thus the key providers of accountability.[22]

As illustrated in Figure 7.1, in 1950, for example, individual investors owned a little over 60 per cent of total value of stocks, financial institutions (mainly banks and insurance companies) had about 12 per cent and corporations 11 per cent. But about 40 years later (in the latter half of the 1980s during the height of the 1987–90 asset bubble), individual investors' share declined to 24 per cent, but financial institutions' and corporations' share rose to more than 40 per cent and 28 per cent, respectively. Investment trusts (the Japanese equivalent of mutual funds), foreign investors and pension funds owned relatively small portions, all less than 10 per cent at any point in time over the 1950–94 period. (Cross-shareholdings at 481 of Japan's biggest companies stood at 46 per cent at the end of January, 1997.[23]) In short, the intercorporate holding of stocks by banks and corporations became quite dominant in the late 1980s, accounting for as much as two-thirds of stocks.

In sum, after the 'departure from banks' phenomenon set in, two governance mechanisms can be credited for corporate accountability: Japanese-style management and mutual oversight through reciprocal shareholdings. It can then be argued that these two institutional set-ups served to fill 'a vacuum of effective corporate governance' created as a result of the enervation of main banks' controls.

5. ADVERSE CONSEQUENCES OF THE MAIN BANK SYSTEM AND JAPANESE-STYLE MANAGEMENT

Whatever the stage-specific effectiveness of the main bank system and

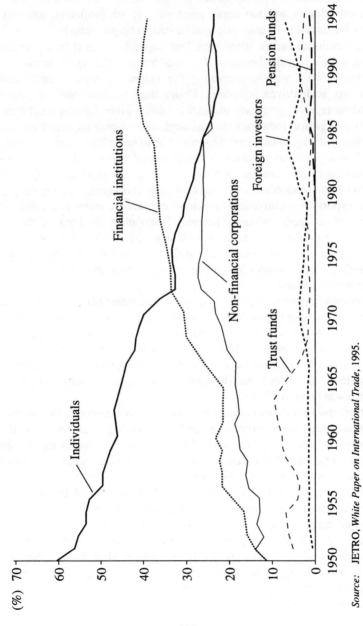

Source: JETRO, *White Paper on International Trade*, 1995.

Figure 7.1   Ownership distribution of Japanese stocks by holder

Japanese-style management, these unique institutions created two major problems which have come to haunt the present Japanese economy: (i) the overcapacity, overdiversification and overstaffing of productive facilities in the non-financial (especially manufacturing) sector (with too many unprofitable subsidiaries and too many employees to be profitable) and (ii) the excessive number of banks (too many banks to be profitable).

As mentioned earlier, when bank-loan capitalism was at its zenith during Japan's heavy and chemical industrialization, the main bank system functioned very well in promoting the *keiretsu* groups to enter capital-intensive, scale-driven industries. Under the so-called 'one-set' principle, furthermore, each group was induced to enter a given (overlapping) range of promising growth industries such as steel, petrochemicals, heavy machinery and shipbuilding. In fact, each *keiretsu* came to resemble a 'semi-economy' in itself. And vigorous rivalries at home forced them to look for overseas markets as vents for excess supplies. The more they produced, and exported, the lower the production cost because of scale economies – hence, the greater their export competitiveness. Japanese exports in those days were often described as '*gohu yushutsu* [torrential exports]'. So long as the world economy grew (as it did during the Golden Age of Capitalism of 1950–90), and so long as the inevitable trade conflicts created by such export-oriented strategy (neo-mercantilist policy) remained manageable, Japanese industry continued to expand.

But such impetuous capacity-building was doomed to cause the problem of overcapacity, once the world economy slumped or once competition emerged from other Asian economies as new suppliers of similar goods and Japan's comparative advantage would erode. (This new chasing-up competition itself was in part created by Japanese multinationals' headlong rush into other Asian countries.) And indeed, the slow-growth era did arrive when Japan's asset bubble was burst in 1990.[24]

Overcapacity was also associated with excessive diversification within the *keiretsu* group. Many corporations ended up holding a large number of subsidiaries (their own suppliers and affiliated firms). So long as Japan enjoyed high growth, these bloated corporations could cross-subsidize less profitable operations with more profitable ones.

Moreover, Japanese-style management has contributed to this trend of corporate overdiversification and self-aggrandizement – and overstaffing. Lifetime employment and the seniority-based system of promotion and compensation required continuous corporate expansion and diversification so as to create new career positions in a hierarchical fashion. Hence, the result was the 'growth-at-any-cost' school of management, a style of management totally incompatible with the present era of slow growth and increasingly globalized market environment.[25] Overcapacity in production is estimated at more than Y80 trillion ($656 billion or about 12 per cent of GDP).[26]

In the meantime, the banking sector, too, was inexorably headed for excess capacity. As Japan's large corporations accumulated internal reserves, banks began to lose major customers for lending. The 'departure from banks' phenomenon was synonymous with the appearance of an excess banking capacity. Having been used as the key policy instrument of bank loan capitalism, however, the banks still felt protected by the government and guaranteed for bailout if anything went wrong. In fact, the Ministry of Finance itself publicly assured that no bank would be allowed to fail.[27] The banks thus came under the spell of moral hazard.

It was against this backdrop that banks' imprudent lending resulted in a short-lived bubble in Japan over 1986–90. The Plaza accord of 1985 soon drove up the yen phenomenally. Fearing a 'high-yen' recession, the Bank of Japan pumped money into the economy. This made the banks awash in liquidity. Having lost many large borrowers, they had to look for new customers. The banks found small- and medium-sized enterprises, real estate firms and construction companies as their new major borrowers. They also channelled loans through non-bank banks (that is, housing loan companies and consumer credit firms), since the latter were less strictly regulated than the banks themselves.

Low interest rates and the abundance of liquidity fuelled the rising prices of stocks and real estate. Many Japanese firms issued new shares at home and bonds (including so-called 'warrants') overseas, but actively put the proceeds back into the market, driving stock prices even higher. This speculative activity was even lauded as *zai-tekku* (financial engineering). The banks became all the more anxious to lend to anyone, especially those who had land, since the value of land as collateral soared due to speculation. The rising stock prices in banks' portfolios increased their capacity to make even more loans. In those days, Japanese banks were accustomed to the 'too important to fail' assurance by the Ministry of Finance. The bubble and its aftermath (so far, approximately $800 billion in non-performing loans) were *nothing but the outcomes of the main bank system gone astray*. Then, an obvious question is: how on earth have the main banks that were supposed to have an oversight capacity for their clients' investment decisions ended up with such imprudent lending activities themselves?

It should be mentioned here that those corporations which became independent from banks in long-term finance did not totally cut off their relations with banks, of course. Banking services for operating funds and short-term loans have certainly been required. Cross-shareholdings with banks did continue to help shield corporations from takeovers and to keep common stockholders at bay by marginalizing their power – hence there was no room left for common shareholder activism through individual proxy votes.

Furthermore, the efficacy of self-discipline, combined with Japanese-style management, led to hubris on the part of Japanese corporations with the 'we know best' attitude. Stockholders' annual meetings came to be held all on the same day so that investors with a diversified portfolio could not attend all the meetings.[28] Also, so-called *sokaiya* (literally, 'general meetings experts'), who can expedite proceedings by unsavoury means, were hired to suppress any questioning from common stockholders. The *sokaiya* had close ties with organized crime (*yakuza*).

In addition, a so-called '*tobachi*' (literally, 'flying') practice – under which brokerage firms' prime customers were guaranteed for profit – was rampant in the securities brokerage industry. In fact, this illegal practice finally cost Yamaichi Securities, Japan's oldest and fourth largest company, its demise after a century's existence in November 1997.

As the bad-loan crisis became worse, a credit crunch soon ensued in late 1997. The large *keiretsu* businesses with close ties with their main banks were able to have their loans renewed, since their payment failure meant the collapse of the banking industry. Small and mid-size businesses were the ones which had to bear the full brunt of the credit crunch. Hence, the government had to step in and provide loan guarantee facilities for them. Almost all (more than 90 per cent) of these handicapped companies that apply for the loans are said to be able to secure guarantees – hence they received loans. Another and new bureaucrat-driven form of corporate finance has been in the making.

6. JAPAN'S BIG BANG: A FINALE TO THE MAIN BANK SYSTEM AND THE *KEIRETSU* SYSTEM?

In November 1996, then Prime Minister Ryutaro Hashimoto announced that Japan's financial industry would have its own Big Bang – analogous to Britain's a decade earlier – to set itself free from the shackles of heavy regulations and protection from foreign competition. Japan's financial industry would no longer be secluded; it would have to be integrated with the outside world. Japan's plan is quite dramatic, in the sense that its entire financial sector (inclusive of banking, securities business and insurance) is to be thrown open to market competition.

The Big Bang consists of reforms in three key areas: (i) transactions involving foreign exchange, that is, cross-border capital flows; (ii) securities brokerage businesses and financial product development (derivatives and securitization); and (iii) merging of commercial and investment banking and insurance (that is, removal of the separation of these financial services under Article 65 of the Securities Exchange Law, Japan's equivalent of the US

Glass–Steagall Act of 1933). In April, 1998, the Big Bang was initiated, and all the reforms are supposed to be completed by 2001.

Given the comprehensiveness of the reform, the Big Bang will have a significant impact not only on Japan's financial sector but also more widely on the Japanese economy as a whole. In particular, it will vastly alter the Japanese system of corporate finance and governance.[29]

The immediate impact is, of course, on the financial industry. Already some drastic changes have been observable. For starters, there has occurred a sudden market penetration by foreign financial institutions, an event that was unthinkable just a few years ago. The financial industry, especially securities brokerage, used to be closed for foreign participation.

In this regard, investment trusts (the Japanese version of mutual funds), notably those marketed by American investment firms, such as Merrill Lynch, Fidelity, Morgan Stanley, Goldman, Sachs & Co. and Citigroup (Travelers Group),[30] initially gained popularity quickly when they were offered for the first time in 1998. Japan's fast-growing individual investor market is soon expected to rival the US market.

Japanese households now possess approximately $12 trillion in personal financial assets, more than half of which were on deposit in banks and the postal savings programme, earning less than 1 per cent interest.[31] Surprisingly, however, they have so far been reluctant to – or at a loss how to – directly shift their assets to securities, not to speak of doing so abroad to take advantage of higher yields. Asset management is therefore emerging as one of the most promising new businesses.[32] Now that controls on commission rates have been completely lifted in October 1999, competition will intensify in the brokerage business. Since Japanese securities firms are thus deprived of comfortable commission incomes from stock retails, they are striving to offer more asset management services.

Furthermore, banks, securities firms and insurance companies will be vying with each other fiercely in providing one-stop financial services (for combined services in commercial and investment banking and insurance) – for the benefit of customers. In addition, some European private banking firms, such as UBS Group and Lombard Odier Holding, both of Switzerland, along with Citibank have also begun to provide private portfolio management for rich Japanese clients (with at least Y100 million in financial assets).[33]

Not only are the foreign institutions eager to capture a huge share of individual assets but they are also keen to introduce new financial products (derivatives and securitized products). They are way ahead of their Japanese counterparts in product development, marketing and risk management. The Japanese institutions are likely to step up their search for foreign alliance partners who can provide know-how in new financial products and services. Partly because the Ministry of Finance used to regard derivatives basically as instruments of gambling (pure speculation) and law evasion, the markets for futures and derivatives have long been retarded in Japan. In fact, it is said that 'fully one-third of the business in Nikkei 225 stock futures is conducted on its Singapore Monetary Exchange (Simex)'.[34]

No doubt, rapid foreign participation in domestic financial services is facilitating the growth of the securities markets in Japan. But, individual investors' interests in stocks and other securities, which are brokered through mutual funds and private banking services, will not raise the level of their consciousness as owners of business enterprises; they are merely interested in diversifying risks and maximizing earnings – without any attachment to the management of business enterprises. In other words, they will be merely trading the 'commoditized' equities American-style:

> A share of stock is not what it used to be. Originally, a share of stock was more than an economic investment, it was an ownership interest in a company embodying both rights and responsibilities. Today, a share of stock is a financial commodity, little different from an ounce of silver or a pork-belly futures contract. The increasing legal and regulatory barriers that prevent stock holders from behaving as owners, coupled with new technologies, that make it less expensive and easier to trade stocks, are transforming the stock market into less of a place to raise capital and exercise corporate oversight than a gambling casino. (Jacobs, 1991, p. 31)

There seem to be, however, some glimmers of investor activism. Japanese individual investors have traditionally behaved very passively as 'patient – or rather captive – shareholders'. With increased participation of more vocal foreign investors, some common Japanese shareholders have begun to be more active and assertive at shareholders' meetings. It is even said that the *sokaiya* are now recasting themselves as born-again shareholder advocates, Ralf Nader style.[35] But given a small fraction (about 25 per cent) of shares held by individual investors at the moment, shareholder activism is not likely to have any significant impact on corporate governance. In fact, even if the entire $12 trillion in personal assets are invested in stocks, not much influence on corporate governance is expected because of the 'commoditization' of equities – unless mutual funds and other institutional investors themselves consciously exercise proxy votes to monitor and influence the management of corporate Japan.[36]

Now that foreign competition is expected to present direct challenges not only on the home turf but also in foreign markets (where Japanese corporations domiciled at home are now free to borrow directly from foreign banks[37]), Japanese banks can no longer have captive customers, individual and corporate alike. They, notably regional banks, still retain a grip on small- and medium-sized firms in the rural areas. But even small entrepreneurs may soon search low-cost loans and banking services. Eventually, those foreign institutions which enter the Japanese market may also compete even in the rural areas. The main bank practice will be significantly weakened – and may even disappear – by the forces of competition, and banking business will be more and more arm's-length oriented.

As mentioned earlier, there are too many banks in Japan, a legacy of dirigiste bank loan capitalism. An excessive supply of banking services is indicated by the fact that 'the biggest 17 Japanese banks combined have only slightly more revenue than the top two in the US',[38] and that 'the most profitable Japanese banks earn a 2 per cent return on equity', while 'top American banks earn five to 10 times as much'.[39]

Hence, the problem of excess banking capacity needs to be addressed if banking reform is to succeed. In 1997, with an eye to streamlining industrial organization, the Japanese government revised the Anti-Monopoly Law in such a way as to allow financial institutions to establish holding companies. The first case of using this new opportunity is the recent unification of Japan's three biggest banks with $1.26 trillion in assets: Fuji Bank, Dai-Ichi Kangyo Bank (DKB) and Industrial Bank of Japan (IBJ) decided to join under a holding company (in the fall of 2000) and realign their operations by creating separate companies, each specialized in different banking services, such as retail, commercial and investment banking. This merger would create the world's largest banking group, nearly one-and-a-half times as much as the current largest, Deutsche Bank AG – and about twice the size of the biggest American bank, Citigroup ($668 billion in assets).

How will this improve corporate performance and governance? Since they have strengths in different areas (namely comparative advantages in different banking functions), business specialization and concentration will bring about benefits by way of scale-cum-scope economies. That is, more efficiency may be gained in part because of a better oversight of the three banks' performance via the newly created holding company and also because this three-way combination forces them into corporate restructuring and cost-cutting. There are, however, some costs of such a huge merger in terms of inevitable turf battles involving personnel management, although the net gains are expected to be positive in the long run.

Hence, other Japanese banks are likely to follow suit lest they be outmanoeuvred. Two other major banks, Sumitomo Bank and Sakura Bank, also have decided to merge by April 2002. Actually, two mid-sized banks (Tokai Bank and Asahi Bank) had made public their intention to set up a joint holding company in the year 2001 much earlier than the Fuji–DKB–IBJ merger, although it did not make much news outside of Japan because of their relatively small size (the two banks when merged will be the seventh largest worldwide). This is perhaps the most effective way of reorganizing the bloated Japanese banking industry, which is after all the very intention of the revised Anti-Monopoly Law. Indeed, the insurance industry appears to ride on the bandwagon: three major non-life insurers (Mitsui Marine and Fire Insurance Co., Nippon Fire and Marine Insurance Co. and Koa Fire and Marine Insurance Co.) are in the process of setting up a holding company to streamline their operations as a single group, Japan's largest so far in non-life insurance.

Bank mergers may be a finale to the main bank system. In fact, IBJ President Masao Nishimura reportedly proclaimed the death of the system, since banks themselves are no longer interested in maintaining their past lending practices which are not bottom-line oriented.[40] The mega-merger plan of Fuji–DKB–IBJ to sell off a third of their shareholdings in corporate customers also signals an end to long-term custodial banking relations. Sumitomo Bank's president is also quoted as saying 'The logic of Japanese corporate groups no longer holds water'.[41] The outcome of these mergers will be a greater emphasis on more profit-oriented arm's-length banking, as the *keiretsu*-based banking weakens. After all, more and more of banks' shares will be traded on the stock exchange on the basis of their profitability and future prospects.

Parallel to this movement in the banking sector, non-financial corporations, especially those large-scale *keiretsu* manufacturers that were at their zenith during Japan's high-growth period may move in the same direction. They are stuck with many unprofitable divisions (internally within themselves) and affiliated subsidiaries (semi-externally). In other words, their organizational size has grown so large that they now suffer diseconomies of both scale and scope. A holding company makes it easier to focus on core operations by separating and eventually selling off unprofitable non-core operations. For example, Toshiba Corporation, a highly diversified manufacturer of electric and electronic goods (ranging from nuclear generators to lap-top PCs to electric razors), has already decided to spin off unprofitable businesses through this mechanism. Many other firms including Hitachi and Sanyo Electric are waiting for Japan's corporate tax code to be revised to introduce a consolidated tax system.[42]

In addition, the problem of proliferation of subsidiaries was also the result of the seniority-based Japanese-style management. Those employees who did not reach the top were normally parked in affiliates. But with or without the holding companies, some companies have already announced their determination to cut their subsidiaries. For example, Sumitomo Corporation (trading) will cut its top subsidiaries from 300 to 150; Mitsubishi Electric (machinery) will reduce domestic units from 180 to 140; Daiei (retailing) will drop 13 of 132 affiliates; and Itohchu Corporation (trading) will cut a third of its 1027 worldwide subsidiaries in the next few years.[43]

The government has lately been enacting a series of new bills (under the so-called 'Industry Revitalization Laws') all designed to revive and enhance competitiveness. For example, liquidation of surplus capacity and assets is promoted by loss-deducting tax measures. The commercial code is also being revised to encourage mergers and acquisitions (M&As). And the tax code is being rewritten to create 'angel' investors for small start-ups.

In short, interestingly, there is thus asymmetry between the banking and the non-banking (manufacturing) sectors in the use of holding companies. The former seeks agglomeration ('bulking up') to reduce the banking capacity, whereas the latter aims at disintegration ('slimming down') at corporate level through the medium of the holding company. In either case, corporate restructuring will be ultimately achieved in terms of reducing overstaffing and selling off unprofitable operations.

In each case, however, the holding company as the owner (stockholder) of separated, individual semi-autonomous units can focus on the profitability of its group. In this sense, a new oversight mechanism is introduced. And the holding company-based organization will be more amenable to M&As and takeovers of its individual units by the outsiders (including foreign participants), since separated business units are much easier to dispose of – and to acquire. Thus this may create a new opening to the hitherto secluded *keiretsu* fortress, and takeovers may occur more frequently.

7. ASSESSMENT

In the wake of Japan's rapidly evolved business environment, then, the conventional main bank-cum-*keiretsu* system has been debilitated as a mechanism of corporate finance and governance. Japanese-style management used to function as a self-regulating entity in which management and employees were highly disciplined and motivated to devote themselves for the interest of their companies as sharing units. However, all these unique Japanese institutions, once acclaimed as the sinews of Japan's economic miracle, were compatible only with, and effective only during, its bygone days of high growth.

The main bank system reached its pinnacle in the mid-1970s and finally became practically disfunctional because corporate Japan no longer needed such a bureaucrat-driven regime of bank loan capitalism. Besides, the banking industry soon got mired in bad debts in the aftermath of the bubble burst. In fact, the bubble itself was created by the then already obsolescent main bank system itself, which came under the spell of moral hazard and the pampering of the Ministry of Finance ('too important *to be allowed* to fail').

And Japanese-style management, which was developed and perfected in Japan's high-growth era, also has became obsolete and is no longer workable;

it has, indeed, brought about the problems of overstaffing, mediocrity and organizational inflexibility. Seniority-based compensation and promotion are now being increasingly replaced by a more merit-based approach (including the use of employee stock options) which recognizes individual initiatives, performance and contributions. Penetration of foreign financial multinationals – and their new products and services – is about to create a consciousness revolution among Japanese savers and wealth holders; they are being awoken to the new opportunities to earn more decent yields on their personal assets. Once Japan's Big Bang integrates its financial sector with the global market, Japanese households will not be likely to passively keep $12 trillion in personal assets at home. Corporate Japan (banks, postal savings, securities firms, insurance companies and corporations alike) can no longer take it for granted that they are captive suppliers of funds. They will soon have to fight for it.

Moreover, intra-*keiretsu* cross-shareholdings have been declining, albeit gradually, and losing effectiveness as a mutual oversight device (or actually they may not have really served as an effective mechanism for corporate governance, as effective as thought to be). But this 'dishoarding' process has a long way to go, since about two-thirds of stocks are still held by financial institutions and non-financial corporations in cross-shareholdings. Unless there is another stock market boom, it is rather suicidal to dump shares on the market. Japan's stock market revival may be in the making thanks to capital inflows by foreign investors and the growth of mutual funds. But this will merely promote the commoditization of securities and will not necessarily enhance the role of stocks as proxy votes that can really influence corporate decisions.

So, how will corporate accountability be ensured? Shareholder activism in Japan is still sporadic and ineffective. M&As have only recently begun to occur and rise. M&As by foreign corporations, as was the case with Renault SA's partial acquisition of Nissan Motor and Ford's takeover of Mazda, are most likely to infuse new managerial ideas into, and strengthen, corporate Japan. The hope, therefore, lies in a continual improvement of the managerial and organizational abilities of Japanese executives and board directors. They are about to go through a drastic corporate restructuring to improve company performances. The possible use of holding companies also holds some promise. But, after all, *self-disciplined management (internal governance) buttressed by the forces of fierce market competition (all the more global) continues to serve probably as the single most effective mechanism for corporate accountability in Japan.*

Japanese corporations can no longer afford to merely pursue the conventional market-share-oriented (that is, company-size-enlarging) strategy at low profits to maximize and maintain employment; they realize that they must become more sharply profit-focused in the interests of shareholders, more of whom are now global investors. Hence, they are modifying, if not totally discarding, the once-touted Japanese-style management, and are groping for a new effective way of running companies suitable for both the present 'Schumpeterian' stage of economic growth and the era of intensifying globalization, especially in the financial sector through Japan's Big Bang reforms.

NOTES

1. Japan's high-growth era at the macro level lasted over 1950–74, coinciding with the Golden Age of Capitalism. At the meso level, however, Japan's growth industries such as automobiles and electronics expanded very rapidly over 1975–90, inclusive of the bubble period of 1987–90. Hence, Japan's high-growth era is meant to cover 1950–90 in this study.

2. This was clearly reflected in the ever-declining equity–total capital ratio throughout Japan's high-growth era; for all industries, it declined from 26.9 per cent in 1950 to 16.1 per cent in 1970, and for the manufacturing sector, it decreased from 31.4 per cent to 19.9 per cent over the same period.

3. It should be noted that in the prewar period Japan did develop thriving securities market capitalism, in which more than half of companies' capital came from issuing shares and bonds before the Great Crash on Wall Street spread depression to Japan.

4. Here, one provision of Japan's Commercial Code has a useful provision: any director can be replaced at any time by a two-thirds vote of the stockholder general meeting. The main bank can make use of this provision in initiating the temporary takeover of a failing firm (Aoki, 1988, p. 149).

5. The present banking crisis has added to its advantage, because many apprehensive savers shifted deposits from banks to the post offices. After all, the postal savings system is government-run; hence the people believe it will never go bust.

6. '[A] large part of the funds thus distributed is destined to such public purposes as housing (about 20 percent), road construction (8–10 percent), transportation and communication (12–14 percent) and construction of other social infrastructure. But a significant sum is reserved for investment in basic industries (as much as 13.6 percent in 1960, but declining to about 3 percent in the decade of the 1970s) and for export promotion and economic cooperation (10 percent or less). The rate of interest charged then was 6.5 percent for the term of 25 years for the funds channeled from the Trust Fund Bureau, which of course was below the rate charged by commercial banks for loans or the fixed rate of return on debentures' (Tsuru, 1993, pp. 109–10).

7. The first sharp decline in par-value right offering occurred in 1972, accounting for 26.6 per cent of total issue. It then returned to higher levels for a while, but again sharply declined to 8.5 per cent in 1984, then swung back to 61.5 in 1991. Based on a table in Ide (1998, p. 83).

8. Patrick (1994, p. 371) succinctly sums up: '[The Ministry of Finance] used regulatory restrictions and economic incentives to severely *inhibit* corporate bond issues and the development of a secondary market. Essentially, only public utilities and long-term credit banks could issue bonds in any quantity, and this was done mainly through non-arm's length placements. Equity issue was expensive for management-controlled firms, both because dividends were paid out of after-tax profits while interest payments were a deductible expense, and because the pre-war custom of new stock issue at par rather than market prevailed well into the 1970s. The issuance of commercial paper for short-term finance was not allowed until 1987. Business, growing rapidly and always in need of new loans for working capital and fixed investment, had no choice but to borrow from banks.'

9. In terms of these Japanese experiences, moral hazard can be classified into two types: 'socially justifiable moral hazard' and 'degenerative moral hazard' (see Ozawa, 1999a).
10. The framework developed by Shigeto Tsuru (1993) specifies the sources and uses of funds for a main bank-affiliated firm as follows:

$$D - R + S = V \qquad (7.1)$$

Where D: depreciation allowances
    R: replacement investment
    S: internal reserves (retained earnings)
    V: new investment.

When the firm is on a rapid growth path, D is necessarily larger than R, creating a surplus. Its high growth also brings profits, part of which are retained as S. But its need for funds to finance V will be greater than $D - R + S$. Hence, long-term bank loans (L) are required:

$$V = D - R + S + L \qquad (7.2)$$

Eventually, the firm successfully grows to a point where $S - V$ becomes positive, creating 'net internal surplus of the firm', namely

$$(NS > 0) = (D + S) - (V + R) \qquad (7.3)$$

Now that the firm has accumulated a substantial amount of NS, how to use NS becomes an important decision. NS can be used for a variety of activities, including: (i) repayment of debt to banks, (ii) R&D expenditures, (iii) direct foreign investment, (iv) diversification of business activities, and (v) financial investment in securities and land. 'When we view the entire economy, composed of numerous firms, the aggregate of NS found its destinations in all these directions as the high-growth period progressed' (Tsuru, 1993, p. 185).

11. Retained earnings accounted for as much as 53 per cent of the sources of funds in Japan over the 1983-87 period, for example. By comparison, 72 per cent of the sources of funds in Germany came from retained earnings, 66 per cent in United Kingdom over the same period, as cited in Baums (1994).
12. 'As a fraction of all securities issued by Japanese companies, overseas issues [reached] nearly 50 percent by 1985' (Kester, 1991, p. 188). As far as bonds are concerned, 'within three years of the revision of the Law, the value of bonds issued abroad exceeded the value of bonds issued domestically' (Weinstein and Yafeh, 1998, p. 637).
13. Japan's postwar growth has gone through four evolutionary stages (Ozawa, 1992): stage I (1950 to mid 1960s) was built on the 'Heckscher–Ohlin' industries which are labour-intensive (such as textiles, sundries and other low-wage goods; stage II (late 1950s to early 1970s) involved the 'non-differentiated Smithian' industries (such as steel, petrochemicals and synthetic fibres, heavy machinery and shipbuilding); stage III (late 1960s to the present) has been dominated by the 'differentiated Smithian' industries (such as automobiles and electronics); and stage IV (early 1980s onwards) is represented by the 'Schumpeterian' industries (such as biotechnology, new materials and information technology). The main bank system was mainly used during stage II non-differentiated Smithian industries which were highly capital-intensive. And Japan is currently in the incipient stage of Schumpeterian' growth.
14. '[The company is] an independent inventor-entrepreneur without any connection with *zaibatsu* groups initially or thereafter. Sakichi Toyoda ... obtained L100,000 from a British company, Pratt Brothers, as royalty income for his patents on the automatic loom and handed this entire sum over to his son, Kiichiro, telling him to make use of it as R&D funds for founding a new venture of manufacturing automobiles; and, thus, a tradition was established in the Toyota Motor Company not to rely on external finance for investment purposes' (Tsuru, 1993, p. 191). It should be mentioned that Toyota does have relations with the Mitsui group, but we cannot say that Toyota was closely monitored by the Mitsui Bank (now the Sakura Bank). More appropriately, we can probably say that it is a privilege

for any bank to serve for Toyota.

15. 'In 1984, Matsushita Electric Industries ... paid out less than 10 percent of its earnings in dividends, retaining the balance for reinvestment. As one consequence, Matsushita has been growing in sales nearly 15 percent a year and doing so without incurring the risks and costs of bank borrowings' (Abegglen and Stalk, 1985, p. 187).

16. Even by European standards, as illustrated by the recent merger between Daimler-Benz and Chrysler which revealed a huge discrepancy in executive compensations between the partners.

17. These comparative figures are from the results of a survey published in 'Executive Pay: the party ain't over yet', *Business Week*, 26 April 1993, p. 60.

18. 'Share Options', *The Economist*, 7 August 1999, pp. 18–20.

19. In general, moreover, those who own or manage businesses in Japan have traditionally been conservative and reserved, avoiding any appearance of selfishness and conspicuous consumption. In the words of William Lockwood (1954, p. 284):

> By comparison with the value standards prevailing among many other peoples, perhaps most of them, social position and prestige in Japan are less dependent on display of material wealth. In this respect Japanese society is comparatively democratic, however hierarchical and authoritarian in other respects. The well-to-do classes of modern Japan, although living on a plane far above the masses, have generally failed to exhibit those tendencies to extravagant, conspicuous consumption ... Their work habits, the frugality, and even the sense of 'calling' displayed by many Japanese businessmen have sometimes recalled to Western observers the rationalistic Protestant ethic which contributed so powerfully to the rise of modern capitalism in Europe.

20. A high degree of competition in the Japanese market seems to be paradoxical, since the domestic markets were heavily protected in those days. But the existence of the *keiretsu* and government competition policy created the so-called 'reserved competition' phenomena (see Ozawa, 1997).

21. Their sense of long-term commitment is evident in the fact that the Japanese corporation usually paid dividends as a percentage (usually 10 per cent) of the par value of shares regardless of their profitability and that even when it did not make any earning, it often went out of its way to 'borrow to cover the dividend payment and thus meet the investor's expectations and maintain their ability to raise equity funds' (Abegglen and Stalk, 1985, p. 184).

22. In theory, cross-shareholding is supposed to be effective for mutual monitoring. But I wonder why this mechanism did not work at all during the asset bubble of the late 1980s when the major banks were all engaged in rather reckless lending practices. Why didn't their closely affiliated firms raise red flags? After all, they were the banks' major shareholders. *The Economist* ('Big Bang: A whopping explosion', a survey of Japanese finance, 28 June 1997, pp. 1–18) observes: 'shareholders have not been able to make banks concentrate on profitable lending. Bank shares in Japan are particularly tightly held, making it hard for outsiders to apply pressure' (p. 7). Anderson and Campbell (1999) investigated the relation between performance and executive turnover for 111 banks between 1976 and 1996 and found no relation between stock returns and executive turnover except in the 1990s. Hence they conclude that governance mechanisms have not provided sufficient incentives to Japanese bank executives.

23. *The Economist*, op. cit.; p. 7.

24. Japan did experience a slump immediately after the first oil crisis of 1974. But it quickly recovered and continued to expand, especially as its assembly-based industries (automobiles and electronics) became its stellar exports.

25. As *The Economist* puts it somewhat hyperbolically, 'Japan's old growth-at-any-cost school of management assumed that it was always better to diversify than to face stagnation or (heaven forbid) redundancies – even if that meant entering fields where the company had no production facilities, no technology, no suppliers, no customers and no competence whatsoever. Because of their past addition to investment, many Japanese firms are also still

burdened with too much capacity, too much labour and too much debt', *The Economist*, 'Japan's growth companies', 26 June 1999, p. 69.

26. 'Government sets out competitiveness, job plans', *Nikkei Weekly*, 28 June 1999, p. 2.
27. Until the failure of Hanwa Bank in November 1996, a mid-sized regional bank, no Japanese bank had gone out of business since the Second World War. Even faltering banks were protected under the so-called '*goso sendan* [convoy]' policy, which compelled stronger banks to help out weaker ones.
28. This practice still persists even today. According to the *Nikkei Shimbun* (Japan's version of *The Wall Street Journal*) 1374 listed companies held their shareholders' meetings on 29 June 1999, accounting for 88 per cent of the total. Nissan, which was partly acquired by Renault SA, was among 109 listed companies that held their meetings on 25 June 1999, as cited in Stephanie Strom, 'Nissan Shareholders' Meeting Takes on Some Western Trappings', *New York Times* (www.NYTimes.com), 26 June 1999.
29. In this respect, some claim that it is far more extensive in impact than Britain's big bang itself, which was basically confined to the London Stock Exchange.
30. Another US broker, Charles Schwab Corp., has most recently (June 1999) joined the fray by forming a 50–50 joint venture with the Mitsubishi group (Tokio Marine & Fire Insurance Co., Bank of Tokyo–Mitsubishi and others).
31. In fiscal 1998 (April 98–March 99), only 7.9 per cent of total individual financial assets were in stocks and 6.5 per cent in securities, while as much as 55 per cent and 27 per cent were in deposits and insurance, respectively ('Private bankers find plenty of wealth to manage in land of low interest rates', *Nikkei Weekly*, 23 August 1999, p. 1).
32. It is reported that less than 3 per cent of Japan's total personal assets are in mutual fund-type investments. 'More than 50 percent of the total is locked up in multi-year certificates of deposits (CDs) at banks with annual yields of around 0.25 percent.' 'US Investment Firms Can't Woo Japan', *New York Times* (www.NYTimes.com), 16 May 1999.
33. At this point, however, Japanese households are not plunging into the securities markets. Once burnt when Japan's last asset bubble popped in 1990, and because of the current decade-long slump in the Japanese economy, they are only gingerly testing the new water, and there is no massive shift out of bank deposits into securities as yet. In fact, Goldman is sponsoring a weekly half-hour (rather 'soapy') TV drama, 'Money Angels', to educate the public, especially Japanese homemakers, about the basics of household financial planning. ('One Japanese TV, the ABC's of Money', *New York Times* (www.NYTimes.com), 4 July 1999.) Furthermore, even if yield rates on securities and interest rates are higher overseas, they are weary of the exchange risks involved in overseas investment, especially because of their current expectations about the future rise of the yen (as of this writing). Foreign exchange transactions have long been monopolized by specially designated banks, which therefore reaped fat commissions. Corporations and individuals are now free to engage in foreign exchange transactions, holding overseas bank accounts (until April 1998, only banks were permitted to have overseas accounts; and any overseas investment more than Y5 million had to obtain permission from the Ministry of Finance). Besides, Japan's income tax codes on financial earnings are such that individual investors feel uncomfortable about shifting funds overseas lest they be charged for tax evasions (Hasegawa, 1997).
34. 'A survey of Japanese finance: A whopping explosion', *The Economist*, 28 June 1997, p. 1.
35. 'Crackdown Spurs a Makeover of Japan's Corporate Racketeers', *New York Times* (www.NYTimes.com), 11 August 1999.
36. Such a massive participation of individual investors in Japan's stock exchanges, if it occurs, would surely introduce high volatility in stock prices. This is because 'In August [1999], individuals accounted for 16% of trading on Japanese exchanges, but they hold only about 4% of their assets in stocks, and only 10% even when mutual funds are included. In the U.S., in contrast, individuals hold about 60% of their assets in stocks directly or through mutual funds' (Bill Spindle, 'Japan's Brokers Brace for Industry "Big Bang"', *Wall Street Journal*, 8 September, 1999, C1).
37. Only those Japanese firms which had a foreign subsidiary were qualified to borrow directly overseas. But to set up a foreign subsidiary, they first had to secure permission from the MOF.

38. Peter Landers, 'Japanese Banks to Form Colossus', *Wall Street Journal*, 20 August, 1999, p. A7.
39. 'U.S. Bankers See No Threat in Planned Japanese Behemoth', *New York Times on the web* (www.NYTimes.com), 21 August 1999.
40. As cited in Fumiyo Nagaoka, 'Banks shedding cosy relations with clients', *Nikkei Weekly*, 4 October 1999, p. 15.
41. Cited in Peter Landers, 'Sumitomo, Sakura to Merge Into Mammoth Bank Designed to Survive Japan's Transformation', *Wall Street Journal*, 15 October 1999, p. A10.
42. As reported in 'Lifetime-employment system unravels as downsizing fever grips corporate Japan', *Nikkei Weekly*, 7 June 1999, p. 1.
43. 'Japan: No Room at the Top', *Business Week*, 9 August 1999, p. 50.

REFERENCES

Abegglen, James C. and George Stalk, Jr (1985), *Kaisha: The Japanese Corporation*, New York: Basic Books.

Anderson, Christopher W. and Terry L. Campbell II (1999), 'Corporate governance of Japanese banks', paper presented at the 35th Annual Conference on Bank Structure and Competition, the Federal Reserve Bank of Chicago, 5-7 May.

Aoki, Masahiko (1988), *Information, Incentives, and Bargaining in the Japanese Economy*, Cambridge: Cambridge University Press.

Aoki, Masahiko and Hugh Patrick (1994), *The Japanese Main Bank System: Its Relevance for Developing and Transforming Economies*, Oxford: Oxford University Press.

Aoki, Mashiko, Hyung-Ki Kim and Masahiro Okuno-Fujiwara (1997), *The Role of Government in East Asian Economic Development: Comparative Institutional Analysis*, Oxford: Clarendon Press.

Baums, Theodor (1994), 'The German banking system and its impact on corporate finance and governance', in Masahiko Aoki and Hugh Patrick (eds), *The Japanese Main Bank System*, Oxford: Oxford University Press, pp. 409-49.

Berle, Adolph, Jr and Gardiner C. Means (1932), *The Modern Corporation and Private Property*, New York: Macmillan.

Genay, Hesna (1999), 'Japanese banks and market discipline', *Chicago Fed Letter*, No. 144, August.

Hasegawa, Keitaro (1997), *Big Bang de Nihon wa kookawaru* (How the Big Bang will Change Japan), Tokyo: Tokuma Shoten.

Ide, Masasuke (1998), *Japanese Corporate Finance and International Competition: Japanese Capitalism versus American Capitalism*, London: Macmillan.

Jacobs, Michael T. (1991), *Short-Term America: The Causes and Cures of Our Business Myopia*, Boston, Mass.: Harvard Business School Press.

Kester, W. Karl (1991), *Japanese Takeovers: The Global Contest for Corporate Control*, Boston, Mass.: Harvard Business School Press.

Lockwood, William W. (1954), *The Economic Development of Japan: Growth and Structural Change 1868-1938*, Princeton: Princeton University Press.

Ohno, Tai'ichi (1978), *Toyota Seisan Hoshiki: Datsu-Kibo no Keiei o Mezashite* (Toyota Production System: Toward Non-Scale-Driven Management), Tokyo: Daiyamond.

Ozawa, Terutomo (1992), 'Foreign direct investment and economic development', *Transnational Corporations*, **1**(1) (February), 27-54.

Ozawa, Terutomo (1997), 'Japan', in John Dunning (ed.), *Governments, Globalization, and International Business*, Oxford: Oxford University Press, pp. 377–406.

Ozawa, Terutomo (1999a), 'The rise and fall of bank-loan capitalism: institutionally driven growth and crisis in Japan', *Journal of Economic Issues*, **33**(2) (June), 351–9.

Ozawa, Terutomo (1999b), 'Bank loan capitalism and financial crises: Japanese and Korean experiences', in Alan Rugman and Gavin Boyd (eds), *Deepening Integration in the Pacific Economies: Corporate Alliances, Contestable Markets and Free Trade*, Cheltenham, UK and Northampton, MA: Edward Elgar, pp. 214–48.

Patrick, Hugh T. (1994), 'The relevance of Japanese finance and its main bank system', in M. Aoki and H. Patrick (eds), *The Japanese Main Bank System*, Oxford: Oxford University Press, pp. 353–408.

Tsuru, Shigeto (1993), *Japan's Capitalism: Creative Defeat and Beyond*, New York: Cambridge University Press.

Weinstein, David E. and Yishay Yafeh (1998), 'On the costs of a bank-centered financial system: evidence from the changing main bank relations in Japan', *Journal of Finance*, **53**(2) (April), 635–72.

Womack, James P., Daniel T. Jones and Daniel Roos (1990), *The Machine that Changed the World*, New York: Macmillan.

8. Reforming corporate governance: redirecting the European agenda*

Erik Berglöf

1. INTRODUCTION

Calls for corporate governance reform are reverberating throughout Europe in the wake of scandals like Bremer Vulkan and Metallgesellschaft in Germany, Banesto and Seat in Spain and Ferruzi in Italy. But also less spectacular corporate governance failures like that of Navigation Mixte and Suez in France have led to demands for reform. Another source of reform pressure is the ongoing integration of European capital markets, and the perception that differences in corporate governance patterns inhibit investors from taking advantage of the single market. Harmonization and greater transparency, the argument goes, would improve the liquidity of the less-developed equity markets of continental Europe.

There is also outside pressure for reform from international, primarily US, institutional investors increasing their presence in European corporations. So far these institutions have kept a low profile, but they are beginning to question incumbent management. More importantly, their arrival has unleashed competition for global savings among recipient countries in Europe. One crucial element in the attractiveness of a particular country is its system of corporate governance.

In response to these calls for reform, many member states, such as Germany, France, Italy and Sweden, are rewriting their corporate laws, and many more are reviewing the requirements for firms to be listed on exchanges. The Cadbury and Greenbury Committees, the Viénot Committee and the initiatives from the Belgian Stock Exchange, Amsterdam Stock Exchange and European Securities Dealers Association are all responses to perceived deficiencies in corporate governance arrangements.

What are the issues on the reform agenda? Topics in individual countries include strengthened minority protection, voting caps and limits on the share of capital held by certain types of investor, and the imposition of one share, one vote. Another set of proposals is intended to increase the liability of directors and activate institutional investors in corporate governance. At the

European Union level, initiatives to harmonize the structure and control of corporations, takeover bid procedures and employee rights have effectively been halted. A number of proposals, such as the draft fifth, tenth and thirteenth company law directives, are still on the table, but the prospects for their adoption are bleak. The most ambitious harmonization project, the European company statute (*Société Européenne*), would provide an optional structure for companies recognized in all member states, but subject to the law of home states. The regulation specifies terms of incorporation, minimum capital requirements, two options for board structure, allowable restrictions on voting rights, and reporting requirements. A related draft directive defines the rights of the employees in the company which chooses this form of incorporation. Despite some recent attempts to revive the idea, hopes for *Société Européenne* currently appear dim.

Reform is in the air. This new zeal is understandable, but before dismantling existing institutions and tampering with fragile relationships, reformers must step back and consider the underlying issues. Too many reform initiatives have been partial and poorly conceived, undertaken without considering the fundamental interdependence between corporate law and corporate finance, and between corporate governance and the rest of the economic system. This relationship has only recently been subjected to systematic analysis, and few strong conclusions can yet be drawn. However, we can now discern the outlines of a basic conceptual framework for thinking about corporate governance reform. This paper sketches out the emerging framework and uses it to interpret observed patterns of corporate law and corporate finance in Europe. In an effort to redirect the zeal of reformers, the paper suggests some basic principles that should guide policy reform.

How we tackle reform of corporate governance has implications not only for western Europe, but also for the countries of eastern Europe in transition from socialism to market economies. In the absence of functioning corporate laws, and with corporate control in the hands of insiders, firms find it difficult to raise outside finance. Without outside finance, and the pressure from outside investors, little deep restructuring and strategic investment are taking place. These countries are closely watching ongoing reforms and are searching for blueprints.

The article briefly surveys recent literature on corporate governance that links corporate law and corporate finance. It makes use of the basic dichotomy between two generic forms of finance – control-oriented finance and arm's-length finance – and discusses their implications at the level of the financial system. In order to understand corporate governance in Europe, it first describes existing patterns of corporate ownership and finance (Section 3), and then outlines the most important corporate law traditions (Section 4). Section 5 discusses the observed patterns of law and finance, and how they combine in corporate governance arrangements. It also discusses the implications of these arrangements for economic growth and investment. Finally, in Section 6, some conclusions are drawn for reformers.

2. CORPORATE LAW AND CORPORATE FINANCE

The failure of efforts to reform corporate governance at the level of the European Union and the problems of implementing reform in individual member states can only be understood once we recognize how deeply rooted corporate governance arrangements are in national economic systems, and how strongly corporate law and corporate finance are related in these systems. The recent corporate finance literature provides some useful concepts and a framework for thinking about these relationships. This section goes back to the basic finance decision of the individual firm and how this choice of finance influences various aspects of the financial system.

The starting point of the literature is the basic agency problem of capitalism: that is, the credibility problem facing entrepreneurs or firms when they seek to convince outside investors to contribute funds. Competition in factor and output markets may mitigate this agency problem, but in itself competition is insufficient; market signals are generated after funds have been committed. *The role of corporate governance is to ensure that these signals and other relevant information are actually translated into investment decisons*: for example, by replacing management following poor performance or closing down unprofitable units. Competition and corporate governance are also likely to be substitutes, in the sense that when competitive signals are strong the relative importance of corporate governance is less, and vice versa.[1] If the classic agency problem cannot be eliminated, and competition is not sufficient to constrain managers, what can the firm do to commit to pay investors back? This is the fundamental challenge of corporate governance addressed in the recent corporate finance literature.

2.1 Two Generic Forms of Finance

In some primitive or theoretical world, the firm and its investors would sit down and agree on *both* specific financial contracts and a set of legal rules and institutions to enforce these rules. In reality, and in the finance literature, parties normally negotiate their contracts *given* a specific legal environment. There are two generic approaches to this contracting problem in the corporate finance literature. Either one or more investors are given influence over strategic decisions in the firm (control-oriented finance) or management finds ways of committing to efficient actions and to share in the proceeds from these actions (arm's-length finance).[2] The two forms of finance are often combined in the individual firm, giving rise to additional agency problems – in particular, between controlling shareholders and minority shareholders.

In deciding which contractual arrangement to choose, parties weigh the benefits and costs of control. Holding large blocks not only requires wealth, but also implies abstaining from diversification opportunities; controlling owners in large corporations are seldom well diversified, not even in the United States (Demsetz and Lehn, 1985). To induce investors to give up diversification opportunities and hold, or assemble, control blocks to exercise corporate governance, other investors may have to allow large stakeholders to extract private benefits from the firm. By giving up discretion, management may also weaken its incentives to engage in entrepreneurial activity.[3] Yet another cost of control-oriented finance is reduced liquidity: when financial instruments are concentrated into a few hands, they are often viewed as more difficult to trade; stocks of closely held companies are less liquid than those of widely held corporations, and stocks that form part of control blocks are less liquid than those that do not.[4] The costs of control can be reduced by separating ownership and control – for example, by issuing shares with different voting rights or through pyramiding – but only at the expense of aggravating agency problems.

2.2 Financial Systems

The choice between the two generic forms of finance, and their specific corporate governance arrangements, has ramifications not only for the individual firm, but also for the rest of the financial system (Table 8.1). Arm's-length finance implies dispersed ownership of debt and equity, and thus promotes liquid markets. Investors in such arm's-length financial systems are prone to portfolio orientation, and the market for corporate control operating over the public exchanges is an important mechanism for the correction of managerial failure. Systems where control-oriented finance dominates have more concentrated ownership structures in individual firms and less liquid markets. Control-oriented financial systems also breed control-oriented investors; opportunities for diversification are less and the costs of trading tend to be high. The market for corporate control operates outside the public exchanges in the form of trades in large blocks. While control changes may be hostile in the eyes of incumbent management, the terms are negotiated between the controlling owner and the outside investor.

The choice between arm's-length and control-oriented finance also influences the nature of conflicts in the financial system. With arm's-length finance as the most important source of funding, the predominant conflict is likely to be between management and investors. However, under control-

Table 8.1   *Financial systems and capital structure*

| | Type of financial system | |
	Control-oriented	Arm's-length
Share of control-oriented finance	High	Low
Financial markets	Small, less liquid	Large, highly liquid
Share of all firms listed on exchanges	Small	Large
Ownership of debt and equity	Concentrated	Dispersed
Investor orientation	Control-oriented	Portfolio-oriented
Use of mechanisms for separating control and capital base	Frequent	Limited (often by regulation)
Dominant agency conflict	Controlling vs minority shareholders	Shareholders vs management
Role of board of directors	Limited	Important
Role of hostile takeovers	Very limited	Potentially important

oriented finance, conflicts are more likely to occur between different classes of investors: that is, between holders of control and investors with arm's-length financial instruments. The basic issue of the two agency problems is the same: how to convince investors that they will be repaid in the future. However, the concrete manifestations of agency problems in a widely held firm often differ substantially from those in a closely held firm with a controlling shareholder, and conflicts in owner-managed firms are different from those in firms with professional management without substantial owner-ship stakes. Minority investors in a control-oriented financial system also have fewer opportunities to make use of the outside 'exit' option provided by liquid markets than in an arm's-length financial system with liquid capital markets.

The role of various corporate institutions, such as the board of directors and the general shareholders' meeting, also depends on the predominant form of finance. When firms are closely held, proxy voting and other procedures in the general shareholders' meeting and the composition of the board of directors are less important; outside directors should not be expected to take independent stands when the controlling owner can hire and fire them at will. In addition, the two forms of finance probably also place different demands on the general legal environment and enforcing institutions. Both rely on property rights, but the role of courts is likely to differ. Arm's-length finance should place greater demands on courts by requiring detailed enforcement of specific rights to assets and cash flows, whereas control-oriented finance merely requires the protection of voting rights. However, the viability of control-oriented finance is also related to the protection of arm's-length investors: when ownership is concentrated, controlling owners rely on the legal protection of minority shareholders in order to commit not to exploit them.

We thus see that financing patterns potentially influence the evolution of the legal system. They determine the nature of conflicts between the firm and its investors, and between investors, which in turn has implications for the structure and function of the board of directors and general shareholders' meeting. In a similar vein, the importance attached to fiduciary duties and rules for minority protection reflects the capital structure of firms and the liquidity of markets for the instruments issued. Equally important, when there are clearly identifiable owners with controlling stakes, lawmakers may choose to abstain from regulation and court involvement. For example, instead of providing detailed rules for how many members there should be on the board, how they should be elected, and when they should be fired, lawmakers may choose to delegate these decisions to controlling owners, when there are such owners. The poor liquidity of capital markets for corporate instruments has also made lawmakers less inclined to let courts rely on the information produced in these markets.

So far we have assumed that corporate finance affects corporate law, but the influence also goes the other way. The legal framework does influence the viability of different financial arrangements and the trade-off between corporate governance and liquidity, either *directly* (for example, through restrictions on the size of stakes or types of control mechanism allowed) or *indirectly* by affecting investors' incentives to take on controlling blocks. A recent survey of the corporate governance literature by Shleifer and Vishny (1996) argues that concentration of ownership is an unavoidable outcome of shortcomings in the legal system: in the absence of well-functioning corporate law, concentration of ownership is the only way to commit not to steal from the company. Companies in countries with poor protection of minority share-holders should therefore have more concentrated ownership structures than countries with more protective, and better enforced, rules.[5] To test the provocative proposition that law determines finance, Shleifer and Vishny have joined forces with two other researchers, Rafael La Porta and Florencio Lopez-de-Silanes. In an ambitious study (La Porta et al., 1996a, 1996b) they compile data on investor protection, ownership and financing patterns, and a number of other variables in 49 countries. We will draw on this study in the rest of this article.

Without taking a stand on the issue of causality, at least for now, the most important conclusion from this literature is the strong interconnectedness between different aspects of corporate governance arrangements, and in particular the strong relationship between corporate finance and corporate law. In order to understand corporate governance in Europe, we thus need to look at both how firms are financed and the legal environment in which they operate. The following section describes the basic ownership and financing patterns in some European countries.

3. CORPORATE FINANCE IN EUROPE

While much has been said about the differences across countries in governance systems, there is a growing consensus about certain common features in corporate finance across countries, at least in mature market economies. Internally generated funds universally provide most of the investment capital to firms, and bank loans are the most important external source of finance (Mayer, 1990). Intermediated finance strongly dominates direct finance with the possible exception of the United States – the only country where corporate bonds play an important role in financing the corporate sector.[6]

Despite these similarities, most observers, and participants, agree that there are important differences across financial systems. We suggest here that *it is the relative importance of markets and institutions in monitoring the use of funds, rather than their roles in the supply of funds, that distinguishes financial systems.* For example, bank finance in the United States is not the same thing as bank finance in Japan, and the role of markets in monitoring firms differs between the United Kingdom and Germany. Unfortunately, these differences are not captured by traditional financial statistics and therefore require other data.

The data on ownership in European firms are still rather poor and comparability is limited. A first idea of the differences can be obtained by looking at Table 8.2, which presents ownership concentration of the three largest owners in the ten largest private firms in fourteen EU countries (La Porta et al., 1996a). Of course, the very largest firms may not be representative, not even of large firms. These data are also primitive in the sense that related owners have not been grouped, and possible differences between share of equity capital and voting shares are not recorded. Nevertheless, it is striking that ownership concentration is very high – 46 per cent is on average held by the three largest owners in the 49 countries covered by the study. The average would most probably be even higher if larger samples were taken. In addition, the variation across countries is considerable.

Table 8.3 summarizes some studies of ownership of equity in non-financial

Table 8.2   Ownership concentration in listed firms (ten largest firms)

Country	Ownership by the three largest shareholders in private firms	
	Mean	Median
Ireland	0.39	0.55
UK	0.19	0.15
Belgium	0.54	0.62
France	0.34	0.68
Greece	0.67	0.68
Italy	0.58	0.60
Netherlands	0.39	0.31
Portugal	0.52	0.59
Spain	0.51	0.50
Austria	0.28	0.28
Germany	0.48	0.50
Denmark	0.45	0.40
Finland	0.37	0.34
Sweden	0.28	0.33
Total average (49 countries)	0.46	0.45

Source: La Porta et al. (1996a).

corporations for more complete samples of large firms in six OECD countries. The samples and methodology differ across studies, but one feature stands out – the high concentration of ownership in continental European and Scandinavian countries, as compared to the United Kingdom and United States. If only quoted companies are considered, 79 and 85 per cent of the companies in France and Germany, respectively, had one owner with stakes larger than 25 per cent (Franks et al., 1995). The corresponding figure for the United Kingdom was 16 per cent. In fact, the overwhelming majority of listed companies on the European continent are closely held. Comparisons over time are not always available, but evidence from, for example, France, Germany and Sweden shows an increase in ownership concentration of listed firms during the 1970s and 1980s (Berglöf, 1988).

Table 8.4 attempts to take a closer look at the identity of controlling holders. Unfortunately, comparisons here are even more difficult. The

Table 8.3   Ownership concentration in listed firms (all listed firms, %)

Largest owner's share	France (1982) (1)	Germany (1985) (2)	Italy (1993) (3)	Spain (1990) (4)	Sweden (1987) (5)	UK (1990) (6)
>50	55	66	89	49	42	5
30–50					31	
25–30			9			29
		23			12	
20–25				49		
15–20	42					
10–15			2		11	27
5–10		12				30
					4	
<5	2			2		9

Sources: (1), (2), (5) and (6) from Berglöf (1988); (3) from Barca (1995); (4) from Galve Gorriz and Salas Fumas (1993).

samples are different, and what constitutes a controlling shareholder varies across countries and should ultimately depend on the dispersion of shares in the individual firm. Nevertheless, the table reveals the strong influence of family and entrepreneurial ownership on the European continent, here represented by France, Germany and Sweden. The continuing importance of families in control of large corporations is one of the central features distinguishing continental European systems from those of the United Kingdom, and the United States for that matter.[7] Institutional shareholders – in particular, non-financial corporations and banks – also play an important role in monitoring in the former countries. The significance of family control does not seem to have markedly decreased over the last two decades, whereas non-financial corporations in many countries have become more important as large blockholders.[8]

In practically all European countries, institutional shareholders have become more important at the expense of private individuals (Table 8.5). However, the types of institution holding shares, and possibly exercising

Table 8.4   The identity of controlling owners (%)

	France[a] 1982	Germany[b] 1980	Sweden[c] 1985
Individuals	42.3	34.5	36.0
Non-financial enterprises		17.3	25.0
Investment companies			26.0
Banks		12.2	
Insurance companies		2.5	6.0
Government	18.0	14.2	
Foreign owners	39.6	17.3	
Others		2.0	7.0
Total	100.0	100.0	100.0

Notes:
[a] Data refer to 249 firms with a majority shareholder (out of 500 largest firms).
[b] Majority shareholder in listed firms.
[c] Largest shareholder in 107 largest privately owned firms.

Source: Berglöf (1988).

control, are quite different. In the United Kingdom, the growth of pension funds over the last two decades has been spectacular, whereas increases in institutional shareholdings in Germany have come primarily from non-financial enterprises and foreign investors. The strong portfolio orientation of institutional investors in the United Kingdom contrasts sharply with the control orientation of this investor category in, for example, Germany. This difference in the orientation of institutional investors is closely linked to the observed variations in the functioning of financial markets.

Investors on the European continent and in Scandinavia have made use of a number of mechanisms to separate capital contribution from control. Holding companies are important ingredients in corporate governance in many countries, particularly in Belgium and Germany (Wymeersch, 1994). Closed-end mutual funds and dual class shares have been the prime vehicles of control in Sweden (Isaksson and Skog, 1994). In Germany and Sweden, and particularly in Italy, pyramiding, whereby chains of firms (sometimes as many as ten or fifteen) own each other, allowing the ultimate controlling owner to minimize its capital stake without affecting the concentration of control, plays an important role.[9] Proxy votes held by banks on behalf of small investors and cross-holdings of shares are other ways of concentrating control in Germany (Wymeersch, 1994). Voting trusts and

Table 8.5   Ownership of listed stocks by sector (as of 31 December)

		Households	Non-financial corporations	Government institutions	Financial institutions	Foreign owners
France	1977	41	20	3	24	12
	1992	34	21	2	23	20
Germany	1970	28	41	11	11	8
	1993	17	39	3	29	12
Italy	1993	32	22	28	14	4
United Kingdom	1969	50	5	3	36	7
	1993	19	2	1	62	16
Japan	1970	40	23	0	35	3
	1993	20	28	1	42	8
United Sates	1981	51	15	0	28	6
	1993	48	9	0	37	6

Sources: Barca (1995); Berglöf (1988); Lannoo (1994); International Capital Markets Group (1995).

special golden shares serve the same purpose in Dutch corporate governance. Despite legal restrictions, corporations in France have complicated cross-holding arrangements to ensure concentration of control, and the government has maintained potential influence in large privatized firms through golden shares.

The concentration of ownership seems to be related to the importance of equity and debt markets, and to the willingness to list firms on public exchanges. Table 8.6 relates external capitalization,[10] numbers of listed firms and initial public offerings, and total debt,[11] to GNP and population in EU countries. Unfortunately, due to differences in reporting, these figures are often hard to interpret and sometimes directly misleading. However, the United Kingdom clearly stands out in a European comparison, with a large number of firms listed, a high external capitalization and high debt relative to GNP and population. In general, the markets of continental Europe seem to play a more limited role, with the Netherlands as an important exception.[12] Sweden is also characterized by a relatively large and active stock market, despite heavily concentrated ownership.

There are also differences in the nature of the market for corporate control. In the United Kingdom, hostile takeovers mounted through purchases in the official market play an important role. On the European continent, such transactions are rare. In Germany, as in Holland, no truly hostile takeover attempt has succeeded. Since the regulatory changes in the wake of the failed

Table 8.6   External capital markets

Country	External capitalization/GNP	Domestic firms/population	Initial public offerings/population	Debt/GNP
Ireland	27.40	20.00	0.75	0.38
UK	100.07	35.68	2.01	1.13
Belgium	16.84	15.50	0.30	0.38
France	23.06	8.05	0.17	0.96
Greece	7.14	21.60	0.30	0.23
Italy	8.03	3.91	0.31	0.55
Netherlands	52.19	21.13	0.66	1.08
Portugal	8.04	19.50	0.50	0.64
Spain	16.59	9.71	0.07	0.75
Austria	6.39	13.87	0.25	0.79
Germany	12.75	5.14	0.08	1.12
Denmark	21.36	50.40	1.80	0.34
Finland	25.12	13.00	0.60	0.75
Sweden	50.78	12.66	1.66	0.55

Source: La Porta et al. (1996b).

takeover attempt of Société Générale, hostile takeovers of larger firms in Belgium have basically come to a halt. French authorities have made a point of activating the market for corporate control, and a considerable number of takeovers have taken place against the will of incumbent management. Sweden had only four successful hostile offers during the 1980s, a period characterized by substantial corporate restructuring (Isaksson and Skog, 1993). In general, takeovers in continental Europe are used as a mechanism to withdraw firms from the stock exchange rather than as a device to change control. Most control-related trading in Europe occurs in large blocks outside official markets. There is, however, evidence that this trade is at least as important as that taking place on official exchanges in countries with arm's-length type arrangements.

This brief characterization shows important differences among European countries in terms of ownership concentration in individual firms, the identity of these owners and the role of institutional owners. In addition, the number of firms and the capitalization of equity and debt markets differ considerably. These differences have implications for how control is transferred in the financial system, but also for the nature of conflicts and the role of corporate institutions and corporate law.

4. CORPORATE LAW IN EUROPE

To understand corporate governance arrangements in Europe, and how to reform these arrangements, it is not enough to look at patterns of corporate finance. We must also study variations in corporate law. This section briefly discusses the legal origins of European corporate laws and identifies two broad corporate law traditions. We then look at some evidence for how the various systems protect investors.

The European Union countries span a wide range of legal origins. Comparative legal scholars normally distinguish between common law and civil law systems, with the law in the former systems being made primarily by judges and in the latter by scholars and legislators in the tradition of Roman law (David and Brierley, 1985). Within the latter group, a further distinction is made between French and German civil law countries. The Scandinavian countries have had considerable influence from German civil law, but they are normally classified as a separate family of civil codes. Common law systems are normally found in countries with an Anglo-Saxon tradition: in Europe, primarily the United Kingdom and Ireland.

These differences in legal origins are reflected in corporate laws and the institutions enforcing these laws. While most countries regulate minimum capital requirements, structure and composition of boards, and responsibilities of the general shareholders' meeting in limited liability companies, these similarities conceal deep-rooted differences in legal frameworks. Furthermore, the relative importance of private and public limited liability companies differs substantially. Wymeersch (1994) identifies two broad corporate law traditions in Europe – a *company-based* and an *enterprise-based* legal system. In the company-based system, the focus is on the firm as a legal entity and the relationship between it and its investors, while the enterprise-based tradition places greater emphasis on the physical entity (for example, the individual plant with its buildings, equipment and workers) and often takes a broader view of the stakeholders. This classification resembles to some extent the distinction made in the economics literature between the 'nexus-of-contracts' view, which analyses the contracts between the various investors, and the 'property rights' paradigm, where the specific assets at the core pay an important role in bargaining (Hart, 1989). While the classification into the two types of system may exaggerate differences and obscure important variations within each category, it seems to capture significant elements of existing regulation, self-enforced rules and social norms.

The company-based system is primarily associated with the United Kingdom, while the enterprise-based system is best represented by Germany and the Netherlands, but can also be found in Switzerland and Austria.[13] In terms of legal origin, Anglo-Saxon common law systems have company-based systems, whereas systems of German origin tend to have enterprise-based corporate laws (the Netherlands is an exception in that it belongs to the French tradition). French-origin legal systems have traditionally had enterprise-based corporate laws, but some of these countries – primarily France and Belgium – now find themselves in transition, largely in response to government intervention. The Scandinavian countries, which traditionally have had features of enterprise-based corporate legal systems, are also undergoing change in important respects. We will return to these transitional systems, but for now we will briefly describe the most important features of the two systems corresponding most closely to the two types – the United Kingdom and Germany, respectively.

4.1   United Kingdom: a Company-based System

Regulation in the United Kingdom – whether statutory or by self-enforced codes of conduct – views securities markets as playing an important role in monitoring and disciplining firms. The market provides an objective valuation of the firm and protects shareholders against the abuses of management, primarily through the takeover mechanism. An active, liquid market is a prerequisite for efficient monitoring, and market manipulation and insider dealing are severely punished. Securities regulation in areas such as disclosure requirements, accounting standards and auditing procedures is ambitious. The City Takeover Code, with its strong protection of minority shareholders, is one of the most elaborate sets of rules governing the takeover process. Furthermore, legislation discourages holdings of large stakes by institutional investors, and in addition these investors respect self-imposed limits on the concentration of ownership.

In such a system, the structure and functioning of the board of directors are viewed as crucial, reflected in a vast literature on the optimal size and composition of boards. In the absence of a controlling shareholder, boards of directors are essentially self-appointed. The increasing equity ownership by institutional investors with a tradition of portfolio orientation has further intensified the discussion and led to the establishment of audit committees and special committees reviewing corporate policies in such areas as remuneration and business ethics (Cadbury Report, 1992). Boards in UK companies have also become more non-executive, with technical expertise and general industry knowledge, rather than financial stakes, being viewed as important criteria in the selection of directors. The positions of chairman of the board and chief executive officer are becoming separated in an increasing number of firms.

Conflicts of interest in corporate governance are viewed as a serious problem. For example, while equity holdings by banks are allowed, the

Bank of England strongly discourages controlling stakes in manufacturing companies. Stakeholders other than shareholders, such as creditors or employees, are seldom represented on the board. Such board representation is perceived as driving the firm away from maximization of shareholder value. In particular, takeovers are typically initiated and negotiated by management without involving other stakeholders, not even major shareholders. As compared to German law, English corporate law is characterized by few explicit provisions for the protection of minority interests. Group law – that is, the legal rules applying when one firm is controlled by another – is merely viewed as a special case of company law (Prentice, 1993).

4.2 Germany: an Enterprise-based System

The German-style enterprise-based legal system places less emphasis on the role of the market. A relatively small number of firms are listed, and there is an even smaller share of listed firms with a majority of shares actively traded.[14] Securities market regulation has largely been neglected. Supervision is weak and enforcement rare. For example, German authorities have been reluctant to require officially organized supervision of public issues other than initial public offerings, semi-annual disclosure of information and the regulation of insider dealing.[15] There is no explicit takeover regulation, and no strong need for such regulation seems to be perceived. (Few hostile takeovers have been attempted, and not a single one has succeeded in the traditional sense; given the concentrated ownership structure of German firms and the extensive use of proxy shares, no dramatic increase in such takeover activity should be expected.)

The well-known two-tier board structure in Germany, with a supervisory board (*Aufsichtsrat*) and a management board (*Vorstand*), has been extensively described and analysed in the legal literature. Company law assigns a key strategic role to the *Aufsichtsrat*, which appoints the *Vorstand*. However, even though the supervisory board can play an important role in some critical situations, and has done so historically, the current consensus seems to be that its role in monitoring management is limited. Some recent corporate governance failures have led to calls for reform and activation of the *Aufsichtsrat*. However, the supervisory board cannot be expected to function as an independent board of directors in the Anglo–American sense. In large companies, half of the members are representative of the employees, and the rest of the board is *de facto* appointed by the controlling owner, if there is such an owner.

Corporate lawmakers and supervisory authorities seem to have taken conflicts of interest, at least those between shareholders and creditors, more lightly than their counterparts in the United Kingdom. Commercial banks frequently hold equity stakes in debtor firms, and ofen vote the proxies of bearer shares deposited with them. As a result, a comparatively large share of equity holders are legally presented at general shareholders' meetings.[16] In the relatively small number of firms where ownership is widely dispersed, these proxy votes give the three large commercial banks – Deutsche Bank, Commerzbank and Dresdner Bank – potential control over voting at these meetings. The large banks also organize the most important markets for securities trade. Whether or not banks have used their positions to exercise corporate governance, and the possible effects of such bank intervention, are currently subjects of intense debate in Germany, but few observers question their potential influence.[17]

There is a stark discrepancy between the rudimentary securities markets regulation and the elaborate laws affecting the structure of enterprises and groups of companies.[18] The legislation on codetermination is another example of the emphasis placed in German law on the enterprise itself and its stakeholders, rather than the nexus of contracts between investors.[19]

4.3   Systems in Transition

The legal system of the Netherlands has some features of a company-oriented system: in particular, securities regulation is close to UK practices. This is largely due to the presence on the Dutch stock market of the large binational companies listed on international exchanges. In most other respects the system is enterprise based, but of a rather different type than in Germany. A number of specific control instruments, such as voting trusts and golden shares, have been developed to preserve control in firm, mostly Dutch, hands; a large number of hostile takeovers have been attempted, but all have failed. The legislation on insider trading is of recent date, and its enforcement has been weak (Wymeersch, 1994). Apparently, the large institutional investors have not pushed for reform to the same extent as their UK counterparts. Dutch law requires a two-tier board structure where the supervisory board elects itself. The Netherlands also has elaborate codetermination laws.

Some countries on the European continent, primarily Belgium and France, find themselves in transition with features of their legal systems being altered. Belgium has become increasingly enterprise oriented, especially after the takeover legislation in the wake of the failed attempt on Société Générale de Belgique. This legislation largely emulates the City Takeover Code, but rather than fostering takeover activity, it has led controlling shareholders to reinforce their positions, essentially ruling out hostile takeovers on the bulk of Belgian enterprises. The increasing foreign influence, mostly Dutch, German and French, has further reinforced the enterprise-based nature of the system. This orientation is reflected in the operation of the market for corporate control, with most transactions taking place outside the dormant Brussels stock exchange.

The situation in France is rather different. Even though most of the legal thinking is still strongly influenced by an enterprise-based doctrine, regulators have since 1965 systematically attempted to introduce elements of company-based systems (Wymeersch, 1994). The attempts to open up the market have primarily been motivated by a desire to protect minorities. Disclosure requirements and accounting standards have been comparatively strict, and rules on insiders and takeovers have evolved considerably in response to changes in the operation of markets. State agency supervision is important. Strong tax subsidies have attracted large numbers of small shareholders to the stock exchange, and the large-scale privatizations have been another important instrument in changing ownership and trading patterns.[20] Recent shareholder activism has also put unprecedented pressure on management in some firms to consider the interests of smaller shareholders.[21]

The recent attempt to separate the positions of chairman of the board and president has not been successful; very few companies have undertaken such a separation.[22] The French government has also outlawed a number of specific control techniques. In particular, autocontrol by a parent company through holdings by subsidiary, or cross-holdings, has been restricted. Double voting rights and voting caps for loyal investors have been forbidden, and preferential subscription rights can no longer be waived. The French financial system has become more open through these reforms, but issuers and investors have found ways of circumventing many of the restrictions. There is also strong emphasis on the desirability of a controlling core group of shareholders (*noyeau dur*) with privileged information rights. The restrictions on the concentration of credits are limited, and combinations of debt and equity holdings are allowed and common among larger banks.

Sweden, like the other Scandinavian countries, has had a control-oriented financial system strongly influenced by German corporate law. Corporations only have one tier of boards, and employee representation is required in large and medium-sized firms. However, during the 1980s the Swedish financial system underwent considerable deregulation, and financial markets expanded rapidly. Securities regulation has developed in the direction of the United Kingdom.

4.4 Investor Protection

This brief description of corporate legal systems in Europe illustrates the important differences in the significance attached to various potential conflicts between stakeholders, and the relative importance of different corporate institutions, such as the board of directors and general shareholders' meeting. However, these differences in corporate laws do not necessarily imply differences in the protection of investors. The various rules and institutions may well substitute and complement each other in ways that produce the same outcome. In order to say something about differences in the level of investor protection, we need to find suitable measures.

Needless to say, quantifying differences in corporate laws across countries is difficult, if not impossible. Nevertheless, La Porta et al. (1996a) attempt to compare the level of investor protection in different financial systems. The 49 countries covered by the study are classified into four categories depending on the origin of legal codes: Anglo-Saxon common law and the civil codes emanating from France, Germany and Scandinavia. Table 8.7 presents the findings for just 13 European Union members classified by legal origin, and thus does not do justice to the scope of the study. This small subsample precludes statistical testing, and conclusions are only meant to be suggestive. However, in terms of aggregate statistics, these countries turn out to be reasonably representative of the entire sample.

The authors distinguish between shareholder and creditor protection, and identify legal rules under each category. Legal codes are classified either using a binary zero–one variable or, when this is possible, by a number indicating, for example, the percentage required to call a shareholders' meeting. The 'anti-director' column (column (7)) aggregates the different measures for shareholder protection, supposedly, the higher is the number, the more protected are shareholders. Judging from the data, shareholders are best protected in common law countries, but most vulnerable in French civil code countries. Scandinavian and German codes fall in between. This is the same pattern as for the entire sample in La Porta et al. (1996a), where the difference between countries with French legal origins and the other countries covered by the study is also statistically significant.

Creditor protection is even more difficult to measure along such simple dimensions. The creditor collective is more heterogeneous in terms of contracts with the firm, and rules protecting one set of creditors may infringe on the rights of other creditor categories. The rights included by La Porta et al. are restrictions for going into reorganization, automatic stay on secured assets (creditors cannot reach assets in a bankrupt firm until the court procedure is finished), debtor-in-possession (management stays in control during bankruptcy reorganization), absolute priority to secured creditors over other claimants (including workers and state) and legal reserve requirements (the percentage of total share capital mandated by law). French-origin countries' investors again fare significantly worse than those in other countries in terms of protection. However, creditors in German and Scandinavian firms are at least as well protected as their counterparts in the Anglo-Saxon countries. These patterns are not as clear in the EU subsample.

These differences in basic legal rules would be of little significance if laws were not enforced, and possibly laws with poor investor protection could be enhanced by effective enforcement. To examine whether there are such

Table 8.7   *Some measures of investor protection in European Union countries*

	Shareholder protection						Creditor protection					
	(1)	(2)	(3)	(4)	(5)	(6)	(7)	(8)	(9)	(10)	(11)	(12)
Ireland	0	0	0	0	1	0.10	3	0	1	1	1	0.00
United Kingdom	0	1	0	0	1	0.10	4	1	0	1	0	0.00
Average	0	0.5	0	0	1	0.10	3.5	0.5	0.5	1	0.5	0.00
Belgium	0	0	1	0	0	0.20	0	0	0	1	1	0.10
France	0	1	1	0	0	0.10	2	0	1	0	1	0.10
Italy	0	0	1	0	0	0.20	0	1	1	1	1	0.10
Portugal	0	0	0	0	0	0.05	2	0	1	1	1	0.00
Spain	0	0	1	0	1	0.05	2	0	0	1	1	0.20
Average	0	0.2	0.8	0	0.2	0.12	1.2	0.2	0.6	0.8	1	0.10
Austria	0	1	1	0	0	0.05	2	1	0	1	1	0.10
Germany	0	0	1	0	0	0.05	2	1	0	1	1	0.10
Netherlands	0	0	1	1	0	0.10	2	1	1	1	1	0.20
Average	0	0.33	1	0.33	0	0.06	2	1	0.33	1	1	0.13
Denmark	0	0	0	0	1	0.10	3	1	0	1	1	0.25
Finland	0	0	0	0	0	0.10	3	0	1	1	1	0
Sweden	0	0	0	0	0	0.10	2	1	1	1	1	0.20
Average	0	0	0	0	0.33	0.10	2.66	0.66	0.66	1	1	0.15

Notes:
(1) one share, one vote required; (2) proxy by mail allowed; (3) shares blocked before general shareholders' meeting; (4) cumulative voting for directors; (5) an 'oppressed minority' mechanism is in place; (6) percentage of share capital required to call an extra shareholders' meeting; (7) anti-director rights; (8) restrictions for going into reorganization; (9) automatic stay on assets; (10) secured creditors paid first; (11) management stays in reorganization; (12) legal reserve required as percentage of capital.

Source: La Porta et al. (1996a).

differences in enforcement, La Porta et al. make use of the 'Rule of Law' index compiled by the rating agency International Country Risk (ICR). This index supposedly represents investors' assessment of country risk, and it has been used by a number of other studies to compare levels of law enforcement. If anything, poor enforcement seems to reinforce the weaknesses of investor protection in countries with French-origin legal codes. In fact, countries with Scandinavian and German-type legal systems fare best on this measure, with Anglo-Saxon countries as a close third. We now turn to the

economic implications of these differences in corporate law and investor
protection.

5.   CORPORATE LAW AND CORPORATE FINANCE: DO THEY MATTER?

But do the variations in corporate governance arrangements and the strong
correlation between corporate law and corporate finance really matter? In
particular, does corporate governance influence 'real' variables? La Porta et
al. (1996a, 1996b) suggest that the level of investor protection and legal origin
influence ownership concentration, and thus access to finance and capital
costs. In this section, we briefly discuss some evidence regarding the effects
of the choice between the two generic forms of finance, and financial systems,
before returning to La Porta et al.

Unfortunately, our understanding of what explains these large variations in
corporate governance systems and how they influence economic performance
is still very limited. Indeed, it is typically difficult to compare the performance
of individual corporate governance arrangements even within systems. There
is no uncontroversial way to measure performance, and even when there is
some agreement on the appropriate measures and their interpretation, the
more difficult problem remains to establish cause and effect: for example,
whether successful firms seek arm's-length finance, or whether arm's-length
finance lowers capital costs and thus makes firms more profitable.

However, some progress has been made in understanding differences in
economic behaviour of governance arrangements. In particular, the study by
Hoshi et al. (1990, 1991) comparing firms inside and outside the Japanese
financial *keiretsu* sheds some light on differences in how firms cope with
financial distress: that is, shortfalls in cash flows. The authors show that firms
that are members of *keiretsu*, a specific form of control-oriented finance, have
lower profitability and less variability in cash flows, and their investments are
less sensitive to variation in cash flows. The presumption is that group
financial institutions and other member firms come to the rescue when a firm
experiences liquidity problems.

Another set of evidence is provided by a study of firms financed through
junk bonds – a specific form of arm's-length finance – in the United States
(Asquith et al., 1994). These authors assembled information on the capital
structure for a sample of such firms: in particular, on the structure of debt
finance, and how the firms were affected by financial distress. According to
the study, banks virtually never forgave debt; to the extent concessions were
made, they came from holders of public debt. Firms with more complex debt
structures were more likely to go into formal bankruptcy. Perhaps most

surprisingly, more solvent and better-performing firms did not fare better in financial distress. Junk bond financing is admittedly a rather special form of finance, but the evidence suggests that *a firm's capital structure is at least as important as its general economic health in explaining the outcome of liquidity problems.*

These studies focus on two specific forms of corporate governance arrangements – arm's-length and control-oriented finance, respectively – and the observations may depend on the context: that is, on the properties of the financial system in which a particular financial arrangement has been set up. Kaplan (1994a, 1994b) attempts to compare systems of corporate governance across countries by studying the probability that the management of a corporation is replaced when a firm is experiencing problems. He demonstrates that, for a given shortfall in a firm's cash flows, deterioration in its performance or fall in its stock price, there are no significant differences in the likelihood that a manager is replaced in Germany, Japan and the United States. Perhaps even more surprising, the effect on managerial compensation is approximately the same, in percentage terms. In other words, these *corporate governance systems appear to be equally good, or equally bad, in correcting managerial failure.* Kaplan and Minton (1994) show in subsequent work that even when the outcome is the same, the mechanisms for achieving this outcome may differ greatly. For example, in Japan, managerial turnover is typically brought about by intervention from the company's main bank. The same result in the United States is probably achieved through actions by large shareholders or a hostile takeover by an outside investor.

The problem with the Kaplan study, and most other studies, of cross-country performance differences in corporate governance is that it focuses on two, or at the most three, mature market economies likely to have the best-functioning governance arrangements. To see whether larger samples would bring out the economic effects better, we return to La Porta et al.

The differences in investor protection identified by La Porta et al. seem to matter, in the sense that there is a strong correlation between legal origin and ownership concentration. Countries with French origin have a much more concentrated ownership, at least in the ten largest listed firms covered by study (see Table 8.2 for the EU subsample). Higher ownership concentration is likely to imply higher cost of capital in terms of both diversification opportunities forgone and less liquid markets for corporate financial instruments. In La Porta et al. (1996b) the authors show that, indeed, countries with legal systems that provide better protection to investors have more external finance in the form of higher-valued and broader capital markets (as measured in Table 8.6). Interestingly, large companies seem to be able to raise the external finance they need more or less in all countries covered by La Porta et al., whereas small and medium-sized firms appear more vulnerable to weaknesses in legal protection of investors. The limited extent of capital markets reinforces the problems of poor legal protection by worsening the outside, 'exit' option available to holders of minority stakes. Judging from La Porta et al., French civil law countries appear to be stuck in this vicious circle.

La Porta et al. do not seek to explain the relationship between finance and 'real' variables such as investment and economic growth, but rather the correlation between legal arrangements and corporate finance. However, when combined with the recent literature on finance and growth, their findings are at least suggestive. In a large cross-sectional study, King and Levine (1993) show that *financial sector development, measured as the level of financial intermediation and share of private ownership in the financial sector, is the most important among a large number of factors explaining economic growth*. Thus, to the extent that weaknesses in basic legal arrangements – in particular, corporate law – inhibit the development of the financial sector, they are indeed likely to have an impact on 'real' variables.

However, the importance of corporate governance may also depend on other aspects of the environment in which firms operate. If, for example, competition and corporate governance are indeed substitutes, this suggests a correlation between financial systems and industrial organization; in industries where competition is working well, corporate governance is likely to be less important. However, in industries where strong competition is unlikely to develop, effective corporate governance is going to be particularly important. The corollary for financial systems is that, in countries where competitive forces in industry for some reason are weak, the demands on corporate governance are going to be stronger, and vice versa.

The study by La Porta et al. is just a first step in explaining the relationship between law and finance; in general, the authors raise more questions than they answer. However, their contention that causality goes from legal origin via corporate law to ownership and financing patterns has very strong implications. The higher concentration of ownership, the smaller and less liquid capital markets, the different functioning of markets for corporate control and the different nature of conflicts between investors would all be explained by the original decision to adopt, or impose, a specific legal system. Indeed, there are several reasons to believe that legal origins are more fundamental than both corporate laws and financing patterns. For example, it is hard to argue that all of Latin America adopted French civil codes because of some efficiency argument, or that the members of the British Commonwealth somehow found common law most suitable to their basic economic conditions.

However, caution is warranted in drawing policy conclusions from the findings of La Porta et al. Their measures of investor protection are still crude, and possibly biased by an Anglo-Saxon view. Indeed, the notion of 'anti-director measures' already suggests a focus on conflicts between management and shareholders, and the stress on the rules strengthening the board of directors and the general shareholders' meeting assumes that these corporate institutions are indeed important to the decision-making process in firms. Furthermore, the rather naive view that more investor protection is always better can be subjected to criticism. More likely, excessive protection is likely to stifle entrepreneurial activity and managerial initiative; what is an optimal level of investor protection is ultimately an empirical issue, and it should vary across industries and over the life cycle of the firm.

More fundamentally, it cannot be ruled out there is some third underlying factor that explains both legal origin and corporate financing patterns, and that has shaped the interplay between them. Clearly, one plausible candidate for such an underlying factor is the role of the state. It is well known that under the French system the state plays a very important role, potentially influencing both legal practices and financing patterns. Another possibility is that certain forms for organizing economic activity, particularly the family firm, have travelled with legal practices and thus come to mould both corporate law and corporate finance.

Yet another problem for public policy is that, even if we believed the strong claims of La Porta et al. regarding, for example, the French civil law system, it is not clear what policy conclusions can be drawn. If legal origin, or some underlying third factor, is indeed so powerful in explaining costs of capital and, ultimately, economic growth, and if this basic condition has been so resilient to economic forces and previous reform attempts, what can corporate governance reform achieve? It also remains to explain how certain countries, such as Italy, have managed to develop so strongly over the last 30 years despite apparent weaknesses in basic legal structure and investor protection.

6. IMPLICATIONS FOR REFORM

There are three important broad conclusions from our discussion. First, existing corporate governance arrangements span a wide range of legal and financial systems. At one end of the spectrum is the German system, with its strong presence of control-oriented finance, concentrated ownership and illiquid capital markets supported by an enterprise-based corporate law of its own civil law origin. At the other end, we find the arm's-length financial system of the United Kingdom, with dispersed ownership, liquid capital markets and a company-based corporate law within a common law tradition.

Second, there is a strong correlation between corporate law and corporate finance. Countries with control-oriented financial systems tend to have enterprise-based legal systems. Perhaps more fundamentally, these countries have a civil law tradition, either German or French. The Scandinavian countries form a separate category of a distinct legal origin with, on the one hand, control-oriented financial systems and enterprise-based corporate law systems and, on the other, a greater susceptibility to influence from the Anglo-Saxon company-based corporate law tradition and arm's-length corporate finance.

Third, the variation in corporate governance arrangements and the close relationship between corporate law and corporate finance are of crucial importance for investment and economic growth. Policy-makers should be concerned. They should also beware of the risks involved in meddling with intricate and fragile governance arrangements. Our understanding of the basic relationships is still limited. In the following, we outline some potential implications for corporate governance reform in Europe.

- *The corporate governance problems in some European countries appear sufficiently grave to warrant the calls for reform.* The evidence on the perfomance of different systems is still far from satisfactory, but there are strong indications that there are serious weaknesses. Corporate governance reform is likely to be most urgent in countries, and industries, where competitive forces are weakest.

- *Corporate governance reform is, and should remain, primarily a national issue.* Given the considerable variation in corporate law and corporate finance within Europe, the subsidiarity principle should have a strong bite. Most issues are best settled at the level of individual member states.

- *Regulators cannot rely on competition between regulatory systems to harmonize corporate governance patterns.* The physical presence rule for determining the legal domicile within the European Union, and a number of well-known cultural factors, severely limit such mobility. More fundamentally, the apparent interconnectedness between legal systems and financing arrangements, and between these arrangements and other aspects of the economy, impedes competition among regulatory frameworks.

- *Partial corporate governance reform is unlikely to succeed.* Dismantling individual parts of these systems and tampering with fragile relationships within the systems could easily set in motion unforeseen, and undesirable, reactions. Given the strong interrelationships among the various aspects of corporate governance arrangements and their embeddedness in the larger economic system, partial reform is in any case likely to be ineffective.

- *Real corporate governance reform will require fundamental changes in both legal and economic systems.* The strong explanatory power of legal origin, or some factor associated with legal origin, suggests that for reform to have a major impact it must address these deeper issues. Needless to say, such reform is risky. If our understanding of the relationship between corporate law and corporate finance is still limited, we know even less about the connection between corporate governance arrangements and the larger economic system.

- *Reform should attempt to address stated objectives directly rather than meddling with specific corporate governance arrangements.* For example, if the objective is to improve the liquidity of stock markets, restrictions on ownership concentration are likely to be costly ways of achieving this goal. Promoting entry, and trade across exchanges, will be more effective, and lead to less deterioration in corporate governance. Indeed, more liquid exchanges facilitate the accumulation of control blocks and improve the information content of stock prices.

- *Improved investor protection is a worthwhile objective for corporate governance reform in Europe.* While maximal investor protection cannot be desirable in general, as a guideline for reform in many European countries, better protection of shareholders and creditors – in particular, for holders of minority stakes – seems reasonable.

- *Restrictions on specific investor categories are generally undesirable, and will often be circumvented anyway.* With the possible exception of the banking sector, voting caps and limits on the share of equity of certain institutional investors in individual firms do not seem warranted. In particular, possible gains in liquidity or investor protection are likely to be achieved at the expense of corporate governance. The problem is typically that institutional investors are not too active, but rather too passive.

- *Restrictions on deviations from one share, one vote should probably be avoided.* Whereas mechanisms like dual class shares and pyramiding weaken incentives, they often do promote effective control and liquidity. Forbidding their use will force controlling owners either to diversify or to hold larger stakes, and thus reduce the number of traders in secondary markets.

- *Efforts to harmonize the structure and control of corporations at the level of the European Union are unlikely to succeed.* Corporate governance reform, if undertaken, would probably extend beyond issues of finance to the functioning of labour markets and firm organization. Finding the necessary political support for such changes is difficult.

- *Even if adopted against all odds, the Société Européenne is unlikely to have a major impact on corporate governance.* While some firms may opt out of other forms of incorporation – for example, to avoid codetermination requirements – ownership structures are unlikely to change. Indeed, new untested corporate forms could conceivably reduce the liquidity of financial instruments, at least temporarily.

- *A voluntary 'code of conduct' for firms, suggested by some lobbying groups, is probably a non-starter.* Such a proposal fails to address the fundamental differences in corporate governance arrangements. Moreover, a voluntary code would affect only a small number of large companies, most of which already span borders, and therefore would be of little consequence for liquidity. In any case, the Commission is unlikely to endorse this initiative.

- *A European Commission 'Corporate Governance Policy' should focus on transparency and data collection.* It should monitor that the Transparency Directive (88/627/EEC) is transposed and enforced by member states. Furthermore, the Commission, possibly through Eurostat, could play a useful role in assembling the information eventually produced by the directive. As we learn more about the relationship between corporate law, corporate finance and 'real' variables, such a database could prove valuable in providing input to debate on governance reform.

- *One way of enriching the corporate governance debate at the level of the Commission would be to involve not only Directorate General XV (internal market and financial services), but also Directorate General III (industrial policy and competitiveness).* Corporate governance is about decisions directly affecting the management and organization of companies. DGXV, however, is currently deadlocked on issues of legal harmonization and incompatibility of different company laws. Approaching corporate governance as an issue of horizontal industrial policy, and as such under the auspices of DGIII, should pave the way for a new and more constructive debate. And improving the effectiveness of governance mechanisms is a task of utmost importance to the long-term efficiency and growth of European industry.

NOTES

*   Reprinted, with permission, from *Economic Policy*, **24**, April 1997.
1.   Aghion et al. (1996) present the theoretical basis while some empirical results can be found in Nickell et al. (1996).
2.   For example, Aghion and Bolton (1992) and Hart and Moore (1994), respectively.
3.   Aghion and Tirole (1994) and Burkart et al. (1994) have analysed this trade-off.
4.   The most conspicuous evidence is perhaps the difference between different classes of the same stock: high-voting shares are normally much less liquid than low-voting shares. Bolton and von Thadden (1996) and Pagano and Röell (1995) analyse the trade-off between liquidity and control.

5. While this idea seems to capture the observed correlation between the degree of elaboration of securities regulation and the concentration of ownership, it does not explain the widespread use of various mechanisms for increasing control beyond the level of capital contributed (for example, through pyramiding or dual class shares). If anything, the share of capital, relative to the amount of control exercised, seems to be lower in countries with concentrated ownership.

6. Mayer's study suggests that the United Kingdom and the United States rely more heavily on internal funds than France, Germany and Japan. However, Corbett and Jenkinson (1994), using the same methodology but more recent data, do not observe these differences for France and Germany – Japan stands out as the exception with a much higher share of external finance. Rajan and Zingales (1994), based on firm-level data for large corporations in the G7 countries, find little difference in the relative importance of debt and equity finance.

7. France is a notable exception, where family control has decreased markedly in importance during the 1980s and early 1990s.

8. With the exception of France, where tax subsidies have provided households with strong incentives to own equity, share ownership has become increasingly institutionalized in Europe. However, on most of the European continent the accumulation of institutional shareholdings has taken place either in the banks themselves or in institutions controlled by the banks.

9. See for Germany, Franks and Mayer (1994); and for Italy, Barca (1995).

10. The measure 'external capitalization' attempts to adjust market capitalization for differences in the proportion of equity held by insiders. By using only the proportion of outsider equity to better capture the importance of markets, the higher the insiders' share, the more misleading is the unadjusted measure of market capitalization. La Porta et al. (1996b) calculate the proportion of market capitalization attributable to outside finance by using the data from Table 8.2 and calculating the average stake of the three largest shareholders. While this procedure probably overestimates the share of outsiders, it is at least conceptually better than the uncorrected measure.

11. Total debt is measured as the total bank debt in the economy and the face value of outstanding corporate bonds.

12. The high market value and relatively high liquidity of Dutch exchanges can primarily be attributed to a small number of very large multinational firms. Royal Dutch Shell alone accounted for 34 per cent of capitalization in 1991. Together with four other large international Dutch companies, Shell had 33 per cent of the turnover. In Switzerland the high capitalization and turnover are primarily reflections of the country's well-developed financial sector. In Germany, the top five companies accounted for 47 per cent, and the ten largest companies for 63 per cent, of total turnover (Wymeersch, 1994).

13. In an interesting passage, Baums (1994) describes how during the nineteenth and early twentieth centuries there was a nexus of contracts view in German law, at least in legal theory, but after the Second World War this view was abandoned. Under the current doctrine other stakeholders, especially employees, are members of the firm (*Unternehmen*).

14. Baums (1994) estimates that only 38 German firms are actively traded, in the sense that more than 75 per cent of the shares are not in close hands.

15. Germany has now accepted disclosure of large transactions and large block holdings in line with the EC directive (Wymeersch, 1994).

16. Gottschalk (1988) adds up the shares held by the banks on their own account, their proxy holdings and the shares held by the banks' investment companies. He finds that banks represented more than four-fifths of all votes in shareholder meetings. In the case of Siemens, a widely held firm by German standards, 60 per cent of all shares were represented at the general shareholders' meeting in 1987. Deutsche Bank voted 17.8 per cent, Dresdner Bank 10.7 per cent, Commerzbank 4.1 per cent, and all other banks 32.5 per cent. Foreign owners are less likely to be represented at the general shareholders' meeting. As in many other large German firms, foreign ownership increased substantially in Siemens during the 1980s, and in 1990 it accounted for 43 per cent of total equity (Baums, 1994).

17. For example, Edwards and Fischer (1994) ascribe a limited role to banks in corporate

governance, while Gorton and Schmid (1995) find empirical support for positive bank influence.

18. The significance of the law on groups of companies, *Konzernrecht*, reflects the ownership structure of German firms. According to a study referred to in Baums (1994), as many as 90 per cent of all domestic stock corporations and more than 50 per cent of all German partnerships are members of groups of two or more firms.

19. The Codetermination Acts (*Mitbestimmungsgesetze*) apply to firms with more than 500 employees. In companies with more than 2000 employees, one-half of members are elected by the employees. In groups of firms, the employees of dependent firms are allowed to co-elect the employee board members of the top (governing) company (Baums, 1994).

20. However, the initial dispersion of shares has been reduced considerably by subsequent trading.

21. As witnessed, for example, in the Viénot Report on corporate governance in France.

22. French company law allows both two-tier and single-tier boards, but the chief executive officer is considered the dominant authority.

REFERENCES

Admati, A., P. Pfleiderer and J. Zechner (1993), 'Large shareholders' activism, risk sharing, and financial market equilibrium', mimeo, Stanford University.

Aghion, P. and P. Bolton (1992), 'An "incomplete contract" approach to bankruptcy and the financial structure of the firm', *Review of Economic Studies*.

Aghion, P. and J. Tirole (1994), 'Formal and real authority in organisations', mimeo, Nuffield College, University of Oxford.

Aghion, P., M. Dewatripont and P. Rey (1996), 'Corporate governance, competition policy and industrial policy', mimeo, ECARE, Université Libre de Bruxelles.

Asquith, P., R. Gertner and D. Scharfstein (1994), 'Anatomy of financial distress: an analysis of junk bond issuers', *Quarterly Journal of Economics*.

Barca, F. (1995). 'On corporate governance in Italy: issues, facts and agenda', paper presented at OECD conference on The Influence of Corporate Governance and Financing Structures on Economic Performance.

Baums, T. (1994), 'Corporate governance in Germany – system and recent developments', in M. Isaksson and R. Skog (eds), *Aspects of Corporate Governance*, Stockholm: Juristförlaget.

Berglöf, E. (1988), *Owners and Their Control over Corporations: A Comparison of Six Financial Systems*, Stockholm: Ministry of Industry.

Bolton, P. and E.-L. von Thadden (1996), 'The ownership structure of firms: the liquidity/control trade-off', mimeo, ECARE, Université Libre de Bruxelles.

Burkart, M., D. Gromb and F. Panunzi (1994), 'Large shareholders, monitoring and fiduciary duties', *Quarterly Journal of Economics*.

Cadbury Report (1992), *Report of the Committee on the Financial Aspects of Corporate Governance*, London: Gee.

Corbett, J. and T. Jenkinson (1994), 'The financing of industry, 1970–89: an international comparison', CEPR Working Paper No. 948.

Crémer, J. (1995), 'Arm's length relationships', *Quarterly Journal of Economics*.

David, R. and J. Brierley (1985), *Major Legal Systems in the World Today*, London: Stevens.

Demsetz, H. (1968), 'The cost of transactions', *Quarterly Journal of Economics*.

Demsetz, H. and K. Lehn (1985), 'The structure of corporate ownership: causes and consequences', *Journal of Political Economy*.

Edwards, J. and K. Fischer (1994), *Banks, Finance and Investment in Germany*, Cambridge: Cambridge University Press.

Franks, J. and C. Mayer (1994), 'The ownership and control of German corporations', mimeo, London Business School.

Franks, J., C. Mayer and L. Rennebog (1995), 'The role of takeovers in corporate governance', mimeo, London Business School.

Galve Gorriz, C. and V. Salas Fumas (1993), 'Propriedad y resultados de la gran empresa española', *Investigaciónes Económicas*.

Gorton, G. and F. Schmid (1995), 'Universal banking and the performance of German firms', mimeo, Wharton School.

Gottschalk, A. (1988), *Der Stimmrechtseinfluss der Banken in den Aktionärsversammlungen von Grossunternehmen*, WSI-Mitteilungen.

Grossman, S. and O. Hart (1980), 'Takeover bids, the free-rider problem, and the theory of the corporation', *Bell Journal of Economics*.

Hart, O. (1989), 'An economist's perspective on the theory of the firm', *Columbia Law Reviewed*.

Hart, O. and J. Moore (1994), 'A theory of debt based on the inalienability of human capital', *Quarterly Journal of Economics*.

Holmström, B. and J. Tirole (1993), 'Market liquidity and performance monitoring', *Journal of Political Economy*.

Hoshi, T., A. Kashyap and D. Scharfstein (1990), 'The role of banks in reducing the costs of financial distress in Japan', *Journal of Financial Economics*.

Hoshi, T., A. Kashyap and D. Scharfstein (1991), 'Corporate structure, liquidity, and investment: evidence from Japanese industrial groups', *Quarterly Journal of Economics*.

Huddart, S. (1989), 'The effect of a large shareholder on corporate value', mimeo, Yale University.

International Capital Markets Group (1995), *Who Holds the Reins?*, London: ICMG.

Isaksson, M. and R. Skog (1994), 'Corporate governance in Swedish listed companies', in T. Baums, R. Buxbaum and K. Hopt (eds), *Institutional Investors*, Berlin: Walter de Gruyter.

Kaplan, S.N. (1994a), 'Top executive rewards and firm performance: a comparison of Japan and the US', *Journal of Political Economy*.

Kaplan, S.N. (1994b), 'Top executives, turnover and firm performance in Germany', *Journal of Law, Economics and Organization*.

Kaplan, S.N. and B.A. Minton (1994), 'Outside activity in Japanese companies: determinants and managerial implications', *Journal of Financial Economics*.

King, R. and R. Levine (1993), 'Finance and growth: Schumpeter might be right', *Quarterly Journal of Economics*.

Lannoo, K. (1994), 'Corporate governance in Europe', mimeo, Centre for European Policy Studies.

La Porta, R., F. Lopez-de-Silanes, A. Shleifer and R.W. Vishny (1996a), 'Law and finance', NBER Working Paper No. 5661.

La Porta, R., F. Lopez-de-Silanes, A. Shleifer and R.W. Vishny (1996b), 'Legal determinants of external finance', mimeo, Harvard Institute of Economic Research.

Mayer, C. (1990), 'Financial systems, corporate finance, and economic development', in Glenn Hubbard (ed.), *Asymmetric Information, Corporate Finance, and Investment*, Chicago, IL: National Bureau of Economic Research, Chicago University Press.

Nickell, S., D. Nicolitsas and N. Dryden (1996), 'What makes firms perform well?', mimeo, Institute of Economics and Statistics, University of Oxford.

Pagano, M. and A. Röell (1995), 'The choice of stock ownership structure: agency costs, monitoring and liquidity', mimeo, Université Libre de Bruxelles.

Pagano, M. and B. Steil (1996), 'Equity trading I: the evolution of European trading systems', in *European Equity Markets*, London: Royal Institute of International Affairs.

Prentice, D. (1993), *Groups of Companies in the EC*, Hamburg: De Greuyter.

Rajan, R. and L. Zingales (1994), 'What do we know about capital structure? Some evidence from international data', mimeo, University of Chicago.

Shleifer, A. and R.W. Vishny (1986), 'Large shareholders and corporate control', *Journal of Political Economy*.

Shleifer, A. and R.W. Vishny (1996), 'A survey of corporate governance', NBER Working Paper No. 5554; forthcoming in *Journal of Finance*.

Wymeersch, E. (1994), 'Elements of comparative corporate governance in Western Europe', in M. Isaksson and R. Skog (eds), *Aspects of Corporate Governance*, Stockholm: Juristförlaget.

9. The changing corporate governance paradigm: implications for developing and transition economies*

Erik Berglöf and Ernst-Ludwig von Thadden

The rapidly growing literature studying the relationship between legal origin, investor protection, and finance has stimulated an important debate in academic circles. It has also prompted many applied research projects and strong policy statements. This article discusses the implications of this literature, particularly for developing and transition economies. It concludes that its focus on small investors is too narrow when applied to these countries. This group of investors is unlikely to play an important role in most developing and transition economies. External investors may still be crucial, but they are more likely to come in as strategic investors or as creditors. The article proposes a broader paradigm, encompassing other stakeholders and mechanisms of governance, to help improve the understanding of the corporate governance problems facing these countries and lead to policy recommendations that compensate for the weaknesses of capital markets.

Corporate governance has dominated policy agendas in developed market economies for more than a decade, lately in continental Europe and Japan especially. In the transition economies corporate governance took some time to rise to the top of the policy agenda, but since the mid-1990s it has been among the most hotly debated issues. In the wake of the Asian crisis corporate governance has also become a catchphrase in the development debate. Governments and stock exchanges are competing to produce corporate governance guidelines, and the Organisation for Economic Co-operation and Development (OECD) is about to publish its own principles.

But how important is corporate governance? Some rank it among the most

* Paper for World Bank Conference on Development Economics, 28 and 29 April 1999. Printed with permission from the World Bank. The authors are grateful to the Center for Advanced Study in the Behavioral Sciences, Stanford, California, for providing such a stimulating environment for writing this article, and to Masahiko Aoki, Bernard Black, Florencio Lopez-de-Silanes, Joseph Stiglitz and two anonymous referees for their comments.

important policy issues; others claim that its effects are of the second order. These differences in opinion may reflect the fact that people mean different things by the term. Another explanation could be that corporate governance is not always important, but that when it matters, it matters very much. Corporate governance certainly seems to be more important in some phases of a firm's life cycle than in others. It is also likely to matter more in some contexts or some phases of economic development than in others.

Ultimately, of course, when and how much corporate governance matters is an empirical question. A recent series of articles has begun to address these issues from a comparative empirical perspective, promising more precise definitions of the corporate governance problem and better measures of its impact on economic growth (La Porta and his coauthors 1997, 1998 and 1999b; for simplicity, we refer to these three main articles as La Porta and his coauthors where a more precise reference is unnecessary). The authors of these articles – Rafael La Porta, Florencio Lopez-de-Silanes, Andrei Shleifer and Robert Vishny – raise important questions about the interaction between law and finance and, more broadly, about the role of institutions in economic development.

The articles by La Porta and his coauthors have already given rise to a cottage industry of research on the interaction between law and finance. Recent contributions analyse the effects of legal rules protecting investors and of the general quality of the legal system on, for example, the development of the financial system (Levine, Loayzy and Beck, 1998), the impact of macro-economic shocks (Johnson et al., 1998), the cost of capital (Lombardo and Pagano, 1999) and corporate behaviour and industrial growth (La Porta et al., 1999a; Rajan and Zingales, 1998; Carlin and Mayer, 1999). In many cases the explanatory power of the legal variables is very strong, suggesting important implications for policy.

La Porta and and his coauthors document statistically and explain theoretically cross-country variations in ownership concentration and financing arrangements. Their main argument is that when the legal framework does not offer sufficient protection for outside investors, entrepreneurs and original owners are forced to maintain large positions to align their incentives with those of other shareholders (Shleifer and Vishny, 1997). Thus countries with poor shareholder protection would be expected to have more concentrated ownership structures. La Porta and his coauthors find support for this hypothesis, and they argue that differences in investor protection have implications for corporate behaviour and economic growth.

In this article we discuss how the findings in this rapidly growing literature should be interpreted. In particular, what are their implications for developing and transition economies? Although the recent contributions have raised a range of interesting questions and expanded the empirical base from which economists form their theories and draw policy implications, the analysis is incomplete and normative conclusions are often premature. The analysis is incomplete mainly because it focuses on only one group of actors in corporate governance – small outside investors. The fate of corporations is also, and possibly should be, determined by other actors, inside and outside the firm. The net of empirical investigations must therefore be cast wider. We recognize the ingenuity and importance of this first generation of empirical corporate governance papers, but so far, few general conclusions can be drawn.

DEFINING THE CORPORATE GOVERNANCE PROBLEM

The recent literature is based on the premise that the main corporate governance problem is self-interested management and weak, dispersed shareholders. The need to raise external finance determines the structure of the firm and the legal framework in which it operates. Here the literature follows a long tradition. In the quest to understand the interaction between the legal framework and corporate governance, however, the contributors have shown that the empirical context from which they derived their world view is highly unrepresentative when taken beyond the United Kingdom and the United States. A rapidly growing body of cross-sectional studies and comparable country studies demonstrates clearly that the widely held firm is a rare phenomenon in most countries (see La Porta et al., 1999b; and Barca and Becht, 1999).

Most firms, even listed ones, have a dominant owner. Moreover, this shareholder is very often involved in the management of the firm. Sometimes, though rarely, a bank will play this role, but in most cases a family or the state holds the dominant stake. This pattern is strong on the European continent and even more pronounced in developing countries. In transition economies ownership structures still are not well established, but widely held firms are extremely rare, even in countries that opted for early mass privatization through vouchers.

The realization that the closely held firm is the dominant form of governance profoundly affects how we conceive of the corporate governance problem and its policy implications. In the debate about ownership and control the focus shifts from conflict between management and shareholders to three-way conflict among managers, minority investors and holders of large blocks of shares. Furthermore, the identity of investors comes into play, and it becomes important who monitors them, what their incentives are, and how they are constrained by the legal framework. When the firm is closely held, the emphasis shifts from shareholder-oriented governance institutions, such as takeovers, general shareholder meetings, and boards of directors, to a broader set of devices for redesigning ownership and control, such as cross-ownership, block trading, dual class shares, managerial networks and pyramiding of shareholdings. And in the analysis of capital market activity the paradigm of the competitive stock market must be abandoned in favour of models of bilateral negotiations, blockholder conflicts and market design. In particular, with closely held companies, takeover markets operate very differently. Hostile takeovers are often impossible when one owner controls the majority of the shares, and most control transactions take place outside the official exchanges.

What are the policy implications of the findings of La Porta and his coauthors? There are several possible interpretations. A naive and optimistic interpretation is that legal rules protecting minority shareholders should be strengthened. This recommendation should be particularly uncontroversial for developing and transition economies, where these laws are likely to be weakest. La Porta and his coauthors list features of rules that would achieve this result, such as forbidding deviations from the one-share–one-vote rule or allowing proxy voting by mail. Then corporations would be controlled more efficiently, or at least controlling owners would be able to sell off some of their equity, allowing them to better diversify their portfolios and making stock markets more liquid. The remaining problem would primarily be one of implementation and possibly enforcement.

A deeper, but also more pessimistic, interpretation is that protecting investors is indeed very important, but that the rules for doing so are generated by different legal systems – with the most important distinction being between civil law and common law systems – that the laws in any legal system are highly complementary, and that investor protection can therefore be improved only by reforming the entire legal system. Such reforms are complex, however, and may not be an option for many transition economies. Moreover, in most countries the choice of the legal system either is pre-determined (as in many former colonies) or has already been made, if only half-heartedly and imperfectly. Finally, because the necessary legal reforms cannot be restricted to isolated changes in corporate law, important stakeholders may resist legal reform, making it even more difficult.

To make policy recommendations therefore requires defining the corporate governance problem in a particular country with respect to its prevailing institutions. The predominant corporate governance problem in a transition economy is likely to differ from that in a developing country, which in turn differs from that in a developed market economy. Corporate governance issues also vary substantially across developed market economies (see, for example, Berglöf, 1997; Gugler, 1998; and Barca and Becht, 1999). These differences will affect the implementation of policies to improve corporate governance.

An interesting case in point is the problem of corporate transparency. According to the market-based view of corporate governance, transparency about ownership and control arrangements is unambiguously a good thing. On the basis of several measures proposed by La Porta and his coauthors, many countries are deficient in this respect. Prompted by criticism about such deficiencies, the European Commission passed its Transparency Directive in 1993 to increase corporate transparency in the European Union. But this directive appears to have achieved little, if anything (ECGN, 1998). Most firms – even countries – in Europe seem to have found ways around the restrictions imposed by the commission. This outcome suggests that piece-meal introduction of legislation advocated by the market-based corporate governance view may not work in economies organized along other lines.

One reason for this difficulty is that the focus of corporate finance theory for so many years – the widely held corporation – is, as we argued above, a rare phenomenon. But the understanding of the closely held firm, corporate groups and the markets in which controlling blocks are traded is still limited, and analysis of the mechanisms for separating ownership and control has only just begun. In particular, little is known about how to preserve the powerful incentives of owner-managers, especially in family firms, while strengthening the protection of minority shareholders. Furthermore, almost all corporate finance theory assumes that firms operate under the constraint of a functioning civil and criminal justice system. Such theories must fail in environments where large-scale fraud and theft are standard business practice, as in Russia and in some African countries.

More generally, however, an important shortcoming of the new corporate governance literature is that it restricts its attention to control by the providers of capital, and often even further to control by equity holders. In a legalistic sense this restriction may be justified, because equity holders formally 'own' the firm unless it is bankrupt, in which case ownership of the firm, or of parts of it, may switch to other providers of capital. The implicit argument that those who own the firm should control it, however, is flawed in many respects. Most important – and this is, of course, at the heart of the traditional corporate governance literature – there is a big difference between *should* and *does*. More generally than in the traditional literature, however, this difference relates not only to the conflict between top management and equity holders. Other groups inside and outside the firm exert significant influence on at least some decisions by the firm. These include the employees (sometimes formally represented through worker councils or other institutions), middle and higher management, trade unions, firm-specific suppliers or buyers, other large firms that are not linked to the firm by equity stakes, the public and the government.

In this article we therefore argue that the market-based corporate governance approach not only should be broadened to include the problem of owner-controlled firms and large blockholders, but also should be generalized to a model of multilateral negotiations and influence-seeking among many different stakeholders. Such a model must integrate checks and balances between stakeholders and outside constraints and must take into account the effects of a country's legal and political system on these checks and balances.

Even if there is theoretical reason to believe in the view that ownership with all its costs and benefits belongs to equity, this view is not dominant in most economies other than the United Kingdom and the United States. So, the broader notion of corporate governance offers some hope for understanding other economies better, particularly developing and transition economies, where anonymous stock markets are unlikely to promote the necessary entrepreneurial activity and corporate restructuring. It suggests that other mechanisms, such as product market competition, peer pressure, or labour market activity, may compensate for this weakness or, more realistically, may be more promising targets for legal or political reform than the stock market. Of course, investor protection will still be important, particularly if strategic investors are needed to restructure companies, but it becomes one policy goal to be weighed against others. In the long run protecting small foreign investors may also help attract international portfolio investment, but this source of funds is highly volatile and cannot be the centrepiece of a development programme.

This broadening of the perspective on corporate governance implies that the empirical focus of La Porta and his coauthors on ownership concentration and corporate law, although operationally and statistically useful, is likely to be too narrow. La Porta and his coauthors are silent on the roles of suppliers, employees, product markets and management networks and on the bodies of law that affect the workings and interactions of these agents, such as labour or competition law. In particular, they leave corporate governance isolated from product and labour markets. Also largely overlooked is the interaction between corporate governance arrangements and the political system. In most developing countries 'crony capitalism' may be a much more important problem than the protection of minority shareholders, mainly because dominant family owners of business groups are influential politically. Because powerful business families have often succeeded in influencing legislation and regulation, policy recommendations to simply change the rules may be insufficient.

LAW AND FINANCE

La Porta and his coauthors pursue an ambitious agenda in their three main articles. They want to establish systematic, even causal, links between the legal framework and financing patterns – and, ultimately, corporate performance and economic growth (Figure 9.1). They classify legal origins as Anglo-Saxon, French, German and Scandinavian, or simply common law (Anglo-Saxon) and civil law (the three others). The authors view legal origin as exogenous, that is, handed down through history or imposed from outside. In their view the legal origin shapes corporate law, particularly the extent to which it protects external investors, and corporate law influences firms' choice of financial arrangements. The implicit claim is that these financial arrangements, in conjunction with the legal framework, then affect corporate behaviour and performance.

Legal origin $\rightarrow$ Corporate law $\rightarrow$ Financial $\rightarrow$ Corporate behaviour
(Common or (Shareholder arrangements and performance;
civil law) and creditor   economic growth
 protection;
 enforcement)

Figure 9.1 A causal chain from legal origin to economic growth

La Porta and his coauthors presume that the elements of the causal chain can be quantified and observed. In particular, the authors assume that corporate law can be meaningfully reduced to a set of measures, often binomial, that capture the degree of investor protection. They offer eight indicators of shareholder protection and five of creditor protection (Table 9.1). They supplement these measures with more or less generally accepted indices of 'rule of law' and quality of accounting standards (Table 9.2). La Porta and his coauthors establish a strong correlation between legal origin, investor protection and ownership concentration; when they control for investor protection, the significance of legal origin disappears, suggesting that legal origin affects finance primarily through investor protection. They also identify some potentially interesting differences between countries at different levels of development. We return to these differences later.

Many lawyers have been critical of the classification of countries by legal origin. They find the distinction between common law and civil law particularly superficial. Common law countries have a high degree of codification (in the United States, for example, many of the rules protecting investors are described in the Uniform Commercial Code and creditor protection is defined in part by the Bankruptcy Code of 1978), and civil law countries have developed powerful bodies of case law.

In classifying countries, La Porta and his coauthors draw on an admittedly controversial standard textbook in comparative law (Watson, 1974). Analysts

Table 9.1   Indicators of investor protection

Shareholder protection	Creditor protection
One share, one vote	No automatic stay
Proxy by mail allowed	Secured creditors paid first
Shares not blocked before meeting	Restrictions on going into
Cumulative voting and proportional	reorganization
presentation	Management required to leave in
Oppressed minority	reorganization
Preemptive rights to new issues	Legal reserve requirements
Percentage of share capital needed	
to call an extraordinary	
shareholders meeting	
Mandatory dividends	

Source: La Porta et al. (1998).

have challenged the classifications of some countries and have emphasized the differences within the groups. But even if the labels used by La Porta and his coauthors can be legitimately criticized, the strong correlation remains to be explained. A few reclassifications would not radically change the results.

Another criticism by legal professionals is that La Porta and his coauthors use biased or misleading measures of the quality of corporate law. Qualitative judgements obviously lie behind the measures of investor protection, but in principle it should eventually be possible to agree on the appropriate characterizations. Even if the measures were accurate, the danger is, of course, that the quantifiable aspects of the law provide a biased picture or that the conceptual framework used for identifying these measures is flawed.

Different legal systems find different ways to compensate for their weaknesses. For example, mandatory dividends are rare in common law countries but common in civil law countries, particularly in the developing world, indicating that they are intended to compensate for poor protection in other respects. Moreover, the problem of investor protection could have more dimensions than the measures capture. For example, junior and senior creditors may have very different interests, and laws that protect one group may harm the other. Again, even if these biases do exist, critics must explain the systematic and strong correlation that La Porta and his coauthors establish.

Another, potentially more serious criticism relates to the causality claim: that corporate finance drives corporate law and not the other way around. It is

Table 9.2   Indicators of enforcement

Efficiency of judicial system
Rule of law
Corruption
Risk of expropriation
Risk of contract repudiation
Rating on accounting standards

Source: La Porta et al. (1998).

easy to come up with examples showing how corporate law, as written and as enforced, has been shaped by financial structures. Countries with a tradition of strong bank involvement in corporate control have often found effective ways of accommodating this tradition in legal practice (as in Japan and Sweden). Similarly, in countries where closely held firms predominate, legislators and regulators have often found it unnecessary to specifically regulate the composition of boards of directors. When there are clearly identifiable controlling owners, they are believed to be better suited – and to have the right incentives – to make optimal decisions about board composition. The response of La Porta and his coauthors to this criticism is that legal origin, if not corporate law, is highly exogenous – indeed, often imposed by colonial powers. The fact that countries with one legal origin (civil law) score significantly worse on the measures the authors use must still be explained.

The causality issue brings up another possible problem with the interpretation of the results. It could be that the correlation between legal origin and financing arrangements merely reflects the influence of a third exogenous variable, such as the role of the state or the nature of the political system. In other words, the poor performance of countries with French legal origin would reflect the strong French tradition of state intervention or the French political system; what was imposed on Latin American countries was not just the legal tradition but the entire system of government. A similar underlying variable could be fundamental differences in the relationships between stakeholders in society (Roe, 1999). But it is not clear how such differences are transferred across countries and cultures. All these explanations challenge the interpretation of the results, but they still leave a strong correlation between origin, however broadly defined, and investor protection and financing arrangements.

La Porta and his coauthors (1999b) follow up their previous two articles (1997 and 1998) by describing in greater detail the cross-country differences in ownership and control of listed firms in a smaller number of countries where data were available. The authors go to considerable trouble to document both direct control and indirect control (when a firm is controlled by another firm, which in turn may be controlled by a third entity, and so on). This requires information on the use of such control mechanisms as dual-class shares, pyramiding and cross-ownership. The authors show that except in the United Kingdom and the United States, the overwhelming majority of listed corporations have a controlling owner who in many cases is actively involved in management. As expected, in countries with a common law origin firms are more widely held.

These findings are consistent with and highly complementary to those of parallel work in the European Corporate Governance Network (summarized in Barca and Becht, 1999 and Gugler, 1998). This network strives to establish data comparable across countries, at least for Europe. The contributors have access to better-quality data than La Porta and his coauthors do, though for a smaller number of countries. Their data allow a more detailed description and analysis of the corporate governance problem in individual countries.

The European Corporate Governance Network studies show some shortcomings in the quality and comparability of the data used by La Porta and his coauthors. The picture that emerges is nevertheless similar, with a strong concentration of ownership and extensive use of mechanisms for separating ownership and control. The studies show that banks are more – and the state less – important in corporate governance in Europe than in the world as a whole. In addition, the country studies in Barca and Becht (1999) suggest that La Porta and his coauthors underestimate bank control by missing channels for influence other than direct ownership. In some countries banks have managed to circumvent formal restrictions on ownership by establishing independent investment companies (Sweden) and informal constraints by using proxy votes (Germany). Banks' most important source of influence is typically their role as concentrated creditors.

Nevertheless, the qualitative and quantitative assessments by Barca and Becht (1999) and Gugler (1998) raise some fundamental questions about the interpretation of the findings of La Porta and his coauthors. There are undoubtedly situations where better investor protection seems highly desirable; stories of controlling owners exploiting minority shareholders abound in some countries (Italy is the favourite example in the literature; see Zingales, 1995). But blockholders on the whole appear to be important monitors of management and often participate actively in management themselves (these studies suffer from an obvious problem of endogeneity: does ownership determine performance or vice versa?). The jury is out on whether concentration of ownership is good or bad for performance; in some countries, such as Austria, the Netherlands and Spain, companies with concentrated ownership do worse than those with dispersed share holdings, while in others the reverse seems to be true (Gugler, 1998). Roe (1999) raises the legitimate point that, if there are any benefits from large blockholders, better legal protection should, if anything, lead to the formation of *more* large blocks, not fewer.

It is easy to find examples of laws that seem unfair to holders of minority blocks, and the European Corporate Governance Network studies point many of them out. But the basic legal framework is seldom challenged – at least not from within the countries. Could these countries really have lived for decades or even centuries with laws that have the gross inefficiencies suggested by La Porta and his coauthors without recognizing their fundamental weaknesses? In particular, why have controlling owner-managers been willing, year after year, to absorb the large costs associated with these inefficiencies without pushing for legal reform? Are the laws protecting minorities really as hard to change as La Porta and his coauthors seem to suggest? After all, any policymaker could walk down the list in Table 9.1 and propose reforms that supposedly would improve the protection of investors.

Implicit in the articles by La Porta and his coauthors is a political economy story in which managers and large blockholders effectively block legal reform. In some cases this interpretation seems highly plausible. For example, dual-class shares are crucial in the exercise of control in many countries (such as Sweden), and preventing deviations from the one-share–one-vote rule would seriously undermine the influence of existing holders of high-voting stock and result in substantial redistribution of wealth (voting shares typically trade at a substantial premium). Reforms applied *ex post* understandably meet with strong resistance, but *ex ante* legislation could also have important redistributive effects (see Zingales (1999) for an explanation of why inequality may feed resistance to stronger investor protection).

The political economy story may explain why inefficient laws remain in place for long periods, but the many remaining puzzles suggest that we need to better understand the conceptual framework underlying the studies by La Porta and his coauthors before interpreting their observations and drawing policy conclusions.

CORPORATE GOVERNANCE AND THE FIRM

Corporate governance can be defined as the set of mechanisms that translate signals from product and input markets into firm behaviour. This definition focuses on two elements: the signals generated outside the firm and the control structures inside the firm to execute decisions based on those signals. The definition is deliberately broader than the more traditional ones, which focus on the conflict between outside investors and top management (for example, those of Shleifer and Vishny, 1997 or Tirole, 1998). It reflects the importance of recognizing at the outset that control over a firm's course involves more than these two groups of actors.

Despite its theoretical flavour, this definition of corporate governance has important practical implications. It opens the firm, and its management, to pressures from sources other than shareholders. It also emphasizes the need to look at corporate governance within the wider context of product market competition and corporate links. The definition further suggests that the various forces that affect a firm's behaviour may be substitutes as well as complements in pushing the firm toward efficiency. In this section we place La Porta and his coauthors' view of corporate governance in the broader context of this definition and relate it to the modern theory of the firm.

Samuelson (1957) once remarked that in a competitive economy it would not matter whether capital hires labour or labour hires capital. Indeed, if inputs are homogeneous and the only signals from markets are competitive prices that leave no quasi-rents to producers, the only function of corporate ownership is to determine a profit-maximizing production plan and distribute firm revenues according to marginal productivity. In reality, the signals from factor and product markets are richer and more ambivalent than that, the operation of firms generates substantial quasi-rents, at least in the short run, and labour input in particular is heterogeneous and difficult to control. So ownership does matter.

But even if the focus is limited to the ownership arrangement most common in most economies – ownership by capitalists – the analysis of corporate governance is less straightforward than often claimed. There are two extreme forms of capitalist ownership: the widely held firm and the firm fully controlled by a family with no outside ownership. In between is a continuum of firms with more or less concentrated ownership. The corporate governance problem of the widely held firm has been studied extensively, both theoretically and empirically; Roe (1994) has characterized it in the United States as one of 'strong managers, weak owners'. This type of firm relies on anonymous finance using primarily arm's-length contracts and third-party intervention through the market for corporate control.

The family firm has a different corporate governance problem. Although there may be conflicts between owners and hired managers, these problems are probably of minor importance; owners are generally believed to be well equipped to control the operations of their firm. The corporate governance problem in the family-held firm arises precisely because there is no outside interest in the firm. Owner-managers sometimes fail to recognize business opportunities or pitfalls, particularly in times of change, where outsiders would see them and intervene; the fall of such well-known firms as Wang in the United States and Grundig in Germany can be attributed to this type of governance failure. Corporate governance also becomes an issue when there is a succession problem or when the firm decides to raise funds outside the family. In these important but rare situations the lack of links to the capital market may significantly reduce the value of the firm if outsiders are reluctant to buy assets of which they know little and over which they have little control. The corporate governance problem in the pure family firm can therefore be characterized as one of 'strong managers, no outsiders'.

The corporate governance problem in the closely held firm is again different. The main conflict is that between the controlling owner and the minority shareholders. The financing pattern mixes arm's-length finance by minority investors with control-oriented finance, that is, finance by an outside investor who takes a controlling stake to directly affect investment decisions. Small shareholders will usually find it difficult to challenge large shareholders directly because of the difference in the size of their stakes. Moreover, when ownership of financial instruments is concentrated, there are fewer traders in the markets for these instruments; that makes them less liquid, which in turn reduces the value of the exit option of small shareholders (Bolton and von Thadden, 1998). In the closely held firm, then, corporate governance problem is one of 'strong blockholders, weak minorities'.

So far we have discussed the relationship between the firm and its share-holders, and between controlling and non-controlling shareholders. Share-holders are only one class of investors, however. Creditors obviously also contribute funds to the firm. So do suppliers and sometimes even employees (as in Russia today). The state, too, often offers outside funding – voluntarily, by default (unpaid taxes) or through subsidies in response to stakeholder pressure.

The objectives of the law become more complex for creditor protection than for shareholder protection. There are at least four potential inefficiencies: debtor–creditor law may be too hard or too soft on management or controlling owners, and it may favour inefficient liquidation (when continuation would be optimal) or inefficient continuation (when liquidation would be optimal) (Berglöf, Roland and von Thadden, 1999). In addition, conflicts typically arise between creditors in cases of bankruptcy, depending on the types of their loans and their relationship with the firm. But conflicts may also exist much earlier if different creditors have different lending experiences and intervention capacities. Thus creditors can and will seek to influence a firm in distress in different ways and with different objectives. The simple goal of maximizing creditor protection provides little guidance for the design of corporate law.

We have focused on external finance, but internal finance is more important in most developed countries and is particularly important in countries with widely held firms (Mayer, 1990). In the closely held firm, however, the distinction between external and internal finance may not be straightforward. The owner's contribution to the firm is typically viewed as internal, even if the firm and its owner are legally separated through limited liability. But when the owner-manager turns to distant family members or friends and acquaintances, at what point does internal finance become external finance? And should the finance provided by the group bank in the financial *keiretsu* in Japan or bank-led corporate groups elsewhere be regarded as internal or external?

The consideration of internal finance provides a richer perspective on corporate governance than the traditional shareholder perspective and brings us back to Samuelson's (1957) question: who owns the firm and who should own it? Internal funds are the engine of most firms' operations. They crucially influence a firm's ability to compete, invest, and grow, and at the same time they determine the rents and quasi-rents enjoyed by management, lower-level employees and other stakeholders. According to the corporate governance model of La Porta and his coauthors, centred on external investor protection, corporate governance law should focus mainly on helping small investors get as much control over these funds as possible. But shouldn't the law also protect management and owner-managers?

Clearly, if the primary objective of policy is to protect corporate insiders, as it has been until recently in some developing countries, the answer to this question is trivially affirmative. But even if the law has subtler objectives, such as efficiency, the answer is not necessarily negative, because the protection of external investors comes at the expense of managerial incentives and discretion. As Burkart, Gromb and Panunzi (1997) argue, when managers are tightly controlled, their willingness to exert effort and take initiative may be weaker, because controlling outsiders cannot commit to respecting managerial quasi-rents generated through managerial initiative. In the closely held firm this trade-off also applies to the owner-manager or large blockholder. Restrictions on the discretion of these actors also are costly for efficiency, and maximum protection of minority investors is most likely to be less than optimal.

Building on the literature on ownership and control developed by Grossman and Hart (1986) and Hart and Moore (1990), one can push this argument even further. If the presumption of the corporate governance model of La Porta and his coauthors is true and top management is indeed the *de facto* residual claimant to corporate profits – through private benefits deriving from power, the choice of pet investment or public relations projects, or outright diversion of funds – then it may well be efficient for management to also have some of the residual control rights formally associated with ownership (Hellwig, 1998). The point here is not to advocate the formal transformation of capitalist companies into labour-managed companies in the sense of Samuelson (1957), but merely to observe that modern capitalist corporations resemble labour-managed firms in this one important dimension and that this may be efficient. In this sense, legislation designed to rein in managerial power may have unwanted consequences for efficiency.

Other arguments based on similar general considerations make the same point: that outside intervention in management may reduce efficiency. It has been argued, for example, that if internal finance is such an important source of capital, management (possibly as a representative of other stakeholders) should have a role in preventing certain outside investors from grabbing internal funds. According to this popular view, outside investors do not necessarily take into account the long-term interest of the firm and financial markets are excessively oriented toward the short term. Theoretically, this argument can be shown to be sound if there are asymmetries of information in the capital market (Stein, 1988; von Thadden, 1995). But the empirical evidence relating to short-sightedness is mixed.

It is only logical to extend the discussion of managerial incentives to the broader group of all stakeholders. The main argument here builds on the insight that many stakeholders of a firm – particularly employees, customers and suppliers – make firm-specific investments and that these investments are practical only if protected by implicit contracts that will not be breached (Shleifer and Summers, 1988). But if the firm is owned by anonymous share-holders who can sell their stakes on the stock market, the shareholders cannot credibly commit to not breaching these contracts, because once the firm-specific investment has been made and an outsider proposes a high takeover price, it is optimal for them to sell out. According to this reasoning, stakeholders will not invest sufficiently if they are not given some protection against breaches of contract.

The stakeholder perspective clearly has its dangers, especially when taken to extremes. Deviations from the goal of maximizing 'shareholder value', allow management to hide behind diffuse objectives and open possibilities for individual stakeholder groups to capture excessive rents (for a forceful critique along these lines see Jensen, 1993; for a more balanced scepticism see Tirole, 1998). Yet the point is not that shareholders should be disenfranchised to the benefit of another stakeholder group. The theory we have discussed suggests instead that many different stakeholder groups should play their part in corporate governance and that what counts is the delicate balance among them.

This balance typically depends on the broader legal and political environ-ment in which firms operate – not only, as La Porta and his coauthors suggest, on the design of corporate law. Thus the entire nexus of laws affecting firms in a country matters in the analysis of corporate governance. It is no coincidence, for example, that Germany's infamously weak shareholder protection laws go hand in hand with relatively strict competition policies, far-reaching labour participation laws, two-tier boards favouring extensive managerial networks and tax laws favouring corporate cross-ownership.

Whether or not a good normative argument can be made for a stakeholder perspective, in many countries, if not most, stakeholders do share in rents and take part in decision making. This pattern is particularly striking in many transition economies, often as a result of privatization, but it is also a feature of most continental European countries. In fact, employee participation is very strong in the firms considered by many to have the most advanced corporate finance arrangement in the capitalist world, those with venture capital finance (for analyses of this arrangement in a corporate governance perspective see Aoki, 1998 and Rajan and Zingales, 1998). Thus the broader concept of corporate governance we have proposed here not only has theoretical appeal, but also is empirically relevant for comparative institutional analysis.

CORPORATE GOVERNANCE AND ECONOMIC GROWTH

La Porta and his coauthors implicitly claim that the legal system and the protection it provides to external investors strongly influences the behaviour of firms and, ultimately, corporate performance and economic growth. Figure

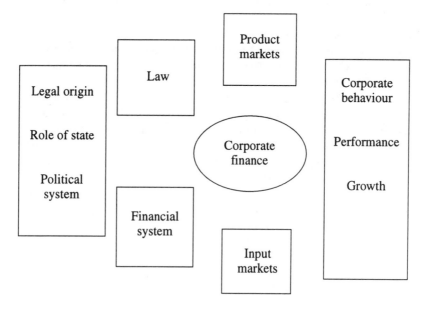

Figure 9.2   Financial system and growth – an enlarged causal model

9.2 attempts to make explicit an enlarged causal model allowing for exogenous factors other than legal origin and a two-way causal relationship between the legal and financial systems. It also incorporates the influence from input and product markets suggested by our definition of corporate governance.

Few empirical studies have directly tested the claim of La Porta and his coauthors, but many have looked at individual links in the figure. This section discusses some of these empirical studies in the context of a broader model relating corporate governance to economic growth.

The discussion in the previous section focused on the balance between management and different classes of investors, but our definition of corporate governance suggests that signals from input and product markets affect investment decisions, through many channels. Obviously, the intensity of these signals should be important. The more competitive are product markets and the stronger is the bargaining power of suppliers, the more likely they are to influence the firm's behaviour. But if management or the controlling owner is somehow shielded from these pressures, the strength of the signals may not matter. Corporate governance, market competition and pressures from suppliers may be both complements and substitutes. The legal framework may thus have a double role, in reinforcing the signals and in improving the mechanism whereby they are channelled into investment decisions. In evaluating the impact of legal mechanisms and drawing policy implications, one should take both functions into account.

Whether product market competition and corporate governance are substitutes or complements is ultimately an empirical issue. Some recent research has investigated this question. Nickell (1996) and Nickell, Nicolitsas and Dryden (1997) study the relative importance of shareholder pressure (the existence of a leading shareholder), debt pressure (measured as leverage) and intensity of competition and whether these forces substitute for or reinforce one another in a sample of British firms. They find some support for the substitution hypothesis. A study of Russian firms finds that competition has little impact – or even a negative impact – on restructuring (Earle and Estrin, 1998). The authors lacked data on corporate governance, but the general impression from the study is that this mechanism was very weak at the time. Brown and Brown (1998) suggest that when the regional fragmentation of markets is taken into account, the effect of competition should be stronger. One interpretation of the Russian experience is that for competition to affect firm behaviour requires at least a minimum of corporate governance. Below that minimum, the question of whether product market competition and corporate governance are substitutes or complements may not be crucial for policy as long as both have a positive impact; competition policy becomes even more important if corporate governance is weak.

Another literature has studied the impact of the financial system on economic growth. King and Levine (1993) show that among a large number of variables related to growth, measures of two aspects of the financial system are economically the most significant: the share of private institutions in financial intermediation and the size of the banking sector. Later contributions have refined these measures and attempted to better control for reverse causality (Levine, Loayza and Beck, 1998). If anything, the impact of financial variables becomes stronger when scrutinized more closely. Levine, Loayza and Beck (1998) also attempt to link the earlier findings to those of La Porta and his coauthors. They suggest that the degree of investor (more specifically, creditor) protection explains the development of the financial sector. Indeed, the measures of creditor protection used by La Porta and his coauthors come out strongly significant.

Another set of contributions has focused on the impact of the regal and financial systems on corporate behaviour rather than performance. Rajan and Zingales (1998) show that under certain assumptions industries dependent on external finance are more developed in countries with better protection of external investors. Rajan, Servaes and Zingales (1998) present evidence that corporate governance affects the degree of diversification of firms. La Porta and his coauthors (1999a) show that firms in common law countries pay more dividends than their counterparts in civil law countries.

All these findings suggest that investor protection strongly influences firm behaviour and probably economic performance and growth. Nevertheless, any policy recommendations must be country-specific, based on analysis of the dominant ownership and control structures and the larger economic system in which they operate.

IMPLICATIONS FOR DEVELOPING COUNTRIES

Developing countries as a group are probably even more heterogeneous than developed market economies in their basic legal frameworks, corporate ownership structures and financial systems. This heterogeneity suggests that few general implications can be drawn for these countries, but there are other important considerations in applying to the developing world the insights from the literature inspired by La Porta and his coauthors.

Although La Porta and his coauthors do not focus on the development problem, they provide data for 22 developing countries (excluding the Asian newly industrialized countries) and control for GDP per capita in their regressions. These data lead to some interesting observations. As expected, there is a development effect, with several variables, such as rule of law and quality of accounting standards, positively correlated with GDP per capita.

But investor protection does not seem to improve with level of development. In fact, creditor protection is strongest in the least developed countries. La Porta and his coauthors interpret this observation as reflecting the reliance on collateral in these economies. But the crucial issue is, of course, whether the letter of the law really matters where enforcement is poor.

There are relatively few listed firms in most developing countres, and in these firms ownership and control is strongly concentrated (La Porta et al., 1999b; for Asia see also Claessens, Djankov and Lang, 1998). The variation across countries is substantial, but with few exceptions firms have a controlling owner, family-controlled firms are important, and many large firms are members of business groups. Business groups are a notable feature of many developing economies (see Granovetter, 1994; Khanna and Palepu, 1999; or Khanna and Rivkin, 1999). They are organized through extensive cross-ownership, are often dominated by a controlling family, and often have good contacts in the government (see, for example, Bhagwati, 1993 on India, and Fisman, 1998 for Indonesia).

Shareholder protection laws may not be a relevant criterion for assessing the workings of capital markets in such economies, because the group-based corporate structure in developing economies is usually seen as a response to lack of capital market institutions. The most comprehensive empirical study of business groups in emerging economies that we know of, Khanna and Rivkin (1999), finds that in three of the seven economies with large numbers of business groups (India, Indonesia and Taiwan, China), group membership has a statistically significant, positive impact on firm profitability, while the impact is indistinguishable from zero in the other four (Brazil, Chile, the Republic of Korea and Thailand). So business groups, with all their opacity, lack of outside accountability, and insider dominance, at least do not seem to harm their shareholders, given the environment in which they operate.

More generally, we believe that the corporate governance problem in our broader perspective is an equilibrium problem: the absence of organized markets and small investors gives rise to substitute constructs such as business groups, but these substitutes prevent capital markets and market-based corporate shareholdings from emerging. In such a situation, modifying corporate law according to the guidelines of La Porta and his coauthors is likely to have little effect and may even be counterproductive.

The consideration of business groups sheds light on another important aspect of the literature inspired by La Porta and his coauthors. This literature presumes that external finance constrains the growth of firms. In most developed market economies that is probably true for at least some important industries. However, internal finance is more important, and new issues of equity and debt are relatively rare events in firms, though bank debt is often used. In developing countries the actual or potential role of external finance is less clear. Finance, internal or external, will help only when firms have access to profitable projects with sufficiently low risk. But the risk premium is high in many developing countries (in part, of course, because of weaknesses in investor protection, rule of law, enforcement and transparency). If such projects were available, firms would probably draw on internally generated funds before pursuing external sources. Here, business groups play an important role: a group, by channelling resources between its firms, relaxes the liquidity constraint at the firm level. This mechanism is enhanced if the group contains a bank as is often the case. Again, legal reform may be harmful, if it disrupts these channels without establishing new, reliable ones (which is quite likely to be the outcome at least in the short run – see, for example, Blanchard and Kremer, 1997 for the case of transition economies).

One feature that stands out in most studies of ownership and corporate control in developing countries is the close ties between business interests and government, often called crony capitalism – or as Bhagwati (1993) put it nicely for India, the economy is enmeshed in a 'Kafkaesque maze of controls'. Although crony capitalism is not a corporate governance problem in the traditional sense, it affects corporate governance in our broader concept, because large family owners often use their influence to limit competition, to obtain favourable finance from the government and in other ways to alter the game in their favour. With soft budget constraints a common part of the picture, crony capitalism can be a strong deterrent to outside investors, particularly when a country is exposed to macroeconomic shocks.

Some of La Porta and his coauthors' indicators relating to rule of law capture elements of crony capitalism, but this political dimension needs to be developed further. For example, Johnson et al. (1998) show that the measures for rule of law explain a significant part of the variation across countries in effects from the Asian crisis.

A question worth exploring is why the ownership structures that lead to crony capitalism in developing economies do not do so in continental Europe. The answer should be closely related to the issues addressed by La Porta and his coauthors. The strength and quality of government is likely to be part of this answer, but such features as tax law and competition law certainly also play a role. Crony capitalism requires remedies other than investor protection, but corporate law might be able to help dismantle some of these unhealthy structures by offering opportunities for broadening or phasing out current ownership.

IMPLICATIONS FOR TRANSITION ECONOMIES

The research programme of La Porta and his coauthors was triggered largely by the transition experience; several of the authors have been deeply involved in Russian institutional reform. Yet their data set includes no transition economies. Although this omission is understandable given the state of data for these countries, it is nevertheless unfortunate. The lessons from this body of work are important for transition economies, though it is dangerous to take them at face value.

The transition economies have widely varying histories and institutional set-ups, but they also share important features. They all have a large sector of formerly state-owned enterprises that need to be restructured and in many cases phased out. They all need new enterprises to emerge in underdeveloped parts of the economy, particularly the service sector. And they all inherited a dysfunctional legal system, with many having to construct basic institutions from scratch.

The new enterprises have very much the same problem, or lack of problem, as those in developing countries do. Still at an early stage of the firm life cycle, they are unlikely to face the problem of intergenerational transfers anytime soon, and liquid markets are therefore relatively unimportant. These firms may not even be financially constrained. The problem of the emerging private sector is instead the lack of market signals and managerial accountability in much of the formerly state-owned sector. Many of the newly privatized enterprises need strong outside investors to execute painful restructuring, but the dominant pattern in Central and Eastern Europe and the former Soviet Union is insider control. In the absence of well-functioning laws, managers with or without shares can effectively expropriate minority investors (who often entered more or less by default through mass privatization or insider privatization schemes). In this situation protection of external investors is crucial; outsiders must be able not only to accumulate stakes but also to exercise control.

While better investor protection is likely to be very important in many transition economies, particularly in the former Soviet Union, the formal legal text is likely to matter much less than in developed market economies. The Russian corporate law provides an interesting example. The original document, prepared in collaboration with Western advisers close to La Porta and his coauthors, was strongly inspired by Anglo-Saxon thinking. The approach taken in the law is very similar to that advocated by La Porta and his coauthors – in fact, the legal text is close to perfect according to their criteria listed in Table 9.1 (Linnarud, 1998). The drafters of the law clearly recognized the limited capacity of the Russian legal system and the need for flexibility: they focused on self-enforcing legal rules and left large holes to be filled by case law (see Black and Kraakman, 1996; and Hay and Shleifer, 1998).

The problem is that the cumbersome procedures and weak enforcement powers of the courts deter investors from bringing suits (Russia ranks 82 out of 99 countries in the 1999 Transparency International Corruption Perceptions Index). The lack of cases has left the large holes in the legal text unfilled, leading to great investor uncertainty. Furthermore, a potentially harmful conflict between the Anglo-Saxon case law doctrine and the Russian legal tradition has manifested itself in the past few years. Russian courts typically have very high evidentiary standards, relying on documentary evidence, and rarely consider circumstantial evidence adequate, unlike in the United States, for example. For this reason, Russian courts dismiss many cases that would be decided in the United States, a tendency that reinforces the other obstacles to building up a sufficient body of case law. And finally, many lower-level courts in Russia are simply corrupt, so that case law based on their rulings is often worthless.

Poor investor protection and concentration of ownership undermine the liquidity of equity markets, a problem that the designers of privatization programmes in many countries appear to have underestimated. They emphasized speed and equity, expecting appropriate corporate governance structures to emerge in due course. But when markets for corporate control are illiquid, initial ownership and control structures become very sticky, something that seems to be at the core of the governance problem in many transition economies. The overwhelming finding in transition economies, at least in Central and Eastern Europe, is that outside, preferably foreign, investors are crucial in bringing about deep restructuring (for an early survey, see EBRD, 1996).

Another important feature of the economic environment in many transition economies, particularly in the former Soviet Union, is the persisting, even worsening, problem of soft budget constraints (Berglöf and Roland, 1998; Schaffer, 1998). The large size or number of formerly state-owned enterprises often forces the government to give in to pressures to refinance the loss-making entities. Weakness in the banking sector also contributes to the lack of financial discipline. The softness of budget constraints weakens the need to seek outside finance and thus the pressure to restructure, sustaining inefficient governance structures.

The predominant corporate governance problem of the large firms in transition economies can thus be summarized as 'omnipotent managers, little resistance'. Improved investor protection can help to attract outside capital and force restructuring, but the overriding issues in most transition economies seem to be law enforcement and government commitment to economic reform (see Dewatripont and Roland, 1997). To be effective, measures to strengthen investor protection must be combined with efforts in other areas – hardening budget constraints, eliminating government corruption, reconsidering the workings of the court system.

In fact, the Russian example suggests that such measures may not even be sufficient. There is much evidence that many large privatized firms in Russia are being run by veritable kleptocrats uninterested in managing these firms for profit. Their real goal, and their comparative advantage, is to plunder the firms' assets and transfer the loot abroad, if necessary by using brute force against opposition (see Black, Kraakman and Tarassova, 1999 for a well-informed and vivid description).

In this situation the normal paradigm of corporate governance – fine-tune the checks and balances on individual self-interest and opportunism – changes its meaning so completely that corporate finance theory no longer applies. In particular, advice to protect minority investors or increase corporate transparency seems to be largely irrelevant, as long as the society's basic rules of economic and political interaction are Leviathan. It is hard to imagine any checks on kleptocratic insiders if the entire political system has proved unable or unwilling to confront them.

GENERAL IMPLICATIONS

La Porta and his coauthors have highlighted many issues crucial for understanding the relationships between laws, financing arrangements and economic growth. The literature shows strong correlation, both statistically and economically, between variables in these areas. Although the issues of causality and the possibility that underlying factors explain these observations have not been resolved, the contributions of La Porta and his coauthors challenge academics and policymakers alike.

We defined corporate governance as the mechanisms translating signals from product and input markets into corporate behaviour. The pressure generated by external investors is just one of these mechanisms. Others include monitoring by employees, suppliers and competitors and within corporate networks; the government also influences the transmission of signals, directly or through the framework it provides for corporations. That all these stakeholders do influence decisions in firms has strong normative implications for the role of law, particularly investor protection. The pressures from different stakeholders may push corporations away from efficiency and profit maximization, in which case strengthened investor protection may be a welcome countervailing force. But these mechanisms can also substitute for, or complement, monitoring by external investors.

The law can affect these trade-offs and the accompanying costs and benefits. But these costs and benefits are multidimensional, and the law, particularly corporate law, must be careful not to focus excessively on outside investors. The optimal governance arrangements reflect delicate trade-offs between the costs and benefits of concentrated holdings, employee participation, management structures, corporate networks and other institutional features of the economy. For example, concentration of ownership improves incentives to monitor management and aligns incentives of owner-managers with those of the rest of the shareholders. Its costs come from the agency problems between concentrated owners and minority owners and from the reduced liquidity of shares. Liquidity can be improved by issuing shares with different voting power. But improved liquidity comes at the cost of separation of ownership and control, and the resulting worsening of the agency problem. Table 9.3 brings together our (perhaps oversimplified) characterizations of the predominant governance problems in different types of firms.

Table 9.3   The corporate governance problem defined – a simple classification

Widely held firm	Closely held firm	Family firm	Transition economy firm	Developing country firm
Strong managers	Strong blockholders	Strong managers	Omnipotent managers	Strong managers
Weak owners	Weak minorities	No outsiders	Little resistance	Related investors

The lessons of La Porta and his coauthors apply primarily to systems in which widely held firms dominate and to some extent in transition economies, where the predominant conflict is between managers and external investors. Whether the protection of external investors in Anglo-Saxon systems is too strong or too weak is hard to say, and there is likely to be important variation across countries with such systems. In many transition economies, particularly those of the former Soviet Union (excluding the Baltic countries), external investors appear excessively weak and the law should aim to strengthen them. For improved investor protection to affect restructuring, however, budget constraints must be hardened, the courts must be more active in settling business disputes, and governments must maintain or create broad political support for economic reforms while making sure that product and factor markets work sufficiently well to provide meaningful signals to firms.

The conceptual framework underpinning La Porta and his coauthors is less well suited to the analysis of corporate governance in countries with mostly closely held firms, even though most of the measures of investor protection also apply to conflicts between controlling owner-managers and minority investors. The evidence is inconclusive on whether the protection provided is excessive or insufficient. La Porta and his coauthors find significant differences among countries with civil law systems, such as between France and the Netherlands. The literature suggests that some countries in continental Europe give too little protection to minority investors. Italy is the most frequently cited example; for other countries, such as Belgium and Sweden, the verdict seems less clear. But there is a general perception that investor protection is weak in many continental European countries. Pressure to reform corporate governance in these countries is particularly strong from US-based institutions desiring to diversify their portfolios internationally. Yet, as we have argued, economic theory does not provide unambiguous guidance in this respect. So policy recommendations must be preceded by careful investigations of the web of relationships governing corporate decision making.

It is less clear that investor protection is a first-order problem in most developing countries. The most important economic policy challenges in most of these countries are fostering an environment for good investment projects, strengthening human capital, accumulating physical capital and improving government accountability. The policy mix for reforming corporate governance will then depend very much on the roles played by markets and different stakeholders. Clearly, better protected investors and functioning financial markets will be part of the solution. In some countries, such as the Republic of Korea, policies to reform corporate governance seem possible and important, while in others their urgency is less clear. In all countries, however, the problem is likely to be one of enforcement rather than of changes in the law.

In the optimistic interpretation of the findings of La Porta and his coauthors countries can achieve reforms of corporate law and investor protection by changing the text of laws and improving their enforcement. The deeper and more pessimistic interpretation is that legal origin determines investor protection and that changing this protection requires changing the basic legal system, a complex task. A similar but conceptually different interpretation is that other, more fundamental factors explain the observed correlation between legal origin, corporate law and investor protection. If these factors involve the role of the state or deeply ingrained relationships between different stakeholders, reforms will be even harder to undertake and will certainly require changes in the society beyond those suggested by the framework of La Porta and his coauthors.

POLICY IMPLICATIONS

The policy implications of La Porta and his coauthors are less immediate than a superficial reading would suggest, particularly for developing and transition economies. Nevertheless, despite the constraints and caveats that we have outlined, we are convinced that there is scope for economic policy on corporate governance. Indeed, it has become very popular to adopt corporate governance guidelines. Many OECD countries have done so, and the OECD itself has issued a set of principles (most guidelines are available on the European Corporate Governance Network's Web site, at http:/www.ecgn.ulb.ac.be).

The current draft of the OECD guidelines (OECD, 1999) is an interesting document. Although it still focuses on minority shareholders and that rare species, the widely held corporation, it shows a clear evolution in thinking compared with earlier versions and with other documents produced by the organization. The preamble recognizes the contextual nature of corporate governance and its dependence on the legal, regulatory and institutional environment. Moreover, the guidelines acknowledge the need to consider stakeholders other than minority shareholders; one of the five basic principles deals with this issue.

The problem with the OECD guidelines, particularly when applied to developing and transition economies, is that they cover a broad range of rules and principles without specifying clear priorities among them. And since the guidelines presume the existence of many of the institutions lacking in these countries, they also fail to provide priorities across policy areas. Moreover, even the watered-down language of these prescriptions is often too ambitious for policymakers. Nevertheless, the OECD guidelines provide a useful start. The following paragraphs therefore give our view of the priorities for developing and transition economies.

- *Any international guidelines must recognize the international differences in governance systems.* Generalizations are often more harmful than helpful. Ownership and control structures differ tremendously, and so do the roles of governance institutions and the basic mechanisms for correcting governance failures. General principles nevertheless should be articulated, particularly when they are unlikely to be expressed locally. At the least, they will force domestic actors to make their own preferences explicit.
- *The general accounting rules and transparency requirements of the OECD guidelines should be a benchmark.* Transparency in ownership and control arrangements is desirable, particularly for improving the liquidity of shares and attracting foreign investors. It is hard to see how such disclosure can have any significant social costs, and the benefits seem substantial. The puzzle is why companies in need of external finance have not implemented these guidelines on their own, which would presumably lower their cost of capital. The failure of the Trans-

parency Directive of the European Union also suggests much resistance or inertia. Either companies do not need (or want) outside funds, or disclosure has substantial private costs. One hypothesis is that insiders to these arrangements are concerned that their legitimacy would be undermined.

- *Protection of external investors is more important in transition economies than in developing countries.* The emphasis in La Porta and his coauthors on external investor protection is most appropriate in transition economies where many managers have entrenched themselves in formerly state-owned companies. But the pressure for change will not come from small shareholders or takeover threats in anonymous equity markets. Instead, it must come from strategic investors with large stakes, or even from the labour force, political authorities or other groups.
- *The development effect from any programme that focuses solely on the plight of small shareholders is likely to be very small.* Poor access to external funds may not be a binding constraint for most firms in developing countries. Even where it is, small, anonymous shareholdings will not be the dominant source of capital in most cases. Most finance is likely to come through family ties or, possibly, peer group arrangements. The same holds for transition economies. That is not to say that protection of small shareholders should not be part of corporate governance, only that it should not be the main focus.
- *Protection of creditors is more important than protection of shareholders in developing and transition economies.* While debt is the dominant source of external finance in developed market economies, equity is more important in developing countries. But developing country firms typically raise equity not in public markets but through family ties or personal relationships. In the short term any substantial growth in external finance is likely to take the form of debt, probably from banks. Recent studies show a strong link between creditor protection and development of the banking sector. In most transition economies companies have been unsuccessful in raising external finance, but their need for it is great. While strategic shareholders are important for restructuring, most external capital in these countries, too, is likely to come as debt.
- *The short- and medium-term emphasis in investor protection should not be on creating liquid markets for shares and corporate bonds.* The reason is not that liquid markets and liquidity are undesirable, as is sometimes argued. Liquid markets generate information and facilitate control transactions in many developed market economies. In developing economies liquidity is most important when families have to sell

out, but this does not seem to be a first-order problem in the short and medium term. In some transition economies liquid equity markets could help strategic investors build positions, but it is not clear that insiders will play their part by issuing shares.

- *In the long term liquid securities markets can be important for attracting foreign portfolio investment.* These markets are hard to create, take time to develop, and are difficult to sustain. In most countries they are not an important source of finance. The recent problems in Asia and Russia have shown how volatile these markets are, but the vulnerability of countries to this volatility seems to be closely related to how well protected external investors are. Foreign portfolio investment may be the type of investment where investor protection matters most. It has important benefits in relieving domestic capital constraints, and its lure can provide important incentives in implementing governance reform.

- *Reforms focusing on enforcement are more important - and more difficult - than changes in the letter of the law.* This obvious point needs to be made. Enforcement is the outcome of a large set of interrelated formal and informal institutions. Unfortunately, our knowledge is still limited of how these institutions interact, to what extent they are substitutes or complements, whether they can be successfully transplanted from one country to another and so on.

- *Reforms must recognize the complementarity of different parts of the law and of different political institutions.* In countries with weak law enforcement the legal protection and legal obligations of economic actors must differ from those in countries with strong enforcement. The efficiency of legal procedures, such as the scope of criminal or civil law in business court cases or the use of circumstantial evidence in court, will depend on the country's overall legal framework and political structure.

- *In many contexts the most immediate concern is to protect stakeholders other than shareholders.* In many transition economies, especially Russia, the main governance problem is entrenched managers' outright theft from, or at least failure to pay, the government and employees. Ruthless managers also exploit suppliers and customers locked into inherited relationships. In many developing countries weak labour laws discourage firm-specific investment by employees and may also undermine general skill formation. An approach favouring non-financial stakeholders could allow managers and individual stakeholders to exploit blurred corporate objectives and paralyse decision making. But corporate governance reform must strike a balance between financial and non-financial stakeholders and recognize the needs and the potential value added of stakeholders other than shareholders.

- *Implementation and enforcement of fundamental corporate governance reform will in many cases require external conditionality.* Governments in developing and transition economies are generally weak. This weakness has many sources, but an important one, particularly in transition economies, is the political deadlock over key reforms arising from their distributional effects. External conditionality can relieve these political constraints. The European Union has played a crucial role as an outside anchor to the institutional reform in Central and Eastern Europe. Unfortunately, EU membership has not been on the cards for most of the former Soviet Union. Conditionality from the international financial institutions should be systematically used, though it can never have the same leverage. Explicit or implicit conditions from foreign investors are also important, but this pressure is likely to be less consistent and less coordinated. Here OECD and other guidelines may be useful.

- *Effective corporate governance reform will often require a combination of threats and co-option of the main actors.* Given the weakness of governments and the absence of credible outside anchors in most developing and transition economies, fundamental reform will not take place against the will of the main actors. Pivotal groups will somehow have to be co-opted. Threats may even be necessary. In the extreme case of Russia renationalization of strategic assets followed by renewed privatization may be the only way to break the resistance to reform. This strategy has obvious reputational consequences, however, and the government may not be strong enough to act on such a threat.

REFERENCES

Aoki, Masahiko (1998), 'A theoretical foundation for comparative corporate governance', Department of Economics and Center for Economic Policy Research, Stanford University, Stanford, CA.

Barca, Fabrizio and Marco Becht (eds) (1999), 'Ownership and control: a European perspective', European Centre for Advanced Research in Economics and Statistics, Free University of Brussels.

Berglöf, Erik (1997), 'Reforming corporate governance: redirecting the European agenda', *Economic Policy*, **24**, April, 93–123.

Berglöf, Erik and Gérard Roland (1998), 'Soft budget constraints and banking in transition', *Journal of Comparative Economics*, **26**, 18–40.

Berglöf, Erik, Gérard Roland and Ernst-Ludwig von Thadden (1999), 'The hypothetical creditors' bargain', Stockholm Institute of Transition Economics and East European Economies (SITE), Stockholm School of Economics.

Bhagwati, Jagdish (1993), *India in Transition: Freeing the Economy*, Oxford:

Clarendon.

Black, Bernard and Reinier Kraakman (1996), 'Self-enforcing model of corporate law', *Harvard Law Review*, **109**, 1911–81.

Black, Bernard, Reinier Kraakman and Anna Tarassova (1999), 'Russian privatization and corporate governance: what went wrong?', Stanford Law School, Stanford University, Stanford, CA.

Blanchard, Olivier and Michael Kremer (1997), 'Disorganization', *Quarterly Journal of Economics*, **112**, November, 1091–26.

Bolton, Patrick and Ernst-Ludwig von Thadden (1998), 'Blocks, liquidity and corporate governance', *Journal of Finance*, **53**, February, 1–25.

Brown, Annette and David Brown (1998), 'Does market structure matter?', SITE Working Paper, Stockholm Institute of Transition Economics and East European Economies (SITE), Stockholm School of Economics.

Burkart, Mike, Denis Gromb and Fausto Panunzi (1997), 'Large shareholders, monitoring and the value of the firm', *Quarterly Journal of Economics*, **112**, August, 693–728.

Carlin, Wendy and Colin Mayer (1999), 'Finance, investment and growth finance, investment and growth', Discussion Paper 2233, Centre for Economic Policy Research, London.

Claessens, Stijn, Simeon Djankov and Larry H.P. Lang (1998), 'Who controls East Asian corporations?', Policy Research Working Paper 2054, World Bank, Financial Sector Practice Department, Washington, DC.

Dewatripont, Mathias and Gérard Roland (1997), 'Transition as large-scale institutional change', in David Kreps (ed.), *Advances in Economics and Econometrics: Theory and Applications: Seventh World Congress, Volume 2*, Cambridge: Cambridge University Press.

Earle, John and Saul Estrin (1998), 'Privatization, competition, and budget constraints: disciplining enterprises in Russia', SITE Working Paper, Stockholm Institute of Transition Economics and East European Economies (SITE), Stockholm School of Economics.

EBRD (European Bank for Reconstruction and Development) (1996), *EBRD Transition Report*, London.

EBRD (1998), *EBRD Transition Report*, London.

ECGN (European Corporate Governance Network) (1998), 'Corporate governance and disclosure in a transatlantic perspective', Centre for Economic Policy Research and European Corporate Governance Network, Brussels.

Fisman, Raymond (1998), 'The incentives for rent-seeking: estimating the value of political connections', Harvard School of Business, Harvard University, Cambridge, MA.

Granovetter, Mark (1994), 'Business groups', in Neil J. Smelser and Richard Swedberg (eds), *Handbook of Economic Sociology*, Princeton, NJ: Princeton University Press.

Grossman, Sanford and Oliver Hart (1986), 'The costs and benefits of ownership: a theory of vertical and lateral integration', *Journal of Political Economy*, **94**, August, 691–719.

Gugler, Klaus (1998), 'Corporate governance and economic performance', Department of Finance, University of Vienna.

Hart, Oliver and John Moore (1990), 'Property rights and the nature of the firm', *Journal of Political Economy*, **98**, December, 1119–58.

Hay, Jonathan R. and Andrei Shleifer (1998), 'Private enforcement of public laws: a theory of legal reform', *American Economic Review*, **88**, May, 398–403.

Hellwig, Martin (1998), 'On the economics and politics of corporate finance and corporate control', Economics Department, University of Mannheim, Germany.

Jensen, Michael (1993), 'The modern industrial revolution, exit and the failure of internal control systems', *Journal of Finance*, **48**, July, 831–80.

Johnson, Simon, Peter Boone, Alisdair Breach and Eric Friedman (1998), 'Corporate governance and the Asian financial crisis', Massachusetts Institute of Technology, Cambridge, MA, Sloan School of Business.

Khanna, Tarun and Krishna Palepu (1999), 'Emerging market business groups, foreign investors, and corporate governance', NBER Working Paper 6955, National Bureau of Economic Research, Cambridge, MA.

Khanna, Tarun and Jan W. Rivkin (1999), 'Estimating the performance effects of networks in emerging markets', Harvard Business School, Cambridge, MA.

King, Robert and Ross Levine (1993), 'Finance and growth: Schumpeter might be right', *Quarterly Journal of Economics*, **108**, 717–38.

La Porta, Rafael, Florencio Lopez-de-Silanes, Andrei Shleifer and Robert Vishny (1997), 'Legal determinants of external finance', *Journal of Finance*, **52**, 1131–50.

La Porta, Rafael, Florencio Lopez-de-Silanes, Andrei Shleifer and Robert Vishny (1998), 'Law and finance', *Journal of Political Economy*, **106**, 1113–55.

La Porta, Rafael, Florencio Lopez-de-Silanes, Andrei Shleifer and Robert Vishny (1999a), 'Agency problems and dividend policies around the world', Economics Department, Harvard University, Cambridge, MA.

La Porta, Rafael, Florencio Lopez-de-Silanes, Andrei Shleifer and Robert Vishny (1999b), 'Corporate ownership around the world', *Journal of Finance*, **54**, 471–517.

Levine, Ross, Norman Loayza and Torsten Beck (1998), 'Financial intermediation and growth: causality and causes', World Bank, Washington, DC.

Linnarud, Christina (1998), 'Corporate governance and shareholder rights in the Russian law', Master Thesis, Department of Finance, Stockholm School of Economics.

Lombardo, Davide and Marco Pagano (1999), 'Legal determinants of the cost of equity capital', Paper presented at the 1999 *Journal of Financial Intermediation* Symposium, Cornell University, Ithaca, NY, Department of Economics, University of Salerno.

Mayer, Colin (1990), 'Financial systems, corporate finance, and economic development', in R.G. Hubbard (ed.), *Asymmetric Information, Corporate Finance, and Investment*, Chicago and London: University of Chicago Press.

Nickell, Stephen (1996), 'Competition and corporate performance', *Journal of Political Economy*, **104**, August, 724–46.

Nickell, Stephen, Daphne Nicolitsas and Neil Dryden (1997), 'What makes firms perform well?', *European Economic Review*, **41** (3–5), 783–96.

OECD (Organisation for Economic Co-operation and Development) (1999), 'OECD principles of corporate governance', Draft, Paris: OECD.

Rajan, Raghuram and Luigi Zingales (1998), 'Financial dependence and growth', *American Economic Review*, **88**, June, 559–86.

Rajan, Raghuram and Luigi Zingales (1999), 'The tyranny of the inefficient: an inquiry into the adverse consequences of power struggles', University of Chicago Graduate School of Business.

Rajan, Raghuram, Henri Servaes and Luigi Zingales (1998), 'The cost of diversity: diversification discount and inefficient investment', University of Chicago Graduate School of Business.

Roe, Mark (1994), *Strong Managers, Weak Owners: The Political Roots of American Corporate Finance*, Princeton, NJ: Princeton University Press.

Roe, Mark (1999), 'Political preconditions to separating ownership from control; the incompatibility of the American public corporation with social democracy', Columbia University School of Law, New York.

Samuelson, Paul (1957), 'Wages and interest: a modern dissection of Marxian economic models', *American Economic Review*, **47**, 884–912.

Schaffer, Mark (1998), 'Do firms in transition economies have soft budget constraints? A reconsideration of concepts and evidence', *Journal of Comparative Economics*, **26**, 80–103.

Shleifer, Andrei and Lawrence Summers (1988), 'Breach of trust in hostile takeovers', in A.J. Auerbach (ed.), *Corporate Takeovers: Causes and Consequences*, Chicago and London: University of Chicago Press.

Shleifer, Andrei and Robert Vishny (1997), 'A survey of corporate governance', *Journal of Finance*, **52**, 737–83.

Stein, Jeremy (1988), 'Takeover threats and managerial myopia', *Journal of Political Economy*, **96**, 61–80.

Tirole, Jean (1998), 'Corporate governance', CEPR Discussion Paper 2086, Centre for Economic Policy Research, London.

von Thadden, Ernst-Ludwig (1995), 'Long-term contracts, short-term investment and monitoring', *Review of Economic Studies*, **62** (213), 557–75.

Watson, Alan (1974), *Legal Transplants*, University of Virginia Press.

Zingales, Luigi (1995), 'What determines the value of corporate votes?', *Quarterly Journal of Economics*, **110**, 1047–73.

Zingales, Luigi (1999), 'Legal systems and financial development', University of Chicago Graduate School of Business.

10. The state, law and corporate governance: the advantage of forwardness

John W. Cioffi and Stephen S. Cohen

1. INTRODUCTION

To be sure, we no longer live in the world of stable and somewhat self-contained national political economic systems of the 'golden age' of postwar capitalism (see, for example, Shonfield, 1969; Cohen, 1969). Just as assuredly, however, we do not live in a world in which the state has withered away under the relentless pressure of these international markets and the intense competitive pressures they transmit so effectively (Berger and Dore, 1996; Vogel, 1996; Weiss, 1998). In particular, the nation state remains the geographical and organizational base of the corporate firm – the very institutional agent that transmits much of the pressure exerted by globalization through investment decisions and responsive restructuring. The laws propounded by the state constitute the structural determinants of corporate governance institutions and these institutional structures define and mediate the opposing interests and the power relations within the corporation. It is this continued and close relationship between the nation state and the corporate firm under conditions of globalization that concerns us here.

Corporate governance has become an increasingly salient subject of political and theoretical debate in the wake of rapid economic and techno-logical change and recurrent crises in the global economy. Yet the relationship among globalization, economic adjustment and the industrialized countries' corporate governance systems remains underdeveloped in the field of comparative political economy. This lacuna is unfortunate because through the lens of corporate governance we can begin to see the structural inter-dependencies among global markets, national political economic arrange-ments, and the structure and operation of the corporate firm. The combination of transformative change alongside substantial institutional resilience and continuity constitutes one of the central puzzles presented by globalization. In this chapter we will present a preliminary approach to analysing by combining the perspectives of corporate governance and comparative political economy.

We limit our analysis to the advanced industrial countries and do not address the governance problems confronting the less-developed countries (LDCs). The LDCs, including (former) 'Asian tigers' such as Indonesia and Thailand, face development and governance problems of another order than the more developed countries. The LDCs must grapple with the fundamental issues of instituting the rule of law and establishing functional political and legal institutions before dealing with the higher-level issues of the substance of corporate governance regimes.

This distinction between LDCs and the industrialized countries stands Alexander Gerschenkron's argument for the 'advantages of backwardness' on its head (Gerschenkron, 1962). The capacity of the advanced industrial states to fashion complex institutional frameworks and enforceable legal relationships constitutes a critical 'advantage of forwardness' enjoyed by the leading economies and leaves the LDCs increasingly disadvantaged.[1] Corporate governance systems represent just such a complex institutional framework at the very centre of national political economies and provide substantial advantages of forwardness. However, these advantages are not identical across the industrialized countries. They vary among different political economic regimes that globalization has brought increasingly into open competition. In this chapter, we are concerned with the impact globalization has had on the institutional features and advantages characteristic of each model and vice versa.

The chapter has three parts. First, we reconceptualize the functional and institutional definition of corporate governance. In doing so, we critique and depart from the dominant theoretical definition of corporate governance developed in neoclassical economic theory as the institutions regulating the relationship between managers as agents and shareholders as owners and principals. The mediation of the principal–agent relationship between shareholders and managers is a core feature of any governance regime, but this is only one relationship within a more complex whole. As comparative analysis immediately makes clear, the ideal of corporate governance as contained within a bilateral relationship between managers and shareholders is characteristic of the neo-liberal Anglo–American political economies. Once the more statist political economies such as Japan or France, and the neo-corporatist systems of Germany, the Netherlands and Scandinavia are included in the analysis, the models and definitions supplied by neoclassical economics, however elegant, become untenable.

Second, we focus on the central role of law and regulation in providing the framework of corporate governance. Corporate governance regimes are the product of intense political and economic pressures ultimately embodied in legal relations, processes and institutions. This more encompassing view of the structural composition and operation of corporate governance leads to a more complex juridical model of corporate governance regimes as a tripartite structure comprised of financial market and securities regulation, company (or corporate) law and labour law. These areas of law function as mechanisms of politics and policy in the constitution and development of corporate governance regimes as a core institutional feature of the political economy.

Third, we examine recent formal changes in corporate governance regimes according to type of political economic organization among neo-liberal, neo-corporatist and statist models of political economy. We find both significant cross-systemic parallels and variations in corporate governance reforms. Substantial changes in financial market and securities regulation have not been matched by changes in company and labour law. This fact reveals the varying impact globalization has had on national political economic structures and begins to account for the patterns of change and continuity we see in industrial economies. Based on these findings, we briefly analyse the developmental trajectories of different political economies and suggest the significance of these varying paths for the process of globalization and national economic adjustment.

2. GLOBALIZATION, THE STATE AND THE CORPORATION

2.1 Globalization as Syndrome

Globalization is more a syndrome than a unified process or phenomenon. As such it is comprised of a set of political economic developments.[2] First, the scale and scope of international trade has grown substantially as a share of global GDP and this growth has sharpened product market competition to an unprecedented degree (Irwin, 1996). This intensifying competition has revealed the relative efficiencies and competitiveness of firms and national economies alike. The expansion of direct foreign investment has further driven this increase in trade, while fostering greater financial and economic openness around the world. The intensification of cross-national competition in trade eroded oligopolistic arrangements as well as the stable relations among the state, labour and capital that had prevailed in many industrialized countries.

Second, capital markets have become truly global, driven by the revolution in digital communications technology and the plummeting costs of executing financial transactions. The emergence of these markets has circumscribed demand-side Keynesian policies and intensified competition among nations and firms for external financing from the growing streams of international investment (Frieden, 1991; see also Hall, 1999; O'Brien, 1992). The development of global markets also created the potential for newly mobile capital to engage in 'regulatory arbitrage' by moving to jurisdictions with the most favourable (or most lax) regulatory regimes (see, for example, McKenzie and Lee, 1991; compare Vogel, 1996, pp. 31–8).

Third, state policies have maintained these open markets for materials, goods, capital and more recently for services, despite the tensions and dislocation caused by globalization. This policy trend manifests itself at the national level through the elimination of currency and capital controls and lowered tariffs. Internationally, the political dimension of globalization is most clearly revealed in the economic integration of Europe into the European Union as an authoritative political and economic entity, the creation of the WTO, and the negotiation of regional trade treaties such as NAFTA (compare Hall, 1999).

Fourth, production has become increasingly cross-national as the value chain is splintered, reorganized, and relocated around the globe to exploit comparative advantages in different locales (Cohen and Guerrieri, 1995; Borrus and Zysman, 1997). The explosive development of microprocessor and communications technologies and the extension and deepening of international capital markets further allowed the increasingly rapid development and dramatic reorganization of complex multinational firms and production networks. This conjunction of technological, economic and political factors produced the broad economic phenomenon called globalization.

2.2 Globalization and Convergence Theories

The increasing attention garnered by corporate governance systems presents a striking paradox. First, at the very time in which global forces are identified as driving economic change, the institutional structures and microeconomic processes of the firm under national law have emerged as increasingly important. Second, within a global economy and international markets marked by rapid change and integration, as the private sector in general and large corporations and capital markets in particular loom larger and more important in domestic and global economies, the more intertwined private institutions become with the state's role in structuring the firm and markets through law and regulation. Any discussion of the evolving institutional architecture of corporate governance must take into account this central fact.

According to much popular belief and economic theory, globalization should force corporate governance regimes to converge on a set of best practices and institutions as determined by competitive international markets. First, the greater efficiencies obtainable under alternative governance regimes should register as increasing opportunity and capital costs on economies and firms that failed to adjust. This should increase the general domestic demands for (or receptiveness to) liberalizing reforms that will be exploited by state actors reliant on economic prosperity for political survival and thus very sensitive to popular pressure (see Keohane and Milner, 1996; Frieden and Rogowski, 1996). Second, key economic actors should press for systemic reform through political means as the competitive disadvantages of the extant governance regime become clearer (see Moran, 1991). Third, suboptimal corporate governance regimes and practices should attract and retain less capital than those more favourable to shareholder interests in short-term returns. The anonymous and spontaneous pressure of global capital markets should therefore induce corporate change through this loss of external finance and force the adoption of informal and contractual means to attract external finance (compare Millstein, 1998). The outcome of each of these scenarios is ultimately the same: the inescapable pressure of market forces will transform overly regulated, moribund economies and bloated states into lean, liberalized competitors in international markets or face stagnation and relative decline.

These arguments neither adequately describe nor explain developments in corporate governance throughout the industrialized world. The intensification of competition in product and capital markets certainly drives corporations to become more efficient, innovative and profit-seeking. However, each of these arguments for convergence misses key features of today's international economy. First, the view that autonomous international markets drive their own development and erode the power and capacities of nation states ignores the fundamental fact that international markets are defined by the interaction of national politics and nationally based actors. International markets are at least as much the product of deliberate policy choices as they are of autonomous economic forces. The globalization of corporate activities, production and investment notwithstanding, corporations and investment funds remain very much rooted in their home countries and defined by their domestic political and legal environments (see Doremus et al., 1998; compare Zysman, 1994, 1995).

Second, path dependency remains an extremely powerful force that buttresses established institutions and practices.[3] Four factors influence the power of path dependence. One is the *number of institutional features that must be changed* to effect reform. A second factor is the *number of political actors and organized interests* incorporated within or implicated by the institutional structure. This factor includes interest groups as well as the level of fragmentation of the state's structure (for example, federalism, parliamentary unified government, separation of powers, autonomous activist courts, independent administrative agencies) that increases the number of political actors and veto points capable of blocking institutional change.

Likewise, the *intensity of interests in a given institutional structure* will determine how actively these organized political forces will pursue or resist institutional change. Lastly, the *relative power of these political actors and organized interests* to shape or block policies and institutional change determines whether institutional reform is politically feasible.

Third, these theories of globalization and convergence ignore the role of different institutional structures in creating *comparative* economic advantage. Different institutional and organizational structures endow national economies with divergent capacities and competitive advantages in certain markets and industries (Soskice, 1999; Zysman, 1994; Zysman and Tyson, 1983; see generally Porter, 1990). Such institutionally rooted comparative advantages are not only a powerful factor in the growth of international markets; they are also a factor in the path dependence and maintenance of divergent political economic models. Comparative advantage contributes to institutional path dependency by lowering (or eliminating) the cost of maintaining alternative institutional arrangements and thus the demand for legal and institutional change.

National political economies institutionalize comparative advantage and path dependencies that persist despite, and perhaps because of, globalization. To some extent, globalization encourages increased specialization of industrialized economies as complementarities develop throughout the global economy. Specialization of national economies, whether in specific industries or market niches, is contingent on the incentives and comparative advantages created by different institutional structures. Rapid adjustment and incentives to take financial risks have endowed the United States with one set of specialized advantages in high tech and sophisticated services. 'Patient capital' and incentives to improve labour productivity and the labour skill base provided the institutional bases for Japanese lean production techniques (Womack, 1991; Aoki, 1994; Brown et al., 1997; compare Gilson and Roe, 1997) and German 'diversified quality production' strategies (Streeck, 1991, 1992; see also Soskice, 1992, 1999).[4]

Corporate governance provides an ideal illustration of each of these dimensions of path dependence. Corporate governance regimes are the nexus of multiple, often interpenetrating, institutions and bodies of law that may make the alteration of one feature at a time exceedingly difficult, while simultaneous reforms would impose enormous political (and perhaps economic) costs and technical burdens. In addition, corporate governance regimes configure and institutionalize the basic interests and incentives of the most powerful political and economic actors in industrial societies: capital, management and labour. The power of the actors and constituencies directly involved in corporate governance and the intensity of their interests in any attempts to change the governance regime further increase the costs of institutional change. Outcomes of conflicts over corporate governance reflect the relative power of these opposing interests in the political system.[5] State structure also determines the strength of institutional path dependency. Separation of powers, activist independent courts and federalist structures each create multiple veto points in the political process and render significant institutional change difficult to achieve over the strenuous objection of a powerful interest group or political actor. Path dependency does not preclude reform of some of the more dysfunctional features of different national economies, but it does undermine sweeping theories of convergence towards the neo-liberal model and provides a compelling argument that national political economies and governance regimes will remain significantly distinct.

Domestic complementarities among factors of production and their organization form the basis for the emerging global division of labour and thus, to a significant extent, for globalization itself. Thus, globalization and the governance of multinational enterprises remain firmly dependent upon the policies and legal institutions of the state, even as state policies are increasingly informed by international economic competition. However, we still face the question of which domestic institutions and structural components of corporate governance systems will remain relatively insulated or resilient and which are most susceptible to change.

3.   CORPORATE GOVERNANCE AS INSTITUTIONAL FRAMEWORK

3.1   Corporate Governance as the Nexus of Institutions

Corporate governance, as the nexus of law, markets, public and private hierarchies, and national and international political economies, provides an ideal vantage point to analyse the evolving relationships among states, markets and firms in an era of globalization. Globalization is frequently described as a sort of economic juggernaut overpowering national economic policies, institutions and practices and imposing deregulation and liberalization by blind and irresistible force. Such a caricature of complex political and economic realities fails to capture the continuing interdependence of the global economy and domestic politics, on the one hand, and of domestic political processes and microeconomic institutions, on the other. Corporate governance embodies these interdependencies in an especially rich fashion by linking the microeconomic structures and activities of the corporate firm to the macroinstitutional structures and processes of politics and law. Globalization has neither overpowered national institutions, nor left them untouched and unchanged. The task, then, is to identify the patterns of stability and change that characterize the relationship between corporate governance regimes and globalization.

The view of 'corporate governance as nexus of institutions' proposed here incorporates a broader range of political, legal and economic institutions, actors and interests into the analytical framework than is typical of most corporate governance studies. The vast bulk of the large and growing literature on corporate governance has focused exclusively on the relation between shareholders and managers from the perspective of economic theory. This literature has recognized the cross-national differences among corporate governance systems, but has largely ignored the political dynamics that created and perpetuated them.[6] Comparative political economy has long focused on the complex interactions among political and economic institutions and on the behaviour of actors within institutional frameworks, but has largely ignored the subject of corporate governance.[7]

The political economic model of corporate governance presented here conceives of corporate governance as a tripartite structure comprised of corporate (or company) law, financial market regulation and labour law.[8] Together, these elements incorporate and mediate among the principle interests and collective actors in the corporate structure and constitute what we call the national corporate governance regime. From this vantage point, corporate governance is no longer narrowly defined as the legal and institutional relationship between managers and shareholders, but as the juridical framework constituting the actors and interests within the corporate firm by allocating and structuring power and authority among capital, management and labour. The parsimonious definitions and models of economic theory give way to a more contextual description of the political origins of governance regimes and the analysis of more complex institutional structures and interactions. The recognition of the autonomous influence of politics and law on the development of governance regimes also confounds assumptions concerning the autonomous and overpowering influences of global markets and theories of political economic convergence that often flow from them. This chapter challenges these assumptions and theories by placing the contemporary development of corporate governance as a set of institutional arrangements and power relations. It does so in a more explicitly political analytical framework, revealing the sources of institutional resiliency that deflect market pressures for change and convergence.

3.2 The Limits of the Neo-liberal Model of Corporate Governance

The 'finance model' of corporate governance dominates the mainstream of Anglo–American legal, economic and management scholarship.[9] In short, the finance model maintains that the corporation exists for the primary benefit of its shareholders. In this view, as holders of the most subordinate claims to the corporate assets and income, shareholders bear the 'residual risk' of the business venture and are least capable of protecting their interests through *ex ante* contract (see Williamson, 1993; Macey, 1991). Governance structures and practices that maximize shareholder value ensure the protection and satisfaction of more senior claimants while rewarding shareholder risk-taking.

Conversely, allowing other claimants or constituents to participate in the control of the corporation presents a clear externalities problem. Other constituents would not internalize the risks to the shareholders' investment and would thus tend to take risks otherwise regarded as imprudent and use the corporation's paid-in capital as a source of rents. This set of incentives would thus increase the risks, lower expected returns, and reduce the amount of equity investment in the aggregate. Neoclassical economics, therefore, holds that shareholders are in the best position to govern the firm prudently and profitably – and thus presumably in the broader social interest (see Friedman, 1962).

Corporate governance structures and associated investment risks affect debt financing much less. Bank loans and investment grade bonds are secured by collateral and the interest income, which must be paid on pain of default, is not subject to withholding by management. Indeed, financial systems such as those in Germany, France and Japan have generated more than enough capital. The policy and economic question posed by low levels of equity investment in these economies is whether continental Europe and Asia fail to generate adequate levels of equity financing and thus limit their financial systems' ability to absorb the higher levels of risk associated with innovation. In short, do these governance systems provide *an adequate supply of the wrong type of capital* and create excess risk aversion?

This economic analysis of risk assumes a linear relation between degree of risk and the amount of investment. Also, risk is assumed to be risk of appropriation through rent-seeking. However, both assumptions may be incomplete. First, economic risk also encompasses macroeconomic and sectoral conditions that determine the safety of an investment and its returns. Non-liberal political economies often create institutional structures and pursue policies to lower aggregate risk in the economy and increase aggregate investment through the systematic reduction of uncertainty as to future conditions. This structuring of the political economy to reduce risk and uncertainty in order to increase capital investment in large, complex and long-term ventures has been and, we believe, still remains vital to development of economies. This suggests that the risk–investment relation is not linear, but varies disproportionately with the systemic reduction of risk and the development of institutions to accomplish this end. However, to our knowledge, neoclassical theories of corporate governance have produced no empirical analyses of this interaction among institutions, risk and investment.

Within the institutional logic of the finance model emerges the overarching conceptual and normative principle of the economic theory of the corporation and corporate governance: shareholder primacy (see, for example, Hart, 1993; Macey, 1991). The firm's objective is to maximize the wealth of the shareholders; all other interests, economic and social, are logically and legally subordinated. From this perspective, the function of corporate governance addresses the principal–agent problem created by the separation of ownership (shareholders) and control (management) (Berle and Means, 1932). In order to benefit from the efficiencies of functional specialization in increasingly complex firms, a class of professional managers, separate from the diffuse class of shareholders, came to control the modern, large-scale corporation. The conflict of interest between these managers and a diffuse class of shareholders constitutes the classic governance problem the American corporate governance regime was designed to redress. Shareholders face enormous collective action problems in monitoring and exercising control over corporate affairs, thereby raising the recurrent problem of shirking and rent-seeking by management. The economic, technological and institutional dynamics that gave rise to the modern firm thus generates a governance problem: how to reassert accountability and control over the managers to maximize the interests of the shareholders where power is concentrated in the manager-agents? A technological and technocratic problem of management becomes a legal, regulatory and political problem of power and accountability that remains a central problem of corporate and economic governance. The rich literature in neoclassical and transaction cost economics devoted to corporate governance largely devotes itself to the analysis of this principal–agent problem and the design of responsive governance structures.

The primacy of shareholder interests derives directly from the established categories and norms of Anglo–American corporate law and is rooted in and reinforced by the institutional structures of the American political economy: fiduciary duties remain enforceable by or on behalf of shareholders alone (see Bratton, 1992, 1993). Securities and financial market regulation enforce transparency and fragmentation of ownership to facilitate efficient market transactions. Labour law enshrines contractual, arm's-length relations between unions and employers within fragmented collective bargaining arrangements with no formal institutional representation structures within the firm or at the sectoral level (see Rogers, 1990).

The theoretical arguments for the priority granted to shareholder interests mask the distribution and exercise of political power underlying the principle of shareholder primacy as a legal norm (see Streeck, 1990). The structure and substantive content of rights in the American finance model reflect the political and ideological conditions under which American corporate law and political economy developed. To state matters simply, rights embody interests, and interests implicate politics. The systematic exclusion of labour from political and economic governance is replicated in the absence of labour interests within corporate governance. Even assuming, *arguendo*, the superior efficiency of the American model of corporate law and firm governance claimed by economic theory, it is clear that cross-national variation in legal regimes and their distinctive developmental 'paths' or 'trajectories' over time cannot be explained by economic models (see Hall, 1999; Zysman, 1994, 1995). Hence, a political analysis is needed. Yet politics does not fit within the narrow confines of the finance model, except, perhaps, as exogenous rent-seeking that distorts otherwise efficient and rational market processes.

The importance of political power in the structure and development of corporate governance regimes becomes clear in comparative perspective. The corporation cannot be reduced to a generic optimal form, severed from context, regarded as spontaneously self-created out of ideal market forces, and upheld as an exemplar of institutional efficiency (see Lazonick and O'Sullivan, 1997; compare North, 1990). Political, legal and regulatory institutions frame the economic relations within the firm and define to a substantial extent the institutions and processes governing it (see, for example, Gourevitch, 1996; Roe, 1991, 1993b, 1996). The political dimension of the corporation and its governance becomes more concrete when the role and institutionalization of labour relations is viewed in relation to corporate governance. The formal incorporation of labour or employee interests in firm governance substantially alters the legal structure of governance institutions and the balance of power within them. Where employee interests are incorporated through board representation or works councils, the firm becomes a pluralist organizational structure in which conflicts must be managed through negotiation rather than appeals to hierarchical legal norms. This mode of organization poses a fundamental legal problem. The norm of shareholder primacy conflicts with the very structure and functions of such governance institutions and therefore deprives them of the single normative ordering of interests that drives the neo-liberal model.[10]

Prior to the EU's Works Council Directive, codetermination had been closely correlated to neo-corporatist modes of political economic organization. Just as the 'business unionism' and absence of labour representation in firm governance in the United States reflect the fragmented institutions and market-based organization of the American political economy, the institutions of firm governance bear the stamp of their development within neo-corporatist regimes of continental Europe. Indeed, these institutions of codetermination may be accurately labelled as 'micro-corporatism' (compare Assmann, 1990; Streeck, 1984). These micro-corporatist arrangements are held in place by the distribution of political power that favours labour to a far greater degree than in the United States and the United Kingdom. However, neo-corporatist polities are not distinguished by the relative power of organized labour and social democratic parties alone. Centre-right Christian democratic parties built neo-corporatist political economies to ensure the social and political stability necessary for long-term economic growth and to prevent the pathological politics of the past. The social democratic left did not impose these institutional arrangements, though, as in the case of German codetermination, it did extend them (see Thelen, 1991).[11] Further, the development and perpetuation of divergent corporate governance regimes under both right and left of centre governments indicates that they have broader support than that of the unions and the political left.

4. GLOBALIZATION AND MODALITIES OF GOVERNANCE

Globalization forces states to confront conflicting policy imperatives. The effects of globalization are equivocal; they may generate demand for greater state intervention as well as for withdrawal from interventionist governance strategies. One set of market forces presses for reduced government intervention in economic affairs to raise short-term profitability and returns to capital. Yet, political and economic demands grow for increased state oversight of economic institutions and processes as globalization gives rise to an international economy that is at once more complex, interdependent and volatile (Rodrik, 1997; compare Dunning, 1997, p. 4; Katzenstein, 1985).

Just as economic phenomena may be too complex for effective regulation, they may also be too complex for adequate self-ordering through autonomous market processes. This problem of complexity is also reflected in the increasing volatility of international markets. Governing economies and firms under conditions of rapidly shifting macroeconomic demand and intensifying product market competition distinguishes the contemporary economic environment from that prevailing in the postwar era of mass production, Keynesianism and active state intervention in industrial development (see Streeck, 1987, 1991). The increasing volatility of increasingly international markets underscores the mutual vulnerability of national economies to events, policies and practices around the world. Once again, this problem, illustrated in all its urgency by the Asian crisis and subsequent cross-national 'contagion' of financial panic, cuts both ways. The volatility and vulnerability generated by globalization has led to calls for greater regulation of global financial markets that national governments are loath to impose and even more unlikely to agree upon. These interconnected problems of complexity, volatility, vulnerability and interdependence thus impel both more and less state intervention in economic matters.

Nowhere are the cross-currents of politics, policy and globalization more in evidence than in the Asian financial crisis. If there has been an event providing the conditions to impel the liberalization and deregulation of national political economies, this is it. The implosion of protected and opaque financial systems, the revelation of wasteful and profoundly inefficient allocation of capital, and the absence of any accountability for economic failure until disaster had struck, led many to predict the imminent death of the Asian model of economic development.

What has been striking in the fallout of the crisis is the absence of a clear, systematic pattern of structural changes and outcomes at the national and international levels. First, despite the extraordinary conditions favouring the reform and liberalization of the Asian economies, no consistent trend of liberalization has emerged. Japan, Korea, Taiwan, Thailand and Malaysia have been struck by the crisis in different ways and have adopted different policy responses to stabilize their political and economic systems. Of course, it may be too early to tell the long-term repercussions of these policies and whether they all will ultimately lead in the direction of liberalization. However, the preliminary evidence does not indicate that they are converging, much less converging on the liberal model.

Second, the relief measures imposed by the IMF and the World Bank revealed the inevitable entanglement of governments and financial systems. Once again, national governments bailed out the domestic banks – this time by transferring tens of billions of dollars of bad debts to the state as security for international loans. The governments were also forced to nationalize, restructure and consolidate failing institutions. The lesson is that governments cannot afford to let banking and financial systems fail. Preventing such failure will always require some level of intervention by the state, but in times of crisis this intervention in the financial sector becomes intensive and extensive, and not 'global'.

Third, the Asian crisis underscored just how difficult it is to substantially change governance regimes. The political character and sensitivity of these institutions has been laid bare along with the enormous difficulty of the technical task of creating new legal and institutional frameworks. Finally, the best conditions to compel governance reforms – a serious systemic crisis – may also be the worst. The Asian economies are so vulnerable to financial collapse, deflation and the contraction of credit that the state must intervene in finance to prevent the seizing up of the entire system. No sensible lender using rational market criteria would lend in these crisis-ridden environments. Under these conditions, 'cronies', insider deals and financial opacity may be indispensable tools to repair the economy.

The growing interdependence of national economies brought about by globalization creates the most vexing problems of policy and governance precisely because the territorially defined nation state remains the basic constituent political unit in the world economy and the source of institutional order. Threats of cross-national externalities due to the misfeasance or malfeasance of public and private actors increase the possibilities for cross-national or global economic crisis, while the international system of nation states has no ready institutional response to these new threats. Some sort of state action is inevitable to address problems of systemic risk and to improve the competitiveness of domestic firms and domestically based multinational enterprises in global markets. The question then, is what form of intervention and at what level?

Intervention at the international level has been and is likely to remain piecemeal. Nation states have not been willing to part with a sufficient degree of sovereignty to create anything approaching a global system of economic governance, let alone of corporate governance. Even the EU, which has altered the political and economic geography and geometry of the world economy and substantially altered economic institutions of its member states, has been unable to harmonize European company law and corporate governance standards and structures – despite more than 25 years of effort (see Rhodes and van Apeldoorn, 1998; Schaede, 1995; Buxbaum and Hopt, 1988, pp. 259–69). International trade agreements and rules alter the relationship of individual countries and global markets, but play, at most, an incidental role in shaping corporate governance regimes. International bodies such as the IMF and World Bank play a significant role in the developing world, particularly in times of crisis, but virtually none in the developed countries that define the standards and institutional models of corporate governance. Finally, no international system of governance has emerged to constrain the forces of global capital markets in currencies, portfolio investment, or foreign direct investment. The primary creator and enforcer of institutional order – including the order reflected in trade agreements – remains the nation state. We simply have not seen international bodies or rules supplanting national institutions (see Panourgias, 1999).[12]

5. POLITICAL ECONOMY AND FORMAL LEGAL AND REGULATORY CHANGE

Given the absence of a global legal and regulatory framework, the relation of corporate governance to globalization must be sought at the level of the national political economy. We therefore compare corporate governance developments cross-nationally. We focus on the formal institutional and legal changes in corporate governance regimes because they are the most enduring and indicative of the depth of political economic change.[13]

Globalization affects different institutional components of corporate governance regimes to different degrees and, among countries, the degree of impact varies. Two categories of variables describe these dynamics. One category is composed of the tripartite institutional structure of corporate governance regimes: the structures of (1) corporate law, (2) financial market regulation and (3) labour law. A second set of variables is constituted by different types of political economic systems. We divide political economic regimes into three basic types: (1) neo-liberal, (2) neo-corporatist and (3) statist. We combine these sets to construct Table 10.1. The table describes the characteristic features of these systems during the late 1970s and early 1980s, prior to the burst of globalization in the later 1980s and 1990s. Of course, Table 10.1 reduces extremely complex and individually distinctive national systems to a rough heuristic scheme. However, these generalizations do capture the characteristic features of the underlying national level institutions. By focusing specifically on the five most important countries illustrative of the political economic typology in Table 10.1, we come up with Table 10.2 to show recent developments in each of the core institutional components of their governance systems.

A comparison of these tables gives us a rough idea of the cross-national trends of legal and institutional change in corporate governance regimes. Of our tripartite governance model, the financial markets and financial market regulation have changed most substantially under the pressure of globalization, labour law (with the significant exception of the EU Works Councils Directive) has changed very little, while corporate law shows a moderate degree of change. This is in keeping with our description of corporate governance and its relation to political economy.

Financial system reforms and international financial flows have driven globalization. As the most important juncture between national economies and international markets, domestic financial systems are most susceptible to change in response to international market pressures.[14] The institutional arrangements integrating labour into the political and economic system are fundamental to the structure and political stability of national political economies and thus most resistant to exogenously induced change. Company law functions as a juridical mechanism mediating between the capital and labour market structures and should thus display an intermediate degree of change in response to the globalization of capital markets.

5.1 The Transformation of Financial Markets

Financial market regulation reveals a pronounced trend in favour of increased formal regulation and codification, improved transparency and disclosure,[15] and regulatory oversight of securities markets. This is consistent with the hypothesis

Table 10.1 Traditional character of corporate governance by type of political economy

	Financial market regulation	Corporate/company law	Labour law
Neo-liberal (US and UK)	• Legalistic regulation designed to correct market failures and facilitate market processes (in the US); • Strong emphasis on transparency and disclosure rules; • Fragmentation of equity ownership stakes and financial services (in US by law); • Pension and tax laws encouraged development of large equity holding pension funds.	• Law is permissive with few mandatory rules (wide latitude for charter-defined corporate structures and governance processes); • Shareholder primacy enshrined in fiduciary duties enforceable by private rights of action and active market for corporate control; • Legal limits on network structures discouraging/prohibiting cross-shareholding, director interlocks, and business associations as sectoral coordinating; • Well developed market for corporate control.	• No codetermination at the board or works councils levels and strict separation of labour relations and firm management (sharp distinction between corporate and labour law); • Fragmented labour organization with no sectoral or peak bargaining between employers and unions; • Weak protection for labour organizing (and strict restrictions on strikes in UK).
Neo-corporatist (Germany)	• Moderately weak transparency and disclosure rules; • Legalistic regulation structures institutional frameworks for private interest bargaining; • No separation of banking and securities business, financial system centralized at core with substantial number of	• Mandatory rules structure the corporation and governance processes; • Corporate interests legally superior to shareholder interests, corporation responsible for stakeholder employees, few effective privately enforceable legal protections for shareholders; • Corporate networks underpinned by cross-shareholding, interlocking	• Interpenetration of labour relations and firm management through board and works councils codetermination (blurred boundaries between company and labour law); • Centralized labour organization and employer association, legal facilitation of sectoral/industry level bargaining; • Strong protection for labour

decentralized smaller institutions;
- Private pensions insignificant and not encouraged by policy.

Statist

(France and Japan)

- Weak transparency and disclosure rules;
- Administrative officials vested with extensive discretion over financial regulation (including discretionary allocation of capital);
- Highly centralized and concentrated bank-dominated financial systems;
- Private pensions insignificant and not encouraged by policy.

directorships, and strong employers and sectoral business associations;
- Weak market for corporate control.

- More mandatory rules than neo-liberal systems, but informal regulatory and inter-firm relationships have most powerful impact on corporate structures;
- Shareholder interests subordinate to 'corporate interests' and state policies, responsibility for stakeholder employees split between firm and state, virtually no effective privately enforceable legal protections for shareholders;
- Virtually no market for corporate control and state plays substantial role in industrial and sectoral organization through discretionary administrative power and/or control of finance.

organization (but not necessarily for strike activity).

- *De facto*, if not *de jure*, separation of labour and strategic management of firm and few formal veto rights for employees, though firm paternalism toward employees common;
- Fragmented organized labour limiting coordination in bargaining (but more centralized employer associations to facilitate and coordinate state policies including incomes policies through patterned bargaining);
- Weak protection for autonomous labour organizing.

323

Table 10.2   Recent changes in corporate governance regimes by country

	Financial market regulation	Corporate/company law	Labour law
United States	• Institutional investors given more power and influence by reform of SEC proxy rules to allow greater communication and cooperation in governance activism, 1995 legislation grants institutional shareholders 'lead shareholder' status to curb alleged excesses in shareholder litigation (ineffective); • Treasury Department ruling requires ERISA pension funds to vote their shares as a fiduciary duty; • Federal Reserve and Treasury Department sanction erosion of Glass–Steagal separation of banking and securities business (though repeal repeatedly blocked in Congress).	• Wave of anti-takeover statutes in the late 1980s and early 1990s, and judicially sanctioned anti-takeover devices weaken market for corporate control as disciplinary mechanism; • Takeover litigation during the 1980s strengthens fiduciary duties to shareholders in most significant jurisdictions; • NY Stock Exchange and SEC exempt most stock option plans from shareholder approval, continuing pattern of US law giving shareholders comparatively few rights to vote on important corporate decisions.	• No significant legislative change; • Courts further weaken legal rights to organize.
United Kingdom	• 'Big Bang' of 1986 deregulates financial services and opens securities brokerage and trading to greater market competition; • 1986 Financial Services Act reregulated financial services sector through increased codification of rules focusing on fraud; • In 1997, government proposed creation of a single regulatory body, the Financial Services Authority, overseeing securities markets; • Increasing harmonization of with UK financial law EU Financial Services and Capital Adequacy Directives further increases codification of securities law but without substantial change.	• 'Super Code' of 'voluntary' best practices for corporate governance and issued as an appendix to the London Stock Exchange listing rules combines Cadbury, Greenbury, and Hampel Committee reports, and an Exchange disclosure rule that has induced significant compliance by large firms; • Increased use of non-executive and independent directors and independent board committees; • Greenbury Report recommends greater disclosure and shareholder approval of executive and board compensation – too soon to determine impact; • Fiduciary duties remain weakly developed as shareholder litigation rare, Cadbury silent on conflicts of interest, and UK Companies Act silent on duties and role of directors (though obligation is to shareholders as group).	• 1997 accession to the EU Social Policy Agreement extends Works Councils Directive to UK; • Increasing juridification and codification of labour relations under EU pressure; • No other substantial legal change.
Germany	• Disclosure law passed in 1998 to increase transparency by allowing firms to issue financial statements using IAS or US GAAP	• Courts inferred existence of fiduciary duties to shareholders, but law remains undeveloped and ineffective, conceptions of corporate interest distinct from	• Court rulings strike down attempts to circumvent board

	• only (no 2d report using German rules); • Securities Trading Law of 1995 requires disclosure of parties owning or controlling 5 per cent of stock, but has limited effect because of loopholes; • KonTraG proxy voting rules more protective of shareholders, induce banks to create voting procedures and offices to reduce conflicts of interest; • Neue Markt for small cap securities issues requires use of IAS reporting standards.	• shareholder interest persist; • KonTraG statute (only major company law reform) requires: • Auditor hired by and reports to supervisory board instead of by management board; • Limit on bank equity holdings to 5 per cent or give up right to vote deposited proxies and shareholder primacy recognized as duty of custodian bank voting proxies; • Effectively requires 1 share, 1 vote; • Power of cross-shareholding reduced by barring these shares from voting in board elections; • Stock repurchases allowed for first time.	• codetermination; • No other significant change in law.
France	• French government reforms financial regulation to give up most discretionary power over allocation of finance; • EU increasingly restricts state's ability to finance and bail out firms; 1988 and 1989 legal reforms expand COB power to oversee and enforce disclosure and reporting requirements; 1988 law establishes stock exchange authorities, the CMF and SBF, whose powers over time expand to include regulation of listing, brokerage, and tender offers.	• 1989 COB and exchange rules create bidding and disclosure procedures for tender offers; • Introduction of freezeout and appraisal rules to protect minority shareholders; • Law requires shareholder vote on wide range of corporate decisions (newly important given other legal changes); • Proxy voting reform to facilitate shareholder voting and weaken management control over voting (too early to discern impact); • Private litigation enforcement mechanisms for shareholder rights considered but either rejected (for example, class action) or not yet enacted.	• EU Works Council Directive introduces a weakened form of the institution to France (after initial failed attempt in 1980s); • No other significant change in law.
Japan	• To date, very little disclosure and transparency reform, virtually no practically enforceable shareholder rights (despite some rise in litigation); • Ministry of Finance has used discretionary control over lending to small and medium-sized firms to maintain employment despite recession and excess capacity; • New financial services regulatory body created in 1999 and required use of IAS financial reporting rules starting in 2000, but too early to judge effect.	• No major changes in law, though Keidaren has released a policy statement endorsing corporate governance practices favouring shareholder interests; • Despite creation of independent securities regulatory body and government pledge of more stringent securities and banking regulation, bank and keiretsu group finances remain opaque and tightly interwoven; • Government in 1999 pledged legal and policy reforms to eliminate constraints on market for corporate control, including acquisitions by foreign buyers, but no action taken yet.	• No change in law, labour relations remain largely non-legalistic; • Continued economic slump has compelled some firms to lay off 'lifetime' employees and middle managers.

that globalization's primary impact has been on the financial system, and capital markets have provided the mechanism through which it influences national economies. However, this schematic account also reveals that globalization's impact has not taken the form predicted by economic theory. Globalization is often described as eroding the significance of law and regulation by compelling countries to engage in competitive deregulation and inducing a shift to market-driven contractual forms of governance. What appears striking is the pattern of re-regulation and juridification of governance areas, even in the most neo-liberal countries. Indeed, the neo-liberal systems appear most inclined to pursue what Steven Vogel has described as 're-regulation not deregulation' (Vogel, 1996; see also Buxbaum, 1987; Kubler, 1987).

The European Union has driven the juridification trends in Europe as harmonization efforts and implementation of EU directives require either replacement or codification of formerly tacit understandings and informal self-regulation. The introduction of powerful new regulatory bodies and the expansion of the powers wielded by extant regulatory agencies, however, cannot be explained solely by EU integration. EU directives and legal harmonization have not required the development of new administrative and regulatory capacities. Further, we see evidence of this development beyond the borders of the EU in Japan. Finally, Britain's experience with financial services deregulation and the 1986 Financial Services Act, preceding the EU's financial services harmonization, indicates that the increasing regulatory stringency and legalism in the securities markets has independent sources (see Vogel, 1996, pp. 93–119; see also Woolcock et al., 1991).[16]

The growth of formal legal rules and regulation serves three interrelated functions. First, they serve to govern behaviour in (1) highly complex and (2) rapidly changing environments where customary practices cannot form over time to provide an alternative basis for legal standards of behaviour. Financial markets fulfil both criteria, especially within the EU where global economic changes have been compounded by EU-wide economic and political integration. Second, formal legal rules restrict the discretionary power of state actors needed for the development of markets and market savvy firms, and in keeping with the liberalizing political ideology ascendant in the industrialized nations during the 1990s. Conversely, legalistic rules constrain the types of anti-competitive and other rent-seeking behaviours that flourished under unaccountable bureaucrats and poorly supervised self-regulatory regimes. Third, they prevent market failures and information asymmetries in order to facilitate market transactions and provide a framework for the stable expectations and credible commitments necessary for a functional market. In addition, increased competition among European exchanges brought about by EU integration and globalization has prompted tightened regulation and higher disclosure standards.

Intriguingly, the United States' modest reforms of financial market regulation suggest convergence toward the European model of universal banking and a concentrated financial sector. Two trends predominate. First, the financial sector is consolidating. Banks are merging with each other, to compensate for the erosion of their core corporate lending business, and to achieve greater economies of scale made possible by the development of information technology. American banks also have intensified their efforts to supply a full range of financial services, from retail and commercial banking to brokerage and investment banking services. The United States has witnessed a far-reaching reconcentration of finance, the likes of which have not been seen since the Guilded Age of the nineteenth century. American financial institutions are seeking to expand the scale of their operations and to increase the *scope* of their services by acquiring or forming subsidiaries to provide brokerage services in the belief that these strategies will enable them to better compete in global markets.[17] Banks have pursued this strategy with increasing intensity since 1988 when a Federal Reserve Board decision took effect and permitted them to use this ruse to circumvent the long-standing separation of banking and brokerage under the Glass–Steagall Act (Litt et al., 1990). Thus, the United States appears to be converging on the universal banking model exemplified by Germany.[18]

This consolidation and concentration of the financial sector is a global phenomenon. A similar dynamic has emerged in Europe and more recently in Japan. German banks seeking higher returns on capital have begun to move aggressively into investment banking. Led by Deutsche Bank's acquisitions of Morgan Grenfell in Britain and Bankers Trust in the United States, the 'big three' German universal banks are increasingly interested in the growth of securitized finance in Germany and the financial sector profits that go with it. That Deutsche Bank was compelled to seek investment banking expertise in the United States and the United Kingdom testifies to the comparative advantages acquired in different institutional settings and the difficulty of recreating such complex competencies under different political economic conditions.[19] The formation of Hypovereinsbank, now Germany's second largest, also indicates a broad restructuring and increased concentration of the financial sector. In France, the hostile takeover of the Paribas investment bank by BNP, a larger commercial bank, also reflects the European trend towards integrated financial services emphasizing securities dealing and investment banking. However, as a systemic issue, consolidation is less a transformation in the already concentrated European and Japanese financial systems than it is for the traditionally – and intentionally – fragmented American financial system.

The neo-liberal economies of the United States and Britain are experiencing a second, and potentially more far-reaching, form of financial concentration through the rise of institutional investment funds. Pension funds and mutual funds have arrested and reversed the dispersion of shareholding characteristic of the Berle and Means corporation that formed the basis of managerial capitalism in neo-liberal economies. The percentage of equity of the 1000 largest public corporations held by institutions in the United States has gone from approximately 25 per cent in the early 1970s, to 46.6 per cent in 1987, to 58.8 per cent in 1996. More important for corporate governance, over 25 per cent of equity in the 1000 largest public corporations is held by large, and generally public, pension funds with longer time horizons, lower portfolio turnover, and thus greater incentives to become active in firm governance (The Conference Board, 1997, tables 8 and 19). The market power of these vast institutional holdings is double-edged. The very size of institutional holdings makes them increasingly illiquid but therefore raises the incentives for governance activism as the remaining strategy to improve the performance of their investments (see Hawley and Williams, 1994, 1996).

This increasingly concentrated pooling of investment capital and the governance power that goes with it carry potentially profound international consequences (see Buxbaum, 1991, 1994). Anglo–American institutions own between 35 per cent and 45 per cent of equity traded on the Paris Stock Exchange and have been repeatedly credited with pushing French managers to focus on shareholder value through corporate restructuring and a wave of major corporate mergers and hostile takeover activity that has shaken the French economic elite (see Davis Global Advisors, 1998, pp. 52–4).[20] Hence, it would be inaccurate to attribute the transformation in governance taking place in France to the general phenomenon of globalization. The power of institutional investors derives from their *organizational form* as large-scale equity holders, and national legal structures and institutional arrangements determine this form in the first instance.

In the United States, the increasing power of institutional investors is not solely a matter of scale and type of investment, but also of government policy expressed through legal reforms. First, changes in SEC proxy rules have encouraged funds to cooperate in corporate governance activism, thereby sanctioning informal tactics likely to be more effective. Second, pension funds now have a legal *duty* to remain knowledgeable and reasonably active in corporate governance. Third, institutional investors were given greater power over shareholder litigation – though they have not taken up this role with any frequency (see Grundfest and Perino, 1997). The failure of these policies to effect substantial change in corporate governance is not surprising, given the institutional bias favouring liquidity over control in the United States (Coffee, 1991). However, the consistent and distinctive policy initiatives to empower institutional investors are striking in their attempts to foster and use concentrated financial power within a 'political model' of corporate governance (compare Pound, 1993). To date, the increasing size, activism and international investments of institutional investors represents a set of legal and historical developments unique to the United States and, to a lesser degree, Britain.[21] Yet the rise of institutional investors may substantially transform the institutions and dynamics of governance around the world as industrialized countries seek to meet the dual challenge of improving governance while providing for aging populations. Shareholder capitalism has taken on an identifiable and functional institutional form.

In the statist political economies, globalization and the elimination of capital controls that preceded it have eroded the capacity of the state to control the allocation of finance as a policy mechanism. Neither France nor Japan can utilize their ministries of finance for the highly interventionist industrial policies of the past. France gave up the capacity to allocate and ration credit in the mid-1980s as the political costs of choosing economic winners and losers began to rise throughout the 1970s and 1980s and as the 'national champions' created with these financial mechanisms of policy proved increasingly uncompetitive (see Deeg and Perez, 1999). The stunning growth of the Japanese economy and the success of its export-oriented industrial firms reduced the relative power of the state's control over credit and finance in an economy awash with cash and rapidly inflating asset prices.

However, the state remains a powerful actor in both these economies. The French state has maintained substantial, though subtly deployed, discretionary power over industrial organization and the wave of mergers sweeping France. The BNP–Paribas merger that transformed the French financial sector also signalled the French government's policy choice to allow market forces and, in particular, a new market for corporate control to reshape French finance. The BNP–Paribas, Total-Fina–Elf Aquitaine and Carrefour–Promods mergers are creating a new breed of national champion shaped more by market forces than state fiat and intended to be more competitive in international markets.[22] Japan's Ministry of Finance has recently used its remaining control over finance to condition credit for small and medium-sized enterprises on their retaining otherwise redundant workers. Having failed to end the recession through halting and haphazard demand stimulus policies, the state has returned to the use of traditional policy levers, but seemingly without a long-term industrial policy.

Japan and the rest of Asia present non-trivial special cases that require separate mention. Yet even these special cases illustrate the central importance of domestic politics in a globalizing economy. Japanese financial consolidation has only begun in earnest in mid to late 1999 after a decade of economic stagnation and financial crisis. Given the enormity of Japan's debt crisis (possibly as much as 1 trillion US dollars in bad debts), resolving it would have taken enormous political and bureaucratic will and strength. Japan in the 1990s has evidenced neither. A political crisis initiated by the crash of the bubble economy and pervasive corruption scandals shattered the long-ruling

Liberal Democratic Party and ended its virtual monopoly on power (see Vogel, 1996). What followed was a rotating succession of weak and unstable coalition governments unwilling and unable to take difficult and divisive policy decisions. At the same time, the esteem and authority of the powerful bureaucracies was weakened by the crash and recurrent corruption scandals. Under these conditions, no political resolution could be found to unwind the debt crisis and restore the financial system to health. As a consequence of this political failure, Japan has not been capable of undertaking the kind of financial reforms to improve transparency, disclosure and accounting for fear of exposing and intensifying the severity and breadth of the crisis. The result has been political and economic stasis. As discussed above, the rest of the Asian NICs have recapitulated this general pattern in varying degrees and permutations. Change in the corporate governance regimes of Asia has been slow, sometime erratic, and always accompanied by intense political wrangling. Consequently, it is premature to characterize the evolution of finance and corporate governance in Asia.

5.2 The Equivocal Case of Company Law

Company law reveals a moderate but surprisingly variable degree of cross-national change. In the neo-liberal economies of the United States and the UK, this moderate change is unsurprising because they are supposed to supply the model for globalization induced convergence. However, the substance of the changes that have occurred in these countries confounds the mainstream convergence theories. In the United States, the political and legal reaction to the hostile takeover boom generated anti-takeover laws and legally sanctioned anti-takeover devices that effectively restored much managerial power of the *status quo ante*.[24] Conversely, the rise of institutional investors after the end of the takeover boom has driven extra-legal changes in corporate governance by increasing the use of independent board members, independent board committees and direct dealings between investment funds and managers that has reinforced managerial sensitivity to shareholder values. At the same time, however, the American governance regime has allowed – or encouraged – the use of stock options as executive compensation that has effected a vast redistribution of wealth to managers (*The Economist*, 1999, p. 26). Despite attacks on these compensation schemes as excessive and vulnerable to managerial conflicts of interests, the politics and economics of the American corporate governance regime have been incapable of restraining this flow of money. Rather, the New York Stock Exchange with the SEC's blessing reduced transparency and shareholder control by exempting a wide range of options plans from shareholder approval.

The comparison between France and Japan is the most startling. As in securities regulation, French company law has changed with surprising swiftness and magnitude.[24] Company law reforms have appropriated Anglo-American company law structures to a surprising degree, given the *dirigiste* and *colbertiste* traditions in economic policy and governance. Most surprisingly of all, these changes in law and state policy have triggered a dynamic market for corporate control, including tender offers and hostile takeover battles reminiscent of the United States.[25] The state has not completely relinquished its grip upon industry and the economy. Foreign institutional investors hold 35 to 40 per cent of the French equity market, but the French government retains extensive powers to block control transactions and intervenes selectively in merger and acquisition activity. Hence, the state has overseen the process of sectoral consolidation to ensure that French industry remains largely in the hands of French managers as a deliberate policy choice (Iskandar, 1999). The result of this combination of liberalizing and interventionist policies has been the creation of a new breed of more competitive 'national champions' created by market forces.[26]

In contrast, Japanese company law and corporate governance has remained largely unchanged through an economically disastrous decade. The market for corporate control is flat. Friendly acquisitions are exceptional; and hostile takeovers are non-existent. Legal protection for shareholders remains feeble and the procedural and institutional mechanisms to protect the nominal rights that do exist virtually preclude bringing claims against management. Cross-shareholdings within keiretsu groups remain common and account for up to 60–70 per cent of shares (Davis Global Advisors, 1998). Informal practices have not evolved to compensate for the absence of legal change. Board composition, structure and practices continue to be dominated by management and interlocking directorates among *keiretsu* insiders. Prospects for substantial change and reform in the near to medium term are remote (ibid.).

5.3 The Resilience of Labour Market Structures

Of the juridical components of corporate governance, labour law remains the most stable. In Europe, where organized labour has far more power than in the United States and Japan, labour interests continue to exercise substantial influence over the dynamics of national politics and economic policy. The core interest of labour is the manner in which labour law structurally constitutes and integrates labour interests and organized labour into the political economy. Globalization has certainly altered the balance of power between capital and management on one side and labour on the other. Europe's basic labour laws and labour market institutions, such as centralized and sectoral bargaining, forms of codetermination and job protection, were almost all developed from the 1950s until the 1970s. These were the institutional developments that endowed labour with substantial political and economic clout. Changes in labour law and labour relations during the 1980s and 1990s have generally been concerned with marginal incremental measures concerning the flexibility of internal labour markets and wage-bargaining structures.

Labour politics have been at the core of the deadlock and stasis that have characterized the contemporary politics of corporate governance in Germany and Europe as a whole. What is most striking, amid the predominantly neo-liberal rhetoric of the globalization debate, is the stability of codetermination in Germany (see Rhodes and van Apeldoorn, 1998; Roe, 1998), and the expansion of works councils' codetermination in Europe through the EU itself The interests represented in the German corporate governance regime – management, banks and labour – are powerful actors within the political process and can easily thwart political initiatives to increase their accountability to and the power of shareholders. The interests of each of these factional beneficiaries of the German governance regime interlock in mutually reinforcing ways. Banks maintain control over the domestic capital markets. Labour remains shielded from competition over wages in the core export-oriented industries through the continuation of sectoral collective bargaining between strong industrial unions and employers' associations. Management remains essentially invulnerable to takeover threats and shareholder pressures. This 'governance coalition' straddles the political divide between the CDU–CSU and the SPD and thus provides an ideal example of the sort of quasi-public institutional arrangements that underpin Germany's exceptionally stable consensus politics and the deadlock that often results from them (compare Katzenstein, 1987, pp. 58–80).

More broadly, proposals for an EU directive on harmonizing company law and corporate structure have been blocked over the role of labour within the firm. For over 25 years, the EU has debated, and failed to promulgate, its draft Fifth Directive adopting a pan-European company law amid conflicts over mandatory works councils and labour codetermination (see Rhodes and van Apeldoorn, 1998; Schaede, 1995; Buxbaum and Hopt, 1988, pp. 259–69). Moreover, further confounding the theory that globalization is driving convergent liberalization is the EU's adoption of the Works Council Directive requiring that member nations adopt works council legislation giving employees a direct voice in the management of firms. While not nearly as protective of worker interests as Germany's Works Council Act,[27] the Works Council Directive does introduce another dimension to the governance of European firms. The introduction of works councils devolves power and legal authority within the corporation downward to the employees and their representatives. This reallocation of authority effectively circumscribes the power of the management, the board of directors and shareholders. The proliferation of works councils thus alters the structure of governance in precisely the opposite direction predicted by economic theories.

Even in countries like the United States and Japan in which labour is not nearly so powerful and well entrenched, labour has played a role in shaping the development of corporate governance and cushioning the sometimes harsh mechanisms and pressures of market forces. In the United States, labour interests mobilized in resistance against corporate takeover activity joined with managerial interests in pressing for protective anti-takeover legislation – though labour's political weakness was clearly reflected in the statutes' expansion of managerial powers without any grant of power to employees and their representatives. Japanese corporate governance law does not mandate any formal employee representation or provide significant job protection; nor does Japanese politics give labour much power. Yet, despite a decade of economic stagnation and industrial overcapacity, management has been extremely resistant to mass lay-offs. This resistance reflects state policy discouraging firings to prevent political instability and further erosion of aggregate demand, but it also reflects the ingrained norms of the postwar corporate governance system in which insider and employee interests were paramount in the organization and operation of the corporate firm.

In Japan and throughout the industrialized countries, the striking lack of change in the legal structures of labour law and labour relations indicates the extremely sensitive political character of these institutions and their connection to corporate governance regimes. This absence of formal change certainly does not imply that labour relations and the relative strength of labour, management and capital has not changed since the 1970s. Obviously they have. Yet this absence of formal change indicates that states, politicians and policymakers have been unwilling to incur the political costs of such a course or have not found fundamental labour market reform to be necessary or desirable. Thus, for both economic and political reasons, labour market institutions and their interrelationships with corporate governance have proved strikingly resilient.

5.4 Legal Structures vs. Legalistic Enforcement

We summarize the changes in corporate governance in Table 10.3 and add the category of legalistic enforcement (which was only implicit in Tables 10.1 and 10.2). The structure of legal institutions and their role in enforcing legal relations inhibit dramatic changes in corporate law and corporate governance. Fiduciary duties of directors and dominant shareholders remain under-developed in Germany, and the procedural law discourages (and often precludes) enforcement of rights through litigation (Kim, 1995). German governance law recently has been changed by the enactment of the KonTraG

Table 10.3   *Degree of change in corporate governance law by country and category*

	Financial market regulation	Corporate/ company law	Labour law	Legalistic enforcement
United States	Moderate/low	Moderate/low	Low	Low
United Kingdom	High (form of law and institutions)	Low (formal change)	Low	Low
	Moderate (substantive law)	Moderate (informal/self-regulatory change)	(High during the confrontation between Tories under Thatcher and unions in the early 1980s)	
Germany	Moderate	Moderate/low	Low	Low
France	High	High/moderate	Low	Low
Japan	Low	Low	Low	Low

law (Control and Transparency Law), to reduce the percentage of shares needed to vote for an independent investigation of firm affairs from 10 per cent to 5 per cent.[28] However, the procedural rules and substantive duties of officers and directors have not been altered to increase the availability or viability of shareholder actions as a governance mechanism. This describes a fundamental choice for politicians and policymakers around the world. The Anglo–American model of governance operates against a backdrop of common law and common law courts that have buttressed the institutions of shareholder capitalism. This feature of governance is both political and strictly legal in character. Common law systems, and nowhere more so than in the United States, have granted substantial *authority* and *autonomy* to courts to fashion legal doctrines, rules of law and remedies. This institutional pattern is comparatively unusual. While it would be an exaggeration to describe civil law courts systems as essentially bureaucratic, these systems do constrain significantly the discretion of judges and courts compared to latitude of common law courts. Thus, the attempts to fashion doctrines of fiduciary duties protective of shareholder interests have been halting and unsuccessful.

Judicially driven reform is unlikely to occur for several reasons. First, few countries are likely to place the same degree of power in the hands of unelected and politically unaccountable judges as the United States. Constitutional and legal traditions and norms of parliamentary sovereignty define the legitimate role of courts and, under such conditions, courts are unlikely to significantly reform governance institutions without substantial statutory changes by legislatures. Courts can step in where the political costs are not excessive and particularly in case where legislatures would like to resolve issues without taking on the political costs. Thus, courts have become more active in many areas, such as civil and criminal rights that are peripheral to the fundamental distribution of political economic authority and power, but have not moved to alter these core institutional structures and relationships underpinning the political economy.[29]

Second, the comparison of liberal political economic systems and the neo-corporatist and statist systems reveals a basic choice among governance mechanisms (compare Soskice, 1999). The liberal paradigm of law, exemplified by common law rights, requires a hierarchical set of legal entitlements enshrined as rights that can be predictably enforced through legalistic, adjudicative methods. In the neo-corporatist economies, law fashions institutional settings and mechanisms for bargaining among conflicting interests and adjustment of differences. Formal rights form a backdrop, often more procedural in character, that creates the structure and incentives for negotiation and bargaining among constituted actors. Legal rights as defined here in the liberal sense are common and prevalent in neo-corporatist systems as well, but the basic function of law diverges in the liberal and neo-corporatist settings. This creates powerful path-dependent effects in the juridical structure of governance regimes.

The position and function of courts *vis-à-vis* the legislative and executive institutions (whether or not they are unified) is a basic feature of the constitutional and political economic orders. Changing the role of courts and adjudication with respect to corporate governance would require funda-mental restructuring of the constitutional, political and economic orders *simultaneously*. Barring profound dysfunction in the governance regime, the political and economic parties to such a restructuring are unlikely to expose themselves to the costs of such a battle. Recent legal developments in the United States and Germany bear out this analysis. The courts have fashioned new doctrines of fiduciary duties designed to govern the behaviour of managers and dominant shareholders, and to curb conflicts of interest in Germany's opaque and centralized financial and governance systems (Kim, 1995; see also Kondgen, 1994; Assmann, 1990). But these incremental and very modest judicial innovations have not been accompanied by any significant legislative action and there has been little change in the structure and practice of German corporate governance. In the United States, where the judicial enforcement of formal rights and fiduciary duties forms the core of the corporate governance system, attempts to reduce reliance on and the prevalence of litigation have met with limited success. Cross-nationally, the reluctance to empower courts to a greater degree, and rely on privately enforced rights as core mechanisms of governance, has been mirrored in the empowerment of alternative public or quasi-public institutions to enforce improved governance practices. These include the creation or increased power of securities regulators and stock exchanges to construct and enforce substantive and procedural rules governing the practices and structures of corporate governance.

Third, and finally, viewed from abroad (and often at home), the United States' litigation-prone governance system is viewed as pathological and litigation as something of an American disease.[30] Litigation and litigious tactics are frequently seen as wasteful, destabilizing and counter-productive in producing stable and mutually acceptable conditions for policy implementation and economic coordination, and as corrosive of consensual social relations.[31] Moreover, litigation-driven governance mechanisms are frequently criticized in the United States and abroad as ineffective (see, for example, Romano, 1991; Coffee, 1985). Thus, the demand for the adoption of an American-styled legal framework for corporate governance lags behind the rhetoric of liberalization and reform (compare Charkham, 1994).

The use of law and regulation to structure markets and firms (that is, markets and hierarchies) is becoming an increasingly important, and perhaps dominant, mode of state intervention in the advanced industrial economies.[32] Structuring economic institutions and relations through law has the potential to satisfy both political and economic demands on policymakers and managers, while avoiding more direct (and distortionary) modes of intervention such as state ownership, bureaucratic control over finance and credit, and broad discretionary regulatory powers. The governance structures and bargaining fora created by corporate governance law function to this end. The legal mechanisms of corporate governance *restructure* markets and market relationships in the private sphere. They do not *supplant* the market. However, these reconfigured institutional arrangements take distinctive forms in different countries and among the most resilient of these institutional arrangements are those of national corporate governance regimes. These legal frameworks and regulatory policies have provided the institutional foundation necessary for the development of large, complex corporations and the domestic and international markets within which they are situated. Hence, the emerging international economic order and domestic politics remain highly interdependent, even as the *modalities* of economic regulation and governance evolve.

5.   CONCLUSION

This comparison of corporate governance regimes under the pressures of globalization reveals patterns of institutional development that support some preliminary and conjectural conclusions about the relationship between national political economies and globalization. First, we do see significant financial market reforms and increasing securities market regulation driving the development of more transparent and liquid investment flows and ownership structures both domestically and internationally. The construction of the institutional framework for increasingly marketized and securitized finance appears well under way across a wide range of political economies. These market-facilitating institutional arrangements form the channels through which signals, and shocks, from the global capital markets feed into national economies. Through these markets and the domestic institutions that constitute them, national economies are becoming increasingly integrated into a global economy. Once we turn to company and labour law, the picture becomes substantially more complex. We see substantial continuity and institutional resilience with varying degrees of transformation in company law but very little change in labour law. Political actors have been unwilling or unable to alter these fundamental arrangements at the base of their political and economic orders.

These differences among areas of law lead us to conclude that the impact of globalization has not and most likely will not produce convergence but globalization will produce a new set of differentiated political economic systems integrated into global capital markets. Among these divergent systems, the patterns of change and stability revealed here suggest two potential sets of outcomes. First, we see indications of two divergent hybrids of the neo-liberal economic model and the neo-corporatist model.[33] The neo-liberal model appears to be forming more centralized and concentrated financial systems shaped primarily by unmediated market forces favouring the development and interests of strong financial actors, particularly *vis-à-vis* labour. This form of political economic organization is adjusting to global markets in which the deliberate policy of fragmenting markets, investments and ownership interests is no longer appropriate. Whether this change in the structure of neo-liberal shareholder capitalism has any significant effect on the governance and functioning of these economies remains to be seen.

The development of the neo-corporatist model, exemplified by Germany, suggests that shareholder interests are gaining in marginal power and importance, but in an institutional setting in which the forces of global capital markets are mediated by firm and labour market structures. These micro-corporatist institutional structures counterbalance the interests of key political economic interests and actors at the level of the firm where flexible adjustments to changing market conditions are more efficient (Thelen, 1991). There is thus greater flexibility and adjustment capacity in the neo-corporate model than usually is recognized. This flexibility, in addition to the political resilience of these institutions, accounts for the relative stability of neo-corporate regimes.

The evolution of the statist political economies remains subject to greater uncertainty and presents us with the most important puzzle revealed by the foregoing analysis. Of each of the three broad models of political economy considered here, the statist mode of organization appears most at odds with globalization. The statist political economies of Japan and *dirigiste* France provide our cases in point. Statist policies of planning and targeted financing have become liabilities in economic adjustment at the same time that global financial markets and the elimination of capital controls have effectively forced the abandonment of state-channelled finance as a mechanism of industrial policy in both Japan and France. The similarity ends there. In France, the state pushed through financial liberalization and has successfully reformed much of its securities and company law along Anglo–American lines. This would suggest that the developmental path of the statist political economies, once deprived of their statist policy mechanisms and lacking the dense networks of institutional structures that have developed in neo-corporatist systems, 'tip' towards minimalist, neo-liberal organizational forms. Yet the French state, for all its legal liberalization, retains very substantial discretionary power over industrial organization and the outcomes of market processes. Japan has been prevented by the depth of its financial crisis, the legacy of its government institutions and its political disarray from pursuing effective reforms.

In short, the evolution of the statist political economies to date reveals an equivocal and ambiguous picture of the impact of globalization on economic and corporate governance regimes. And in this ambiguity lies the unsettled and unsettling character of our age. There is, as yet, no clear theoretical or political alternative to the stark logical and substantive austerity of neo-liberalism and deregulation. However, as the above analysis suggests, national political institutions remain powerful and distinctive determinants of political economic adjustment. Globalization does not control the development of national institutions any more than nations govern globalization.

NOTES

* Prepared for the Conference and Symposium on Corporate Governance and Globalization, St Mary's University, Halifax, Canada, 17–19 September 1999. The authors would like to thank Professor Gavin Boyd and the Frank H. Sobey Faculty of Commerce for their support and encouragement of this contribution. This paper is adapted in significant part from two earlier conference papers (Cioffi, 1998a, 1998b). The themes explored in those papers are extended here and developed in the context of globalization and international markets.

1. In recent years, the American economic boom has generated substantial neo-liberal triumphalism that associates such advantages of forwardness with the neo-liberal political

economic model, and the American model in particular (see, for example, Murray, 1999). Our scepticism regarding such claims will become amply clear.

2. Each of the listed characteristics may have its own etiology in whole or in part independent of those of the other features of globalization. The simultaneous emergence and sum total of the interactions among these political, institutional, and economic factors constitute globalization. A more thorough analysis of the historical and functional relationships among these characteristics of globalization is beyond the scope of this paper.

3. Some of the more sophisticated economics and law and economics scholars have recognized and elaborated upon the importance of path dependency in the development of corporate governance regimes (see Bebchuk and Roe, 1998; Roe, 1997). For a more general analysis of path dependence and economic institutions, see North (1990).

4. Further, neo-corporatist institutional arrangements are conducive to the provision of public goods and the coordination of complex factor inputs needed to combine sophisticated production processes and industries with egalitarian policies (see Soskice, 1992,1999). This, however, takes us beyond the scope of the present paper.

5. Of course, the relative power of these interests varies among different political economic systems: varying constellations of powers within different corporate governance regimes alter the politics but not the fact of path dependency.

In addition, this truncated account relies on a simple incomplete public choice theory. Institutions are also buttressed by ideational constructs that Peter Hall has described as the 'interpretive dimension' of institutions. Institutions that have endured and the interests they serve are seen as legitimate and become the bases of habituated routines that constrain actors' conceptions of alternative institutions and practices (compare Hall, 1999, pp. 160-61). Attempts to alter such arrangements run counter to established social norms that foster political mobilization and resistance. For example, German supervisory board codetermination may, to many observers, appear inefficient, but it is regarded as sacrosanct by the polity at large and as legitimate, and even beneficial, by many German managers. Even those German managers who are critical of the institution do not seriously consider its repeal or reform. In contrast, it is hard to conceive of American managers adopting such a tolerant view of worker authority imposed on them by law.

The neo-classical principal–agent perspective on corporate governance has begun to take hold in continental Europe where legal scholarship and economic policymaking had long resisted the concepts of shareholder value and shareholder rights as the hallmark of short-term, neo-liberal economics. For a major compilation of recent scholarship indicating this trend, see generally, Hopt et al. (1998).

6. Although a growing body of work explores the influence of politics on corporate governance (see, for example, Roe 1991, 1993a, 1993b, 1994; Romano 1987, 1993a, 1993b; Black 1990; Grundfest 1990; compare Black, 1998; Pound, 1993), it unduly minimizes the institutional sources of comparative advantage, the political import of labour interests, and the autonomous role of the state and law in the development of corporate governance. The work of Mark Roe is a noteworthy exception in that he views the politics as constitutive of national corporate governance systems. Further, in his most recent work, Roe identifies the power of labour interests in social democracies as a fundamental determinant of the financial and corporate governance systems (see Roe, works cited above, and 1998, 1999). However, even in this excellent and pathbreaking work, politics, political institutions and labour interests are treated as interfering with the economically rational ordering of the governance regime, finance and corporate ownership.

7. For exceptions, see, for example, Deeg and Perez, 1999; Rhodes and Appeldoorn, 1998. Some recent work of comparative political economy skirts the subject of corporate governance but does not directly engage it (see Hall, 1999; Soskice, 1999). In addition, these comparative and political analyses tend to miss the centrality of legal structures and institutions in the constitution, operation and development of corporate governance regimes.

8. Labour has been almost entirely ignored in the American corporate governance literature. In comparative perspective, however, the importance of labour interests in different governance regimes become strikingly apparent. Institutional arrangements such as codetermination, centralized wage bargaining, mandatory participation in worker training

programmes, and other aspects of labour relations has a substantial impact on governance structures and practices.

9. See, for example, Romano (1993b); Williamson (1985, 1996); Easterbrook and Fischel (1991); Chandler (1977). For purposes of this brief review, we do not distinguish among the neoclassical (see, for example, Coase, 1937; Jensen, 1976, 1989; Easterbrook and Fischel, 1991), the transaction cost economics (see, for example, Williamson, 1985, 1996), and property rights (see, for example, Hart, 1993; Hart and Moore, 1990, Grossman and Hart, 1987) variants of the finance model of the firm and corporate governance. Likewise, we do not begin this description of neoclassical economics at its logical starting point, the theory of the firm on which the finance model is built.

10. Despite their obvious structural differences, this is true for both codetermined boards and works councils. Works council laws take a set of subjects, such as working conditions and lay-offs, and subject them to bargaining between managers and employee representatives. Within this zone of legal competence, works councils effectively suspend shareholder primacy. We distinguish between collective bargaining by unions and bargaining between works councils and management on the ground that in the latter case, all parties are 'insiders' within the firm and thus have no broader, extra-firm agenda. This is particularly important in countries with sectoral collective bargaining where intra-firm representational structures and supra-firm institutions (industrial unions and employer associations) mutually reinforce and complement each other. In these systems, works councils can provide a governance mechanism that increases flexibility in adjusting to economic and technological change (see Thelen, 1991, 1993; Turner, 1991).

11. In this respect our analysis differs from Mark Roe's recent work (1999) arguing that social democracy is the primary determinant of national governance regimes and determines the resultant patterns of ownership and control. There is certainly a correlation between the presence of significant social democratic parties and neo-corporatist institutions. However, for most of the postwar period and almost the entire period of postwar reconstruction and institution building, the centre-right was in power in continental Europe. Social democratic parties were consistently in power only in the Scandinavian countries. Likewise, statistical political economics of Japan and France were also constructed by centrist coalitions devoted to developmental policies.

    Likewise, we disagree with Roe (1998) on the role board codetermination has played in discouraging financial transparency and thus the development of securitized finance. He argues that workers' representatives on the board discourage information flows to the board because the workers will use this information to extract additional rents from the firm in wage bargaining. The theory is questionable on historical and analytical grounds. Once upon a time, the United States had a powerful labour movement, yet this did not prevent the United States from achieving financial transparency through stricter disclosure rules and accounting standards than in other countries. Further, German codetermination and company law binds the employee representatives to a duty of confidentiality, arguably mitigating the variety of opportunism assumed in Roe's analysis. Finally, sectoral bargaining such as that characteristic of the German labour relations system does not extract *firm-specific* rents.

12. The failure of the Multilateral Agreement on Investment provides an illustrative case. Intended to provide an analogue to the GATT and WTO in the area of cross-border investment, the negotiations disintegrated in a welter of national and regional conflicts and intense attacks by NGOs hostile to globalization. This failure of institution building shows both the continued power of nationally based interest groups to derail international negotiations over the formal organization of globalization, and how regional and supra-national entities such as the EU may increase conflict over the creation of institutions of global scope (see Henderson, 1999). Further, the fate of the MAI indicates the politically sensitive and divisive character of rules and institutions relating to investment flows. As controversial as trade liberalization has been in many countries, the valorization and empowerment of capital through financial liberalization has generated far more fear.

13. This leaves the analysis vulnerable to the criticism that the most significant and meaningful of corporate governance developments have been informal and market-driven. This is

possible. However, managers may quickly reverse informal practices such as voluntary termination of cross-shareholding and interlocking directorships, increased financial disclosure and board reform if conditions change – say a substantial decline in the American stock market and/or another global financial crisis.

14. Liberalized trade has a negligible impact on cross-national capital flows, while liberalization of capital controls, financial services and capital accounts substantially increase them (see Tamirisa, 1999).

15. Although Germany at first appears to be lagging somewhat in improving transparency, one consultancy has recently commented that German firms had been waiting for passage of legislation that permitted them to adopt US GAAP or IAS without filing a second set of financial statements using German accounting rules before switching to more stringent accounting standards (see Davis Global Advisors, 1998). In addition, the German Neue Market, the 'new market' for small cap high-tech stocks requires use of IAS.

16. Similarly, the almost baroque character of the American legal and regulatory systems adds further support to the proposition that liberalization breeds legalism through the proliferation of legal rules and formal enforcement mechanisms (compare Kagan, 1991, 1997). Kagan has argued persuasively that divided government (that is, separation of powers and federalist structures) drives the growth of legalism as political actors and institutions seek to lock in legislative and policy deals through codification and as the resultant conflicts between branches and levels of government open political space for courts to become more activist and autonomous. This certainly helps explain the highly developed legalistic modes of regulation and governance in the United States and Germany. Although they are configured very differently, both have some degree of separation of powers and both are federalist systems. However, the increasing codification and formalization of law in the United Kingdom, with its unified parliamentary system and strong central government, suggests that legalism has a functional cause in addition to a structural one.

17. The formation of Citigroup, the mergers of Bank of America and NationsBank and of Chemical Bank and Manufacturers Hanover, to mention only a few of these groundbreaking transactions, reveal a financial sector in search of economies of scale and volume of assets and transactions. Whether the assumed benefits of scale economies driving this movement are in fact real or realizable is another matter.

18. For years, repeal of Glass–Steagall has been on the Congressional agenda. At first repeal was resisted by the financial institutions who saw their protected markets threatened. In recent years, the fight has been over who will regulate the new universal financial institutions: the Federal Reserve or the Treasury Department.

19. This difficulty is further underscored by the fact that its British venture is widely regarded as a failure and that Deutsche Bank's acquisition of Bankers Trust has been greeted with substantial scepticism by commentators – though the merger appears to have worked better than anticipated.

20. In 1999, foreign shareholders own 61 per cent of Total and 51 per cent of Elf Aquitaine (Tagliabue, *New York Times*, 1 September 1999).

21. Both economic interests and demographic concerns are driving interest in funded and invested pension funds in Europe. However, the deadlock between supporters of traditional state-delivered pay-as-you-go public pension programmes and those seeking to introduce privately invested pensions has not been resolved anywhere in Europe. Nor has Japan adequately addressed the future needs of its graying population. These conflicts are entirely political and they will only be resolved through politics and policy.

22. As the BNP-Paribas–Société General hostile takeover battle revealed, the French state has adopted a deliberate policy of allowing market forces to compel consolidation and adjustment if managers cannot come to voluntary agreements. The outcome, in which BNP won control over Paribas through a hostile bid exposes Société Général to acquisition by a foreign bank. The French state could have blocked any of the bids and imposed a resolution, but *chose* not to (compare Ford, Peter (1999), 'Europe Answers Walmart Threat', *Christian Science Monitor*, 1 September, p. 1).

23. For an overview of the American hostile takeover movement and political and legal

responses thereto, see Alcalay (1994); Wallman (1990, 1991); see also essays collected in Blair (1993); Bhagat et al. (1990); Schleifer and Vishny (1990). For a comparison with the European conception of 'corporate constituencies', see Conard 1991.

24. It should be noted that, technically speaking, there is no distinction in French law between securities and company law; they are part of the same legal code (see Fanto, 1998, 1997).

25. These developments challenge cultural theories of political economic behaviour. The rapidity with which the formerly closed and mutually supporting French political and economic elite has embraced adversarial relations and tactics obliterate the image of the French political economy as overdetermined by a shared and ingrained culture of elitism.

26. This was especially clear in the consolidation of the French petroleum sector as French government officials oversaw the cross-national merger of Total with Belgium's Petrofina and as the resultant entity, Total-Fina, takes over the much larger (and traditional 'national champion') Elf Aquitaine. Likewise, other large cross-border mergers by French firms have left the French acquirer in the dominant position.

27. In Germany, works councils are a more significant institution in the governance of firms than the codetermined Supervisory Board (see Lutter, 1982; compare Thelen, 1993).

28. KonTraG, Law on the Control and Transparency in Business, Gesetz vom 27.4.1998, BGBI. I, S.786 vom 30.4.1998; see Siebert (1999).

29. One obvious counter-argument to this analysis is the leading role of the Italian courts in bringing down the corrupt political order in the scandals of the late 1980s and early 1990s. Yet, for all the extraordinary impact of the Italian courts on the Italian party system, the core institutions of the political economy and the state bureaucracy were left largely untouched.

30. See Kagan (1997); for an excellent analysis of the exceptional character and dynamics of the American case, see Kagan (1991).

31. This point was stressed repeatedly in a series of interviews conducted by the authors with senior legal academics and policymakers. This attitude is not unique to Germany. In more statist economic systems, such as Japan and France, governance has been organized and coordinated through discretionary authority of administrative bureaucrats and the law is designed to promote this form of state power. In Japan, for example, the number of lawyers is kept artificially low to discourage litigation and to preclude the emergence of legalistic socio-economic relations (see Haley, 1986, 1991). Thus, globalization and the concomitant increase in private sector autonomy, arms'-length relations and legalistic governance mechanisms should pose an especially difficult challenge for the more statist political economies and provide an important set of test cases for our thesis that globalization increases the importance of law.

32. We address only the structure of and the state's relationship to governance institutions, that is, the structural allocation of power and authority within the private sphere. We do not address the role of the state in containing negative externalities through command and control regulation. Modern social regulation, such as environmental, discrimination, consumer protection, and so on, lies outside the sphere of corporate governance. However, there are approaches to regulation that utilize the structural mechanisms described here (see essays in Hopt and Teubner, 1985, especially Teubner, 1985).

33. Soskice (1999) has also theorized that globalization is inducing a form of bilateral convergence. However, we are not as confident as he is in this outcome, as our discussion indicates.

REFERENCES

Alcalay, Roger E. (1994), 'The Golden Age of Junk', *The New York Review of Books*, **26** May, 28–34.

Aoki, Masahiko (1994), 'The Japanese firm as a system of attributes: a survey and research agenda', in Masahiko Aoki and Ronald Dore (eds), *The Japanese Firm: The Sources of Competitive Strength*, Oxford and New York: Oxford University Press.

Assmann, Heinz-Dieter (1990), 'Microcorporatist structures in German law on groups of companies', in David Sugarman and Gunther Teubner (eds), *Regulating Corporate Groups in Europe*, Baden-Baden: Nomos Verlagsgesellschaft.

Bebchuk, Lucien Arye and Mark J. Roe (1998), *A Theory of Path Dependence in Corporate Governance and Ownership*, Center for Law and Economic Studies, Columbia University School of Law (unpublished draft dated 6 May).

Berger, Suzanne and Ronald Dore (eds) (1996), *National Diversity and Global Capitalism*, Ithaca: Cornell University Press.

Berle, Adolf A. and Gardiner C. Means (1932), *The Modern Corporation and Private Property*, New York: Macmillan.

Bhagat, Sanjay, Andrei Schleifer and Robert Vishny (1990), 'Hostile takeovers in the 1980s: the return to specialization', *Brookings Papers on Economic Activity*.

Black, Bernard S. (1990), 'Shareholder passivity reexamined', *Michigan Law Review*, **89**(3) (December) 520-608.

Black, Bernard (1998), 'Shareholder activism and corporate governance in the United States', in Peter Newman (ed.), *The New Palgrave Dictionary of Economics and the Law*, London: Macmillan, New York: Stockton Press.

Blair, Margaret (ed.) (1993), *The Deal Decade: What Takeovers Mean for Corporate Governance*, Washington, DC: The Brookings Institution.

Borrus, Michael and John Zysman (1997), 'Globalization with borders: the rise of Wintelism as the future of global competition', *Industry and Innovation*, **4**(2) (December).

Bratton, William W. (1992), 'Public values and corporate fiduciary law', *Rutgers Law Review*, **44**, 675.

Bratton, William W. (1993), 'Public values, private business, and U.S. corporate fiduciary law', in Joseph McCahery, Sol Picciotto and Colin Scott (eds), *Corporate Control and Accountability: Changing Structures and the Dynamics of Regulation*, Oxford: Clarendon Press, New York: Oxford University Press.

Brown, Clair, Yoshifumi Nakata, Michael Reich and Lloyd Ulman (1997), *Work and Pay in the United States and Japan*, New York and Oxford: Oxford University Press.

Buxbaum, Richard (1987), 'Juridification and legitimation problems in American enterprise law', in Gunther Teubner (ed.), *Juridification of Social Spheres: A Comparative Analysis in the Areas of Labor, Corporate, Antitrust and Social Welfare Law*, Berlin and New York: Walter de Gruyter.

Buxbaum, Richard M. (1991), 'Institutional owners and corporate managers: a comparative perspective' (The Fourth Abraham L. Pomerantz Lecture), *Brooklyn Law Review*, **57**(1) (Spring), 1-53.

Buxbaum, Richard M. (1994), 'Comparative aspects of institutional investment and corporate governance', in Theodore Baums, Richard M. Buxbaum and Klaus J. Hopt (eds), *Institutional Investors and Corporate Governance*, Berlin and New York: Walter de Gruyter, Chapter 1.

Buxbaum, Richard M. and Klaus J. Hopt (1988), *Legal Harmonization and the Business Enterprise: Corporate and Capital Market Law, Harmonization Policy in Europe and the U.S.A.*, Berlin and New York: Walter de Gruyter.

Chandler, Alfred D. (1977), *The Visible Hand: The Managerial Revolution in American Business*, Cambridge, MA and London: Belknap Press.

Charkham, Jonathan P. (1994), *Keeping Good Company: A Study of Corporate Governance in Five Countries*, Oxford: Clarendon Press.

Cioffi, John W. (1998a), 'Political incorporation: the comparative political economy of corporate governance and juridical structure', paper presented at the Law & Society Association Annual Meeting, 4 June, Aspen, Colorado.

Cioffi, John W. (1998b), 'The political logic of corporate governance: the constitution of the firm in comparative perspective', paper presented at the Law & Society Association Annual Meeting, 5 June, Aspen, Colorado.

Coase, Ronald H. (1937), 'The nature of the firm', *Economica*, **4**, 386.

Coffee, John C. Jr (1985), 'The unfaithful champion: the plaintiff as monitor in shareholder litigation', *Law and Contemporary Problems* (Summer).

Coffee, John C. Jr (1991), 'Liquidity versus control: the institutional investor as corporate monitor', *Columbia Law Review*, 1277.

Cohen, Stephen S. (1969), *Modern Capitalist Planning: The French Model*, Cambridge: Harvard University Press.

Conard, Alfred F. (1991), 'Corporate constituencies in Western Europe', *Stetson Law Review*, **21**, 73.

The Conference Board (1997), *Institutional Investor Report*, **1**(1) (July).

Davis Global Advisors (1998), *Corporate Governance 1998: An International Comparison* (June).

Deeg, Richard and Sophia Perez (1999), 'International capital mobility and domestic institutions: corporate finance and governance in four European cases', unpublished paper presented at the Conference on the Political Economy of Corporate Governance in Europe and Japan, Robert Schulman Center, Europe University Institute, 10–11 June.

Doremus, Paul N., William W. Keller, Louis W. Pauly and Simon Reich (1998), *The Myth of the Global Corporation*, Princeton: Princeton University Press.

Dunning, John H. (1997), *Alliance Capitalism and Global Business*, London and New York: Routledge.

Easterbrook, Frank H. and Daniel R. Fischel (1991), *The Economic Structure of Corporate Law*, Cambridge, MA and London: Harvard University Press.

The Economist (1999), 'Cutting the cookie', 11 September, p. 26.

Fanto, James A. (1997), 'The role of corporate law in the adaptation of French enterprises', paper prepared for the Cross-Border Conference on Corporate Governance, Center for Law and Economics of Columbia Law School, 17–18 March.

Fanto, James A. (1998), 'The role of corporate law in French corporate governance', *Cornell International Law Journal*, **31**(1).

Frieden, Jeffery A. (1991), 'Invested interests: the politics of national economic policies in a world of global finance', *International Organization*, **45**(4), (Autumn), 425–51.

Frieden, Jeffery A. and Ronald Rogowski (1996), 'The impact of the international economy on national policies: an analytic overview', in Robert O. Keohane and Helen Milner (eds), *Internationalization and Domestic Politics*, New York and Cambridge: Cambridge University Press.

Friedman, Milton (1962), *Capitalism and Freedom*, Chicago: University of Chicago Press.

Gerschenkron, Alexander (1962), *Economic Backwardness in Historical Perspective: A Book of Essays*, Cambridge, MA: Belknap Press of Harvard University Press.

Gilson, Ronald J. and Mark Roe (1997), 'Lifetime employment and the evolution of Japanese corporate governance', Center for Law and Economic Studies, Columbia University School of Law, Working Paper No. 126 (September).

Gourevitch, Peter A. (1996), 'The macropolitics of microinstitutional differences in the analysis of comparative capitalism', in Suzanne Berger and Richard Dore (eds), *National Diversity and Global Capitalism*, Ithaca: Cornell University Press, pp. 239–59.

Grossman, Sanford J. and Oliver D. Hart (1987), 'One share/one vote and the market for corporate control', NBER Working Paper No. 2347, Cambridge, MA: National Bureau of Economic Research.

Grundfest, Joseph A. (1990), 'The subordination of American capital', *Journal of Financial Economics*, **27**.

Grundfest, Joseph A. and Michael A. Perino (1997), 'Securities litigation reform: the first year's experience: a statistical and legal analysis of class action securities fraud litigation under the Private Securities Litigation Reform Act of 1995', unpublished report (27 February) (available on the Web at http://securities.stanford.edu/report/psira_yrl/)

Haley, John O. (1986), 'Administrative guidance versus formal regulation: resolving the paradox of industrial policy', in Galy R. Saxonhouse and Kozo Yamamura (eds), *Law and Trade Issues of the Japanese Economy*, Seattle: University of Washington Press.

Haley, John O. (1991), *Authority without Power: Law and the Japanese Paradox*, New York: Oxford University Press.

Hall, Peter (1999), 'The political economy of Europe in an era of interdependence', in Herbert Kitschelt, Peter Lange, Gary Marks and John D. Stephens (eds), *Continuity and Change in Contemporary Capitalism*, Cambridge: Cambridge University Press.

Hart, Oliver D. (1993), 'An economist's view of fiduciary duty', *University of Toronto Law Review*, **43**, 299.

Hart, Oliver D. and John Moore (1990), 'Property rights and the nature of the firm', *Journal of Political Economy*, **98**, 1119–58.

Hawley, James P. and Andrew T. Williams (1996), 'Corporate governance in the United States: the rise of fiduciary capitalism, a review of the literature', paper prepared for the OECD.

Hawley, James P. and Andrew T. Williams, with John U. Miller (1994), 'Getting the herd to run: shareholder activism at the California public employees retirement system (CalPERS)', *Business and the Contemporary World*, **6**(4).

Henderson, David (1999), *The MAI Affair: A Story and Its Lessons*, London: The Royal Institute of International Affairs.

Hopt, Klaus J. and Gunther Teubner (eds) (1985), *Corporate Governance and Directors' Liabilities: Legal, Economic, and Sociological Analyses on Corporate Social Responsibility*, Berlin and New York: Walter de Gruyter.

Hopt, Klaus J., Hideki Kanda, Mark J. Roe, Eddy Wymeersch and Stefan Prigge (eds) (1998), *Comparative Corporate Governance: The State of the Art and Current Research*, New York and Oxford: Oxford University Press.

Irwin, Douglas A. (1996), 'The United States in a new global economy? A century's perspective', *American Economic Review, Papers and Proceedings*, **86**(2) (May), 42.

Iskandar, Samer (1999), 'Three wiser men: the French government and the business community can learn important lessons from the drawn-out takeover battle in the banking sector', *Financial Times*, 30 August, p. 11.

Jensen, Michael C. (1989), 'Eclipse of the public corporation', *Harvard Business Review* (September–October), 61–66.

Jensen, Michael C. and William H. Meckling (1976), 'Theory of the firm: managerial behavior, agency costs, and ownership structure', *Journal of Financial Economics*, **3**.

Kagan, Robert A. (1991), 'Adversarial legalism and American government', *Journal of Policy Analysis and Management*, **10**, 369.

Kagan, Robert A. (1997), 'Should Europe worry about adversarial legalism?', *Oxford Journal of Legal Studies*, **17**(2) (Summer), 165–183.

Katzenstein, Peter J. (1985), *Small States and World Markets: Industrial Policy in Europe*, Ithaca: Cornell University Press.

Katzenstein, Peter J. (1987), *Policy and Politics in West Germany: The Growth of a Semisovereign State*, Philadelphia, PA: Temple University Press.

Keohane, Robert O. and Helen Milner (1996), 'Introduction', in Robert O. Keohane and Helen Milner (eds), *Internationalization and Domestic Politics*, New York and Cambridge: Cambridge University Press.

Kim, Hwa-Jin (1995), 'Markets, financial institutions, and corporate governance: perspectives from Germany', *Law and Policy in International Business*, **26** (Winter), 371–405.

Kondgen, Johannes (1994), 'Duties of banks in voting their client's stock', in Theodore Baums, Richard M. Buxbaum and Klaus J. Hopt (eds), *Institutional Investors and Corporate Governance*, Berlin and New York: Walter de Gruyter, Chapter 18.

Kubler, Friedrich (1987), 'Juridification of corporate structures', in Gunther Teubner (ed.), *Juridification of Social Spheres: A Comparative Analysis in the Areas of Labor, Corporate, Antitrust and Social Welfare Law*, Berlin and New York: Walter de Gruyter.

Lazonick, William and Mary O'Sullivan (1997), 'Corporate governance and corporate employment: is prosperity sustainable in the United States?', Jerome Levy Economics Institute, Working Paper No. 183 (January).

Litt, David G., Jonathan R. Macey, Geoffrey Miller and Edward Rubin (1990), 'Politics, bureaucracies, and financial markets: bank entry into commercial paper underwriting in the United States and Japan', *University of Pennsylvania Law Review*, **139**, 369–453, 383–403.

Lutter, Marcus (1982), 'The German system of worker participation in practice', *Journal of Business Law*, (March), 154–61.

Macey, Jonathan R. (1991), 'An economic analysis of the various rationales for making shareholders the exclusive beneficiaries of corporate fiduciary duties', *Stetson Law Review*, **21**, 23.

McKenzie, Richard B. and Dwight R. Lee (1991), *Quicksilver Capital: How the Rapid Movement of Wealth Has Changed the World*, New York: Free Press.

Millstein, Ira M. (Chair), OECD Business Sector Advisory Group on Corporate Governance (1998), *Corporate Governance: Improving Competitiveness and Access to Capital in Global Markets, A Report to the OECD by the Business Advisory Group on Corporate Governance*, OECD: Paris (April).

Moran, Michael (1991), *The Politics of the Financial Services Revolution: The USA, UK, and Japan*, New York: St Martins Press.

Murray, Allan (1999), 'Asia's financial foibles make American way look like a winner', *Wall Street Journal*, 8 December, pp. A 1, A 13.

North, Douglass C. (1990), *Institutions, Institutional Change and Economic Performance*, Cambridge, New York and Melbourne: Cambridge University Press.

O'Brien, Richard (1992), *Global Financial Integration: The End of Geography*, monograph, Royal Institute of International Affairs, Chatham House Papers, London: Pinter Publishers.

Porter, Michael (1990), *The Competitive Advantage of Nations*, New York: Free Press.

Pound, John (1993), 'The rise of the political model of corporate governance and corporate control', *New York University Law Review*, **68**, 1003.

Rhodes, Martin and Bastiaan van Apeldoorn (1998), 'Capitalism unbound? The transformation of European corporate governance', *European Journal of Public Policy*, **5**(3).

Rodrik, Dani (1997), *Has Globalization Gone Too Far?*, Washington, DC: Institute for International Economics.

Roe, Mark J. (1991), 'A political theory of American corporate finance', *Columbia Law Review*, **91**, 10.

Roe, Mark J. (1993a), 'Takeover politics', in Margaret Blair (ed.), *The Deal Decade: What Takeovers Mean for Corporate Governance*, Washington, DC: Brookings Institution, pp. 321–53.

Roe Mark J. (1993b), 'Some differences in corporate structure in Germany, Japan, and the United States', *Yale Law Journal*, **102**, 1927.

Roe, Mark J. (1994), *Strong Managers, Weak Owners: The Political Roots of American Corporate Finance*, Princeton, NJ: Princeton University Press.

Roe, Mark J. (1996), 'From antitrust to corporate governance? The corporation and the law', in Carl Kaysen (ed.), *The American Corporation Today*, New York and Oxford: Oxford University Press.

Roe, Mark J. (1997), 'Path dependency, political options, and governance systems', in Klaus J. Hopt and Eddy Wymeersch (eds), *Comparative Corporate Governance: Essays and Materials*, Berlin and New York: Walter de Gruyter.

Roe, Mark J. (1998), 'Codetermination and German securities markets', in Klaus J. Hopt, Hideki Kanda, Mark J. Roe, Eddy Wymeersch and Stefan Prigge (eds), *Comparative Corporate Governance: The State of the Art and Current Research*, New York and Oxford: Oxford University Press.

Roe, Mark J. (1999), 'Political preconditions to separation of ownership from control: the incompatibility of the American public firm with social democracy', unpublished draft, Columbia Law School, 1 June.

Rogers, Joel (1990), 'Divide and conquer: further "reflections on the distinctive character of American labor laws"', *Wisconsin Law Review*, (1) (January–February), 1.

Romano, Roberta (1987), 'The political economy of takeover statutes', *Virginia Law Review*, **73**(111) (February).

Romano, Roberta (1991), 'The shareholder suit: litigation without foundation?', *Journal of Law, Economics, and Organization*, **7**(55).

Romano, Roberta (1993a), 'A cautionary note on drawing lessons from comparative corporate law', *Yale Law Journal*, **102**, 2020.

Romano, Roberta (1993b), *The Genius of American Corporate Law*, Washington, DC: The AEI Press.

Schaede, Ulrike (1995), 'Toward a new system of corporate governance in the European Union: an integrative model of the Anglo-American and Germanic systems', in Barry Eichengreen, Jeffrey Frieden and J. von Hagen (eds), *Politics and Institutions in an Integrated Europe*, Berlin and New York: Springer Verlag.

Schleifer, Andrei and Robert W. Vishny (1990), 'The takeover wave of the 1980s', *Science*, (August), 745–9.

Shonfield, Andrew (1969), *Modern Capitalism: the Changing Balance of Public and Private Power*, 2nd edn, London and New York: Oxford University Press.

Siebert, Ulrich (1999), 'Control and transparency in business (KonTraG): corporate governance reform in Germany', *European Business Law Review*, **10**(1,2)

(Jan./Feb.), 70–75.

Soskice, David (1992), 'The institutional infrastructure for international competitiveness: a comparative analysis of the U.K. and Germany', in A.B. Atkinson and R. Brunetta (eds), *The Economics of the New Europe*, International Economic Association Conference Volume: 1992.

Soskice, David (1999), 'Divergent production regimes: coordinated and uncoordinated market economies in the 1980s and 1990s', in Herbert Kitschelt, Peter Lange, Gary Marks and John D. Stephens (eds), *Continuity and Change in Contemporary Capitalism*, Cambridge: Cambridge University Press.

Streeck, Wolfgang (1984), 'Co-determination: the fourth decade', in Bernhard Wilpert and Arndt Sorge (eds), *International Perspectives on Organizational Democracy* II, Chichester and New York: Wiley.

Streeck, Wolfgang (1987), 'The uncertainties of management in the management of uncertainty', *International Journal of Political Economy*, **17**, 57.

Streeck, Wolfgang (1990), 'Status and contract: basic categories of a sociological theory of industrial relations', in David Sugarman and Gunther Teubner (eds), *Regulating Corporate Groups in Europe*, Baden-Baden: Nomos Verlagsgesellschaft.

Streeck, Wolfgang (1991), 'On the institutional conditions of diversified quality production', in Egon Matzner and Wolfgang Streeck (eds), *Beyond Keynesianism: The Socio-economics of Production and Full Employment*, Brookfield, VT: Elgar.

Streeck, Wolfgang (1992), 'Codetermination after four decades', in Wolfgang Streeck (ed.), *Social Institutions and Economic Performance: Studies of Industrial Relations in Advanced Capitalist Economies*, London and Newbury Park, CA: Sage.

Tagliabue, John (1999), 'Embracing la nouvelle economie: a string of big deals elevates France in Europe and the world', *New York Times*, 1 September, pp. C-l, col. 2, C-17, col. 1.

Tamirisa, Natalia T. (1999), 'Trade in financial services and capital movements', IMF Working Paper, WP/99/89, International Monetary Fund, Policy Development and Review Department (July).

Teubner, Gunther (1985), 'Corporate fiduciary duties and their beneficiaries, a functional approach to legal institutionalization of corporate responsibility', in Klaus J. Hopt and Gunther Teubner (eds), *Corporate Governance and Directors' Liabilities: Legal, Economic, and Sociological Analyses on Corporate Social Responsibility*, Berlin and New York: Walter de Gruyter.

Thelen, Kathleen A. (1991), *Union of Parts: Labor Politics in Postwar Germany*, Ithaca: Cornell University Press.

Thelen, Kathleen (1993), 'Western European labor in transition: Sweden and Germany compared', *World Politics*, **46**, 23.

Turner, Lowell (1991), *Democracy at Work: Changing World Markets and the Future of Labor Unions*, Ithaca: Cornell University Press.

Vogel, Stephen K. (1996), *Freer Markets, More Rules: Regulatory Reform in Advanced Industrial Countries*, Ithaca: Cornell University Press.

Wallman, Steven M.H. (1990), 'Corporate constituency statutes: placing the corporation's interests first', *Business Law Update* (November–December).

Wallman, Steven M.H. (1991), 'The proper interpretation of corporate constituency statutes and formulation of director's duties', *Stetson Law Review*, **21**(1) (Fall), 163–96.

Weiss, Linda (1998), *The Myth of the Powerless State*, Ithaca: Cornell University Press.

Williamson, Oliver E. (1985), *The Economic Institutions of Capitalism: Firms, Markets, Relational Contracting*, New York: Free Press.

Williamson, Oliver E. (1993), 'Organizational form, residual claimants, and corporate control', *Journal of Law and Economics*, **26** (June), 351–66.

Williamson, Oliver E. (1996), *Mechanisms of Governance*, Oxford and New York: Oxford University Press.

Womack, James P. (1991), *The Machine that Changed the World*, New York: HarperPerennial.

Woolcock, Steven, Michael Hodges and Kristin Schreiber (1991), *Britain, Germany, and 1992: The Limits of Deregulation*, New York: Council on Foreign Relations Press, London: Pinter.

Zysman, John (1994), 'How institutions create historically-rooted trajectories of growth', *Industrial and Corporate Change*, **3**(1), 243–83.

Zysman, John (1995), 'National roots of a "Global" economy', *Revue d'Economie Industrielle, un numero special de 1995: Renouveau des Politiques Industrielles dans le Contexte des Economies Globales*, pp. 107–21.

Zysman, John and Laura Tyson (eds) (1983), *American Industry in International Competition*, New York: Cornell University Press.

11. Managing globalization

Gavin Boyd

In globalization the intensification of corporate competition for world market shares and of macromanagement rivalries between governments tends to enhance the significance of comparative institutional advantages and of policies strengthening or weakening structural competitiveness. This observation is suggested by research on the growth effects of institutional factors and of differing mixes of economic policies.[1] Comparative institutional advantages include those deriving from the national system of corporate governance; as globalization continues, however, the influence of a system of corporate governance may be more conducive to corporate emphasis on building globally rationalized systems of production and distribution rather than corporate cooperation with national structural policy concerns. The economic policy mix, meanwhile, may become less functional, because of problems related to or affected by the market and structural changes of globalization. These problems may include the difficulties of maintaining welfare state spending while unemployment increases and capital mobility reduces revenues from corporations.[2]

The structural interdependencies associated with globalization are being made larger and more complex through the transnational production and trading activities of firms, based mainly in the industrialized states. An uneven pattern of market integration is expanding, linking especially North America and Europe. Market efficiencies and failures are thus being internationalized, while the spread of gains, between firms and between countries, exhibits imbalances which have cumulative effects on productive capabilities, growth, employment and the evolution of national policies.

For governments the imbalances in gains from globalization are identified as challenges to enhance structural competitiveness, while resorting to forms of trade policy activism and foreign direct investment policy activism and coping with the manipulations of speculators in world financial markets. The trade policy activism can lead to ventures in managed trade, which may be supported by efforts to strengthen structural competitiveness but which may also be intended to substitute for such efforts. The foreign direct investment policy activism commonly results in competitive investment bidding which,

because of the rivalries between prospective host governments, is advantageous for transnational enterprises with widely dispersed international
operations. The speculation in world financial markets obligates special
concerns about the volatility of portfolio investment flows, and about the
funding of industry for enhanced structural competitiveness.

In varying degrees the endeavours to strengthen structural competitiveness
seek to promote the development of more integrated and more dynamic
political economies, in which widely coordinated entrepreneurship will
evolve in collaboration with responsive policy level objectives, through
consultative interaction. The managements of firms contending for world
market shares, however, have strong incentives to concentrate on building
their transnational production and marketing systems. This concentration may
became more intense in response to international opportunities and problems,
and in response to deficiencies in the performance of home governments.
Another possibility is that the home country attachments and loyalties of
managements and the advice and support of their governments may result in
alignment between their international strategies and the structural endeavours
of those administrations.

The significance of governmental concerns with structural competitiveness
is somewhat obscured in the literature on globalization because an influential
strand of that literature has given prominence to questions about the future of
welfare spending.[3] General increases in welfare costs have been anticipated as
firms shift production operations from industrialized states to lower cost
areas, and decreases in government revenues have been expected as firms
reduce home country activities. Social pressures for greater welfare spending,
it has been argued, tend to become stronger in response to the costs of
globalization, but these pressures may not be given expression in policy
because the preferences of advantaged social groups, although less
representative, may be more influential.[4] The influence of economic ideas
regarding the efficacy of market forces, moreover, may be quite potent at the
policy level, and accordingly may motivate fiscal tightening.[5]

Differences in the structural policies of major industrialized states – in the
scope and effectiveness of these policies – reflect notable contrasts in the
dynamics of policy processes, with mixes of functional concerns and forms of
political trading, as well as degrees of policy learning and experimentation.
Fundamental determinants of the contrasts are beliefs and values in the
national cultures, which remain distinctive despite processes of societal
interpenetration resulting from communication flows and the mobility of
corporate, political and academic elites. The communitarian cultures of Japan
and Germany are conducive to functionally integrated structural policy
endeavours for the management of the interdependencies that increase with
globalization. Strong individualism in the US poses coordination problems,

especially because the trading of political favours is a more active part of the policy process.

Imperatives for international economic cooperation and for widely co-ordinated corporate cooperation become stronger as globalization raises the levels of policy and structural interdependence. In the common interest, imbalances in the spread of gains from global commerce have to be reduced, and this necessitates countering the destructive effects of international competitition which drives weaker firms into decline despite the scope for cooperation that would facilitate improved performance by those firms. The concentration trends which tend to develop as markets are increasingly linked are related to other problems of international market failure, including especially the under-production of global public goods, and these problems set more comprehensive requirements for international economic cooperation.[6] The structural issues which demand engagement, moreover, obligate corporate cooperation, to be sought for in a functional and equitable international balance between competition and cooperation. A problem of government failure of special contextual significance here is the absence of competition policy cooperation.

IMBALANCED GLOBALIZATION

In the cross-border linking of markets through trade and transnational production more competitive firms force weaker ones into declines, thus altering the spread of relative gains from globalization. The complex effects of differences in productivity and differences in competition change, in ways that evidence the functional consequences of contrasts in systems of corporate governance.[7] The combined results reconfigure patterns of structural competitiveness, causing shifts in levels of growth and employment. Diverse structural, trade, foreign direct investment, competition and macroeconomic policies adopted by governments in asymmetric bargaining relationships contribute to all the market linking. The US has superior capacities for leverage in these relationships, and its bargaining strengths in relation to Japan and the European Union are tending to increase while its firms assume greater prominence as agents of global market changes and structural changes. The US's structural competitiveness, however, does not altogether correspond with the level of its bargaining strength. There are imbalances within the US economy, related to the multiple dimensions of its involvement in the globalization process.

Increasing global imbalances, with risks of destabilizing shocks, are in prospect. The US is experiencing the most serious imbalances, and these are tending to become more serious because of the extraordinary strains generated by the very substantial expansion of production at foreign locations; the import drawing effects of high internal demand – sustained by the attraction of high investment inflows and by borrowing against inflated stocks; and the persistence of large current account deficits. Japan is recording large current account surpluses which increase its reserves in US dollars, but the appreciation of the yen which tends to result is restrained by a loose monetary policy and by informal limitations on international use of the national currency. The European Union has modest current account surpluses which reflect growth that is more domestically based, at a level below that of the US, but that is less affected by uncertainties posed by debt burdens and speculation in financial markets.

The US's imbalances, which have grave implications for the world economy, are likely to continue because of the strength of internal demand, the trade effects of upward pressures on the currency associated with the attraction of foreign investment and monetary tightening, and a widening deficit in international investment income, due to deterioration of the net external indebtedness position, which was about 16 per cent of GDP in 1997. The level of internal demand has been related to a rise in stock market wealth of about 40 per cent during 1996–98.[8] Speculative operations which have been responsible for this rise tend to remain very active, and rises in interest rates intended to dampen speculation tend to be moderate, in part because of concerns about the possibilities of currency appreciation that would reduce exports.

Foreign sourcing of intermediate and final products by US firms has contributed substantially to the current account deficits and to changes in sectoral interdependencies in the home economy, which have been reflected in rising shares of imports in domestic consumption, and rises in imported inputs in US manufacturing industries. The proportion of manufacturing production for export (13.4 per cent in 1995) has been lagging somewhat behind the proportion of domestic consumption accounted for by imports (16.3 per cent in 1995).[9] US export performance has been aided principally by superior increases in labour productivity and comparatively lower wage increases, but not significantly by investments in new technology, which overall appear to have had more significance in the international production operations of US multinationals.[10]

Japan, maintaining large current account surpluses, in part through exports to the US, is endeavouring to promote domestically-based growth through fiscal expansion and a loose monetary policy, but the latter leaves the way open for drifts of investment to the US, in response to opportunities for higher yields. The nation's large outward oriented firms have very substantial internal funds for expansion, and thus have reduced their dependence on bank financing, while Japanese banks are drawn toward the investment opportunities in the US. Policy objectives regarding the funding of domestically-based growth tend to be frustrated, and this is all the more serious because of grave weaknesses in the financial sector which have been causing stagnation.[11] The building of international production systems by Japanese multinationals has some deindustrializing effects which are moderated by functional linkages with the home economy, but it must be stressed that there is a difficult structural policy problem: domestic lending by banks has been contracted because of the burdens of bad loans and declining growth, but also because there have been incentives for financial institutions to invest abroad, notably in the US. Recovery would be aided by wide-ranging structural policy cooperation with industrializing East Asian states, especially South Korea, but the development of transnational policy communities and corporate associations for this purpose is not being promoted, mainly because of the intensity of communal attachments and loyalties in the Japanese system of alliance capitalism.

The European Union has a relatively stable modest current account surplus (about 1.5 per cent of GDP, compared with Japan's 3.5 per cent of GDP in 1999), reflecting limited exposure to the disruptive effects of the East Asian financial crises, and less fluctuation in the level of internal demand; growth has been more regionally based, and slack compared with that in the US.[12] A drift of investment to the US, responding to higher US interest rates, has been tending to frustrate the growth objectives of moderate monetary loosening. Moderate levels of outward direct investment, principally from Britain, France and Germany, have contributed to minor degrees of deindustrialization but unemployment has been high because of labour costs and much reliance on labour saving innovations. The development of corporate capacities in line with potentials for rationalization in the Single Market is somewhat restricted by the diversity of systems of corporate governance and the related effects of competing structural policies. The growth opportunities for European firms, moreover, are also affected by the size and competitiveness of the US corporate presence, which in Europe as a whole, on a historical cost basis, was valued at $420,934 million in 1997.[13] The gross product of US nonbank affiliates in the 15 EU members in 1995 was $273.9 billion.[14] Expansion of the US corporate presence, especially through mergers and acquisitions, is a major process of structural change in the Union.

Overall, Triadic structural interdependencies are tending to evolve with greater imbalances, advantageous mainly to the US. Associated changes in bargaining strengths, meanwhile, are altering policy interdependencies, also mainly to the advantage of the US. The US political economy, however, is burdened with problems of governance and lacks a structural policy capability that would be adequate for management of its interdependencies and for the development of a comprehensive system of Triadic economic cooperation.

Issues of corporate governance in this context are linked with larger developmental issues, in which problems of internationalized government failure interact with problems of internationalized market failure.

CORPORATE STRUCTURAL CAPABILITIES

National economic structures and the linkages between them are being shaped more and more by the production and marketing operations of international firms, and the most active ones, based mainly in the US, implement their strategies very independently. The scope for all this multinational activity is very extensive because of the policy orientations of governments, especially the US administration, toward economic openness; their diverse interests in attracting direct investment by large transnational enterprises; and their efforts to enhance the structural competitiveness of their economies, through aid for and advice to their firms. Domestic market strength, providing resources for the support of international operations, has been a decisive factor in the rivalries for foreign market shares, enabling US firms to gain advantages over European firms based in smaller economies, but also over Japanese firms operating in solidarity within industry groups.

Openness to trade and foreign direct investment as a basic principle of growth has been accepted, with qualifications, as a fundamental requirement in the external economic relations of the US and the European Union. The qualifications have been related to concerns about relative gains due to differences in competitiveness and to concessions exchanged on degrees of market openness, as well as to contrasts in forms of government assistance to firms. Shifts in the attitudes of US and European policy communities have been developing in response to the costs and risks of the multiple asymmetries in deepening integration. These have been altering mainly as consequences of corporate contests for world market shares. Japan has remained apart from the uneven Atlantic consensus on economic openness, especially because of intense elite awareness of acute resource deficiencies that entail exceptional vulnerabilities in structural interdependence.

US policy has had the most extensive effects in the international political economy. A free market ideology, aggressively articulated in an agency type system of government, has inspired vigorous advocacy of international trade and investment liberalization, with preservation, in principle, of administrative aloofness from industry and commerce.[15] In Atlantic relations this advocacy has been rather persuasive because of European corporate recognition of the growth potential of regional market integration and because of broad elite awareness of the inefficiencies of state enterprises and interventionist industrial policies. European sensitivities to differences in structural competitiveness, however, have been sources of reservations about the benefits of full economic openness, and European traditions of administrative–corporate cooperation have been seen to have increased significance in the Atlantic and global rivalries for market shares. Official technology enhancement programmes have thus been launched, and combined state endeavours have sought to establish a globally competitive aerospace industry.[16] Rivalries between members of the European Union, however, hinder progress toward the development of a common structural policy. Union firms have thus tended to focus independently on their contests in regional and global markets.[17] Because of generally weaker competitiveness there have been strong incentives to seek links with US firms.

In the absence of a common structural policy European Union concerns with weaker structural competitiveness have to give much attention to external trade policy. The principal effect is to maintain moderate protection of the single market while nevertheless exposing Union firms to international competition. Openness to foreign direct investment, however, and rivalries to attract it, reduce the significance of the protection. Meanwhile, European firms, contending with slack growth in their own area, are attracted by the higher growth opportunities in the US economy, which they enter in minor structural roles. Very large increases in the European direct investment position in the US were recorded in 1998.[18] Some of this outflow may have been influenced by the emergence of social democratic administrations in Germany, France and Britain.

The structural capabilities of US firms are becoming more important for their home economy and for the world economy because of the weaker competitiveness of European Union enterprises, and also, it must be stressed, because of the effects of Japan's economic difficulties on its international firms. Japanese rivalry has become a less significant factor for US enterprises in Europe and, indeed, in East Asia and Latin America. The financing of expansion by US corporations has been aided by large increases in stock market values at home, and although this entails vulnerabilities because of uncertainties about the sustainability of those values, the extensions of international operations add to the resources of the expanding firms for the support of larger scale activities. The increases in international market strengths which are in prospect hold the promise of higher returns, with widely dispersed risks.

In the evolution of international financial markets, US manufacturing and service enterprises, it must be emphasized, are also advantaged, notably through what amounts to preferential funding, based on their growth prospects. Home country investor preferences and the attractions of the US economy for European and Japanese investors are factors in this process. The US stock market, in which speculative operations tend to push assets to high levels, represents about 42 per cent of the world stock market (compared with 9 per cent for Britain and 15 per cent for Japan).[19]

US institutional investors dominate world financial markets, and are well placed to consolidate their strengths in mature and emerging financial markets. The assets of US institutional investors totalled $11,490.2 billion in 1995, that is nearly three times greater than the combined figure for Britain, France and Germany.[20] While exerting more and more influence on the direction of investment flows, the US institutional investors are able to assert preferences to regulatory authorities and policy communities that in effect allow wide freedom for securities trading. This tends to discourage adoption of stricter regulatory arrangements in European financial markets, as these endeavour to compete for the attraction of investment firms. The principal result is that the manipulative operations of speculators tend to move to risk levels that may suddenly become excessive because of unforeseen events. The major US financial institutions have superior resources for risk-taking, while their European competitors have to function with greater caution.[21]

European financial interests and financial policy communities lack the cohesion that would be needed to assert strong demands for effective regulation of the international financial markets and for a common Union financial policy that would ensure more substantial and more stable funding of Union firms. The representation of financial interests in the Union is fragmented, and the development of cross-border links between financial policy communities in the Union is difficult because of the absence of political affinities conducive to collaborative inputs into Union level decision making.

Japan is more seriously disadvantaged than the European Union in the changing dynamics of the international financial system, and has even less scope for initiatives aimed at international regulatory reform.[22] Relative political isolation, the severe problems in the financial sector and heavy dependence on the US market discourage consideration of quests for rapport with European authorities on issues of international financial regulation, and on the European side little has been done to seek understanding with Japanese policymakers on problems of economic cooperation. Japan, however, because of the high degree of integration in its political economy, and the large size of its international net investment position, has greater significance in world financial markets than any individual European Union member.[23]

The shifting balance of power in world financial markets is linked with the changing balance in markets for goods and services, and with its structural implications. The internationalization of financial markets facilitates preferential funding of large firms acquiring oligopoly power and enables high-growth countries to attract much investment, especially if there are prospects of superior short-term yields. Overall, large US international firms tend to become more active agents of structural change, notably in Europe, while efforts by European governments to enhance the structural competitiveness of their economies become less effective, because of the diverse growth retarding factors in the European Union but also because of the increasing strength of the US corporate presence. The US's lack of a structural policy capability remains a problem for its political economy, but does not hinder the expansion of its firms in Europe, and the flow of European investment to the US indirectly facilitates that corporate expansion, without significantly affecting the domestic market strengths of major US firms.

US corporate expansion contributes to structural change on a much smaller scale in Japan, where an exceptionally small presence has been increasing in response to opportunities resulting from the East Asian financial crises of 1997/8. Severe problems in the Japanese financial sector, and difficulties in the international operations of Japanese investment firms, have motivated policy shifts toward increased economic openness. Japan's structural policy capability, however, remains very strong, and as Japanese firms recover from the problems of the late 1990s their capacities to cause structural change through direct investment and trade are likely to become more important challenges to American enterprises, but more in East Asia than in Europe.

INTERNATIONAL ECONOMIC COOPERATION

In the asymmetries of policy interdependence between the US, the European Union and Japan, the American interest in promoting general trade and investment liberalization is the main source of initiatives: superior bargaining strength can be exerted for leverage in separate Atlantic and Pacific inter-actions, without provoking collaboration between the European Union and Japan. But the potential for leverage is limited because of risks of provoking concerted European reactions that would reduce openness to US exports and direct investment, and also because of the dangers of antagonizing Japanese investors holding American securities. These potential constraints may not prevent episodic resorts to dramatized pressures against the trading partners by a US administration seeking wider domestic support.[24] For US international firms producing in Europe, however, the incentives to devote resources to political action for market-opening leverage against the European Union seem to be generally weak and may well be diminishing as stronger market positions are secured in Europe through direct investment.

The European Union's scope for trade and investment policy activism is restricted because of decisional problems in its complex policy processes and its related weaknesses in bargaining capabilities. The management of foreign economic policy tends to be reactive, and unless external challenges are very potent the aggregation of preferences at the Union level is difficult. The potential for consensus building under the leadership of the European Commission is significant, but the persistence of slow growth in the Union and the magnitude of the competitive American presence tend to activate structural policy rivalries between member governments, and these can become more divisive because of competitive investment bidding.

The urgent requirement to reduce the US's large current account deficit could be met by securing reductions of the relatively low effective rates of protection maintained by the European Union. Increased access for US firms could raise exports and perhaps reduce their emphasis on producing in the Union. The leverage that might be necessary for this market opening, however, could provoke negative reactions, and in any case the incentives for US firms to expand production in Europe could become stronger even as successes were achieved in US quests for greater market access.

Japan is a more vulnerable target for US trade policy and investment policy activism, because despite the substantial degree of dependence on Japanese investor confidence the prospects for economic recovery in Japan depend heavily on continued access to the US market. The principal challenge for the US in this relationship, it must be stressed, is to work for more balanced structural interdependence with the integrated Japanese regional production system in East Asia, and to accept the functional logic of regional economic cooperation in that area that could develop in complementarity with the North America Free Trade Area.

The development of an East Asian system of regional cooperation centred on Japan would reduce the degree of US domination in the globalization process, and the US's capacity to exert influence in the Asia Pacific Economic Cooperation forum as a loose association with some potential for the promotion of trade liberalization between East Asia and North America. A rough convergence of interests in US foreign economic policy tends to oppose Japanese initiatives for the formation of an East Asian economic group, and such opposition has a more discouraging effect on the attitudes of Japanese policymakers now than it did before the East Asian financial crises.

The US policy process is not generating consensus for a comprehensive design in response to the challenges of globalization and the opportunities for a more assertive role in the international political economy while European and Japanese foreign economic policies remain basically defensive. Management of the liberally oriented decisional interactions through political trading in the system of divided agency type government entails neglect of structural policy issues while, through the perpetuation of administrative failings, it adds to the incentives for US firms to focus on the development of their international production and trading operations. As these incentives have become stronger on account of Japan's economic difficulties and the persistence of flow growth in Europe, the possible benefits of political action at home, it can be reiterated, evidently tend to assume less significance.

Aggravations of the nation's basic macromanagement problems have to be anticipated. The most prominent difficulty, it must be stressed, is that monetary tightening to dampen unsustainable upward pressures in stock markets tends to cause appreciation of the currency, with adverse effects on exports and, thus, on the current account. A broad functional consensus to achieve a solution fails to emerge because of the absence of institutionally developed peak economic associations. Conflicts between interest groups negatively affected or at risk because of perceived macromanagement failures and the costs of globalization tend to become more intense, further reducing administrative effectiveness.

Coping with the macromanagement problems obligates quests for international economic cooperation, because of the high and rising levels of policy and structural interdependence. The difficulties of economic management, however, while becoming more serious, generate pressures to externalize the costs of those difficulties. This happens through the dynamics of adversarial politics, more so in the US than in major European states, because of its conflicted policy style and its scope for leverage in what is becoming a hegemonic pattern of globalization. In Atlantic relations, then, and in US–Japan interactions, bargaining over questions of economic cooperation or accommodation may well become more adversarial.[25]

Hence there is an urgent need for constructive initiatives by US policymakers and corporate elites. For this a vast and intensive educational endeavour is clearly required, to promote concerted reorientations toward collaborative engagement with basic structural issues. A fundamental part of this endeavour will have to be the encouragement of shifts toward stakeholder concepts of corporate governance, as advocated by Margaret Blair,[26] and what may be called stakeholder concepts of *intercorporate governance*, in which multiple interdependencies between firms are seen as bases for mutually responsive methods of operating, as in the Japanese industry groups.

The educational endeavour will have to have a strong moral thrust, and a profound grasp of the functional imperative for wide ranging entrepreneurial collaboration, in a spirit of solidarity, combined with technocratic–corporate consultative interactions. This can be affirmed with emphasis on its innovative significance, in the public interest, and on the negative effects of distrust and ruthless competition on overall growth and the resolution of market failure problems. The solidarity that will have to be promoted will have to be oriented toward comprehensive engagement with the imbalances in the US's structural interdependencies, so as to bring order into the current account. Meanwhile, the need for fundamental reform in the international financial system will have to be stressed.

A strong moral drive in the educational endeavour will also be necessary because the US liberal political tradition encourages aggressive assertions and pursuits of self-interest which perpetuate problems of governance and cause stresses in the economy: pluralistic stagnation tends to be combined with allocative pressures for fiscal expansion, while intense intercorporate competition results in strong oligopoly power and in large negative externalities associated with outward direct investment. The need for vigorous moral advocacy will have to be emphasized with reference to the greatly increased importance of structural issues for the US and other industrialized states as globalization continues.

International economic cooperation, in perspectives based on the liberal political tradition, has been understood mainly as the collaborative management of macroeconomic policies, in contexts of shallow integration, to increase demand and therefore imports in states with trade surpluses and reduce demand in trade deficit states. Endeavours of this kind have been unsuccessful, because commitments have not been honoured, but in the present context of imbalanced deepening integration the import drawing effects of macroeconomic expansion in a trade surplus state can be lowered by drifts of investment to a trade deficit state where macroeconomic contraction, although lowering demand, attracts financial flows because of higher yields – flows which offset the effects of reducing demand by contractionary measures.

Deepening integration has greatly increased the importance of potentials for structural cooperation, for the development of more balanced and more dynamic interdependencies. Trade and transnational production develop on the basis of structural capabilities, and change those capabilities while linking them across borders. The growth and employment effects, it must be stressed, which assume increasing magnitude as firms increasingly rationalize their operations on a global scale and gain or lose market strengths, have more and more vital significance for each government. The basic policy choices are to strive for advantageous changes through trade and investment measures or to seek extensive corporate cooperation through consultations. In these, incentives for such cooperation can be provided through technocratic sponsorship of exploratory interactions to identify opportunities for concerted entrepreneurship. The development of technocratic capabilities for such sponsorship, especially through surveillance of advances in frontier technology, could be given much prominence. Attempts to alter the spread of gains and losses from globalization through restrictive or promotional trade and investment measures, it could be made clear, would tend to invite circumvention by international firms. These would be dealt with mainly at arm's length in the implementation of interventionist measures, but the consultative structural endeavour would seek their spontaneous cooperation.

It may be argued, especially by public choice theorists, that the rationale for consultative structural endeavours is visionary, and that the principal result of consultative initiatives would be a pattern of informal collusive arrangements, dominated by firms with superior market strengths and exceptional capacities for representation of their interests. For the policymakers the increasing intercorporate cooperation which they were promoting could assume an oligopolistic trend at variance with the public interest. This danger, however, would have to be seen as a challenge for intensive development of technocratic expertise, dedicated to the common good.

The logic of a consultative structural policy is an extension of John Dunning's well-founded argument that governments have responsibilities for influencing the ethos of their political economies, in the public interest, through affirmations of values and through the demonstration effects of macromanagement.[27] In highly individualistic societies, accordingly, shifts to the acceptance of communitarian values thus have to be promoted, and these became more necessary if, in increasingly complex industrialized states, the negative economic and political consequences of aggressive pursuits of self interest have seriously disruptive effects.

The rationale for a consultative structural policy, with its political and corporate dimensions, implies an extended stakeholder concept of corporate governance: managements would be responsive not only to shareholders, workers, suppliers and distributors but also to many interdependent firms and to the national administration. This would not stifle entrepreneurial initiative but would provide an environment for the full development of *alliance capitalism*. A system of *intercorporate governance* with much spontaneous order would evolve.

The constructive US initiatives which can be hoped for would have to seek European and Japanese cooperation. The Atlantic relationship would deserve priority because of its potentials for meaningful communication, the size of the European Union, and the scope for structural partnering that could produce more balanced interdependence. It would have to be emphasized, however, that the Japanese political economy is the most significant model of alliance capitalism, and that Japan would have to play an essential role in the Triadic structural partnering.

INTERNATIONAL FINANCIAL MARKET REFORM

The structural partnering approach to international economic cooperation necessitates very critical assessment of the functional deficiencies in international financial markets and of the governmental and corporate failings contributing to those deficiencies. International financial markets are affected by volatility which major institutional speculators have interests in causing and manipulating. Investments are drawn to opportunities for high yields, especially on a short-term basis, and thus tend to flow more to the US than to Europe and Japan, defeating the growth objectives of monetary easing, notably in Europe, but also in Japan. Meanwhile, large international firms, acquiring global oligopoly power, in effect receive preferential funding. The market manipulators, moreover, while engaging in highly risky and potentially destabilizing operations, diverting funds from productive use, resort to ingenious methods of tax evasion which assist their efforts to attract investment.

Regulatory cooperation between US, European and Japanese financial authorities is weak, especially because of the magnitude and complexity of operations in world financial markets, rivalries to draw international investment, and the interests of the US financial community in dominating those rivalries. Regulatory endeavours are concerned only with restraint on risk-taking by large institutional investors. Only in Japan and Germany are there financial structures oriented primarily toward the funding of national industries, and these are being weakened to degrees by drifts of investment to the US, in search of higher yields.

The independent activities of financial market operators reduce the effectiveness of monetary policies, especially in the US, because of the vast scale of those activities. Monetary tightening to slow growth and reduce speculation begins to lose significance because financial flows through the securities industry can provide cheaper and more substantial funding. On this account, and because of the reduced effectiveness of fiscal policies as well as monetary measures, governments are under pressure to earn the confidence of major operators in world financial markets. These operators, however, it must be stressed, compete for the exploitation of volatility and the exertion of pressures on firms through portfolio switching to force higher earnings.

Structural policy objectives in industrialized states obligate concerns with the funding of national industries and, tacitly, with the basic interests of home country investors in the prosperity of those industries, although these basic interests tend to be overlooked as investors entrust decisions to financial institutions under managements without home country loyalties. International financial markets do show home country bias in investment patterns, due to information problems and prudential considerations, but the main trend is the funding of large international firms that demonstrate high profitability and of prominent firms in higher growth countries. The principal effects, it must be stressed, are enhancement of the capacities of major US international firms to draw global investment, and the increased attractiveness of the US economy as a destination for foreign investment.

Linked with the significance of investment flows in the Triad pattern are issues concerning the stability of the global financial system as it evolves with increasing degrees of concentration. With continuing globalization the dangers of destabilization have become more serious because of the greater magnitude of financial interdependencies, the opportunities to cause and manipulate volatility, and the currently intractable problems of financial management in the US.[28] The risks of a financial crisis in the US are exceptional, it must be emphasized, because of the high level of speculative activity, a high level of corporate debt and the growth in the securities industry that has gone further than in any other industrialized state.

International cooperation for effective regulation and concerted crisis management in world financial markets, with a focus on the centrality of the US's problems, has become imperative, and clearly must be sought by US policymakers. Vigorous representations of concerns to activate quests for such cooperation will have to come from the US financial community and, because of the diverging perspectives of its members, an intense educational drive like that which has become necessary for a consultative structural policy will clearly be necessary. It will be extremely important, moreover, for this drive to enlist the collaboration of European and Japanese policy communities, especially on the basis of their concerns about the stability of the US's role in the international political economy.

The necessary international financial policy cooperation will have to be sought with the objective of institutionalizing it on a sound basis. The international dimensions of financial markets, which has made such cooperation imperative, set requirements for institutional development at an advanced level, to ensure that dedicated collegial expertise will have decisive effects despite contrary representations of preferences by financial groups unresponsive to the public interest.

A vital task for political designing, then, will be to plan an institutionalized link between the European Central Bank and the US Federal Reserve, as the basis for collaboration in lender of last resort operations, in the surveillance of potentially destabilizing trends in world financial markets, and in vigorous advocacy for regulatory reform directed at financial authorities in the USA and Europe. A special target for this endeavour would be the bias toward inaction in the US system, due to the conflicted representation of financial interests, which is made all the more serious by a fragmentation of responsibilities between its official structures.

The European Monetary Union was formed very much on the basis of prolonged policy learning forced by vulnerabilities to the effects of destabilizing US macroeconomic policies, and aided by general recognition that regional market integration had set a requirement for monetary integration. The European Central Bank's primary responsibility to work for regional price stability obligates concerns for the maintenance of monetary policy effectiveness while the Union's securities industries expand and become more closely linked with US financial markets. The structural consequences for the Union have vital significance for the policy communities to which the European Central Bank is in effect accountable. The development of financial markets in Europe can assist the funding of European industries but on balance may well contribute more to the funding of industry in the higher growth US economy, and to speculative operations in that economy that can entail high risks.

Patterns of concentrated ownership in Europe that restrict the development of securities sectors but that enable monetary policy to remain effective and that ensure continuity in the funding of industry have to be evaluated with reference to the long-term significance of larger investment flows to the US if the European stock market becomes much more active. In well institutionalized dialogue the structural considerations underlying the European Central Bank's functions could be communicated very effectively to the US Federal Reserve. The Federal Reserve, it must be stressed, has to reckon with a very serious problem of diminishing monetary sovereignty, attributable to the growth of a securities industry which is linked very actively with that in Europe. Complementary macroeconomic considerations as a basis for dialogue could generate Federal Reserve initiatives to engage with the problem of weakening policy-level capacity to restrain potentially destabilizing speculation in financial markets. This necessary endeavour, deriving motivation from interaction with the European Central Bank, could be at the centre of an Atlantic policy community that would deal with issues of corporate governance on the basis of fundamental structural policy objectives.

PROSPECTS

Central bankers are being held responsible for the integrity of financial systems, more so now than in the recent past because of stresses in world financial markets, but their tasks are becoming more difficult. This is happening, it must be emphasized, because of the internationalization of those markets, the diversification of financial services, the volatility of financial asset prices, the lack of transparency – due especially to the use of derivatives – the reduced significance of traditional banking, and the general increases in vulnerabilities which tend to spread the effects of any financial crisis.[29] The systemic responsibilities which are becoming more demanding will have to be met, to a large extent, by stronger supervisory functions, and if these are to be effective they will have to operate through functional reform of the connections between financial markets and systems of corporate governance. These connections will have to undergo basic changes to serve the needs of the real economies that are becoming more and more interdependent, structurally and at the policy level.

Structural policy concerns related to asymmetries in gains from deepening integration are likely to become more active in the European Union's policy communities, motivating endeavours to enlist cooperation from national firms while competition in the Single Market gives further impetus to concentration trends. The structural significance of the established system of corporate governance will probably become stronger in Germany, because of the degree of integration in its political economy. This, however, will be less likely in France, because of long-standing corporate antipathies toward the policy level, influenced by ideological cleavages and the fragmentation of conservative political groups. In Britain the development of a structural policy capability will probably continue to be prevented by a corporate culture distrustful of government, and by the influence of the financial community as a source of policy advice, indirectly supportive of the market-based system of corporate governance.

Problems in international financial markets, despite their structural significance, may engage less attention in the European Union's policy communities because their significance for constituencies is quite diffuse. The European Central Bank's scope for initiative may therefore assume much importance, but effective use of this capacity in interactions with US monetary authorities will require building solidarity in Union financial policy communities through intensive policy learning activities like those which were necessary to launch the European Monetary System and promote regional market integration. A major cost of failures to engage with issues of vital structural significance in the operation of financial markets will be further substantial drifts of investment to the higher performing US economy, despite its potentially destabilizing stresses.

The US's structural problems, related to the increasing volume of national manufacturing capacity located outside the United States (about 25 per cent),[30] and to the scale of speculative activity by institutional investors, are setting more and more demanding requirements for policy learning which cannot be resolved without corporate learning. Strongly pluralistic policy processes with adversarial qualities seriously hinder policy learning, and this is also made difficult by optimism generated in the atmosphere of stock market upsurges. If the necessary policy learning does not develop through an intensive educational endeavour, with vigorous high level leadership, responses to the basic structural issues are likely to be reactive, incremental, experimental and disjointed.

The involvement of US institutions in world financial markets will undoubtedly become more highly prominent, although the danger of a financial crisis in the US will tend to become more serious, and the official capacity to aid distressed enterprises may well continue to weaken. The imperatives for fundamental reform are assuming international dimensions because the potentially destabilizing speculation which demands the Federal Reserve's attention is becoming a central process in world financial markets. Comprehensive cooperation, especially in Atlantic relations, is becoming more and more necessary, but the gravity of this requirement may not evoke the extensive consensus promotion endeavour that is needed. Public interest that could give impetus to such an endeavour, however, could be aroused by high level efforts drawing attention to the scope for tax evasion in world financial markets, notably through the use of derivatives. The development of highly sophisticated financial instruments, the use of tax havens and tax policy competition between industrialized states is making the problem of tax avoidance more intractable.[31] Meanwhile, trading rules for the regulation of financial markets in one country can be evaded by ordering transactions through another country: trading rules in the US can be avoided by sending orders through London.[32] Altogether, the magnitude of the problems of government failure and market failure in the largely integrated global financial system are making reform in the interests of the real economy more and more necessary, but for the present the intensive educational efforts necessary for effective policy learning are lacking.

Japan must be expected to remain apart from the interactions and inter-dependencies in Atlantic relations, mainly because of the influence of distinctive cultural factors. The scope for constructive US initiatives on structural issues in the world economy is thus likely to remain very significant. Enlightened use of this scope for initiative by seeking collegial structural partnering with Japan could be highly productive, complementing and then merging with the proposed Atlantic partnering. Calls for a new international financial architecture could then be answered at a fundamental level by building a new international structural architecture.[33]

NOTES

1. On comparative institutional advantages and the importance of functional economic policies see Mancur Olson (1996), 'Distinguished lecture on economics in government', *Journal of Economic Perspectives*, **10** (2) (Spring), 3–24.
2. Gunther G. Schulze and Heinrich W. Ursprung (1999), 'Globalization of the economy and the nation state', *The World Economy*, **22** (3) (May), 295–352.
3. Ibid.
4. See J. Rogers Hollingsworth (1997), 'The institutional embeddedness of American capitalism', in Colin Crouch and Wolfgang Streeck (eds), *Political Economy of Modern Capitalism*, Thousand Oaks: Sage Publications, ch. 7.
5. See observations on the evolution of policies in Pete Richardson (1997), 'Globalization and linkages: macro-structural challenges and opportunities', *OECD Economic Studies*, **28** (1), 61, 62.

6. This extends the main line of argument in Inge Kaul, Isabelle Grunberg and Marc A. Stern (eds) (1999), *Global Public Goods*, New York: Oxford University Press.
7. See Colin Mayer, 'Corporate governance, competition and performance', *OECD Economic Studies*, **27** (11), 7-34, and Dirk Pilat (1999), 'Competition, productivity and efficiency', in ibid., 107-46.
8. See *OECD Economic Outlook*, June 1999, pp. 200-203.
9. See Jose Campa and Linda S. Goldberg (1997), 'The evolving external orientation of manufacturing: a profile of four countries', *Federal Reserve Bank of New York Economic Policy Review*, **3** (2) (July), 53-82. On foreign sourcing see Masaaki Kotabe (1996), 'Global sourcing strategy in the Pacific: American and Japanese multinational companies', in Gavin Boyd (ed.), *Structural Competitiveness in the Pacific*, Cheltenham, UK and Northampton, MA: Edward Elgar, pp. 215-39.
10. See Evangelos Ioannidis and Paul Schreyer (1997), 'Technology and non-technology determinants of export share growth', *OECD Economic Studies*, **28** (1), 169-205.
11. See *OECD Economic Outlook*, June 1999, pp. 203, 204.
12. Ibid., p. 205.
13. *Survey of Current Business*, **78** (7) (July) 1998, 43.
14. See Ray Barrell and Nigel Pain (1999), 'The growth of foreign direct investment in Europe', in Ray Barrell and Nigel Pain (eds), *Innovation, Investment and the Diffusion of Technology in Europe*, Cambridge: Cambridge University Press, pp. 19-43. See Hollingsworth, cited in note 4.
15. Ibid., but the aloofness from industry and commerce is qualified by policy-level openness to protectionist pressures. See Robert Z. Lawrence (ed.) (1998), *Brookings Trade Forum 1998*, Washington, DC: Brookings Institution, Part 1.
16. See Jonathan Eaton, Eva Gutierrez and Samuel Kortum (1998), 'European technology policy', *Economic Policy*, **27** (October), 405-38.
17. Structural factors influencing the strategies of Union firms are examined in Pierre Buigues and Alexis Jacquemin (1998), 'Structural interdependence between the European Union and the United States: technological positions', in Gavin Boyd (ed.), *The Struggle for World Markets*, Cheltenham: Edward Elgar, pp. 32-58.
18. See Mahnaz Fahim-Nader (1999), 'Foreign direct investment in the United States: new investment in 1998', *Survey of Current Business*, **79** (6) (June), 16-23.
19. *International Capital Markets*, Washington, DC: International Monetary Fund, 1998, p. 189.
20. Ibid., p. 189.
21. Ibid., see figures for Britain, France and Germany, p. 184.
22. Ibid., p. 92: US mutual fund assets in April 1998 were over $5 trillion, roughly matching Japan's GDP.
23. Ibid., p. 184.
24. See I.M. Destler (1998), 'Congress, constituencies and US trade policy', in Alan V. Deardorff and Robert M. Stern (eds), *Constituent Interests and US Trade Policies*, Ann Arbor: University of Michigan Press, pp. 93-108.
25. The pressures from interests mentioned by Destler are likely to become stronger.
26. See Margaret M. Blair (1995), *Ownership and Control*, Washington, DC: Brookings Institution.
27. See John H. Dunning (1991), 'Governments, economic organization and international competitiveness', in Lars-Gunnar Mattsson and Bengt Stymne (eds), *Corporate and Industry Strategies for Europe*, Amsterdam: North Holland, pp. 41-74.
28. See Alexandre Lamfalussy (1994), 'Central banking in transition', in Forrest Capie, Charles Goodhart, Stanley Fisher and Norbert Schnadt (eds), *The Future of Central Banking*, Cambridge: Cambridge University Press, pp. 330-41.
29. Ibid.
30. Comment by Roy C. Smith in Donald H. Chew (ed.) (1998), *Discussing the Revolution in Corporate Finance*, Oxford: Blackwell, p. 403.
31. See Vito Tanzi (1999), 'Is there a need for a world tax organization?', in Assaf Razin and Efraim Sadka (eds), *The Economics of Globalization*, Cambridge: Cambridge University

Press, pp. 173–86.
32. See Benn Steil et al. (1996), *The European Equity Markets*, London, Royal Institute of International Affairs, p. 61.
33. On proposals for international financial reform see Barry Eichengreen (1999), *Towards a New International Financial Architecture*, Washington, DC: Institute for International Economics. On the rationale for structural partnering see Thomas L. Brewer and Gavin Boyd (eds) (2000), *Globalizing America*, Cheltenham, UK and Northampton, MA; Edward Elgar, Chapters 11 and 12.

Index